The Rise of
Militant Islam

The Rise of Militant Islam

An Insider's View of the Failure to
Curb Global Jihad

Anthony Tucker-Jones

Pen & Sword
MILITARY

First published in Great Britain in 2010 by
Pen & Sword Military
an imprint of
Pen & Sword Books Ltd
47 Church Street
Barnsley
South Yorkshire
S70 2AS

Copyright © Anthony Tucker-Jones 2010

ISBN 978-1-84415-945-1

Typeset in 11/13 Ehrhardt by Concept, Huddersfield, West Yorkshire
Printed by the MPG Books Group in the UK

Pen & Sword Books Ltd incorporates the imprints of Pen & Sword Aviation,
Pen & Sword Maritime, Pen & Sword Military, Wharncliffe Local History,
Pen and Sword Select, Pen and Sword Military Classics, Leo Cooper,
Remember When, Seaforth Publishing and Frontline Publishing.

For a complete list of Pen & Sword titles please contact
PEN & SWORD BOOKS LIMITED
47 Church Street, Barnsley, South Yorkshire, S70 2AS, England
E-mail: enquiries@pen-and-sword.co.uk
Website: www.pen-and-sword.co.uk

Contents

Preface vi

Timeline xi

1. Killing bin Laden 1

2. Goodbye Afghanistan 14

3. The Mountains of Allah 25

4. Seekers of the Truth 35

5. Somalia: a Lesson in Victory 46

6. Yemen: a Nest of Vipers 54

7. Bosnia: Trouble with 'Ragheads' 62

8. Algeria: Sacred Frustration 73

9. Chechnya: Moscow's Running Sore 81

10. Kosovo: a Missed Opportunity 92

11. Lebanon: Cradle of Terror 101

12. The Mahdi and the Pharaohs 108

13. Middle East Sojourn: Saudi Arabia 115

14. East Africa: War is Finally Declared 125

15. Punishing the Taliban 132

16. Tora Bora: Afghanistan Revisited 141

17. Saddam's Terrorists 148

18. Unwelcome Aftermath: International Jihad 155

19. Where's bin Laden? 162

20. Syria: on the Brink 173

21. Iraq: the New Breeding Ground 180

22. Holy Terror: the Rage of Islam 186

Epilogue 193

Glossary of Militant Islamic Groups 197

Notes and References 203

Bibliography 222

Index 231

Preface

The ruling to kill the Americans and their allies – civilians and military – is an individual duty for every Muslim [. . .] in *any* country [. . .] in order to liberate the al-Aqsa Mosque [in Jerusalem] and the holy mosque [Mecca] from their grip.

(Osama bin Laden, World Islamic Front, 22 February 1998)

The threat from terrorism is real, it is immediate, and it is evolving.

(George J. Tenet, Director of Central Intelligence,
7 February 2001)

We calculated in advance the number of casualties from the enemy, who would be killed based on the position of the tower.

(Osama bin Laden, November 2001)

We ask to be near God, we fight you and destroy you and terrorise you.

(The 9/11 Shura Council, 1 March 2009)

I remember sitting in my office in the Old War Office Building when a passing colleague informed me that a plane had flown into one of the World Trade Towers in New York. I had shown little interest and assumed it had been an accident involving a light aircraft. However, all the way home a sense of nagging doubt crept over me that something really dreadful had happened. When I finally arrived I watched transfixed with the rest of the world as the news networks showed the planes crashing into the towers over and over again until you felt numb.

Some argue that 9/11 opened Pandora's box, whereas, in reality, it had been opened long ago. The creation of Israel, American policy in the Near/Middle East and the Soviet invasion of Afghanistan all helped sow the seeds for an anti-Western Islamic terrorist backlash. Furthermore, militant Islamists interpret the Koran as explicitly invoking the use of terrorism: 'Against them make ready your strength to the utmost of your power, including steeds of war, to strike terror into the heart of the enemies of Allah and your enemies.'[1]

This book was written with the intention of showing how, over the past three decades, the West at every step seriously miscalculated its response to the rise of global Jihad. In fact, the Bush and Clinton administrations, despite their best intentions, inadvertently encouraged Islamic militancy in Afghanistan, Bosnia, Iraq, Iran, Lebanon, Pakistan, Palestine, Somalia, Sudan and Saudi Arabia with appalling results.

The concern is that, in the case of Afghanistan and Iraq, the failure to resolve their underlying problems will inspire yet more terrorists. Only the resolution of the Palestinian problem, through the Middle East Peace Process, is capable of finally defusing the wrath of militant Islam. In the meantime, one thing is clear: America will have to handle such states as Iran, Syria and Pakistan with care, for if backed into a corner, who knows how they will react after the precedent of 9/11.

For almost fifty years, as the Cold War heated up, Western intelligence agencies scrutinised every single move of the Soviet Union and its Warsaw Pact allies, ever fearful the Soviets might attack Western Europe. While the nuclear threat of mutually assured destruction kept them apart, ultimately, NATO had something the Soviet Union did not – capitalism – and was able to outspend the Soviets at every turn. The cracks began to show in 1981, when the Solidarity Movement rose up against the Communist government in Poland: instead of taking punitive action – as it had done in Hungary and Czechoslovakia – Moscow refrained from intervening.

The cost for Moscow of keeping its Groups of Forces in Eastern Europe was exorbitant and increasingly unbearable. In 1989 the Berlin Wall came down and West and East Germany took the slow road to reunification. Just two years later the Warsaw Pact unravelled and was formally dissolved in mid-1991. At the same time, the ailing Soviet Union imploded, following a desperate coup to halt decentralisation as the various republics sought to go their own way. The Soviet Union was formally dissolved in late 1991.

Almost overnight, the Soviet threat disappeared – granted, Russia retained her nuclear weapons, but it was felt it would take a decade before a resurgent Russian military could reach the halcyon days of the 1960s and 1970s. The peace dividend in the West was eagerly anticipated as the military presence in Europe was wound down. Unfortunately, London and Washington took their eye off the proverbial ball.

Western intelligence was painfully slow to adapt to this strategic climate change as it sought to identify new enemies to justify its existence.[2] Now that the certainty of a superpower face-off had ended, the new buzz words became 'proliferation of weapons of mass destruction'. Non-Western countries seeking these capabilities were deemed pariah states: they were the new enemy. In the meantime, militant Islam was slipping under the radar largely unnoticed.

Key to the growth of al-Qaeda[3] as a global terrorist organisation was not only the emergence of Osama bin Laden, but also the growing understanding of asymmetrical warfare, which the CIA taught anti-Soviet Jihadists in

Afghanistan in the 1980s, and which was dubbed 'Franchise Terrorism'. Neither was any symmetry recognised between al-Qaeda and the Palestinian Liberation Organisation, Hamas and Hezbollah, which between them had represented the disenfranchised Muslim world through the bomb and the bullet for over three decades.

The CIA's 'blowback' in Afghanistan is well documented. Encouraging Islamic militancy to galvanise the Mujahideen in its war against the Soviet Army inevitably came at a cost. The outcome was reminiscent of the America domino theory and the failed containment of Communism. First, Afghan veterans reduced Algeria to a state of civil war and disrupted Yemen, then foreign fighters taking part in Bosnia's civil war impacted on Kosovo and Europe. Islamists took power in Afghanistan and destabilised Pakistan.

The outcome for the war on terror in Afghanistan and Iraq is clear: the West has to make sure that these countries have strong central governments to ensure that they do not become fertile breeding grounds for terrorism once again.[4] More alarming is the potentially catastrophic impact the war on terror has had on Pakistan – a nuclear power at loggerheads with its traditional enemy India, also armed with nuclear weapons. If Pakistan becomes a failed state, the consequences could be truly disastrous.

Pakistan is victim to its many competing interests. It was already a divided society: these divisions have been greatly aggravated by two lengthy wars on its doorstep. American policies bear some responsibility for helping destabilise its key ally in the region. The Afghan-Soviet war proved a useful training ground for Pakistani-backed Kashmiri separatists waging a brutal insurgency in neighbouring Indian Kashmir. The CIA's money and guns for the Mujahideen were funnelled through Pakistan – a willing pawn in the dying days of the Cold War. For Pakistan, courting America offset the threat of India and distracted criticism over Kashmir and its nuclear arsenal. However, its support for the Mujahideen and then the Taliban has brought the country to its knees. It was caught between a rock and a hard place: the Taliban and al-Qaeda on one side and Washington on the other.

During the late 1990s American attempts to isolate, apprehend or kill the catalyst for Islamic militancy, Osama bin Laden, simply fuelled the mystique surrounding him. America's seemingly ineffective strikes against Sudan and Afghanistan with missile attacks during the 1990s simply reinforced bin Laden's sense of invulnerability. The fact that a young Saudi, whose Yemeni family had made good in Saudi Arabia, then went on to challenge the last remaining super-power, had an allure that went beyond his religious appeal and ideology. In the eyes of the Muslim world, bin Laden was responsible for bringing down the Soviet Union: he and his supporters had bled the Soviet Army dry and then driven it from Afghanistan, and this – in their view – resulted in the Soviet Union falling apart at the seams. To the militants, 9/11 was his crowning glory.

Ironically, attempts to kill bin Laden have only hardened the resolve of his followers to strike against the heartland of the 'Great Satan'. Conversely, if Washington had been successful, 9/11 would probably never have taken place and there would have been no need to invade Afghanistan. There is no denying that removing the Taliban was the right thing to do – after 9/11 America needed a grand gesture – but what to replace the Taliban with has remained a problem ever since.

What is less well known is that the West – seeking to safeguard its economy and fuel supplies – almost undid the House of Saud. America's military presence in Saudi Arabia, so near Medina and Mecca, rightly or wrongly was seen by many devout Muslims as a defilement of all they hold sacred. After the 1991 Gulf War, Washington chose to ignore the warning signs and continued to maintain its considerable military footprint in Saudi Arabia. The fact that the Bush and Saud families were so firmly entwined was missed by no one, especially those in the *madrassahs* or Islamic religious schools. Saudi Arabia soon found itself embroiled in its own vicious terrorist campaign, designed to drive out Westerners and topple the House of Saud.

Similarly, Clinton's desire to safeguard Bosnia's Muslim population opened the floodgates for foreign fighters, allowing in the Iranian Revolutionary Guard (whose presence in Lebanon's Bekaa Valley and support for Hezbollah had so long been a thorn in the side for Israel and America), and even worse – al-Qaeda. Global Jihad came home to roost in America and then Europe. After a number of false starts in America, militants finally succeeded beyond their wildest dreams on 9/11: since then, every European capital has been affected by Islamic militancy in one way or another.

But the West has a short memory when it comes to Islamic militancy. Well before the fall of the Shah and the Iran-Iraq War, Iraq not Iran had a track record of encouraging Islamic militants: afterwards the situation was reversed. Iran's *mullahs*, led by Ayatollah Khomeini, humiliated America in 1979 over the hostage crisis, resulting in an armed stand-off ever since. Washington then went head to head with the Iranian Revolutionary Guard in Lebanon in the early 1980s, again with humiliating results.

Conveniently, the West has forgotten that Osama bin Laden and al-Qaeda do not have the monopoly on Jihad.[5] When Khomeini took power he declared Jihad against the West, the US in particular, for its support of the ousted Shah and Israel. While in exile, in Paris, Khomeini wrote:

> Holy war means the conquest of all non-Muslim territories. Such a war may well be declared after the formation of an Islamic govern-ment [...] It will then be the duty of every able-bodied adult male to volunteer for this war of conquest, the final aim of which is to put Koranic law in power from one end of the earth to the other.[6]

Spurious claims of links between al-Qaeda and Saddam Hussein and ill-founded fears over Iraq's residual weapons of mass destruction holdings, led to a knee-jerk invasion of Iraq, following the defeat of the Taliban. The only purpose this served was to draw Islamic militants to American troops in Iraq and away from the US homeland. More worryingly, it reinvigorated Hezbollah in Lebanon, Syria and Iraq.

Like America, the late Soviet Union and its successor, the Russian Federation, did much to inadvertently foster Islamic militancy. The motive for Moscow's intervention in Afghanistan became a self-fulfilling prophecy: militants sprang up in Tajikistan and Uzbekistan especially in the Fergana Valley. After the collapse of the Soviet Union, and the drift to independence of the Baltic States and the Transcaucasus republics, the Russian Federation became adamant it would shrink no further: but the trend could not be stopped. When Chechnya descended into bloodshed, Russia learned the full meaning of Islamic militancy in and around Grozny and then on the very streets of Moscow. The invasion of Afghanistan came full circle – not only had global Jihad attacked the West, it had also declared war on its old foe once more.

What the attack of 9/11 did herald was a new concerted international war on terror, the like of which has never been seen before, but it has yet to fully defeat the threat of global Jihad or bring its ringleader, Osama bin Laden, to justice. While the results of this 'war' to date have been very mixed, what is clear is that this struggle will be long, if not potentially unending. In many respects, the West deliberately brought this clash of cultures upon itself.

An array of individuals and organisations assisted with this book directly and indirectly. Therefore I am indebted to staff of the former Afghanistan Information Office, British Embassy Cairo, House of Commons Library, House of Commons Research Service, International Maritime Bureau, International Maritime Organisation, International Terrorism and Organised Crime Group, HQ British Forces Cyprus, Jamestown Foundation, US Congressional Research Service, US Council on Foreign Relations and the US Office of Naval Intelligence to name but a few.

In terms of individuals my gratitude goes to Usman Ansari, James Bass, Tony Banks, Iain Ballantyne, Natasha Brown, Dr Christopher Clapham, Pamela Covey, John Daly, Robert de la Poer, Henry Dodds, Charles Dragonette, Julian Gearing, Rupert Harding, Nick Harvey, Phil Holihead, Glen Howard, David Hughes, Dr Stephen Jones, Pottengal Mukundan, Tim Newark, Bill Prince, James Smith, Charles Stuart, Charles Strathdee, Christopher Summerville, Tony Tucker, Alan Warnes and Claire Yorke. To all those who have gone unnamed my heartfelt thanks for your time, expertise and feedback. Lastly, I must thank my hosts over the years in the Mediterranean, Middle East and North Africa; despite the actions of a minority of ardent Islamists the Arab world still remains a very hospitable place that has much to teach us.

Timeline

1928: Egypt – creation of the Muslim Brotherhood by Hassan al-Banna to promote Islamic Shariah law; inspiration for subsequent Islamist movements.

1948: Palestine – creation of the state of Israel, resulting in first Arab-Israeli War. Palestinian Arabs displaced into neighbouring Jordan.

1954: Egypt – Muslim Brotherhood banned after an attempt on the life of President Nasser.

1956: Egypt – Suez Crisis. In support of Britain and France's ill-fated seizure of the Suez Canal, Israel invades the Sinai and reaches Suez. All three withdraw from Egypt in disgrace.

1964: Middle East – creation of the Palestinian Liberation Organisation.

1967: Middle East – Six Day War. Israel launches surprise attacks against Egypt, Jordan and Syria occupying the Sinai, Gaza, West Bank and Golan Heights. Continued occupation angers the Muslim world.

1969: Sudan – emergence of the Sudanese Muslim Brotherhood (formerly the Islamic Charter Front).

1969–70: Israel, PLO's War of Attrition. Yasser Arafat's Fatah becomes the dominant PLO faction.

1970: Jordan – Black September. PLO expelled from Jordan after creating a 'state within a state', moves into Lebanon. Egypt, President Sadat tolerates the Muslim Brotherhood, though it remains illegal.

1973: Middle East – Yom Kippur War. Egypt and Syria launch surprise attacks to take back the Sinai and Golan Heights, resulting in their defeat by Israel.

1975: Lebanon – Lebanese Civil War breaks out.

1978: Lebanon – temporary Israeli incursion into southern Lebanon in response to Fatah attacks.

1979: Afghanistan – Soviet Union invades to prop up Marxist government. The CIA, Pakistan and Saudi Arabia invoke Jihad or Holy War to oppose the

Soviet intervention. Egypt, Israel withdraws from Sinai. Creation of Palestinian Islamic Jihad.

1980: Egypt – creation of Egyptian Islamic Jihad.

1981: Egypt – assassination of President Sadat by militants, following the Egyptian-Israeli peace agreement. Philippines, creation of the Moro Islamic Liberation Front (split from the Moro National Liberation front).

1982: Lebanon – Israeli invasion of southern Lebanon in response to PLO attacks. PLO expelled and scattered across North Africa and the Middle East. Sabra and Shatila refugee camp massacre outrages Muslim world. Hezbollah emerges to oppose the Israeli occupation. Indonesia, creation of Jemaah Islamiyah (terror cells formed 1993).

1983: Sudan – imposition of Shariah law sparks civil war with the Christian south.

23 October 1983: Lebanon – terrorists blow up the US Embassy and US Marine Corps HQ in Beirut.

1985: Sudan – Sudanese Muslim Brotherhood charged with sedition, becomes the National Islamic Front.

1986: Saudi Arabia – Saudis seek to radicalise the PLO as they had done with the Afghan Mujahideen.

1987: Israel – creation of Palestinian Hamas or Islamic Resistance Party (military wing created in 1992).

1987–93: Israel – First Intifada. Palestinian uprising against Israeli rule in the Palestinian occupied territories.

1988: Pakistan – al-Qaeda formed by Osama bin Laden, Muhammad Atef and Ayman al-Zawahiri in Peshawar, to support foreign fighters in Afghanistan. Israel, PLO renounces terrorism. Eritrea, emergence of the Eritrean Islamic Jihad Movement.

1989: Afghanistan – Soviet Union withdraws. Bin Laden and supporters return to Saudi Arabia and begin to criticise King Fahd and his government.

1990–91: Kuwait – First Gulf War. Iraqis invade Kuwait and bin Laden offers his services to help oust them: instead he is expelled from Saudi Arabia and moves to Sudan. Philippines, creation of the Abu Sayyaf Group (split from the Moro National Liberation Front).

1992: Algeria – creation of the Armed Islamic Group or GIA, leading to a bloody six-year insurgency and the spread of Algerian terrorism to Europe.

5 April 1992–29 February 1996: Bosnia – Siege of Sarajevo by Serbian forces, 10,000 killed and 56,000 wounded. Muslim world is angered by Western impotence in protecting Muslim safe havens.

29 December 1992: Yemen – militants blow up a hotel, in an attempt to kill US troops deploying to Somalia.

23 February 1993: US – Ramzi Yousef and his terrorist cell detonate a car bomb in the World Trade Center, New York, killing six and injuring over 1,000.

December 1994: Philippines – Ramzi Yousef allegedly meets Terry Nichols to plot an attack on the Alfred P. Murray Federal Building in Oklahoma City.

1994–95: Philippines – Bojinka Plot. Ramzi Yousef plans to blow up eleven airliners (prototype 9/11), as well as kill the Pope and attack the CIA's HQ in Virginia. The attacks never come to fruition.

7 February 1995: Pakistan – Yousef caught and extradited to the US.

19 April 1995: US – Oklahoma City bombing, 168 killed and over 680 wounded.

26 June 1995: Egypt – militants attempt to assassinate Egyptian President Hosni Mubarak.

11 September 1995: Bosnia – Srebrenica massacre, Serbs kill 7,000 Muslims, outraging the Muslim world, which alleges Western indifference.

26 October 1995: Malta – Fathi Shkaki, the head of Islamic Jihad, gunned down by agents on a motorbike. The act is believed to have been the work of Israel's secret service, Mossad.

13 November 1995: Saudi Arabia – truck bomb explodes outside the Saudi National Guard Communications centre, Riyadh, killing five US servicemen and two Indians.

19 November 1995: Pakistan – Egyptian Embassy in Islamabad blown up, fourteen killed and fifty-nine wounded.

Spring 1996: Sudan – bin Laden is obliged to leave and seeks sanctuary in Afghanistan with the Taliban.

23 August 1996: Afghanistan – bin Laden declares Holy War against American forces in Saudi Arabia.

26 September 1996: Afghanistan – Taliban take power and impose Shariah law.

17 November 1997: Egypt – attack on tourists at the Temple of Hatshepsut (Deir el-Bahri), Luxor, sixty-three killed and twenty-six wounded.

23 February 1998: Afghanistan – al-Qaeda issues a *fatwa* against all Americans, wherever they may be in the world.

7 August 1998: Kenya and Tanzania – truck bombs destroy the US embassies, 252 killed and 5,000 wounded.

20 August 1998: Afghanistan and Sudan – in retaliation for the bombings, America launches cruise missile strikes.

4 November 1998: US – American Attorney General indicts bin Laden and Muhammad Atef on a total of 301 counts of murder, following the East Africa bombings.

7 July 1999: US – President Clinton imposes sanctions against the Taliban in Afghanistan for harbouring bin Laden.

4–16 September 1999: Russia – apartment bombings in Moscow, Buynaksk and Volgodonsk, 300 killed in response to Moscow's actions in Chechnya.

May 2000: Lebanon – following Israel's withdrawal, southern Lebanon is liberated by Hezbollah.

28 September 2000–February 2005: Israel – Second Intifada. Renewed Palestinian uprising.

12 October 2000: Yemen – suicide bombing of the USS *Cole* in Aden harbour.

24 December 2000: Indonesia – Christmas Eve bombings in Jakarta.

28 July 2001: United Arab Emirates – Djamel Beghal, an Algerian member of al-Qaeda, is arrested after it is uncovered that he is planning to crash a helicopter into the US Embassy in Paris.

11 September 2001: US – nineteen terrorists hijack four American airliners and crash them into the Twin Towers of the World Trade Center (New York), the Pentagon (Arlington, Virginia) and a field in Shanksville, Pennsylvania.

6 October 2001: Saudi Arabia – suicide bombing in al-Khobar.

7 October 2001: Afghanistan – Operation Enduring Freedom commences. America and Britain drive al-Qaeda and the Taliban from Afghanistan after they refuse to surrender Osama bin Laden.

20 December 2001: Afghanistan – NATO-led International Security Assistance Force (ISAF) established to help stabilise the country.

22 December 2001: US, Boston – British-born al-Qaeda shoe bomber, Richard Reid, arrested after trying to blow up American Airlines Flight 63 en route to Miami from Paris.

23 December 2001: France – attempted bombing of Paris to Miami flight.

12 March 2002: Pakistan – grenade attack on church in Karachi.

11 April 2002: Tunisia – suicide truck bombing of a synagogue.

8 May 2002: Pakistan – suicide car bombing of French engineers in Karachi.

15 June 2002: Pakistan – suicide car bombing of US consulate in Karachi.

6 October 2002: Yemen – suicide bomb attack on French oil tanker.

8 October 2002: Kuwait – gun attack on US armed forces, one US marine killed.

12 October 2002: Indonesia – Bali nightclub bombings, 182 killed and 266 wounded.

28 November 2002: Kenya – suicide bomb attack on Israeli hotel in Mombasa.

20 March 2003: Iraq – Operation Iraqi Freedom commences, as part of the war on terror – America and Britain seek to overthrow President Saddam Hussein.

12 May 2003: Saudi Arabia – assault and bombing of expatriates in Riyadh.

16 May 2003: Morocco – attack on Jewish centre, restaurant and hotel in Casablanca.

5 August 2003: Indonesia – Marriot hotel bombing in Jakarta, twelve killed and 150 wounded.

9 November 2003: Saudi Arabia – assault and bombing of a housing complex in Riyadh.

15 November 2003: Turkey – bombing of two synagogues in Istanbul.

20 November 2003: Turkey – bombing of British consulate and HSBC bank in Istanbul.

14 & 25 December 2003: Pakistan – two assassination attempts on President Musharraf.

6 February 2004: Russia – Moscow Metro bombing, forty killed and 120 wounded.

11 March 2004: Spain – Madrid train bombings, killing 191 and wounding 1,800.

9 September 2004: Indonesia – bombing of Australian Embassy in Jakarta, nine killed and 150 wounded.

7 July 2005: UK – four bomb attacks in London, three on the Underground, one on a bus, fifty-six killed and 700 wounded.

1 October 2005: Indonesia – Bali bombings, twenty killed and 129 wounded.

11 July 2006: India – Mumbai train bombings, 209 killed and over 700 injured by Lashkar-e-Tayyiba and the Students' Islamic Movement of India.

29 June 2007: UK – London, two car bombs disabled before detonation.

30 June 2007: UK – Glasgow International Airport car bomb attack, one dead and five wounded.

27 December 2007: Pakistan, Rawalpindi – assassination of former Prime Minister Benazir Bhutto, al-Qaeda claims responsibility.

2008: Pakistan – Taliban take control of the Swat, Lower Dir, Shangla and Buner and have a presence in many of the NWFP other districts. Also control North and South Waziristan. Pakistan seeks to reassert control of Bajaur.

17 September 2008: Yemen – car bomb attack outside US Embassy, sixteen killed.

20 September 2008: Pakistan – Marriot Hotel bombing in Islamabad, fifty-five killed and 266 wounded.

26–29 November 2008: India – Mumbai city attacks (including Oberoi Trident & Taj Mahal Palace hotels) carried out by Lashkar-e-Tayyiba, 173 killed and 308 injured.

April 2009: Pakistan – Pakistani government seeks to reassert control of NWFP.

27 May 2009: Pakistan – Lahore bombing by Pakistani Taliban, thirty-five killed and 350 injured.

4, 5 & 7 July 2009: Philippines – bombings on Mindanao Island, seven killed and 66 wounded.

27 July 2009: America – seven men arrested near Raleigh, North Carolina, for conspiracy to commit violent Jihad.

17 August 2009: Russian Federation – Police HQ blown up, Nazran, Ingushetia, twenty-five killed and 164 injured.

October 2009: Pakistan – Pakistani government seeks to reassert control of Waziristan.

2 November 2009: Pakistan, Rawalpindi – bombing near Pakistani Army GHQ carried out by Pakistani Taliban, thirty-five dead and sixty injured.

13 November 2009: Pakistan, Peshawar – car-bomb attack on Pakistani intelligence's regional HQ.

25 December 2009: America – Umar Farouk Abdulmutallab arrested trying to blow up Northwest Airlines Flight 253 en route from Amsterdam to Detroit.

2010: Afghanistan, Iraq, Pakistan, Somalia, Yemen, Gaza and the West Bank remain blighted by Islamic militant groups.

Chapter 1

Killing bin Laden

The world watched in horror and dismay on the morning of 11 September 2001 as Islamic terrorists slammed two airliners into the twin towers of New York's World Trade Center (WTC), one into the Pentagon and a fourth into rural Pennsylvania en route to who knows where. On that fateful day the first aircraft struck the WTC north tower at 8.47 a.m., the second smashed into the south tower sixteen minutes later. By 10.30 a.m. both towers had collapsed into a mass of shattered glass, concrete and steel. Manhattan disappeared under a pall of choking smoke and dust centred on what became known as 'ground zero': a term normally associated with the impact of a nuclear warhead.[1] New Yorkers staggered about their city in a daze of incomprehension and terror.

Less than an hour after the first New York attack, just outside Washington, the third hijacked aircraft flew into the south-west side of the Pentagon at 9.38 a.m. The attack was so precise many initially thought the building had been hit by a missile. About twenty-five minutes later the fourth aircraft came down in Pennsylvania after passengers unsuccessfully sought to regain control of the aircraft.

Initially, al-Qaeda had planned to hijack a total of ten planes, with the intention of crashing them into targets on both coasts of America. These would have included nuclear power plants and tall buildings in California and Washington State. However, the four planes had the desired effect. Internationally, the fear and disgust was palpable and the spectre of such outrages was to haunt every major city around the world for the next decade. America asked itself what it had done to inspire such hatred by militant members of Islam? But behind the scenes, the US government had been expecting such a spectacular attack for almost ten years. Osama bin Laden, leader of al-Qaeda, immediately named as Washington's prime suspect, later said:

> We calculated in advance the number of casualties from the enemy, who would be killed based on the position of the tower. We calculated that the floors that would be hit would be three or four floors. I was the most optimistic of them all ...[2]

With these words he became America's public enemy number one. What most Americans did not realise was that Washington had spent the last four years trying to kill him.

The international community immediately rallied to America. The very next day United Nation's Security Council Resolution (UNSCR) 1368 and General Assembly Resolution 56/1 called for immediate international co-operation to bring the perpetrators to justice. They also called for much broader co-operation against global terrorism in general and this was followed on 28 September 2001 by UNSCR 1373. Enacted under Chapter VII of the UN Charter, it required every member state to undertake seventeen measures against all those who support – directly or indirectly – acts of terrorism.

Also on 12 September, President George W. Bush declared the attacks on the American homeland acts of war and requested Congress provide the resources – to the tune of $20 billion – to fight the terrorists wherever they might be. In the event, Congress doubled this sum. The following day, US Secretary of State, Colin Powell, confirmed that Osama bin Laden, believed to be hiding in Afghanistan, was a suspect.[3]

After British prime minister, Tony Blair, held a meeting with President Bush at the White House on 20 September, Operation Enduring Freedom was born. From the first news of the attacks, Blair was convinced it was the work of al-Qaeda and his immediate response was to offer support to America. Britain's intelligence chiefs, notably the head of the Security Service, Secret Intelligence Service and the Government Communications Headquarters, also flew to Washington for urgent talks with their counterparts.[4] The UK had a good handle on Islamic militant groups because it had tolerated fundraising offices in London.

British intelligence advised that bin Laden was the only one capable of such an attack and that no rogue states were involved. Blair was of the view that simply removing bin Laden from the picture would not be enough – and he was right, as militant Islam was already well established around the world. To some, the spread of Saudi Wahhabism, which preaches a return to the pure and orthodox practice of the 'fundamentals' of Islam, is seen as a threat to more moderate Muslim beliefs. Blair wanted a long-term strategy for dealing with Islamic fundamentalism – or rather, Islamic militancy. Bush told Blair that the focus would be Osama bin Laden and Afghanistan's Taliban government. Washington demanded that the Taliban hand over bin Laden immediately. For the very first time the North Atlantic Treaty Organisation (NATO) invoked its mutual defence clause on 2 October 2001, whereby an attack on a member state is considered an attack on all. Five days later the American- and British-led Coalition began systematic air attacks on the Taliban.

The American people – initially stunned and shocked by the sheer magnitude of this assault on their homeland – quickly recovered and sought to lash out as swiftly as possible at those it held responsible. In early October 2001 the Americans tried to kill Osama bin Laden, his deputy Ayman al-Zawahiri, Khalid Sheikh Mohammed (architect of 9/11) and Mullah Omar, leader of the

Taliban. The al-Qaeda and Taliban hit list was much longer than this, but they were the ones that really mattered and the intelligence community naively hoped that by decapitating al-Qaeda the threat would somehow fade away. Tragically, this was a case of too little too late: 9/11 was, in fact, the culmination of a decade of steadily spreading militant Islam. Memories were short; for few beyond the intelligence and law enforcement circles remembered Ramzi Yousef's dramatic truck-bomb attack on the WTC on 26 February 1993, which had first heralded the transnational Jihad against the United States.[5] His attack predated bin Laden's declaration of war on the American homeland by three and a half years. In that time militant Islam's rise had gone unchecked.

In the immediate aftermath of 9/11, the world's intelligence agencies were asked: who or what is Osama bin Laden and his al-Qaeda organisation? What had motivated his followers to sacrifice themselves and carry out such appalling atrocities? It was clear that the perpetrators saw themselves at war with America, but to what end? What was particularly worrying was that many of the young men now attracted to Islamic militancy were well educated, often to university level. These were not stereotypical disenchanted youths from poverty-stricken backgrounds who had nothing to lose, these were men who could understand, articulate and rationalise their cause and yet willingly die for it.

When the experts briefed the politicians the explanation was far from comforting. Bin Laden, they said, since the mid-1990s, saw himself as the self-appointed defender of oppressed Muslims around the world, leading a coalition called the 'International Islamic Front for Jihad Against the Jews and Crusaders to fight the US'. His battle cry was that the Christian Crusaders led by America were regularly being allowed to defile Islam. He and other Islamists were not so much advocates of a Pan-Arabic world but a Pan-Islamic one – or, more precisely, a Sunni-dominated Muslim world. Bin Laden dreamed of recreating the Islamic caliphate that followed the death of the revered Prophet Muhammad.

Osama bin Laden had clearly articulated his philosophy in the 1990s, calling for the imposition of Shariah law throughout the Arabian Peninsula, holy war against America, for supporting Israel and its occupation of Palestine, and the US military presence in Saudi Arabia (which, by his own admission, would not stop even if American troops were withdrawn).

His aim was to fight injustice perpetrated against Muslims anywhere in the world. In effect, he had tapped into every major Muslim grievance stretching from Europe to the Far East. Militant Islam was the new Marxism or socialism – at war with decadent Western capitalism. To some young Muslims, their faith in this creed was unshakeable.

Islamists believe that Islam is a political ideology, arguing that political sovereignty belongs to Allah and that Shariah or Islamic law should be state law

– hence Islamism. To them, there can be no place for secular governments. Ultimately, this is what Jihadists or Holy warriors are fighting for, as most Islamists believe their goals can only be achieved through violence. However, militant Islam should not be viewed as a single problem, rather a series of interconnected ones, ranging from diverse international and regional political disenchantment to local, student-driven radicalism. Nor is Islam synonymous with Islamism, such a contention would be clearly ridiculous: fortunately, the global voice of the Islamists is in the minority, but in the wake of 9/11, militant Islam was in the ascendancy.

The true impact of 'Franchise Terrorism' had not yet been fully appreciated. The fact that al-Qaeda was, until 9/11, a bit player among many unsavoury militant Islamic groups in Afghanistan, was largely ignored by the Western intelligence agencies. A whole raft of terror groups were training in Afghanistan, which read like an international Who's Who: the Kashmiri separatists, Harakat ul-Mujahidin, Jaish-e-Mohammed, Lashkar-e-Tayyiba, the Islamic Movement of Uzbekistan, Tajik stragglers from the United Tajik Organisation, as well as other Uiguher and Chechen separatist organisations. Although Western intelligence was not really interested in any of them, they regularly caused mayhem on the Indian sub-continent and in Central Asia. The only ones that mattered to Operation Enduring Freedom were al-Qaeda, al-Zawahiri's Egyptian Islamic Jihad, and the Taliban. They, after all, were held responsible for 9/11.

At the time, the question everyone was asking was: where is bin Laden hiding? Kandahar, the Taliban heartland or Jalalabad, were the two most likely locations. If bin Laden was going to run for the Pakistani border and Pakistan's lawless North West Frontier Province, the latter city seemed the most likely. Also, because he and his supporters had now brought a rain of fire down on the Taliban, it seemed likely that he would be unpopular in Kandahar. The worry was that, from Jalalabad, he could easily lose himself in the vastness of the Hindu Kush Mountains.

The chance of finding bin Laden in a vast lawless haystack like Afghanistan seemed remote. The British Joint Intelligence Committee had assessed that he was still in Afghanistan, but exactly where remained open to informed guess-work. The previous three years had been a litany of lost opportunities when it came to killing the world's most notorious terrorist leader. All in all, it was not an auspicious start.

The fact that, within the first twenty-four hours of the air campaign against the Taliban on 7 October 2001 few, if any, high value targets remained, mattered little. In reality, close air support for the advancing Tajik-dominated Northern Alliance proved more productive than bombing the Taliban's ramshackle infrastructure. Those assigned to support Operation Veritas (as the UK's part in America's Operation Enduring Freedom was dubbed) had no expertise in counter-terrorism or Afghanistan. The representatives of the armed forces talked in terms of applied pressure and critical nodes, blind to the fact that Afghanistan had never functioned as a unitary state or had any real infra-structure. Without troops on the ground it seemed probable that the Taliban would simply shrug off the bombing.

A few days later an American kill was indeed confirmed: it was an important one but not the one everyone was hoping for. Perhaps, in Washington's eyes, he was a good second best – the Egyptian Mohammed Atef, bin Laden's operations chief and mastermind behind 9/11. A missile strike, probably directed by US Special Forces on the ground, killed him just outside Kabul. Two other senior Egyptian al-Qaeda leaders were also listed dead: Tariq Anwar al-Sayyid Ahmad and Mohammad Saleh. Another, Anas al-Liby, was rumoured killed, but it later emerged that he had escaped: he was eventually captured in Afghanistan the following year.[6]

As the US-led air campaign gathered pace, several more senior terrorists were claimed, including, it was rumoured, Juma Namangani, leader of the Islamic Movement of Uzbekistan. His forces were openly fighting alongside the Taliban and al-Qaeda against the Northern Alliance. No one in the West cared about his demise but in Russia, Tajikistan, China and Chechnya, it was a different matter. Fighters from the last three countries were among his ranks. Similarly, a senior member of Lashkar-e-Tayyiba was reported killed – good news for the Indian government – but Osama bin Laden easily eluded America's military might.

Few people in the outside world realised that this was not the first attempt on bin Laden's life. America had been attempting to eliminate him since the 1990s. Saudi nationals using assault rifles tried to assassinate him in the Sudanese capital Khartoum in 1994. Before 9/11 it was President Bill Clinton who signed a memorandum instructing the CIA to work with local elements in Afghanistan to capture bin Laden and authorised them to use alternative methods with which to attack al-Qaeda.

To this end, in the mid-1990s, the Central Intelligence Agency (CIA) established an Osama bin Laden Task Force to attempt an assassination using poison. Trying to find bin Laden in the vast wastes of the Afghan mountains proved time-consuming and exhausting for those Special Forces and local agents assigned to the hunt. The CIA even attempted to snatch bin Laden from Afghanistan in 1997, but the mission was to be aborted for diplomatic reasons.[7] Bin Laden was not yet aware that he was under intense CIA scrutiny, or indeed that the National Security Agency[8] was eavesdropping on his mobile phone. This meant that, while he was at Tarnak Farms he stuck to a fairly predictable schedule.

George Tenet, the CIA's Director, was never keen on the kidnap plan. The idea was that Pashtun tribesmen would grab bin Laden and hide him in a cave until US Special Forces could retrieve him. Much could go wrong with such a mission and Tenet firmly believed that Clinton only authorised bin Laden's capture not his death. To the CIA, ambiguity hung over the directive to use lethal force to apprehend bin Laden.

After 9/11, senior Clinton officials vigorously disputed Tenet's contention that he had never been authorised to kill bin Laden. Similarly, it was only after 9/11 that President Clinton confirmed that he had authorised the arrest and, if necessary, the killing of Osama bin Laden, and that America had made contact with a group in Afghanistan to do it. He also admitted that, in the late 1990s, America trained Pakistani commandos for a bin Laden snatch-and-grab raid, but lacked the necessary intelligence to carry it out.

Significantly, the plan to kidnap bin Laden was pre-empted by Tenet's visit to Saudi Arabia to solicit Saudi assistance in dealing with bin Laden. Crown Prince Abdullah said yes, the Saudis would buy off the Taliban to hand him over. However, Washington was instructed to keep the deal secret and bin Laden would not be sent to the US to face trial.[9] Sandy Berger, US National Security Advisor, was informed, and as this seemed a much easier solution to the bin Laden problem, the CIA kidnap plan was cancelled. After Tenet's meeting in Saudi Arabia, Prince Turki held talks with the Taliban in Afghanistan but these came to nothing. Some felt that the kidnap plan was a lost opportunity and that the Saudi offer permitted Tenet to weasel out of covert action against bin Laden.

After the bombing of the US embassies in Kenya and Tanzania, Michael Scheuer, chief of the bin Laden tracking unit, received a visit from Tenet. The Director was visibly shaken that the cancellation of the kidnap plan had come back to haunt him so soon and said: 'I guess we made a mistake.' Scheuer was understandably blunt in his response: 'No, sir, I think *you* made a mistake.'[10]

Following the East African bombings Washington offered $5 million for bin Laden's capture as well as striking his camps around Khost and Jalalabad in Afghanistan with Tomahawk cruise missiles. While America sought to capture or kill Osama bin Laden, opportunities were passed up in December 1998 and February/May 1999 to launch strikes on known locations where he was staying. Ironically, as early as December 1998, Bill Clinton had received a 'President's Daily Briefing' entitled *Bin Laden is Preparing to Hijack US Aircraft and Other Attacks*. While Clinton's response was not recorded, New York's airports were placed on full alert.

When the retaliatory attacks on al-Qaeda training camps in Afghanistan were launched from the Arabian Sea they proved singularly ineffective. The cruise missile attack on Zhawar Kili al-Badr terrorist training camp in 1998 had been clearly botched. According to satellite imagery of the strike, the camp was deserted: rumour had it that Pakistani intelligence had tipped off the Taliban, who had warned their guests to make themselves scarce.

There were at least four more attempts to kill bin Laden between 1998 and 2000. The closest the Americans came was in 1999. On one occasion bin Laden was photographed on a hunting trip but he was accompanied by Arab princes so, for fear of a diplomatic incident, no missile attack was launched. A plan was also concocted in the spring of 1998 to use local tribesmen to attack his Tarnak Farms compound in Kandahar and kidnap him. This was abandoned by June 1998 as nobody at senior level within the CIA wanted to support the mission. In a third incident bin Laden was tracked on the ground for five days, though no missile attack was launched for fear of civilian casualties and the opportunity was lost.

An unarmed, unmanned Predator aerial vehicle or drone located him again at the end of 1999 at a training camp near Khost in eastern Afghanistan. Michael Scheuer, former CIA officer in charge of Alec Station, which tracked bin Laden during the 1990s, recalled:

> We had no doubt over his identity. Bin Laden can clearly be seen standing out from the rest of the group next to the buildings. Nobody at the top of the CIA wanted to take the decision to arm Predator [unmanned aerial vehicle]. It meant that, even if we could find him, we were not allowed to kill him.[11]

In fact, the nearest the CIA ever came to killing bin Laden was in early 1999. On 9 February, acting on a tip-off, CIA tracking teams located a camp close to a large airstrip in the desert south of Kandahar. Richard A. Clarke, Clinton's senior counter-terrorism advisor, observed: 'When word came through that we had a contemporaneous sighting from informants, the counter-terrorism security group met immediately by secure video conference.'[12]

In reality Clinton's options were severely limited as, at that stage, the Predator was not armed, which meant sea-launched cruise missiles were all that could be deployed at such short notice, but the attack on the Khalden training camp in the east of the country the previous year had hardly produced encouraging results.

Nevertheless, a strike was planned for 11 February 1999, but information that visitors from the United Arab Emirates were present stalled the attack. Scheuer alleged that Clarke called a senior figure in the Emirates royal family and conveniently the party moved on and the chance to kill bin Laden was lost.

State-sanctioned assassinations are an emotive issue and a legally grey area, and for many years the CIA was prevented from resuming such Black Ops due to diplomatic and political fall-out. Post 9/11 the CIA was back in business, but what was once done up close and personal is increasingly done at long distance. In fact, in its war on terror, the CIA turned to the aptly named Predator as the platform of choice for delivering a goodnight call to senior terror leaders.[13]

This was most visibly exemplified by Washington's escalating efforts to kill bin Laden.

Dissatisfied with the CIA's poor results, Admiral Scott Frey (Director Operations for the Joint Staffs) and Charlie Allen (in charge of collection priorities for the US intelligence community) came up with a novel way to hunt bin Laden. Why not, they argued, use Predators to regularly loiter over Afghanistan to provide a real-time video feed on suspicious movements.[14] Unfortunately, Predator was then in short supply, being tied up over Bosnia and Iraq; additionally, there was a major hurdle in getting the various agencies to agree to the unprecedented and concerted use of UAVs against terrorists rather than military targets.

Sandy Berger, Deputy National Security Advisor, had to bully the intelligence chiefs to get their act together. The attack on the USS *Cole*, off Yemen, showed that al-Qaeda's war was spreading and by September 2000 the necessary technical means were in place to support a UAV counter-terrorism mission in Afghanistan. The CIA prepared to operate Predator from their HQ at Langley, Virginia, via the military's Central Command or CENTCOM HQ in Tampa, Florida, and a clandestine base in Uzbekistan at Karshi-Khanabad, codenamed K2 (Pakistan would have been the ideal host nation, but a military coup made it impossible). Despite the CIA's reluctance to take the war to al-Qaeda, Ramzi Yousef – mastermind behind the 1993 WTC bombing – had been planning to fly an aircraft into Langley.

Those arguing against using UAVs for such a mission felt vindicated when a Predator was damaged on take-off, causing a row over who would pay for the $4 million system. Between September and December 2000 the CIA, US Air Force and an inter-agency operations team conducted fifteen unarmed Predator reconnaissance missions over Afghanistan.

Afghanistan's ruling Taliban proved wily adversaries. When an old radar picked up a Predator flight they scrambled an ancient, barely airworthy Soviet MiG fighter to intercept it. Operators at Langley and K2 watched with dismay as the Taliban pilot took off and began to circle within 2 miles of the UAV. 'Holy shit, it's going to hit us!' exclaimed the startled operator as the fighter loomed into the UAV's camera: some of those in the control room actually dived beneath their desks.[15] Fortunately, the MiG overshot its target and to the operators' satisfaction, they were able to track a Land Rover in real-time, leaving a known terrorist camp outside Kandahar.

In testimony given by George Tenet in 2004, he said:

> During two missions the Predator may have observed Osama bin Laden. In one case this was an after-the-fact judgement. In the other, sources indicated that bin Laden would likely be at his Tarnak Farms facility, and, so cued, the Predator flew over the facility the next day.[16]

This was a missed opportunity, as Tenet notes: 'It imaged a tall man dressed in white robes with a physical and operational signature fitting bin Laden. A group of ten people gathered around him were apparently paying their respects for a minute or two.'[17]

Former senior White House official, Richard A. Clarke, is convinced that, on at least three occasions in late 2000, Predator found bin Laden. Unfortunately, the US Navy had no attack submarines on station, so no Tomahawk missile strikes could be launched. To make matters worse, the onset of winter in 2000 made it impossible to fly and the Predators were returned to America. But planning immediately commenced for a second deployment.

To get round the problem of not having cruise missiles or aircraft readily available, it was suggested that an armed version of Predator might be used. It would be easier and less risky to deploy than men on the ground and a lot quieter than roaring jet fighter-bombers: in effect, with its long loiter time, the UAV provided an ideal silent assassin. US Special Operations Command also developed plans to deploy an AC-130 Spectre gunship aircraft tasked to kill bin Laden (it has been claimed that AC-130s successfully used Hellfire missiles against specific targets in Serbia and Kosovo). These plans did not come to fruition probably due to the lack of US Special Forces bases in the region from which the aircraft could operate.

Under the direction of General John Jumper, Air Combat Command, weaponisation of the Predator was already well under way. The USAF had been working on mounting the AGM-114 Hellfire laser-guided, fire-and-forget, air-to-surface missile, essentially an anti-tank weapon carried by the Cobra and Apache attack helicopters, on Predator. Its in-service date was scheduled for 2004 but this was dramatically accelerated after discussions between USAF and the CIA. Test firings, using line-of-sight communication, were successfully carried out in late February 2001 at Indian Springs.[18]

The CIA confirmed weapons tests were then conducted between 22 May and 7 June 2001, but with mixed results. Missile fusing proved a problem. At the same time, in an effort to foster inter-agency co-ordination, two exercises were held to examine command-and-control issues and rules of engagement. Dubbed the MQ-1, the combination of Hellfire, Multi-spectral Targeting System and Predator seemed a winner.[19]

Unfortunately, when President Clinton left office, bin Laden remained very much alive and precious time was lost by the new Bush administration. In later years, in response to why he had not done more against al-Qaeda and bin Laden, Clinton remarked bitterly: 'I got closer to killing him than anybody's gotten since.' He also pointed out that he had authorised the CIA to kill bin Laden, whereas the Bush administration 'had no meetings on bin Laden for nine months'.[20]

In April 2001 Richard Clarke briefed the Bush administration's Deputies Committee, headed by the new Deputy National Security Advisor, Steve Hadley. Clarke stated: 'We need to put pressure on both the Taliban and al-Qaeda by arming the Northern Alliance and other groups in Afghanistan.' Adding, 'Simultaneously, we need to target bin Laden and his leadership by re-initiating flights of the Predator.'[21] Ironically, Paul Wolfowitz, Deputy Secretary of Defense, did not grasp the significance of the man he described as 'this little terrorist'. The administration did not fly UAVs over Afghanistan during its first eight months and was still refining the plan to employ the MQ-1 to assassinate al-Qaeda's leadership when the 11 September 2001 attacks on New York and Washington took place.

Washington could not decide whether to re-deploy the unarmed Predator in early summer 2001, while the weather was good, or wait for the armed variant. George Tenet observed: 'Some CIA officers believed that continued reconnaissance operations would undercut later armed operations.' The worry was that the Taliban would detect the flights again, making Predator vulnerable to interception, anti-aircraft fire or surface-to-air missiles. Tenet elaborates:

> Additionally, indications were that the host country would be unlikely to tolerate extensive operations, especially after the Taliban became aware, as it surely would, of that country's assistance to the United States.[22]

Such host-nation concerns were well founded. In June 2005 the Uzbek government imposed restrictions on operations out of the K2 airbase in response to Washington's criticism of its crackdown on protestors in Andijan. American HC-130 aircraft had to be relocated to Bagram airbase in Afghanistan, while cargo aircraft had to be diverted to Manas in Kyrgyzstan.

In the meantime, the key players could simply not agree if armed Predator should be used against those responsible for the numerous previous terrorists attacks. The CIA was concerned it could lead to reprisals against their operatives around the world. George Tenet was arguing a week before 9/11 that it would be a terrible mistake, and it has been alleged that the CIA did not act sooner because the Directorate of Operations were risk averse. After 9/11 there were, understandably, no objections to armed Predator operating as soon as possible over Afghanistan.[23] According to a senior CIA source:

> During the summer, [the] CIA led an inter-agency effort to fully develop the capabilities of the armed Predator and to explore the questions inherent in its use. One question that arose was who would bear responsibility for Predators that might be lost – Department of Defense or CIA[?] While we finally agreed to split the cost evenly, the question was still in negotiation on 11 September 2001.[24]

In the aftermath, US Special Operations Command was granted a budget increase of almost 50 per cent, with $250 million being spent on Predator and another $610 million on the Global Hawk UAV.

In fact, the CIA was authorised to deploy the MQ-1 in early September 2001, but only on reconnaissance missions. Uzbekistan, which had not agreed to allow armed flights, frustratingly held up the delivery of the Hellfire missiles – doubtless while the thorny issue of appropriate rent for K2 was discussed. Just five days after 9/11 the missiles arrived, but the first armed flight did not occur until 7 October 2001, when host-nation approval was finally granted, by which time Afghanistan was under general air attack. In the meantime, the CIA had to make do with reconnaissance flights, which resumed over Kabul and Kandahar on 18 September.

During September and October 2001 there were at least four unsuccessful attempts to ambush bin Laden on the ground. The CIA-guided MQ-1 got off to a good start, killing al-Qaeda's No. 3, Mohammed Atef (alias Abu Hafs), in November 2001 near Kabul. By this stage, two Predators had been lost to icing, leaving sixteen in total, though only one was in the air at any one time. The following month, acting on a tip-off, a Hellfire fired from Predator took out a Range Rover believed to be carrying bin Laden. DNA samples from the body later proved otherwise (the bin Laden family obligingly provided the FBI with swabs for comparison). This was probably the closest the MQ-1 got to killing him before he escaped from Tora Bora and into Pakistan. Two other key al-Qaeda figures, Mohammad Saleh and Tariq Anwar al-Sayyid Ahmad, along with Juma Namangani, were killed around the same time in USAF bombing raids.[25]

On 4 February 2002, a Predator tracked a group of up to twenty people, apparently converging for a meeting, and targeted six suspected al-Qaeda leaders (who it was hoped included bin Laden or his chief lieutenant Ayman al-Zawahiri) near the Zawahr Kili caves. Although the missile killed at least two of the party, it was found not to include any of al-Qaeda's top leadership. Local Afghans claimed that the dead were, in fact, scrap-metal collectors. Three days later an MQ-1 attacked and destroyed a convoy transporting suspected terrorists. Efforts were stepped up and by July 2002 Dale Watson, FBI counter-terrorism chief, was convinced that bin Laden was dead. His faith proved misplaced.

Behind the scenes concern circulated in Whitehall, London, about the legality of such operations. Israel is regularly castigated for assassinating Hamas, Hezbollah and Islamic Jihad leaders. The UK-based CIA liaison officers found themselves having to fend off unwelcome questions regarding the scale and effectiveness of State Department-sponsored counter-terrorist assassination attempts. Not only was Downing Street and Permanent Joint Headquarters not informed about US intentions, there were serious concerns that such operations could potentially be viewed as the illegal murder of non-combatants if target intelligence proved incorrect. In contrast, President Bush was impressed with the MQ-1's efforts, but was disappointed the CIA could only fly a single mission at a time – ambitiously he advocated fifty of them in theatre. George Tenet assured Bush that they were trying to fly two simultaneously.

The MQ-1 was not only used against terrorists. The CIA tried unsuccessfully to kill Afghan warlord Gulbuddin Hekmatyar, after he called for the killing of US troops, on 6 May 2002. A Predator launched its Hellfires into the Shegal Gorge near Kabul, wounding thirty people, but missed its intended target. The month before, security forces in Kabul had carried out mass arrests of Hekmatyar's Hezb-i-Islami party, which was accused of planning bomb attacks on Coalition forces.

Following the attempt on Hekmatyar, the CIA remained cautious about killing terrorists using the MQ-1. Some argue that they had become tied up in legal knots, like Whitehall. While targets and the number of attacks remain highly classified, former CIA official Mike Scheuer has stated that, between May 2002 and February 2005, the MQ-1 fired less than ten missiles. This was not for the lack of targets (the total number of terrorist fatalities has never been revealed) but because of legal constraints.[26]

After 9/11 the CIA's counter-terrorist efforts came under the scrutiny of a joint inquiry conducted by the US Senate Select and House Permanent Select Committees on Intelligence. To add to the indignity, the CIA's Office of Inspector General was then required to endorse the inquiry's findings.[27]

Damningly, the joint inquiry concluded that before 9/11 neither the US government nor the American intelligence community had a comprehensive strategy for dealing with al-Qaeda. The view was that the Director General Central Intelligence 'was either unwilling or unable to marshal the full range of IC resources necessary to combat the growing threat to the United States'.[28] In light of the evidence, the Office of Inspector General had little choice but to agree with this finding.

In particular, co-ordination failures between the CIA and the National Security Agency were identified. The latter was reluctant to share its signals intelligence with the CIA, which hampered the Counter-terrorism Center's efforts against al-Qaeda. It likewise stymied coordination between the CIA and US military.

The US military did not escape criticism either. The Pentagon was censured for its reluctance to conduct operations in Afghanistan or support CIA operations against al-Qaeda before 9/11. As noted, one of the reasons cited for this was the CIA's failure to provide adequate intelligence to support such operations. As a result, the US Defense Department felt it could not put troops on the ground in Afghanistan or conduct cruise missile attacks against bin Laden over and beyond the August 1998 strikes in Afghanistan and Sudan. Disagreements over replacing lost Predator drones also needlessly hampered collaboration between the CIA and US military.

The US government's inquiry concluded that 'the CIA was reluctant to seek authority to assassinate bin Laden and was averse to taking advantage of ambiguities in the authorities it did receive that might have allowed it more flexibility'.[29] Although the US government wanted bin Laden dead as early as August 1998, it had not removed the ban on assassination and did not provide clear direction, or indeed authorisation, to the CIA. These mixed messages ultimately meant that the attempt to kill bin Laden in the late 1990s was doomed from the start and by October 2001 America was at war with Afghanistan.

This muddled state of affairs was clearly a recipe for disaster and allowed bin Laden to elude his hunters with relative ease. The 9/11 Commission found that the CIA and Pentagon had the opportunity to kill or capture bin Laden on five occasions between June 1998 and May 1999, but each time had wavered for fear of the consequences in terms of retaliation or civilian deaths.[30] Killing bin Laden had ultimately ended up a fiasco and Washington paid a bitter price for this failure.

At the time of 9/11 bin Laden was probably in the Kandahar area awaiting the birth of a daughter by his fifth wife Amal al-Sadah. From that point on he was to remain an elusive shadow, who always remained one step ahead of his assassins. Sources close to him claim Amal stayed at his side.

Chapter 2

Goodbye Afghanistan

The last contingents of the Soviet Army, led by Lieutenant-General Boris Gromov, withdrew from Afghanistan over the Amu Darya in 1989. The general waved, smiling from his armoured personnel carrier and once over the bridge at Termez he and his men were greeted with traditional garlands and bread as if heroes. At the time, pundits believed the Soviet Union was economically and morally bankrupt – the Cold War and Afghanistan had seen to that. The West could barely hide its glee.

As far as Washington was concerned, Moscow's humiliation at the hands of the Mujahideen had somehow helped expunge its own shame two decades earlier in Vietnam. Moscow had now been similarly disgraced by a rag-tag army. 'Goodbye and good riddance', 'That's the end of that', was the general sentiment within British and American intelligence circles. Ironically, the Vietnam analogy was to be more accurate than Washington could imagine: just like the corrupt South Vietnamese government, which lasted until 1975, following the US withdrawal in 1972, the Communist Afghan government was to keep the Mujahideen at bay for three years before Moscow finally gave up on it.

Moscow's withdrawal was a historic moment and a turning point in the evolution of militant Islam. Thousands of Arabs had flocked to the country to fight the Soviets, the most significant contributions coming from Algeria, Saudi Arabia and Yemen. The net result was that Jihadists had learned that asymmetrical warfare could be used to bring a superpower to its knees. In the coming years this experience would help fuel violence in Algeria, Bosnia, Chechnya, Kosovo, Saudi Arabia and Yemen.

The rise of Osama bin Laden and al-Qaeda stemmed directly from the ten-year Mujahideen resistance to the Soviet occupation. Osama bin Laden's al-Qaeda subsequently grew out of the Services Office, a clearing house for the international Muslim brigade opposed to the Soviet invasion. The Service Office that recruited, trained and financed thousands of foreign Mujahideen was run by bin Laden and Palestinian religious scholar Abdullah Azzam. Al-Qaeda came into being in the late 1980s.

With the Soviets gone, London, like Washington, had little interest in Afghanistan. The expectation was that President Najibullah's 'puppet' regime would collapse in a matter of weeks or months and that the plucky freedom fighters would take over. They would be hostile to Moscow and everyone would be happy. This was ignoring the fact that the Mujahideen consisted of up to a dozen factions and that their very inability to co-ordinate their efforts had ensured the Soviet Army remained for a decade.

Najibullah's nominally Communist forces – while their morale was an unknown factor – were armed to the teeth. Even if the Mujahideen managed to prevail, it seemed inevitable they would fall out, plunging the battered country into yet more civil war. If that happened, would it not affect Afghanistan's neighbours? In reality, no one cared about troublesome Iran, ostracised since the fall of the Shah in 1979, and any problems for the Soviet Central Asian Republics would be good news – even Pakistan was an uneasy bedfellow because of its armed stand-off with India.

Pravda had first announced the Soviet Union was prepared to commence withdrawing its troops from war-torn Afghanistan on 11 January 1988: this would actually commence on 1 May, contingent on an Afghan-Pakistani agreement. This date was then pushed back when Soviet President, Mikhail Gorbachev, announced that Soviet troops would begin withdrawing on 15 May 1988 to coincide with the next superpower summit, and would be completed by 15 February 1989. The reason for this withdrawal was because Moscow had been bled dry. It announced in mid-1988 that the Soviet armed forces had suffered 13,310 killed, 33,478 wounded and 311 missing (with a slight increase after the withdrawal was completed). The Afghan Army had lost about 20,000, while civilian losses were estimated as high as a million.[1]

One of the primary pre-requisites for waging successful guerrilla warfare is having a secure base from which to operate. The Mujahideen were lucky in that both Iran and Pakistan turned a blind eye to their activities, allowing them to smuggle arms and fighters over their borders. In particular, Pakistan's Inter Services Intelligence (ISI) agency became the conduit for massive quantities of CIA-funded weaponry, as well as hosting innumerable training bases. Both Pakistan and America had been meddling in Afghanistan since the early 1970s, when they trained some 5,000 Islamists, including Gulbuddin Hekmatyar and Ahmad Shah Massoud to counter Daud Khan, who had been seeking to establish a greater 'Pashtunistan'. This training ceased when Khan agreed to build a railway to the Iranian port of Bandar Abbas.[2]

President Zia ul-Haq had been prepared to countenance the CIA taking a role in the war in Afghanistan, because he needed Washington as an ally against Soviet-backed India. The latter was armed to the teeth, having purchased thousands of Soviet-built fighter aircraft and tanks. In particular, he wanted more American F-16 fighters to counter the Indian Air Force. In the early 1980s Pakistan received forty F-16s and subsequently ordered another seventy-one, worth $1.7 billion. This deal eventually became mired in the row over Pakistan's nuclear stance and only twenty-eight aircraft were built and these were never delivered (Pakistan's deposit amounting to almost $500 million was not refunded until the late 1990s).

Zia was a strange bedfellow for Washington – a military dictator of a staunchly Muslim country that was hostile to America; he had little to offer except a conduit to the Mujahideen and therefore the ability to strike at the Soviet Army. However, once maverick Congressman Charlie Wilson, sitting on the powerful Appropriations Committee and the Defense Appropriations subcommittee, decided he liked Zia and the Mujahideen cause, the provision of arms to militant Islam was never an issue. Zia and his intelligence chief, Lieutenant-General Akhtar Abdul Rehman Khan, were not prepared to let the CIA have free reign in Afghanistan or Pakistan. Such a move would have exposed Pakistan's 'neutrality' and made it fair game for Soviet retaliation. Once CIA-funded weapons arrived, they were stored and distributed by Pakistani intelligence.

Just as importantly, the Pakistanis also controlled all the tactics and weapons training for the Afghan resistance. This meant that whenever a new weapon system was introduced, Pakistani operators were instructed first and then passed on their knowledge. Not only did this cause a delay, the upshot was that Washington had no real control over who was being trained – whether they be Afghans or foreign fighters come to join the Jihad. From this perspective it is easy to understand why the CIA and US State Department dragged their feet so long when it came to providing weapons that could kill Soviet fighter aircraft and helicopters. Once the proverbial genie was out of the bottle there would be no getting it back in again. There was never any guarantee that the Mujahideen could defeat the Soviet Army with or without CIA backing, and when they did it was the Fundamentalist groups that were left in the ascendancy. Washington favoured those it saw as moderates, such as Pir Gailani, Ahmad Shah Massoud, Hazrat Mujaddadi and Molvi Nabi, but it was Fundamentalist Gulbuddin Hekmatyar who had the ear of the ISI because they viewed him as the toughest and most vigorous of the leaders.

Ultimately, President Zia manoeuvred himself into such a position that Pakistan was permanently in the driving seat when it came to the prosecution of the Mujahideen war in Afghanistan. While Zia was conscious of American sensitivities about the Fundamentalist resistance groups, they were always the ones in the forefront of the Jihad. Zia and the ISI never had a problem with this and were oblivious to the fact that their support would come back to haunt Pakistan in a violent and destabilising way. According to Brigadier Mohammad Yousaf, head of the ISI's Afghan Bureau, over 80,000 Mujahideen went through Pakistan's training camps (this is roughly the equivalent to eight divisions). When the Afghan Taliban and later the Pakistani Taliban emerged, their rank-and-file fighters were never going to be short of commanders who knew what they were doing, thanks to Zia's legacy.

Covert aid provided to the Mujahideen by Washington expanded from $35 million in 1982 to a staggering $600 million in 1987. On top of that, Saudi Arabia was reportedly matching American funding, which meant that, towards the end of the conflict, $1 billion a year was pouring into the Mujahideen's coffers. This could buy an awful lot of weapons. With Pakistan acting as middleman, it inevitably meant that much, if not all, of this money and weaponry passed through Pakistani hands. It soon became clear that buying weapons through third parties and delivering them through third parties resulted in substantial quantities of these weapons never reaching the Mujahideen. They disappeared en route to Pakistan or ended up in Peshawar's guns bazaar, Kashmir or Central Asia. The region became awash in guns.

The total number of Mujahideen fighting Jihad or holy war against the Soviets and the Democratic Republic of Afghanistan's government is impossible to estimate accurately. In the mid-1980s opposition forces numbered some 90,000, with perhaps 20,000 active fighters supported by fifteen exiled political groups. Later estimates vary wildly, going up to 500,000. However, by 1990, the Mujahideen were assessed to number 120,000, with 40,000 active.

Notably, there were seven main, largely Sunni, resistance groups based in Pakistan at Peshawar, all with an overt Islamic agenda, including Hezb-i-Islami, the Islamic Party of Gulbuddin Hekmatyar. Of the seven Mujahideen political parties headquartered in Pakistan, four were considered Islamic Fundamentalist or Islamist, while the rest were Islamic moderates. The former were to prove the most effective operationally, which meant they got the bulk of the weapons distributed by Pakistani intelligence.

In Afghanistan itself, the Mohaz Melli Islami (National Islamic Front of Afghanistan) operated in the Kandahar, Badakhshan, Ghazni, Wardak and Kabul areas, and the Jebhe Milli Nejad (National Liberation Front of Sibghtullah Modjaddidi) operated in the Jalalabad, Logar and Kandahar areas.[3]

The two main Shia groupings in Afghanistan were the Shura-i-Inquilabi (Revolutionary Council) and the Sazmar-i-Nasr (Organisation for Victory), the latter being the Iranian-backed revolutionary opposition. The Shura ruled the Hazara Jat region as the 'official' government until the mid-1980s. It found itself not only challenged by Sazmar-i-Nasr and Kabul but the Sepha and the Pasadran (Revolutionary Guards) also supported by Iran and the pro-Iranian Hezbollah. Iran provided these groups as well as the Palestinian Liberation Front with G-3 assault rifles, originally built under licence from Heckler and Koch.

Once the radical groups had taken over the Hazara Jat they were able to prevent the Soviets and the Afghan government reasserting control. Although Islamic revolution and religious fanaticism were alien to Afghan traditions, it still took hold and an Islamic republic was created in Nuristan.

Moscow originally intervened in late 1979 to help topple President Hafizullah Amin and install the pro-Marxist government of Barak Karmal. At the time, the Soviet Union's policies towards the Muslim world were dominated by its desire to neutralise revolutionary Iran as an Islamic model that might appeal to Central Asian Soviet Muslims, consolidate its position in Afghanistan, and prevent America re-establishing a foothold in Iran.[4]

Despite viewing revolutionary Shia-dominated Iran as a threat, Moscow adopted a wait and see policy in the Middle East. Similarly, the Soviet Union viewed the outbreak of the Iran-Iraq War in 1980 as far less important compared to the troubles in Poland, the worsening internal economic situation and Afghanistan. Nonetheless, Moscow feared Iraq's invasion of Iran could lead to civil war in Iran and US intervention. Such a civil war might also result in secessionism spilling over into the Soviet Union. Moscow's response was to keep a tight leash on Afghanistan.

The media claimed that the Soviet invasion force for Afghanistan consisted of 90 per cent Soviet Muslim Tajiks, Turkmen and Uzbeks, and only 10 per cent Russian Orthodox Slavs.[5] On the surface this seemed plausible, as the Soviet Central Asian Military District (embracing Kazakhstan, Kyrgyzstan and Tajikistan) and the Turkestan Military District (covering the Turkmen and Uzbek republics) were the ones involved. However, Soviet forces were not manned on a territorial but an all-union basis.[6] In light of this it is doubtful that the bulk of those troops invading Afghanistan were Central Asian or indeed practising Muslims.

Nonetheless, it is likely that the four motor rifle divisions involved were bolstered with Central Asians, especially Tajiks, to make it look like they were going to help the Afghan government rather than take over the country. The divisions undoubtedly included reservists called up from the Turkestan and Central Asia Military districts. These would have been of similar ethnicity as the local Afghan population and not only included Tajiks, but also Kyrgyz, Turkmen and Uzbeks, though most were Uzbeks.

It was rumoured that the Central Asian troops proved unreliable and many were withdrawn shortly after the invasion and replaced by regular conscripts. To be fair, they were poorly trained and had never served with the divisions before, and one division was so poorly equipped that it was replaced shortly after the invasion. In truth, though, the reservists only had a liability of 90 days and were released under these terms at the end of March 1980.

This did not stop the Russians looking down on the Central Asians, with their poorer educational levels and inability to speak Russian, which meant they were inevitably consigned to labour units. This led Russian troops to feel that Soviet Central Asians were not pulling their weight when it came to fighting. While most of the Afghan Army was disarmed, 2,000 Afghan troops were killed resisting and another 40,000 took to the hills, some of whom joined the Mujahideen.

Afghan government and Soviet counter-insurgency tactics – such as destroying crops and terrorising civilians – soon led to hundreds of thousands of people being made homeless. By May 1980 there were 1 million registered refugees in neighbouring Pakistan, but this soared to 3 million registered and another 400,000 unregistered by mid-1987. This huge pool of people provided an ideal sanctuary and recruiting ground for the resistance. Iran also had about 2.5 million Afghan refugees, but was much stricter about border transiting.[7] The refugee problem rendered it impossible for the Afghan government and the Soviet Army to control the rural population.

One of the most notable Mujahideen leaders to emerge was ethnic Tajik Ahmad Shah Massoud, a former engineering student whose forces in the Panjsher Valley withstood numerous Soviet offensives. The valley juts into the Hindu Kush mountain range just 96km north of Kabul and was held by the Tajik-dominated Jamiat-i-Islami, which attracted Pashtun support, particularly in Paktia and Nangarhar to the south-east.

After the invasion, the winter of 1979–80 was reasonably quiet, but in March, May and September there was fierce resistance in Kunar province and in Paktia. By June 1980 the Soviets began the systematic destruction of Afghanistan's agriculture and in September they launched their first offensive against the Jamiat-i-Islami in the Panjsher. Increasing numbers of Afghans took to the mountains, with resistance growing in the eastern and north-eastern valleys and to a lesser extent to the west.

The Mujahideen (Soldiers of God) were so named because they were fighting for Allah in His war against the unbelievers. A Mujahid killed fighting Jihad becomes a martyr or 'Shaheed', and no matter what sins they have committed they go straight to Paradise. For a Muslim warrior there is no greater glory than dying for Islam, and as the Soviets were to discover, this made the Mujahideen a particularly dangerous and tenacious foe. They also learned to fear the Mujahideen battle cry: 'Allah o Akbar. Mordabad Shuravi' – 'God is Great. Death to the Soviets.' Those fighters who survive Jihad are also venerated as 'Ghazi' and Islam promises them rich rewards in Paradise. Moscow was to learn there was no answer to such ideology.

By occupying the bazaar areas of Khost, Jaji (also called Ali Khel) and Urgana, the guerrillas were able to bring arms directly over the Pakistani border by truck instead of pack animal. Under ex-Afghan Army Colonel, Ramatullah Safi, the Mohaz Melli Islami began major operations in the important eastern Paktia province, bordering Pakistan in the summer and autumn of 1983. About 5,000 Mujahideen moved into the bazaar area of Khost that August and the following month occupied Matun and Khurhai in the same area. The result was 300 Soviet and 1,500 Afghan troops were trapped in Khost. However, in three days of fierce fighting, the Mujahideen failed to capture the town.

To the north-east, Massoud and the Soviets held a controversial cease-fire during 1983–84. This rapidly came to an end in April 1984, when the Panjsher VII offensive launched 10,000 Soviet and 1,500 Afghan troops against the guerrillas. Although the Soviets were fighting the war on the cheap, and at an acceptable level, by 1984 the Afghan government had no control over 85 per cent of the countryside, with guerrilla attacks almost a daily occurrence all over the country. Massoud's forces still remained in control after the Soviet's XI offensive and the Mujahideen began to stand and fight for the first time.

Having failed to defeat the Mujahideen in the field, the Soviets tried to strangle their vital supply routes, and in mid-1985 attempted to halt the flow from Pakistan and relieve Barikot, which had been under siege since 1981. By June a Soviet-led force of about 4,000 had succeeded in forcing the Mujahideen to withdraw. The increased guerrilla activity in the Khost area resulted in a major offensive in August–September 1985, involving 20,000 Soviet and Afghan troops spearheaded by *Spetsnaz* Special Forces. They succeeded in driving the Hezb-i-Islami, under Jalulladin Haqani, from the bazaar but failed to break the siege or take Zhawar. Ominously, by December there were 10,000 Mujahideen in the Khost area.

The plight of war-torn Afghanistan horrified the international community as the global media broadcast images of death and destruction into every home around the world. This became a rallying call for thousands of Muslims who were disgusted by what Moscow was doing.

It has been estimated that some 35,000 Islamic militants from forty-three Muslim states poured into the country to fight Jihad against the Soviets. In total, over 100,000 radicals would be exposed to the teaching of Jihad in Afghanistan and Pakistan, providing a vast pool for global Jihad to draw upon.[8] Among them was the half-Yemeni and half-Saudi bin Laden, who had money and, just as importantly, powerful Saudi connections.

Operating out of Pakistan, his lair began to take shape, helping fuel the war not only in Afghanistan but also in Central Asia and Indian Kashmir. In 1986 bin Laden built a tunnel complex for the CIA-backed Mujahideen in the Afghan mountains near Khost. Three years later he set up al-Qaeda to service the needs of Arab militants now firmly ensconced in Afghanistan.

Awareness of foreign fighters infiltrating Afghanistan began to emerge in the late 1980s. Tacitly, the CIA and ISI were happy to train Arab fighters who wished to wage Jihad against the Soviets – certainly, they were viewed by the Americans as little more than mercenaries, and if they made life difficult for the Soviets and helped boost Mujahideen manpower then all the better. The wider implications for the recruiting grounds of Algeria, Bosnia, the Philippines, Somalia and Yemen seemed to go unnoticed.

While the CIA turned a blind eye – or indeed actively encouraged this army of Arabs to flock to Pakistan and Afghanistan – Saudi Arabia took the lead in assembling the recruits. Notably, it was Prince Turki, head of Saudi intelligence who approved the role of bin Laden in helping to recruit, transport, train and indoctrinate Arab Jihadists. Saudi Arabia refused to resume diplomatic relations with the Soviet Union until it withdrew from Afghanistan, although Saudi oil exports to Moscow increased to help pay for Soviet weapons bought for Iraq.

At the time Julian Gearing, Director of the Afghan Information Office, was of the view that the Afghan Mujahideen considered the Arab fighters as more of a liability than an asset.[9] Many of the younger volunteers made up for their lack of military training and experience with reckless enthusiasm – a characteristic that was liable to get those around them killed. Others, particularly the Saudi volunteers, had a habit of turning up in Peshawar or near the front and then going home, having fulfilled what they considered their obligations under Jihad. It seems that few of the Afghan Arabs actually left Peshawar, where they were engaged in relief work. One assessment claims that just forty-four Arab fighters were killed fighting the Soviets, while another 198 died during the offensive against Najibullah's regime at Jalalabad in 1989.[10]

Worryingly for Moscow, Henry Dodds, former Editor of the prestigious *Jane's Soviet Intelligence Review*, also had evidence from US sources that Soviet Central Asians were serving not only with the Soviet Army but also with the Mujahideen.[11] By December 1987 the KGB in Tajikistan was becoming aware that radical Muslims were infiltrating the border and causing a big surge in draft-dodging and desertion from the Soviet armed forces.[12] The local *mullahs* had been preaching in opposition to the Soviet presence in Afghanistan, on the grounds that they were turning Afghans into non-believers. The KGB also alleged that the Islamic clergy were calling for a holy war against Soviet rule. As a result, clandestine Soviet Islamic leaders were placed on trial. Behind the scenes, Moscow knew that a defeat in Afghanistan could have a catastrophic affect on its Central Asian republics. Its fall-back option was to prove extreme.

Intelligence sources in London and Washington seemed largely indifferent to the presence of the foreign fighters, unless they were Iranian or Iranian-backed, such as the Lebanese Hezbollah. America had remained at bitter loggerheads with Iran ever since the fall of the Shah, the Tehran hostage crisis, and the bombing of US forces in the Lebanon. Washington was highly suspicious of Iranian motives in Afghanistan, which were felt to have an anti-American agenda.

This was borne out when Iranian Revolutionary Guards stole half a dozen US Stinger man-portable anti-aircraft missiles in 1987, from a convoy en route to Ismail Khan, whose guerrilla forces were operating near the western Afghan city of Herat.[13] Sceptics argued Washington had cooked this story up to hide the inconvenient truth that Afghan rebels had sold the missiles to Iran, or indeed that Washington traded them in an arms-for-hostages deal with Tehran. Either way, it was felt the weapons would pose a threat to US naval forces in the Gulf.

According to Brigadier Mohammad Yousaf, head of the ISI's Afghan Bureau, he gave explicit instructions to the Mujahideen not to transit Iranian soil with Stingers: nonetheless, Iranian border guards stopped resistance fighters carrying four launchers and sixteen missiles. They were never returned.

Ironically, it was the Soviet Su-25 Frogfoot fighter-bomber's high survivability against the Soviet-designed SA-7 Grail SAM that convinced Washington to supply the Stinger to the Mujahideen. London also provided the inaccurate British Blowpipe. The resistance may have captured some Grail from the Afghan Army, but the Palestinian Liberation Organisation provided some via Beirut. Likewise, some came from Egypt, which manufactured them as the Sakr Eye. However, the Grail was not easy to use and was ultimately few in number, so fortunately was not readily available to other militant groups.

The CIA and Pakistan's President Zia opposed supplying the Mujahideen with Stinger for almost six years on the grounds it would publicly confirm Washington's military backing for the Mujahideen. Its introduction could never be kept a secret and Zia privately feared it could fall into terrorist hands that might target him. Once Stinger was supplied to the resistance, the CIA argued it would inevitably fall into the hands of the Soviets and the Iranians and they were proved right. However, without it, the ISI argued the Mujahideen could never turn the tide in Afghanistan.

In April 1986 the first Stingers began to reach Afghanistan and the Afghan Army made an even greater effort to cut the rebel supply routes across the Pakistan border. In fact, the Afghan Army assumed the burden of the fighting when elements of five divisions – some 15,000 men, supported by 2,000 Soviets – launched a major attack in Paktia province.

Guerrilla leader, Ahmad Massoud, said there were only two things the Mujahideen needed: one was the Koran, the other was Stinger. In total, about 1,000 had been delivered by 1989, and its introduction ended Moscow's ability to conduct heliborne operations with impunity.[14] The Soviets' over-reliance on helicopters (echoing American problems in Vietnam a decade and a half earlier) meant that the Soviet armed forces had no other options when it came to interdicting the Mujahideen's operations, making the war unwinnable and contributing to the decision to withdraw.

Soviet-trained Afghans eventually tried to tackle the Stinger threat by blowing up a weapons dump between the Pakistani capital Islamabad and Rawalpindi in early April 1988. This audacious raid caused 1,200 casualties and destroyed a third of the guerrillas' surface-to-air missile supplies.[15] It was not until the end of 1988 that, in response to reports of Mujahideen groups selling missiles to

Iran, and in the face of thawing relations with Moscow, Washington stopped supplying Stinger missiles.[16]

It was also discovered at this time that Pakistan was host to global Jihadists. In February 1988 – much to Washington's embarrassment – the CIA was forced to own up to training Algerian, Egyptian, Filipino, Libyan, Moroccan, Palestinian, Syrian, Tunisian and Yemeni fighters at a camp in the mountains at Sadda, west of Peshawar, just near the Afghan border. Washington insisted the Pakistanis shut down the camp once it became obvious the fighters were not, in fact, destined for Afghanistan. The CIA pleaded ignorance over the camp's activities, but the Pakistani authorities found it contained non-Pakistani instructors training foreign Muslims.[17]

This proved doubly embarrassing for Washington, which, along with Riyadh, was funding Abdul Rasul Sayyaf's Ittehad-e-Islami Mujahideen faction that held violently anti-western views. Sayyaf had become the leader of the Fundamentalist Alliance in 1982 due to his access to weapons and funding via the Muslim Brotherhood and Saudi Wahhabi groups in the Middle East. America now found itself involved in a scheme to train Arab guerrillas operating throughout the Middle East and Filipino guerrillas fighting against a US-backed Filipino government.

Sulaiman Shah, a spokesman for Ittehad-e-Islami, acknowledged: 'There are some foreign elements. They are people from other parts of the world, but they come here freely and they are free to go back.' Nonetheless, he refuted that the camp was regularly training foreigners who were not intending to fight the Soviet Army: 'This is rubbish,' he said. 'We have nothing to hide. Some groups may have visited the camp, but there is no question of regular training.'[18] No one was fooled and it was evident that the CIA and ISI had dirty hands – deliberately or not. Cynics argued that such activities were undoubtedly taking place in other Mujahideen camps, given the prominent role Islam played in the key resistance groups. At this point, alarm bells should have started ringing: the war in Afghanistan was nurturing global terror groups.

Strangest of all, the Sadda camp was said to be training Filipino Muslims from the Moro National Liberation Front, fighting for a separate Muslim state in the southern Philippines. Sulaiman Shah only acknowledged the presence of about a dozen Filipinos.[19] The Philippines has endured a long-standing Muslim insurgent problem on the southern island of Mindanao, involving the Moro National Liberation Front (MNLF), Moro Islamic Liberation Front (MILF) and Abu Sayyaf (Sword of God).[20] The latter split from the MNLF in the early 1990s and has been labelled a terrorist group by the Philippine government. The MNLF and MILF condemned Sayyaf's activities, which involved kidnap and extortion. In 2001 the Filipino Chief of Staff stated the only way Abu Sayyaf could maintain its level of activity was through al-Qaeda supplying arms, training and other logistical support.[21]

By October 1987 the Mujahideen – with the help of Stinger – had tightened their siege of Khost: its air links had been cut and the town was under severe threat. Khost had been under close siege for three months, with its land communication disrupted since 1980. The inhabitants, including army personnel, were faced with growing shortages, and the civilian population – thought to be about 40,000 – began to flee. Initiated to lift the siege and cut the Mujahideen's supply routes out of Pakistan once and for all, the Mujahideen and the Afghan Army fought a set-piece battle that has been compared to Dien Bien Phu on 18 November 1987.[22]

The war in Afghanistan was televised 'live' in the Soviet Union for the first time on 19 December 1987, with a report on the Afghan government offensive at Khost. There was no mention of Soviet involvement. The decision to televise the fighting appeared to be part of a move by Moscow to prepare the Soviet public for the withdrawal and to show the Afghan Army bearing the brunt of the fighting. Ironically, as soon as the Afghan/Soviet forces withdrew from the Khost area after January 1988, four Mujahideen organisations under Jalulladin Haqani resumed their blockade.

The Soviet-Afghan conflict showed Islamic Jihadists just what can be achieved against a superpower. In the face of the Soviet withdrawal, Afghan President Najibullah warned America that Afghanistan could turn into another Iran if the Islamist forces armed by Washington were permitted to seize power. At a meeting with Gorbachev in Tashkent, Najibullah pointed out that the West should re-evaluate the Mujahideen's political credentials, as they were persisting in fighting even though the Soviets were leaving: 'I ask you,' Najibullah said to Washington, 'with the existence of the Iranian factor today, what would be the consequences if another Iran emerged?'[23] At the time nobody seemed to care, but he was proved right.

Pakistan had also been weakened by this ghastly war. Russian historian, Zhores Medvedev, writing in 1985, noted prophetically:

> The large frontier province of Pakistan has become a semi-autonomous, highly militarised zone, which cannot be controlled effectively by the Pakistan Army and which will remain a source of instability in Afghanistan for many years, playing a similar role to that North Vietnam played for the Vietcong in South Vietnam.[24]

He was right. This region would become the breeding ground for the 'Seekers of the Truth' – better known as the Taliban.

Chapter 3

The Mountains of Allah

Following its withdrawal from Afghanistan, Moscow became increasingly concerned at what it perceived as a reawakening of Islam in Soviet Central Asia, though the truth was that it had never gone away, despite decades of Soviet cultural and religious repression. The largely closed world of Central Asia was increasingly conscious of the wider Muslim community or *umma*, thanks to the growing availability of Islamic literature distributed by Saudi Arabia and Pakistan. At this stage, the Soviet Union had a population of some 50 million Muslims (from a total of 287 million), the majority living in Third World conditions – unrest seemed unavoidable.

Inevitably, the war in Afghanistan spread into neighbouring Tajikistan. The Tajik Islamic opposition looked to Afghan Tajik guerrilla leader Ahmad Shah Massoud, while the Soviet Uzbeks looked to the Afghan Pashtuns, led by Gulbuddin Hekmatyar and later Mullah Omar and the Taliban. While America, Saudi Arabia and Pakistan actively encouraged tens of thousands of radical Muslims from around the world to go and fight the Soviet Army, thousands more studied in the radical *madrassahs* in Pakistan. Although Soviet Tajiks and Uzbeks travelled to Saudi Arabia ostensibly to study at the *madrassahs*, they often joined the Jihad in Afghanistan.

As a result, many Tajik and Uzbek Islamists felt that Islamic revolutions in Central Asia would be triggered by a Mujahideen victory in Afghanistan. Throughout the 1980s Shia Iran had held the monopoly with Jihad, but the Deobandi *madrassahs* in Pakistan were to have a major influence on the Taliban in Afghanistan and, in turn, former Soviet Central Asia. Deobandism (a Sunni sect that had been established in British India, which disliked Shia Islam), spread the word in the Fergana Valley, stretching across eastern Tajikistan, Kyrgyzstan and Uzbekistan.

Sunni Wahhabism from Saudi Arabia also took root in Central Asia, again finding the Fergana Valley a fertile recruiting ground. However, its restrictive creed was not popular with largely moderate Central Asia until the 1980s, when the Wahhabi Mujahideen leaders in Afghanistan wielded greater influence.

The Mujahideen, with ISI backing, infiltrated the Soviet Union, striking across the Amu River between Kilif in the west and Faizabad to the east (an area stretching for 500km and encompassing Turkmenistan, Uzbekistan and Tajikistan). Initially, this was designed to foster Islam by smuggling in

10,000 CIA-supplied Korans translated into Soviet Uzbek. The campaign then escalated into attacks on Soviet shipping on the Amu and Soviet railways. During such attacks, Soviet Central Asian troops were known to defect.

The legacy of the Soviet-Afghan war was that a significant number of Central Asians gained military experience in Afghanistan, which provided a cadre of fighters for the emerging Islamist groups in the Central Asian republics. Those Central Asians drafted into the Soviet Army who had been exposed to the religious fervour of the radicalised Mujahideen soon began to question Moscow's right to rule.

By the late 1908s there were 350 Afghan veterans living in Frunze, the capital of Kyrgyzstan, with a much higher number living in the rural areas. In Tajikistan there were almost 300, and a similar number existed in the Fergana Valley. Kazakhstan seemed to be home to the most veterans with 2,000 alone residing in the capital.[1]

After President Mikhail Gorbachev came to power it was evident the Soviet Union was economically ailing and politically groaning at the seams. Aggravated by the worsening economy, many of the Soviet Union's fifteen republics were clamouring to be free of Moscow's rule after seventy years of chronic mismanagement. Ethnic friction was also a legacy of Stalin's Muslim deportations during the Second World War.

The first real signs of a growing restlessness amongst the Soviet Union's 100 or so different nationalities coincided with Gorbachev's policy of greater openness or *Glasnost*. He recognised the problem when he stated in February 1988: 'We should busy ourselves most thoroughly with the nationalities policy at the present stage. This is a most fundamental, vital question of our society.'[2] It was, in fact, a key issue for the very integrity of the Soviet Union.

Gorbachev's parallel policy of restructuring or *Perestroika* was to have far-reaching ramifications, especially in the Soviet republics stretching from Azerbaijan in the Caucasus to Kazakhstan, Kyrgyzstan, Tajikistan, Turkmenistan and Uzbekistan in Central Asia. Fatefully, he sowed the final seeds for the dissolution of the Soviet Union in July 1988 when he said:

> Greater independence of the Union of republics and autonomous entities is seen by the [Communist] Party in indissoluble connection with their responsibility for the strengthening and progress of our multinational state. The socialist ideal is not a detrimental unification but a full-blooded and dynamic unity set in national diversity.[3]

The Soviet Muslim republics thought otherwise. Far too late in the day, Gorbachev acknowledged:

> The needs for the social, economic and cultural development of certain republics, autonomous entities and ethnic groups were not

fully taken onto consideration [...] This led to public disaffection, which now and then escalated into conflicts.[4]

Despite his efforts at liberalisation, Gorbachev saw Islam as an impediment to modernisation, resulting in yet another Soviet anti-Islamic push. In the name of maintaining the status quo, the Central Asian republic's leaders went along with it for fear of losing their grasp on power.

Islamic intellectuals had begun to stir up anti-Russian feeling even before the Bolshevik Revolution in 1917, Tsarist mismanagement having caused revolts over conscription and famine. Only Tashkent was sympathetic to the Bolshevik cause, setting up the Turkestan Autonomous Soviet Socialist Republic in 1918. Despite the Bolshevik espousal of the right to self-determination, this really meant rule from Moscow once the civil war was over. The resulting Basmachi rebellions in Tajikistan and Turkmenistan were to drag on for over a decade. These were finally suppressed in 1929 with tens of thousands of Tajik, Turkmen and Uzbek rebels fleeing into Afghanistan. Ironically, fifty years on, their descendants would resist the Soviet invasion of Afghanistan, and seventy-two years later, the invasion by the British and the Americans.

In Soviet Central Asia, Islam provided traditional values that were always unfavourable to Sovietisation. Stalin's response was to split Turkestan into five republics, which fractured the various Muslim ethnic groups, in an effort to divide and rule. Some fled to China, as the Soviets moved to stamp out Islam by closing down their places of worship. At the time of the Bolshevik Revolution there were 20,000 mosques; by the mid-1930s there were, officially, less than 100. This repression led to the flourishing of an unofficial Islam in the mountains of Central Asia with unregistered mosques, shrines and *madrassahs*.

During the Second World War the problem of Muslim collaboration with the Nazis was so considerable that the Red Army carried out repressive operations against its own people. In particular, the Muslim population of the North Caucasus and lower Volga suffered after being liberated. At the end of 1943 Stalin ordered the deportation of the Muslim nations, who were arbitrarily accused of collaboration with the occupying forces. For example, in November 1943, the entire Karachai population of Stavropol Krai – some 80,000 people – were forcibly deported to special settlements in Central Asia. In just four days, at the end of December 1943, the Kalmyks were also herded into cattle trucks and moved to Siberia.[5] The same fate befell the Chechen, Ingush, Karabardin, Balkar and Crimean Tartars. Half a million Chechens were exiled to Central Asia and Siberia, a third of whom died. In total, about 1 million people of Muslim extraction were forcibly deported from their ancestral lands.[6]

During Khruschev's reign, from the mid-1950s to mid-1960s, all the deported peoples (with the exception of the Crimean Tartars and Volga Germans) were rehabilitated and allowed to return to their native areas. In parallel, he also instigated the virgin lands project, which witnessed hundreds of thousands of Russians imported into Central Asia, in particular Kazakhstan, thereby sowing the seeds for yet more trouble.

The Soviet Union sought to curry favour with the Muslim states that chose socialism or Marxism as their political ideology in the 1960s. Ironically, some of these – such as Afghanistan, Pakistan, Somalia and Yemen – ended up as hot-beds of Islamic militancy. As Moscow sought to win support among the wider Muslim world, it had to offer the pretence of tolerating Islam at home. This resulted in two religious schools being opened in Bukhara and Tashkent. In the meantime, the Fergana Valley became home to itinerant *mullahs*, who took no notice of Moscow's edicts.

Although the superpowers were cautious about coming into direct con-frontation, this did not prevent serious indirect meddling elsewhere in the world. Time after time, Moscow was able to make good its allies' massive losses. In Asia, both India and Pakistan received Soviet arms in the 1960s. Cynically, Moscow also conducted airlift operations in the late 1960s, in support of a republican faction in North Yemen, while supplying South Yemen at the same time. North Yemen purchased weapons worth $14 billion in the mid-1980s. Major re-supply also took place in 1977–79, in support of Ethiopia in its clash with Somalia, and during the Arab-Israeli Wars of 1967 and 1973. Ironically, Somalia had been a Soviet ally and had received weapons before they had fallen out.

At the height of the Cold War, in the 1980s, the Soviet Union exported arms to numerous Third World countries, worth billions of dollars. The Soviets conducted a substantial re-supply of Syria in 1982–83, following Syrian military losses in Lebanon. When the Israelis invaded southern Lebanon in 1982, they found the Palestinian Liberation Organisation's armoury included old Soviet tanks. Paradoxically, the Soviet Union's huge arms exports did not give Moscow any great or long term strategic leverage. Egypt defected back to the American camp. Libya and Syria became dangerous liabilities, and, while Libya moved to rehabilitate itself with the West, Syria remained a cause for concern.

By now, as the republics of the Soviet Union sought independence, the fate of Nagorno-Karabakh – the tiny Christian-dominated republic in the Caucasus – provided an early warning of what Soviet Muslims could expect. The West's apparent indifference to Moscow's heavy-handedness in the region convinced the Muslim world that it would have to intervene to alleviate the plight of these oppressed peoples.

By the late 1980s, Nagorno-Karabakh's population of 188,000 was pre-dominately orthodox Christian Armenian, with a minority of Muslim Azeris. This made it a Christian enclave in the midst of Muslim Azerbaijan, with long unrealised aspirations of being united with Armenia. Unfortunately, Armenia had exactly the same problem with Muslim-dominated Nakhichevan. Armenia and Georgia are the only Christian states in the Caucasus.[7]

Armenia lived with an appalling legacy of Muslim persecution after the Armenian genocide of 1915–1922 at the hands of the Ottoman Turks.[8] It has been estimated that well over half of the 2 million Armenians living within the Ottoman Empire were annihilated. Under international pressure, Turkey put some of those responsible on trial. The perpetrators said they had done it in the name of Jihad after Sheikh-ul-Islam, the spiritual leader of all Sunni Muslims, had issued a *fatwa* before the Fathi Mosque in Constantinople to kill the Armenians as infidels and enemies to the state.[9] Armenia, trapped between Turkey and the Soviet Union, ended up within the latter, rather than becoming a protectorate of the former.

A formal request by Nagorno-Karabakh in February 1988 to join Armenia was swiftly rejected by the Azerbaijani and Soviet authorities. This was followed by mass demonstrations and violence. The situation reached boiling point the following year, when Moscow deployed 5,000 troops to Nagorno-Karabakh. The situation rapidly spiralled out of control when Azerbaijan gained full independence in October 1991 and the Soviet Union formally dissolved in December. Karabakhi Armenian forces supported by Armenia and Russia were soon able to defeat the ill-equipped Azerbaijani government units. The fighting, in part, was influenced by Soviet Afghan war veterans: by the late 1980s there were 1,220 in the Azeri capital of Baku and 600 in the Georgian capital Tbilisi.[10]

By 1992 Nagorno-Karabakh was fully under ethnic Armenian control and a corridor had been created linking it with Armenia. An Azeri counter-offensive that year recaptured some territory but Armenian forces cut a second corridor in 1993. They then set about creating a security zone around Nagorno-Karabakh; the net result was 35,000 people killed during the conflict and one-seventh of Azeri territory controlled by the Armenians.

It was not until May 1994 that a cease-fire agreement was reached. But progress in the peace negotiations remained largely non-existent, especially after it was discovered that Moscow had provided Armenia with covert military aid during 1994 and 1996. To this day the issue remains a thorn in the side of Armenian-Azeri relations. The Muslim world was dismayed at the violation of Azerbaijan's sovereign territory in favour of its Christian neighbours.

While Moscow was seeking to disentangle itself from its Afghanistan intervention, between 1988–89 there were regular demonstrations across the Soviet Union involving up to 100,000 people. Worryingly, inter-ethnic fighting spread to the Fergana region of Uzbekistan in mid-1989. During this period Soviet troops were sent into Uzbekistan, Kazakhstan and Tajikistan, though half the internal security troops were Central Asia recruits with only 25 per cent actual Slavs. Some 12,000 troops were sent to the Fergana Valley, 16,000 to the

Transcaucasus and 7,000 to Tajikistan. Ironically, Gorbachev found himself in the Catch 22 situation of expounding greater freedom but having to hold the Soviet Union together with waning military muscle.

Moscow's contempt for its five Muslim Central Asian republics was such that when Presidents Yeltsin of Russia, Leonid Kravchuk of Ukraine and Stanislav Shuskevich of Belarus got together on 8 December 1991 to sign the Minsk Treaty, ending the Soviet Union and creating the Commonwealth of Independent States (CIS), they were not consulted. Russia largely abandoned the troublesome former Soviet 'Stans' (Kazakhstan, Kyrgyzstan, Tajikistan, Turkmenistan and Uzbekistan) to their fate. There was to be no rejoicing at their newfound freedom, for it was entirely illusionary. Their leaders found themselves in charge of vast countries they were incapable of running or ruling effectively, especially once the Russians began to leave. Critically, none of them had independent armed forces with which to fend off the growing Islamic movements within their populations.

The following year, Tajikistan fell into a bloody state of civil war and 200,000 ethnic Russians fled. The Tajik government found itself opposed by the Islamic Renaissance Party (IRP), which also had supporters in Kazakhstan, Kyrgyzstan and Uzbekistan. In the face of a clampdown by the Tajik government with the support of Russian troops, 800,000 refugees spilled into Afghanistan, Iran, Pakistan and Russia, along with the IRP's leaders. A coalition was formed with the nationalist Tajik parties to create the United Tajik Opposition (UTO) in 1995, based both in Moscow and Taloqan, Afghanistan. This launched a brutal guerrilla campaign against the Tajik government with assistance from both the Islamic Moment of Uzbekistan (IMU) and Iran.

Russia, Kazakhstan, Kyrgyzstan and Tajikistan signed the Shanghai treaty with China in 1996, designed to substantially demilitarise their mutual borders, and the following year they signed a follow-on treaty, demilitarising the 4,300-mile former Soviet-Chinese border. This did not solve the problem of the vast, largely unpoliced borders with Afghanistan.

Meanwhile, in Afghanistan, the Taliban's drive northwards against the Northern Alliance in 1997 caused consternation among neighbouring countries to the west and north. The fear was that the Taliban would try to spread their messianic message of a Pashtun-based Islamic fundamentalism into Central Asia. In July that year, thanks to the heavy fighting, 9,000 Afghan Turkmen crossed the border into Turkmenistan. Although many of them returned home, the fighting in Afghanistan was now clearly affecting Turkmenistan's border regions.

Tajikistan was alarmed by the Taliban ousting President Rabbani's Tajik-dominated Afghan government from Kabul the year before, and the arrival of the Taliban in northern Afghanistan had a major effect on the Tajik civil war. Fear of the Taliban forced both parties to speed up the peace process. The Tajik government and the opposition reached a settlement in Moscow on 27 June 1997, which also allowed Rabbani and Ahmad Shah Massoud's forces to use Tajikistan as a reception point for Russian military aid. In Tajikistan elections were finally held in February 2000.

In the face of the Pakistani-backed Taliban marching westward through Afghanistan, the Iranians opted to support the Northern Alliance. Moscow had little choice but help step up security in the region with 3,000 troops based at Termez on the Uzbekistan border, 25,000 on the Tajik-Afghan border, and place those in Turkmenistan on high alert. It was at about this point that the Hizb ut-Tahrir al-Islami (HuT) and IMU began to make their presence felt. While HuT was a peaceful movement, the IMU was a guerrilla organisation. HuT found a foothold in the Fergana Valley. Although, after Central Asian independence, Saudi money had been allowed to encourage Islamic teaching, it was suppressed from 1997 and then banned after the Tashkent bombings. As a result, HuT began to attract more followers.

President Karimov of Uzbekistan effectively drove HuT underground after he moved to restrict the freedom of worship in May 1998. Between January 1999 and April 2000, 5,000 people were imprisoned, and a further 10,700 were identified as enemies of the state.[11] This simply pushed many HuT supporters into the arms of the IMU, despite HuT denying any links with al-Qaeda, the IMU or the Taliban.

The IMU emerged from the Fergana Valley under Juma Namangani (real name Jumaboi Ahmadzhanovitch Khojeav) and Tohir Abduhalilovich Yuldashev. Namangani was a Soviet army veteran who had fought in Afghanistan and served with the Tajik IRP guerrillas. The IMU had its roots in the Soviet-era Basmachi rebellions.

The case of Kosim Ermatov exemplified the experiences of many radicalised Central Asians. Born in Uzbekistan, he was conscripted into the Soviet Army and served in Afghanistan until captured by the Mujahideen. After the Soviet withdrawal he went to Pakistan, and with the demise of the Soviet Union, refused to go home for fear of being persecuted by President Karimov's regime. In 1996 he joined the IMU, serving as a driver and a cook. After the Coalition invasion of Afghanistan he went back to Pakistan. In January 2004 he was arrested and extradited to Uzbekistan, where he was sentenced to eighteen years imprisonment.[12]

Following the Taliban taking power in Afghanistan there were a series of explosions in Tashkent in February 1999. The Taliban were blamed, along with Mohammad Solikh (a former Uzbek presidential candidate and head of the banned Erk party) and Yuldashev (former head of the banned Adolat social movement), though at this point the IMU had no history of bombings. It was alleged that Solikh had joined the IMU. Craig Murray, former British ambassador to Uzbekistan, is of a different view:

Most analysts now believe that these bombs were planted either by the Karimov regime or by warring factions within the regime. By blaming Islamic extremists for the bombs, the government was able to step up its efforts to fight back the post-Soviet religious revival. To this end, they closed the religious schools [. . .] pupils and teachers were rounded up and dispatched to the gulags after confessing under torture to having been part of an Islamic plot.[13]

It had been estimated that HuT supporters in Uzbekistan numbered about 8,000, and though half these ended up in prison, only 1,000 were considered genuine adherents.[14]

Also in 1999, several hundred Islamic extremists invaded Kyrgyzstan, including a group led by Namangani, allegedly with a view to creating an Islamic state in the south of the country as a springboard into Uzbekistan. Although they were driven out, they returned to both Kyrgyzstan and Uzbekistan the following year. After yet another Karimov clampdown, the IMU took to the field again, moving their base of operations to Afghanistan. From there, the IMU announced a Jihad to remove Karimov. IMU incursions in 2000 prompted China, France, Israel, Russia and the US to provide counter-insurgency equipment to Uzbekistan and Kyrgyzstan. Washington also declared the IMU a terrorist group because of its alleged connections with Osama bin Laden. According to the US State Department, the group had close ties to al-Qaeda and received al-Qaeda funding.

At this stage, the IMU was assessed to number 2,000 fighters based at Mazar-e-Sharif and Kunduz. In thanks for the Taliban's support, Namangani provided 600 men to help with the assault on Massoud's Northern Alliance forces at Taloqan. In fact, a third of the Taliban attacking force of up to 15,000 men were non-Afghans (4,000 Pakistanis, 600 al-Qaeda fighters).[15]

Not long after 9/11, the Central Asian states – desperate to curtail Islamic militants – offered overflight and other support to the Coalition. In particular Kyrgyzstan, Tajikistan and Uzbekistan provided airbases and hosted coalition troops. On 7 October 2001, just as the air campaign against the Taliban was getting under way, the US and Uzbekistan signed a basing agreement. This permitted the use of Uzbek airspace and the billeting of up to 1,500 American troops at the Soviet-era airbase known as Karshi-Khanabad or K2, just 90 miles north of the Afghan border. In return, Washington agreed that IMU fighters serving with the Taliban and al-Qaeda would be targeted. Due to wrangling over delayed payment for use of the base, plus the Andijan shooting, the agreement was eventually terminated in July 2005.

Namangani was reportedly killed during an air strike in Afghanistan in November 2001 and the IMU scattered. However, in 2002 the US redesignated the IMU a Foreign Terrorist Organisation, as it was assessed to be still assisting the Taliban and al-Qaeda against Coalition forces in Afghanistan. The IMU is also believed to have been responsible for two bomb blasts in the capital of neighbouring Kyrgyzstan in December 2002. The following February, a Kyrgyz court sentenced an IMU member, Sherali Akbotoyev, to twenty-five years in prison for terrorist activities.

In May 2004, Uzbek security forces killed hundreds of pro-democracy demonstrators in the town of Andijan in the Fergana Valley, which led to a souring of relations with the US. Craig Murray, who refuted any Islamist involvement in the demonstrations, recalled:

> Rather to my amazement, the [UK] Joint Terrorism Analysis Centre agreed with me, and in two official analyses of the situation, drawing on all available sources, said that claims of involvement by IMU, al-Qaeda or Hizb ut-Tahrir could not be substantiated.[16]

It was evident that militant Islam – fostered for so long in Afghanistan – had spread to Central Asia. However, it was also clear to many that certain states were using the war on terror as an excuse to crush political opposition, betraying their undemocratic credentials. Washington had little choice but to abandon its military relationship with Uzbekistan.

Many nations have sought to portray their Muslim separatist movements as terrorist organisations: a prime example of this is China's treatment of its Muslim Uighurs. After 9/11 it has been argued that Beijing used the War on Terror as a way of isolating Uighur separatists. Following the Coalition's invasion of Afghanistan, some two dozen Uighurs ended up in US custody. Beijing demanded their return but Washington was concerned they would face persecution if sent home. Those Uighurs taken by the Coalition ended up at America's Guantanamo Bay facility and were accused of supporting the East Turkestan Islamic Movement, al-Qaeda and the Taliban.

While the presence of these Uighur militants in Afghanistan was well known, few in the West took much notice of them. Beijing, on the other hand, was only too keen to stamp out separatism manifesting itself in China's western Xinjiang province. It has a population of some 18 million, of whom 8 million are Uighurs, a Turkic people that have long lived alongside the Han Chinese. Uighurs aspire to an independent homeland known as East Turkestan, in the eastern part of Central Asia. The East Turkestan Republic enjoyed brief independence in the mid-1930s; a decade later, a second attempt at independence was brought to an end once the Communists had won the Chinese Civil War in 1949.

China has found itself in a similar situation as the former Soviet Central Asian republics, in that there has been a revival in Islam among the Uighurs and their Muslim cousins, the Hui. Indeed, following the collapse of the Soviet Union, Beijing feared it, too, would face violent Muslim independence movements, particularly in Xinjiang. Indeed it was almost impossible to keep the radical Islam that had spread through the Central Asian 'Stans' out of Western China.

During the Chinese Cultural Revolution in the 1970s, Beijing had sought to offset the Muslim population in Xinjiang by bringing in ethnic Han settlers. Nonetheless, two key Uighur separatist movements had emerged by the 1990s – the East Turkestan Islamic Movement (ETIM) and the East Turkestan Liberation Organisation (ETLO). However, some sceptics argue that the ETIM and ETLO are figments of Beijing's imagination, providing an excuse to silence political opposition.

In light of those fighters captured in Afghanistan, there can be no denying limited Uighur links to al-Qaeda and the Taliban. The Chinese authorities claim that Hasan Mahsum, founder of the ETIM, met bin Laden in 1999 to solicit support for his organisation. The latter was held responsible for a series of car-bomb attacks in Xinjiang during the 1990s. Certainly in 2002, Washington – keen to keep Beijing on board and following diplomatic arm-twisting by the Chinese – designated the ETIM a terrorist organisation. Three years later, the US State Department claimed the ETIM had links with al-Qaeda and international Jihadist movements.

Stepping up the pressure, the Chinese Government issued, on 15 December 2003, a list of East Turkestan 'terrorists' and 'terrorist organisations' – this included the ETLO and ETIM plus two additional groups, the East Turkestan Information Centre and the World Uighur Youth Congress.

In January 2007, in a blaze of publicity, Chinese security forces attacked an ETIM camp, allegedly with links to al-Qaeda and the Taliban, killing or capturing thirty-five members and seizing a large quantity of explosives. Eighteen months later, simmering Uighur-Han tensions boiled over in July 2009, when riots erupted in the cities of Urumqi and Kashgar, leaving hundreds dead and injured. Beijing's response was a massive security clampdown, employing 20,000 troops, and to blame Uighur terrorists rather than long-simmering racial friction.

Chapter 4

Seekers of the Truth

When the Taliban seized power in Afghanistan, nobody in the West seemed to care. Crucially, Western intelligence suffered a major failure of understanding between how the West and the Islamic community saw Jihad in Afghanistan. From the Muslim perspective, after the Soviet withdrawal, an infidel Communist regime remained in power; whereas Washington abandoned Afghanistan having achieved its strategic goals.

In London and Washington the only lingering and unwanted intelligence concern was the fate of the US Stinger missiles. At least 300 remained unaccounted for and there was a real fear that they might end up in the hands of Iran or a terrorist group such as Hezbollah. Some cynics might argue that the destruction of the bulk of the Mujahideen's missiles stocks in Pakistan had been a CIA-backed operation to head off such an eventuality. The more immediate anxiety was that a commercial airliner might be brought down while transiting Afghanistan's airspace. Washington adopted its usual policy of throwing money at a problem by simply outbidding any interested parties, offering $55 million for their return. It was also assessed that, because of the sensitivity of the battery coolant unit, many of the remaining missiles were time expired, making them inoperable.

In the meantime, the country increasingly became a haven for global Islamist organisations. According to Libyan Noman Benotman, not only did many foreign fighters stay in Afghanistan after the Soviets left, attempts to unseat President Najibullah's regime actually attracted new recruits to the cause of Jihad. The siege of Khost in 1991 involved Algerians, Jordanians, Kuwaitis, Libyans, Palestinians, Saudis, Syrians and Tunisians.[1] At the height of the battle they numbered at least 200 men. This, in effect, was the beginning of the CIA's and ISI's blowback.

Although the Libyans were not involved in the inter-Afghan conflict, post-1992 800 men remained, creating, three years later, the al-Jama'a al-Islamiyyah al-Muqatilah or Libyan Islamic Fighting Group, whose aim was the overthrow of Colonel Gaddafi in Libya. Benotman denied any links between his group and bin Laden.[2] Due to US pressure to leave Afghanistan and Pakistan, the group ended up in Sudan, though Benotman eventually moved to the UK.

Despite warnings of the dire consequences for the country after Moscow had abandoned Afghanistan, a swift Mujahideen victory seemed assured and was something both Washington and London wanted. Journalist Charles Stuart, covering the aftermath, recalls: 'It was widely expected President Najibullah's PDPA (People's Democratic Party of Afghanistan) regime would collapse after the Soviet withdrawal on 15 February 1989.'[3]

However, Pakistani intelligence was firmly of the view that the Mujahideen did not march straight into Kabul, because of a covert American decision that the Fundamentalist-dominated Mujahideen should not be permitted outright military victory. The goal of ousting the Soviets had been achieved – that was sufficient victory for Washington. Indeed, it is true that American officials were alarmed at the prospect of the next government in Kabul being an Islamic Fundamentalist one, with Hekmatyar becoming another Khomeini. It was this that resulted in Washington halting its support to the Mujahideen – not a desire to please Moscow.

Even before the withdrawal, the Mujahideen sought to cripple Najibullah's forces by destroying their supply stocks. In August 1988 they attacked Kilagay, north of Kabul, reputedly killing 700 people, wounding 284 others, and blowing up considerable reserves of ammunition and fuel. The following month, a rocket attack hit the main ammunition depot at Kabul airport, triggering a series of explosions that lasted several hours.

Such losses were quickly replaced via Soviet land and air bridge. 'Sustained by this massive aid,' observes Charles Stuart, 'Moscow underwrote Kabul and the Afghan Army was able to confidently face the Mujahideen.'[4] Indeed, Soviet logistical support to the Afghan government not only provided bread and weapons but also a psychological boost, which helped Najibullah's regime hold on during the dangerous transition period.

In the face of the impending Soviet withdrawal things soon started to go wrong for the Mujahideen, when three key Pakistani supporters were removed from the scene. First, General Akhtar, the ISI's Director, who had overseen the guerrilla war in Afghanistan for eight years was promoted and posted. Similarly, Brigadier Mohammad Yousaf, Akhtar's right-hand man, who had headed the ISI's Afghan Bureau for four years, resigned after failing to gain promotion. It has been claimed President Zia saw Akhtar as a threat and that he also folded to American pressure to get rid of him at the crucial moment. Certainly, Brigadier Yousaf claimed Washington was working behind the scenes to ensure the Mujahideen did not claim final victory because of their Islamic credentials. Ironically, the Taliban were to prove far worse than the ramshackle Mujahideen alliance.

As if this was not enough, Pakistan's Afghan strategy was dealt a catastrophic blow. On 17 August 1988 both Zia and Akhtar were killed in a plane crash, when their aircraft fell mysteriously from the sky. While this was a significant loss for the resistance, the US State Department did not shed a tear. In Washington's eyes, Zia had alienated himself because of his apparent determination to see the

Fundamentalists take power in Kabul and, just as damning, his determination that Pakistan should match India's nuclear weapons. Akhtar, who had unexpectedly joined the flight, was an added bonus. Just as the Mujahideen decided to go over to conventional warfare, Washington put the squeeze on the weapons supplies. All this ensured victory was snatched from the resistance.

Most notably, the entire weapons and ammunition stock held by the ISI for the Mujahideen at Ojhri camp, north of Rawalpindi, blew up in early April 1988. In the space of ten minutes, four months' worth of supplies – some 10,000 tons – were lost, including 30,000 rockets, thousands of mortar bombs, millions of small arms rounds and Stinger missiles. While suspicion fell on Soviet and Afghan intelligence, Moscow was in the process of orchestrating its departure from Afghanistan and lacked motivation. The finger was also pointed at the Al-Zulfikar (The Sword) terrorist group, created by the Bhutto family after Zia had taken power. Formed in Kabul in 1979, it had shared offices with the Palestinian Liberation Organisation.

No one could miss Washington's changing attitude towards the Afghan resistance. In the Muslim world there was a growing perception that America had simply used the Mujahideen to avenge Vietnam and now cared little for the Muslims of Afghanistan. In the wake of the Soviet Army's departure, the only winners in Afghanistan were the Americans – they had seen the Soviet Union humiliated by guerrillas they had financed and armed. They also prevented an Islamic government replacing the Afghan Communists in Kabul. Ironically, even the Soviet Union managed to save face – Gorbachev's diplomacy had won him great respect in the West and the Soviet Army, having faced down Islamic militancy on the battlefields of Afghanistan, had successfully left Najibullah in power. The Mujahideen were left bearing a grudge against both superpowers and if there is one thing an Afghan does not forget, it is a blood feud.

It took three long years after the Soviet withdrawal from the Afghan imbroglio before Moscow's proxy government was finally overthrown. Najibullah's position was decisively weakened in January 1992, when both Moscow and Washington agreed to stop supplying the Afghan Army and the Mujahideen respectively. Najibullah put a brave face on the situation and tried to negotiate with the guerrillas. However, Gulbuddin Hekmatyar's fighters – with easily the largest stocks of weapons – attacked the city of Gardez, the gateway to Kabul. Former Iraqi tanks, supplied by Saudi Arabia (breaking the spirit of the US-Soviet undertaking), spearheaded this assault.

In May 1992 the defenders of Kabul were routed by the forces of three of the major guerrilla leaders – Massoud of Jamiat-i-Islami (with about 12,000 men), Sayed Mansour Nadari, warlord of Baghlan province, and General Abdul Rashid Dostum, leader of the Afghan Uzbek militia (some 40,000 strong). Although Massoud was considered the key figure, it was Hekmatyar's fighters who were first into the city. Even so, to the horror of the ethnic Pashtuns, they lost control of Kabul for the first time in 300 years to the rival Tajiks. Predictably, the victorious Mujahideen quickly fell out.

Nonetheless, there was a sense of triumph among American and British intelligence circles when Najibullah's Marxist regime folded, having so flagrantly toughed it out since the Soviet withdrawal. But the West seemed blind to the possibility that the Mujahideen – who were now highly Islamist – would not be able to bring peace to the devastated country. Nor would it serve the interests of Iran and Pakistan to help a prostrate Afghanistan back onto its feet.

The Mujahideen, after almost a decade and a half of fighting, were completely incapable of forming a coherent government and were to consign Kabul to yet another round of bloodletting. Any post-Najibullah government was stymied by Iran's insistence that it include Iranian-backed resistance movements as well as those bankrolled by America, Pakistan and Saudi Arabia. Understandably, the latter countries were not keen on this, as they did not want to give Iran a greater say in Afghanistan's affairs – especially if it meant a state ruled by Islamic law. Also, the Peshawar-based groups felt they had done the lion's share of the fighting and could see no reason to share the spoils with groups from the west.

In the meantime, a new army was being secretly formed in Pakistan's North West Frontier and Baluchistan provinces, bordering Afghanistan, under the guidance of the ISI. The Pakistanis had backed Hekmatyar but his actions caused the Afghan civil war to drag on, so another Pashtun alternative was needed. Their new creation was called the Taliban Farsi (Seekers of the Truth), under a cleric called Mohammed Omar. Many of the senior Taliban commanders were educated and trained in Pakistan. They developed close relations with the ISI and Pakistan had every reason to support a Pashtun-dominated government in Kabul. The last thing they wanted was a hostile administration run by ethnic Tajiks and Uzbeks.

It could be argued that Ayatollah Khomeini was the architect of the radicalisation of the Mujahideen in Afghanistan and ultimately the father of the Taliban. A delegation from the Pakistani Army visited the holy city of Qum on 14 January 1980, where they were presented to the Ayatollah. He told them in no uncertain terms:

> We are at war against infidels. Take this message with you – I ask all Islamic nations, all Muslims, all Islamic armies and all heads of Islamic states to join the holy war. There are many enemies to be killed or destroyed. Jihad must triumph.[5]

The ISI passed this message on, first to the Mujahideen and then their successors the Taliban. Jihad would finally triumph in Afghanistan – but not by the hand of the Mujahideen. Former Pakistani President Musharraf has since sought to justify the rise of the Taliban:

> When we sided with the Taliban, it was for good reasons: first, that they would bring peace to Afghanistan by bringing the warlords to heel; second, that the success of the Taliban would spell the defeat of the anti-Pakistan Northern Alliance. There was nothing wrong with our intentions, except that we did not realise that once the Taliban had used us to get to power, we would lose influence with them.[6]

He felt that, with the Taliban in power, Pakistan's western border would be secure so it could concentrate on guarding against attack from India.

According to a former intelligence officer, it was never going to be a problem arming the Taliban: 'I was in Peshawar in the early 1990s and the place was awash with guns courtesy of American and Saudi buying power. You name it, they had it, much of it being of Chinese and Egyptian manufacture.'[7]

The CIA had chosen Chinese and Egyptian Soviet-pattern weapons in the first instance because it was easier to mask Washington's assistance, on the grounds that the Mujahideen's weapons could have been taken from the Afghan and Soviet armies. During the early 1980s Egypt was exporting up to $1 billion worth of arms a year: while much of this went to Iraq to support its war against Iran, considerable quantities also ended up in Pakistan and Afghanistan (ironically, the Egyptians were eventually undercut by Russian manufacturers).[8] This proved completely ineffectual against the Soviet Army in Afghanistan.

In fact, with the demise of the Warsaw Pact, many East European countries – particularly Czechoslovakia, Bulgaria and Romania – had warehouses full of weapons they were only too happy to shift for the right price. Staff overseeing the UN's conventional weapons register in New York were aware of the havoc small arms exports were playing with regional conflicts, but the UN was reliant on peer pressure to curtail destabilising small arms sales.[9]

The Taliban emerged from the same Pakistani *madrassahs* that had formerly fired the Mujahideen's supporters with Islamic zeal – the intention being to make Afghanistan an Islamic state. The Soviet-Afghan war and the Afghani civil war had been characterised by appalling atrocities – the Taliban's campaign would prove no different.

It was a minor incident that set the Taliban on the road to power – one that most Western intelligence agencies failed to notice, thereby completely missing its significance. In the summer of 1994 bandits held up a convoy on the highway to Kandahar. With a little encouragement from the ISI, 2,000 religious students slipped across the border, freed the convoy and headed for Kandahar: and so the Taliban was born.

When the Taliban first emerged under Mullah Mohammed Omar, Afghanistan was in a state of total chaos, with the warlords ruling numerous fiefdoms. The Tajiks, under President Burhanuddin Rabbani and Ahmad Shah Massoud, held Kabul and the north-east. Uzbek warlord, General Dostum, controlled the north and Pashtun leader, Gulbuddin Hekmatyar, controlled the south. To the west, Tajik Ismael Khan of the Jamiat-i-Islami, controlled the Herat region. Beneath them were a myriad of bloodthirsty thugs.

Supported by the ISI, the Taliban's rapid march across Afghanistan was quite remarkable. Kandahar was taken in November 1994 and 20,000 Afghan refugees and Pakistani *madrassah* students flocked to Omar's cause. Kandahar is sited on the strategic Spin Boldak road, which runs to the Pakistani city of Quetta. With a population of some 300,000, Kandahar was a fertile recruiting ground for the Taliban. It has a bloody history dating all the way back to Alexander the Great, who founded the city of Alexandropolis in 330 BC to protect his lines of communication.

Within three months, a third of Afghanistan's provinces were in the hands of the Taliban, and they were pushing on Kabul and Herat. Hekmatyar found himself fighting not only Rabbani's forces but also the encroaching Taliban. They stormed Hekmatyar's HQ at Charasiab south of Kabul in the last week of February 1995. However, the following month, Massoud drove them out of southern Kabul. While this was a blow to the Taliban's prestige, it did nothing to dampen their zeal. The Tajiks then moved to help defend Herat and Shindand. Although driven back at Shindand with the loss of 3,000 men, the Taliban mustered 25,000 volunteers – many of them from Pakistan – to attack Ismael Khan's forces. In the face of such a host, in September 1995, Khan quickly abandoned both Herat and Shindand.

The following year, on 26 September, the Taliban swept into Kabul and Massoud's forces evacuated the city. Former President Najibullah, caught trying to escape, was brutally tortured and then hanged. The Taliban imposed the strictest Islamic system in the world. Women were banned from working, while music, all games – including kite-flying (a national pastime) – satellite dishes, TV and video were forbidden. Men without beards were arrested for being un-Islamic.

Understandably, there were mixed emotions in London and Washington. On the one hand, there was quiet satisfaction that Najibullah had got his comeuppance, on the other, disappointment that Massoud – always the darling of the West – had been driven from Kabul. No one recognised the danger the Taliban presented to the Afghan people, Pakistan's North West Frontier Province, Baluchistan, or, indeed, the rest of the world.

Once in power, the Taliban, like their predecessors, refused to recognise the border with Pakistan or drop claims to part of Pakistan's North West Frontier. Nor did the Taliban provide strategic depth, as Islamabad hoped, but rather the violent 'Talibisation' of Pakistan's western border provinces. To make matters worse, over 80,000 Pakistani Islamic militants trained and fought with the Taliban. In 1995 the Pakistani Army had to crush an uprising demanding Shariah law and Indian intelligence reported that Pakistani-trained militants (such as Harakat ul-Mujahadin, Jaish-e-Mohammed and Lashkar-e-Tayyiba, which seek unification of Kashmir with Pakistan) and Afghan war veterans were infiltrating northern India to bolster Kashmiri resistance to Indian rule.

Growing corruption in Pakistan's western provinces extended to the Pakistani armed forces. In the late 1990s, the Pakistani Air Force's second-in-command resigned in protest over alleged corruption in the PAF and Pakistan's navy chief was sacked for alleged corruption. Mounting political violence across Pakistan led to the controversial Anti-Terrorism Bill, allowing shoot-on-sight of suspected terrorists.

In Afghanistan, the Taliban soon overstretched themselves in their pursuit of Massoud and on 18 October 1996 his forces retook Bagram air base and began to shell Kabul. Once again, the Taliban looked to Pakistan, which waived all border controls for thousands of Afghan and Pakistani students from the *madrassahs*, who went to join the fight. Predictably, Massoud was pushed back once more. The Northern Alliance (or United Front – representing Afghanistan's Hazara, Tajik, Uzbek and other ethnic minorities), was largely confined to an enclave in the north-east of the country, protected by the Hindu Kush. The following year, Mullah Omar issued another call to arms, which was answered by 5,000 willing recruits.

In the meantime, Osama bin Laden returned to Afghanistan in May 1996, having been forced from Sudan. His first declaration of Jihad against America for occupying Saudi Arabia was issued on 23 August 1996:

> My Muslim Brothers of the World: Your brothers in Palestine and in the land of the two Holy Places are calling upon your help and asking you to take part in fighting against the enemy – your enemy and their enemy – The Americans and the Israelis.[10]

The following year he was taken under the wing of the Taliban, becoming a guest of Mullah Omar in Kandahar. This was facilitated by Pakistan, which wanted to continue using the Khost training camps for Kashmiri militants waging a guerrilla war in Indian Kashmir. On 23 February 1998, bin Laden gathered his followers at the Khost camp and issued a *fatwa* to kill Americans and their allies – both military and civilian. America and Afghanistan were now on a collision course, as al-Qaeda embarked on a truly global terror campaign. It reportedly had a worldwide network encompassing thirty-four countries.

By 1998, the Taliban controlled 90 per cent of Afghanistan. The wily Massoud returned to his old base in the Panjsher Valley, establishing his capital at Taloqan. However, there seemed no stopping the relentless Taliban tide. On 5 September 1999, Taloqan fell after a four-week siege to 15,000 Taliban troops – 30 per cent of whom were foreigners, including several hundred Arabs under bin Laden, 3,000 Pakistanis and 1,000 Uzbeks from the IMU. In total, al-Qaeda controlled about 3,000 fighters from thirteen Arab countries in Afghanistan.

The Taliban's acquiescence of the presence of al-Qaeda and its complicity in the country's drug trade ensured Afghanistan was by now a truly undesirable state. The United Nation's International Narcotics Control Board identified intensified narcotics production with the economic, social and political collapse caused by over two decades of civil war.

Afghanistan, for long a centre for opiate production, under the Taliban accounted for some 75 per cent of the world's opium. Profits generated from narcotic exports helped to fund the civil war. It was, however, unclear what percentage of revenues actually reached central Taliban coffers – local Taliban warlords probably benefited the most from drug taxes. It is likely that the level of remuneration impacted to a degree on the Taliban war effort against the Northern Alliance and other factions, as well as its support for regional Islamic guerrilla movements in Central Asia and the Indian sub-continent.

Nonetheless, it is unclear just how far the Taliban relied on these revenues to maintain the tempo of their military operations and support for international terrorism. It was self-evident from the level of anti-narcotics activity that neighbouring states were forced to undertake that Afghanistan's narcotics trafficking was a major problem. To the west and east, Iran and Pakistan attempted to crack down on drug-smuggling across their borders. Ironically, Pakistan's success simply resulted in pushing lucrative heroin manufacturing into Afghanistan. Iran, in turn, expended considerable financial and military resources trying to control the well-armed border drug warlords.

The production and smuggling of drugs across Asia also became a vital source of revenue for other terrorist and international criminal organisations. This threatened the security and stability of a region heading for further upheaval. Beyond Afghanistan's borders to the north, in the Central Asian states, Afghan drug money and organised crime assisted pro-Taliban opposition groups, such as the IMU and the former United Tajik Opposition. Also, ethnic Uighurs from China's Xinjiang province (bordering Afghanistan and Tajikistan) were known to have trained in Afghanistan with the IMU. As already noted the Uighurs have been agitating against central Chinese authority for decades, necessitating a number of large Chinese military operations against them.

The scale of the Taliban's drug-trafficking profits and its impact on the civil war is difficult to assess, but intelligence estimates suggest it was substantial. Whatever the amounts involved, drugs were widely deemed a major – possibly critical – source of Taliban military funding. Some Western intelligence estimates indicate that opium provided up to 50 per cent of the Taliban's total financial resources, with the rest coming from trafficking arms, precious stones and fuel. It is estimated that the Taliban were making between $50–100 million per annum from the opium trade and that much of the Taliban's military procurement was financed from this illegal source.

Before the Taliban's ban on opium cultivation in mid-2000, production was tied directly to the war economy, to the extent that poppy cultivation and the opium trade were overseen and taxed by the local Taliban military. The ban was, in part, to placate international donors such as the UN, but it also served the Taliban's own purposes. By restricting supply it increased profit margins and enabled the Taliban to exert a greater control over the trade. It was clear that opium trafficking continued from a stockpile estimated at almost 3,000 tonnes, probably to help the Taliban maintain its military spending.

Most cultivation occurred in the Taliban-controlled areas (predominantly Helmand, Kandahar, Nangarhar and Uruzgan provinces) and it was widely reported that leading Taliban figures were involved. Certainly, the Taliban imposed Islamic taxes on production, refining and transit. Following Mullah Omar's ban, areas of Afghanistan under the control of the Taliban – according to the UN – witnessed a transformation as poppy cultivation almost totally disappeared. Nonetheless, doubts remained whether Omar would keep the ban in place, despite statements to that effect. Significantly, the ban on growing poppies only applied to cultivation.

Reports state that the 2000 crop sold before the ban for as little as $30 per kilo, but that it raised approximately $100 million for farmers and tens of millions of dollars for the Taliban. In contrast, the ban sent prices soaring to a peak of $700 a kilo in early 2001, pushing the Taliban's share even higher. After 9/11 opium prices in Afghanistan plummeted 80 per cent to $140 a kilo – a development due in part to quick selling and tighter border security measures by Afghanistan's neighbours.

Nor was the Northern Alliance innocent of complicity in the drugs trade – its north-eastern enclave was an important channel for narcotics into Central Asia and beyond. Indeed, both opium and heroin continued to be smuggled over the Amu Darya river into neighbouring Tajikistan. Compared to the key Taliban-controlled southern and south-eastern provinces, where most Afghan opium production was concentrated, output from the Northern Alliance areas was small – less than 5 per cent of national production. It was unlikely that the Northern Alliance relied on such revenues for its weapon supplies. However, the arrival in Badakhshan of Mashriqi opium traders and moneylenders reportedly stimulated production and turned the region into a conduit for southern opium and heroin moving north into Central Asia. Security measures and interdiction along the Afghan-Iranian and Pakistani-Iranian borders also encouraged this shift northward.

While the Northern Alliance publicly destroyed opium, the United Nations Drugs Control Project (UNDCP) assessed it made little effort to curtail production, refining and export of heroin in its areas. The UNDCP concluded that opium production had become a crucial segment of the rural economy in the region. Drug cultivation in the Taliban areas was further stimulated in 1998, when Saudi Arabia withdrew crucial financial support for harbouring Osama bin Laden.

In the meantime, on 23 February 1998, bin Laden – in alliance with Ayman Zawahiri's Egyptian Jihad – issued their call to Jihad:

> The ruling to kill the Americans and their allies – civilians and military – is an individual duty for every Muslim who can do it in any country in which it is possible to do it, in order to liberate the al-Aqsa Mosque [in Jerusalem] and the holy mosque [Mecca] from their grip.[11]

On 20 August that year the US launched seventy-five cruise missile attacks against camps run by bin Laden in Khost and Jalalabad. This was in response to the al-Qaeda bombings of the US embassies in Kenya and Tanzania thirteen days earlier. Nevertheless, the Taliban vowed to protect bin Laden.

The UN also acted against the Taliban for harbouring Osama bin Laden and those implicated in the attacks on the Khobar Towers in Saudi Arabia, the US embassies in Africa, the USS *Cole* off Yemen and the earlier attempt to blow up the WTC during the 1990s. The first UN Security Council Resolution 1267 against the Taliban came into effect in November 1999. This banned the Afghan carrier, Ariana Airlines, from operating overseas and required members to freeze Taliban overseas assets.

The US, UK and EU froze at least $400 million of Taliban and terror-related funds. Attempts were under way to stop bin Laden's financing operations in their tracks. Estimates of Osama bin Laden's personal fortune have ranged from nothing to $300 million. The IMF had frozen Afghanistan's reserve gold holdings, worth up to $8 million in 1994. The UN also retained Taliban over-flight fees and aviation taxes to the value of some $15 million. In the wake of the attacks in New York and Washington, the UN also halted almost $2 million of aid to help Afghan farmers seeking alternative crops to poppy cultivation.

The second UNSCR 1333 passed by the fifteen-member council (with only two abstentions – China and Malaysia) came into effect on 19 January 2001.[12] This followed a month's grace to allow the Taliban to comply with demands to hand over bin Laden and close down camps being used as terrorist training centres. While reinforcing 1267, this resolution called on member states to prohibit virtually all international travel by Taliban officials; close down Taliban offices abroad – including those of Ariana Airlines – and downsize Taliban embassies in Pakistan, Saudi Arabia and the United Arab Emirates – the only states to recognise the regime. It also called for a ban on the export of chemical precursors (used in the production of morphine base and heroin) to Afghanistan; a military embargo on the sale or transfer to the Taliban (but not the Northern

Alliance) of arms, ammunition, military vehicles, military equipment or spare parts; and the withdrawal of officials, agents, advisors or other military personnel employed by contract or other arrangement to advise the Taliban. In February 2001, George Tenet, Director of the CIA, warned of the dangers of ignoring the country:

> What we have in Afghanistan is a stark example of the potential dangers of allowing states – even those far from the US – to fail. The chaos here is providing an incubator for narcotics traffickers and militant Islamic groups operating in such places as Kashmir, Chechnya, and Central Asia. Meanwhile, the Taliban shows no sign of relinquishing terrorist Osama bin Laden, despite strengthened UN sanctions and the prospect that bin Laden's terrorist operations could lead to retaliatory strikes against Afghanistan. The Taliban and bin Laden have a symbiotic relationship – bin Laden gets safe haven and in return, he gives the Taliban help in fighting its civil war.[13]

In June 2001 the Taliban threw 25,000 men (including 10,000 non–Afghans) against the Northern Alliance. Massoud, that veteran of the long Soviet war, was a marked man. At the behest of the Taliban, Islamist operatives assassinated him just two days before 9/11. Clearly a deal had been cut: whatever America's response to the coming attacks, the Taliban would continue to harbour bin Laden and his acolytes. Journalist Phil Rees, recalling Ahmad Shah Massoud's assassination, noted that it was likely to have been an al-Qaeda operation:

> Massoud was murdered on Sunday, 9 September 2001. A television team claiming to represent an Arab network in London were about to begin an interview when the man pretending to be a reporter detonated a powerful bomb strapped to his waist. His killing was probably an attempt by bin Laden to undermine the unity of the Northern Alliance and remove its most skilful commander before the United States retaliated for the September 11th attacks. The news of Massoud's death was broadcast around the world on the following day. It was the signal that nineteen al-Qaeda members in the United States had been waiting for. On Tuesday morning they hijacked the four fateful flights.[14]

Chapter 5

Somalia: a Lesson in Victory

The war-torn Horn of Africa became the next focus for the escalating war on terror. Crushing the Taliban in Afghanistan had the effect of scattering the various Islamist groups they had been harbouring like so much chaff in the wind. Though few in number, al-Qaeda supporters are believed to operate in Islamic Somalia, which provides a safe haven and transit point to other countries. US intelligence officials had strong indications that bin Laden was preparing to move there from Afghanistan after 9/11.[1] Following the ousting of the Taliban it was assessed that al-Qaeda might relocate to Somalia.

It was only natural that hapless Somalia should become the next front on the global war on terror. This failed state has no effective central government or security forces, while its long coastline and numerous ports are almost impossible to police. Roughly the size of the state of Texas, it is one of the poorest countries in the world, and its 7.5 million people have been treated appallingly by their leaders over the decades.

Britain tangled with Muslim militants in British-administered Somaliland during the first two decades of the twentieth century. Mahommed bin Abdullah (or Sayyid Muhammed Abdullah Hassan) declared himself the 'Mahdi' or 'Guided One of the Prophet' in 1899. The British dubbed him 'The Mad Mullah' and spent considerable time fighting his Dervishes. Once his stronghold at Shimber Berris was finally destroyed, he died in destitution in the Ogaden in 1921.

After General Mohammed Barre seized control in 1969, Somalia became a Soviet client state. As in so many other Muslim states, the appeal of Socialism proved hollow and crippled the country's economy. Territorial squabbles resulted in Barre going to war with his much larger Christian neighbour, Ethiopia, in 1977–78, over the Ogaden region. Moscow cynically abandoned him, despatching a massive influx of Soviet arms and Cuban troops to ensure an Ethiopian victory.[2] Following Somalia's humiliating defeat, the country drifted into despair, though Barre was not overthrown until 1991.

A fresh bout of fighting broke out in February 1987, which was blamed on increased activity by rebels crossing the border to launch attacks. Finally, a peace treaty was concluded in May the following year, which allowed the Ethiopian Army to re-deploy 30,000 troops northwards. Unfortunately, the Ethiopian-Somali rapprochement had unwanted dramatic results, as at the end of the month, the opposition Somali National Movement launched an all-out attack on northern Somalia, hoping to topple Barre. By October 1988, 1.5 million people had been displaced, 50,000 butchered and 400,000 driven into Ethiopia. By 1989 Ethiopia was still host to almost 350,000 desperate Muslim Somali refugees.[3]

Barre's predictably repressive response to the SNM was such that an appalled Washington withheld $55 million and London $9 million of aid.[4] But beyond this, Western governments showed very little inclination to intervene in Somalia's messy power struggle. No one cared now that the Horn of Africa had lost its Cold War strategic relevance. It would have to reach crisis point before that happened, and then when it did it was to have serious repercussions.

Fighting broke out in the Somali capital, Mogadishu, on 30 December 1989, resulting in 1,500 dead, when the insurgent United Somali Congress opened its assault. The civil war dragged on for another year, by which stage Barre's twenty-one-year rule was almost at an end. The rebels soon overran the countryside and Barre was mocked as 'the mayor of Mogadishu'.[5]

Somalia's bloodthirsty warlords dragged the rest of the country into an ever more vicious civil war. In the capital, General Mohammed Farah Aideed managed to gain ascendancy over his rivals, Muse Sude Yalahow and Ali Mahdi Mohammed. This factional fighting brought the country to its knees and around 300,000 Somalis starved to death as the West looked on.[6] It was estimated that fatalities would rapidly reach 1 million unless the international community acted.[7] Fatefully, the UN agreed to send peacekeepers.

Into this quagmire the UN launched an emergency food relief operation in August 1992, but the warlords simply used the food to sustain their militias. Four months later, President George H. Bush instigated Operation Restore Hope, which was to involve 25,000 US troops. General Aideed soon became hostile to UN peacekeepers when they tried to disarm his militia, and in his eyes seemed to be favouring his rival, Ali Mahdi Mohammed.

Around this point, bin Laden – according to US intelligence reports – sent his supporters to Somalia to help the radical group known as al-Ittihad al-Islamiya (Islamic Unity or AIAI) to seize power. After the fall of Barre, the AIAI had tried to take control of the southern cities of Merka and Kismayo and the northern port of Bosaso, but were unable to overcome the well-armed local clans. Bin Laden's first main attack on American interests in the region occurred when a hotel in Aden, housing American soldiers en route to Somalia, was bombed. The troops had already gone but two tourists were killed.[8]

Living in Sudan from 1991–96, under the patronage of the Islamic regime in Khartoum, bin Laden saw American intervention in Somalia as a threat to Islam, which was in line with his views of the defiling US military presence in Saudi Arabia. As part of his overall campaign, he issued a *fatwa* in 1993 inciting the Somalis to drive the Americans out.[9] He also sent Mohammed Atef (subsequently involved in 9/11) and others to help train the Somalis.

In the meantime, the US force was relieved in May 1993 as planned by a multinational contingent of 28,000 UN peacekeepers under a Turkish general. In a taste of things to come, Aideed's forces successfully ambushed and killed twenty-five Pakistani peacekeepers the following month. Fatefully, the Clinton administration's response was to despatch US Special Forces or Rangers to seize Aideed.

When the US Principals Committee of national security advisors met in the White House on 17 September 1993, General Colin Powell warned President Clinton against mission spread, while Madeleine Albright, ambassador to the UN, argued for increased foreign intervention and nation-building. Anthony Lake, Clinton's National Security Advisor, was concerned that America's participation in muddled UN operations, such Somalia and Bosnia, were detracting America from the future strategic direction of Russia post Soviet Union.

In particular, Somalia remained an unwanted commitment, although the US presence had been drawn down from 35,000 troops at its peak to just 4,700. Mogadishu became a major distraction when Aideed's militia successfully brought down two American Black Hawk helicopters using rocket-propelled grenades and killed eighteen Rangers (America's heaviest losses in a single battle since Vietnam). Sandy Berger, Lake's deputy, recalls:

> It was certainly one of the darkest days of the last eight years. We got called in the middle of the night. I think Tony Lake called the president. It was Sunday morning, 3 October 1993. We came into the White House. The beginning of any of these episodes always has conflicting facts [...] But obviously, as we learned more about this, it was clear we had suffered a terrible loss. It was a very, very difficult day.[10]

Chuck deCaro, a US government media consultant and 'soft war' expert, later told the author that Washington lost the PR war over the 'Black Hawk Down' incident, because it refused to release the helicopter gun camera footage showing US forces inflicting terrible casualties on the Somalis. At the time, the US public did not appreciate that eighteen dead and ninety wounded had been traded for 1,000 Somali casualties.[11] Tony Lake later lamented:

> News organisations have better coverage than the CIA does in many areas. When you're working information through the intelligence system – either through the Pentagon or through the CIA or the State Department – it has to go through layers because people are trying to turn the information into [assessed] intelligence.[12]

Clinton, having previously not taken any interest in the 'seize Aideed operation', was caught completely off guard and did not know what to do. 'Black Hawk Down' prompted immediate Congressional calls for the withdrawal of the remaining US troops. Lake cautioned against abandoning Somalia: 'The message would be: You kill Americans, America withdraws from that situation.'[13] Clinton's line was that his policy towards Somalia and Bosnia would remain unchanged and he opted to withdraw from Somalia slowly. Predictably, the Islamists still came to the same conclusion. Five months later, all US forces had withdrawn and the failed UN peacekeeping mission came to a halt in 1995. Somalia was abandoned to its fate.

Bin Laden took credit for the American deaths and in a CNN news interview acknowledged his men had trained the Somali fighters responsible. Certainly, Aideed's men had somehow learned how to ensure that their rocket-propelled grenades exploded in the air by tampering with the fuses. The fact that America had given up on Somalia convinced bin Laden that by killing more Americans he could drive them out of Saudi Arabia and elsewhere. His followers subsequently escalated their attacks, believing America was weak. Al-Qaeda terrorists are believed to have been involved in killing five US military advisors in a bombing in Riyadh in 1995 and killing another nineteen US military personnel the following year with the Khobar Towers bombing in Saudi Arabia. Bin Laden said of the 'Black Hawk Down' incident:

> It is true my companions fought with Farah Aideed's forces against the US troops in Somalia. But we were fighting against US terrorism. Under the cover of [the] United Nations, the United States tried to establish bases in Somalia so that it could get control over Sudan and Yemen. My associates killed the Americans in collaboration with Farah Aideed. We are not ashamed of our Jihad. In one explosion 100 Americans were killed, the eighteen more were killed in fighting. One day our men shot down an American helicopter. The pilot got out. We caught him, tied his legs and dragged him through the streets. After that 28,000 US soldiers fled Somalia. The Americans are cowards.[14]

With the UN gone, the Islamist AIAI now sought to establish a stronghold in the south, in the Gedo region, near the Kenyan border. From the town of Luuq they recruited ethnic Somalis living over the border in Kenya and Ethiopia, in particular in the long-disputed Ogaden region. During the 1990s, operating from Gedo, some 3,000 AIAI fighters attempted to liberate the Ogaden, resulting in predictable reprisals by the Ethiopian and Kenyan militaries. The situation came to a head in 1996, when the Ethiopian Army assaulted Luuq, killing hundreds of AIAI militants. It transpired that the AIAI had not been altogether popular with the local clans, as it had imposed Shariah law and banned *qaat* (a narcotic used by Somalis and Yemenis).

Having expelled the AIAI, the Ethiopians formed a coalition of Somali factions known as the Somali Reconciliation and Restoration Council, to keep the AIAI out and as a rival to the Transitional National Government in Mogadishu. The Ethiopians considered the TNG as stooges of the AIAI.

Amid the chaos, on 5 June 2006, the Islamic militias aligned with the Union of Islamist Courts (local religious courts) took over Mogadishu. In doing so they ousted a coalition of warlords called the Alliance for the Restoration of Peace and Counter-terrorism, which had been enjoying American financial assistance in return for their support in the war on al-Qaeda. Most Somalis accepted the UIC, as they offered the first semblance of government since 1991. While Shariah law was welcomed, a ripple of unease passed through the international community when Swedish journalist Martin Adler was gunned down on 23 June.

It was at this point that Hassan Dahir Aweys, whom both the UN and US believe has links with al-Qaeda, took control of the Islamic militias. He quickly ousted Abdurahman Osman, a Somali-born US citizen, who was the moderate face of the militias.[15] Aweys announced that he wanted to extend his interpretation of Islamic law to the whole of Somalia. Confusingly, the UIC, under Sheikh Sharif Sheikh Ahmed and Aweys, changed its name on 25 June 2006 to the Islamic Courts Council. Repeating its support of Islamists in Afghanistan and Lebanon, Iran is believed to have supplied the Islamic Courts with weapons (including anti-aircraft weapons and anti-tank missiles). Understandably, relations were not good between the Islamic militias and the nominal national government backed by the UN and the African Union. The militias were particularly unhappy about the government's alliance with Ethiopia – Somalia's one-time enemy. Aweys made it clear that he would only support a government based on the rule of Islam.[16]

By mid-2006 the Islamic Courts held sway over much of the country, until they were driven out by an alliance between the TNG and Ethiopia. Somali interim President, Abdullah Yusuf Ahmad, arrived in Mogadishu on 8 January 2007 – the first time since taking office in 2004. This marked the victory of the Transitional Federal Government over the Islamic Courts. However, the TFG was not able to effectively police the country and the Islamic insurgency gained ground.

During early 2007, operations against the insurgents were supported by US helicopter gunships, which attacked sites close to the Kenyan border. This was Washington's first overt military operation in Somalia since 'Black Hawk Down' and the Americans were thought to be after Fazul Abdullah Mohammed, Saleh al-Saleh Nabhan and Abu Taha al-Sudani, who were believed to be behind the 1998 bombings of the US embassies in Kenya and Tanzania.[17] These attacks were thought to have been conducted from Djibouti, which became America's main regional counter-terrorism base in 2002. Interim President Ahmed's response was that Washington had every right to bomb those who had attacked its embassies.

American suspicions about Somalia harbouring Islamist militants were confirmed when it emerged that the UIC had been sending men to Lebanon and Syria to fight against Israel, in return for training and weapons. According to the UN, some 720 Somali fighters were chosen by Afghan-trained Adan Hashi Farah 'Ayro' and despatched to fight alongside Hezbollah in July 2006. Around 100 fighters returned home with five Hezbollah members. Syria also trained about 200 Somali fighters.[18]

The Islamic Courts' six-month rule during the second half of 2006 had one positive aspect, in that the plague of piracy off Somalia almost ceased. It showed that a functioning Somali government could control the pirates. A youth militia, al-Shabaab, which emerged during the rule of the Courts has since been reported to have links with Somali pirates or indeed may be one and the same.[19]

When al-Shabaab commenced its insurgency in late 2006, it relied on classic guerrilla tactics of hit and run to oppose the Somali government. Most of its attacks in August 2007 were conducted in Mogadishu and targeted the Ethiopian military – the escalating violence created 400,000 refugees, as people were driven from their homes. Although Ethiopian forces withdrew from Somalia in January 2009, removing al-Shabaab's main enemy, attacks against African Union peacekeepers continued. This culminated in attempts to secure Galgadud in central Somalia.

Once the Islamic Courts had been ousted the scourge of piracy quickly re-emerged with a vengeance. The problem was such that in 2007 the UN's World Food Programme had to halt deliveries by sea. The semi-autonomous region of Puntland, in the north-east of the country, seems to be where most of the pirates emanate from, though some also come from Yemen. The simple reason for this is that Puntland is one of the most poverty-stricken areas of the country.

The pirates obviously have links with Somali militias because of the types of weapons they deploy, which include rocket-propelled grenades and light air defence systems.[20] On 27 June 2005 the *MV Semlow*, carrying food supplied by the UN's World Food Programme, was seized some 300km north-east of Mogadishu, on its way from Kenya to Puntland. The pirates demanded $500,000 to release the ship and its cargo of 850 tons of rice. The WFP responded by threatening to suspend its food aid and placing Somalia on a ten-year blacklist if the ship was not returned.

An explicit acknowledgement of Somalia's terror links occurred in mid-April 2009 when a senior Saudi Arabian al-Qaeda leader called on Somali Jihadists to step up their attacks on 'crusader' forces in the pirate-infested Gulf of Aden, and on land in neighbouring Djibouti, which hosts France's largest military base in Africa: 'To our steadfast brethren in Somalia, take caution and prepare yourselves,' said Sa'id Ali Jabir al-Khathim al-Shihri (alias Abu Sufian al-Azdi) in an audio tape, 'Increase your strikes against the crusaders at sea and in Djibouti.' [21]

Saudi al-Shihri was captured near Pakistan's border with Afghanistan in December of 2001 and was one of the first prisoners at the Guantanamo Bay detention camp in Cuba, arriving on 21 January 2002. Following being held there without charge for almost six years, he was released to the Saudi authorities and enrolled in a repatriation and rehabilitation programme. After his release, he went to Yemen and was subsequently described as a deputy leader in a press release from 'al-Qaeda in the Arabian Peninsula'.

By early 2009 al-Shabaab controlled much of southern Somalia, except for Mogadishu. Although its links to al-Qaeda are weak, in February 2008, Washington added it to its list of terror organisations. Although al-Shabaab is led by Sheikh Mohamed Mukhtar Abdirahman ('Abu Zubeyr') it is divided into three geographical areas. On the ground it is thought to muster several thousand fighters and has conducted forced recruitment among fellow Somalis. Foreign fighters have also travelled to the country to join it, including Somalis from the UK and US.[22]

Al-Shabaab fighters have been trained by foreigners and in September 2008 a Shabaab leader issued a video pledging allegiance to bin Laden. In acknowledgement, Ayman al-Zawahiri released a video in February 2009 praising al-Shabaab's seizure of the Somali town of Baidoa. While it is assessed that most Somalis oppose Jihadi Islam, and that it seems unlikely the Somalis would embrace a Taliban-style regime, al-Shabaab's influence remains a worry.[23]

Alarmingly for America, it discovered that al-Shabaab had been drawing funds and recruits from America's Somali community. This link came to light in late October 2008, when Shirwa Ahmed became the first American suicide bomber. He blew himself up in northern Somalia during a series of bombings orchestrated by al-Shabaab.[24]

The FBI warned that America was now facing domestic terrorism from second-generation Somali immigrants, following the revelation that two mosques in Minneapolis had recruited twenty young Somali Americans to travel to Somalia. Certainly, Somali youths in America are susceptible to such recruitment in the face of poor employment prospects, disillusionment with US policies in Afghanistan and Iraq, plus America's backing for Ethiopian incursions into Somalia.

The US Counter-terrorism Center variously estimated America's Somali population as anything from 70,000 to 200,000. 'The exact number of young Somali American men who travelled to Somalia to support al-Shabaab or other Somali factions is unclear,' said Andrew Liepman, the Center's Deputy Director of Intelligence, 'and it is possible that others remain undetected.'[25] He went on to add that, since 2006, US citizens who are Muslim converts had also travelled to Somalia, potentially with a view to attending militant training camps. British universities have also provided recruiting grounds for al-Shabaab seeking educated Somalis.

Al-Shabaab's reach was even shown to extend to Australia, when four Somalis with links to the group were arrested in early August 2009. They were accused of planning a terrorist attack on Sydney's Holsworthy Barracks, in revenge for Australia's military involvement in Afghanistan and Iraq. American forces officially returned to Somalia for the first time since the 'Black Hawk Down' incident on 14 September 2009. Six US Special Forces helicopters conducted a raid to kill al-Qaeda terrorist, Saleh Ali Saleh Nabhan, near the town of Barawe. He was seen as a key terror co-ordinator between East Africa and the Horn of Africa. Kenyan-born Nabhan acted as liaison between al-Qaeda and al-Shabaab, and had been involved in attacks in Kenya (the 2002 attack on a Kenyan beach hotel, popular with Israelis, and an attempt on a tourist flight bound for Tel Aviv on the same day).

It seems that, as in the Lebanon, America's intervention in Somalia ultimately aggravated the situation and gave fuel to bin Laden's contention that America was in the business of dominating Muslim states. Across from the Horn of Africa, Yemen became a trouble spot when al-Qaeda terrorists fled there after the collapse of the Taliban. Osama bin Laden claimed responsibility for the 1992 attempted bombing of US service personnel in Yemen, and then the successful bombing of the USS *Cole* in Aden harbour in 2000. It appeared, in the West, that the spread of militant Islam remained unchecked.

Chapter 6

Yemen: a Nest of Vipers

As with Somalia, Western intelligence never had any great interest in North or South Yemen, other than their half-hearted roles in the Cold War. Notably, the South was used as a Soviet staging post for operations in the Horn of Africa, especially Ethiopia. Moscow signed a treaty of friendship with South Yemen in 1980, which gave it access to naval facilities at al-Mukalla, Khormaksar, and on Socotra Island – all of which posed a potential threat to the Red Sea, the Gulf and Western oil supplies. Saudi Arabia was particularly concerned about the presence of Soviet advisers on its southern borders in both North and South Yemen, especially after the South toppled into chaos in the mid-1980s.

The Yemenis were willing customers for Soviet arms. South Yemen had spent $3.5 billion on Soviet weaponry by 1987, while the North had acquired $1.4 billion.[1] Nonetheless, Moscow's aims were hampered by the two Yemens' hostility towards each other and by internal instability. Having abandoned Somalia in the 1970s, Marxist Ethiopia was always considered a more viable regional ally.

Again, like Somalia across the Red Sea, Yemen has a long and troubled past and is a well-known haven for militants, who have been able to travel with impunity to unstable neighbours such as Somalia and Sudan. The Yemenis themselves have provided a considerable number of al-Qaeda supporters. Their country was also the scene of one of the most infamous incidents in the gathering war on terror.

On 12 October 2000, Islamic suicide bombers attacked the USS *Cole*, which was refuelling at the port of Aden in Yemen. The blast killed seventeen sailors and injured thirty-seven. While the vessel did not sink, it ended up with a 13-metre hole in its hull and $240 million worth of damage. Ever since, US regional security remains very tight for fear of another attack similar to the *Cole* and the French tanker *Limburg*. The attack on the *Cole* also caused a temporary halt in developing relations with the US military. The chief culprit, Saudi-born Abd al-Rahim al-Nashiri, was arrested in 2002.

Yemeni, Ramzi Binalshibh, who had been in Afghanistan with bin Laden in January 2000, was the quartermaster of the 9/11 attacks. He was also a flat-mate of Mohammed Atta in Hamburg. He was finally captured in Pakistan in September 2002. Bin Laden's Yemeni driver, Salim Ahmed Hamadan, who was captured in Afghanistan, was charged with conspiring with al-Qaeda and having knowledge of the East Africa and Aden bombings.[2]

Two of the *Cole* bombers – Yemeni, Jamal al-Badawi and Saudi, Abd al-Rahim al-Nashiri – were sentenced to death in Yemen on 29 September 2004. Four other Yemeni plotters were also jailed for up to ten years.[3] Muhammad Hamdi al-Ahdal (also known as Abu Asim al-Macci) and his associate, Ghalib al-Zaidi – who had been held since December 2003 – were put on trial in 2006. Al-Ahdal was a veteran of Afghanistan and Chechnya and was a former deputy of al-Harthi.[4]

Washington's response to the *Cole* bombing was slow because Bill Clinton was initially focused on negotiating with the Israelis and Palestinians, having been galvanised by the Intifada. Both Clinton and his National Security Advisor, Sandy Berger, later told the 9/11 Commission that the link to al-Qaeda with the bombing was only a 'preliminary judgement'[5] and that they were awaiting direction from CIA Director, George Tenet. The 9/11 Commission concluded that the attack on the *Cole* boosted al-Qaeda's recruitment efforts, especially when Washington failed to respond in the anticipated manner. President Clinton, of course, refutes accusations that he dragged his feet:

> Now, if you want to criticise me for one thing, you can criticise me for this: After the *Cole*, I had battle plans drawn to go into Afghanistan, overthrow the Taliban, and launch a full-scale attack search for bin Laden. But we needed basing rights in Uzbekistan, which we got after 9/11. The CIA and FBI refused to certify that bin Laden was responsible while I was there. They refused to certify . . .[6]

Tenet later denied he had ever held any discussions with Clinton and Berger on the issue of retaliation over the *Cole*. Doubt was later cast on Berger's testimony, when it was discovered that he had stolen and destroyed classified documents from the National Archives during the 9/11 investigation.[7]

Formerly part of the Ottoman Empire, during the First World War North Yemen rose in revolt against Turkish rule. A military coup in 1962 resulted in a five-year guerrilla war. Another coup, five years later, was also the point at which Britain withdrew from the Aden Protectorate, which became South Yemen and the only Marxist Arab state. However, the grafting of Marxist-Leninist doctrine on an Islamic tribal society simply aggravated internal divisions. Britain's only colony in Arabia was established at Aden (including Perim Island) in 1839 because it sits at the mouth of Red Sea, adjoining the overland route to India via Egypt (the Suez Canal had not yet been built).

Tens of thousands of expatriate Yemenis became scattered around the Middle East and fighters from the North went to support Iraq during the war with Iran. By the mid-1980s, South Yemen was largely shunned by the other Arab states and its one-time ally, the Soviet Union. It also came to bloody blows with Oman and North Yemen. The South collapsed in civil war in 1986, with the army siding with the rebels, who won at the cost of 2,000 dead. About 80 per cent of its navy and 90 per cent of its air force and some 145 tanks were destroyed in the two weeks of fighting. The international community was also forced to evacuate 2,000 foreign nationals.

Chaotic South Yemen was on America's state sponsors of terrorism list until 1990, when it united with the conservative North. Unification brought its own problems, most notably the return of 850,000 Yemenis who had been working in the Gulf states and a dramatic fall in foreign aid. Internal political disputes – culminating in the 1994 civil war – further hampered economic growth. Five years on, President Ali Abdullah Saleh became the first elected President of the reunified Yemen (though he had been president since 1990 and president of North Yemen since 1978) and was re-elected in September 2006. In the summer of 2000, Yemen and Saudi Arabia signed an International Border Treaty, finally settling a fifty-year-old quarrel over the location of their mutual border.

Yemen and strife-torn Somalia historically enjoy good relations – ethnic Somalis, for the most part, assimilate easily into Yemeni society, as they share close origins. However, Yemen, like Somalia, has an unsavoury record. During the 1980s, Yemeni Mujahideen fought the Soviets in Afghanistan, and through-out the 1990s Yemeni fighters continued to train in Afghanistan under the auspices of al-Qaeda. Subsequently, they made up the largest nationality of prisoners held at Guantanamo Bay. In addition, Foreign Minister Abu Bakr al-Qirbi stated that Yemen was host to over 1,000 Jihadists.[8]

Washington believes Yemen became troublesome when al-Qaeda members fled there after the collapse of the Taliban in Afghanistan. Nevertheless, even before 9/11, Yemen faced the major problem of how to handle the thousands of Jihadist militants who returned home from Afghanistan. Following 9/11, the Yemeni government sought to clamp down on suspected al-Qaeda members, in an attempt to counter Washington's allegations that it was providing a haven for Islamic militants. Understandably, America remained angry over the bombing of the USS *Cole* and the continuing attacks on US interests in the country. There are about 30,000 US citizens (mainly of Yemeni origin), living in Yemen.

It has been alleged that Yemeni Jihadists returning from Afghanistan were allowed home on the proviso of good behaviour. Subsequently, in August 2002, the Yemeni government formed the Committee for Dialogue to open talks with al-Qaeda sympathisers held in Yemeni prisons. These included supporters of the Aden–Abyan Islamic Army, the al-Houthi rebellion, Takfir Wal-Hajra, al-Qaeda and the Afghan veterans. By June 2005 the government had released 364 suspects.

This deal came apart after a jailbreak in February 2006, when twenty-three terrorists escaped from a high-security prison. Seven months later, a spate of terrorist attacks occurred and since the summer of 2007 terrorist activity has steadily increased. These have targeted Western tourists, culminating in a twin car bomb outside the US embassy on 17 September 2008.

America has a long memory. Osama bin Laden claimed responsibility for the 1992 attempted bombing of 100 US service personnel in Yemen, there to support UN relief operations in neighbouring Somalia. He also boasted openly of providing weapons – probably shipped from Yemen – to the anti-US Somali militias. It was America's humiliation at the hands of the Somali warlords that confirmed to bin Laden the utility of using terrorism and low-technology warfare against US forces abroad.

While the Yemeni government vowed to eradicate terrorism, there remain no-go areas where it has, to some extent, tolerated Islamic extremists. The main radical group in Yemen is not al-Qaeda but the Islamic Army of Aden (IAA). This was directed by Zain al-Abdine al-Mihdar, also known as Abu Hassan, who had fought with bin Laden in Afghanistan, forming his group in the late 1990s. Although it opposes the use of Yemeni ports by the US and other Western navies, the US State Department has not been moved to designate it a Foreign Terrorist Organisation. In contrast, the UK added IAA to its list of proscribed organisations under the Terrorism Act 2000.

Britain also has an unwanted connection with Yemeni militancy. In December 1998, eight young men recruited by the Supporters of Shariah and London-based Egyptian cleric, Abu Hamza, were arrested in Yemen equipped with weapons, explosives, mobile phones and laptop computers. They claimed they were in Yemen to conduct training and attacks against the British consulate in Aden, two hotels and a local Anglican church.[9] Some had also received training in Albania the year before. One of the men was Hamza's son, another his brother-in-law. Alarmingly, it was claimed that up to 2,000 British Muslims had received military training in the UK, Pakistan, Sudan and Yemen between 1995 and 1998. It remains unclear how much of this British intelligence was aware of.

Abu Hamza – another Afghan veteran, according to the Yemeni government – also had links with the IAA. The Yemenis contend that the men they arrested were involved with Abu Hassan's IAA. Some doubt was cast on their confessions, which had been extracted under torture.

Also in late December 1998, sixteen British, American and Australian tourists were kidnapped in Yemen by IAA Islamists, reportedly intent on using them as human shields in support of Iraq, which was under air attack at the time. Yemeni security forces stormed the terrorists' hideout and in the shoot-out four hostages and three kidnappers were killed (including second-in-command,

Osama al-Masri, a member of Egypt's Jihad group), though the head terrorist, Abu Hassan, was captured.[10] He was subsequently executed.

At the same time, Washington gained permission for US warships to refuel in Aden, after it was decided that it would pose fewer problems than using Djibouti or Jeddah. The Yemeni government was offered $80 million as a sweetener. However, one of the bombers of the US embassy in Kenya, Mohamed al-Owhali, had already warned US investigators that bin Laden's next planned attack would be a US warship off Yemen. The first attempt to sink a US warship occurred on 3 January 2000, when a boat overloaded with explosives set off to attack the destroyer USS *The Sullivans*, but it sank before reaching its target. The second attempt had much better results.

US experts believe the IAA is not closely linked with bin Laden and therefore unlikely to have been the perpetrator of the attack on the *Cole*. Furthermore, the organisation was decapitated when its leader was executed. While the IAA was one of three groups to claim responsibility, it is believed that 'supporters' of bin Laden were behind the attack. Al-Qaeda was also blamed for the attack on the French tanker, *Limburg*.

As a result of the *Cole* bombing, US pressure has been such on the Yemeni government that, in some instances, US forces have been given a free hand. During 2002, the Yemeni Coast Guard apprehended over 1,000 people entering the country illegally from the Horn of Africa. All this was the result of the deployment of the Combined Joint Task Force-Horn of Africa and the Combined Task Force-150. The most notable military operation in the region was the interception of a Cambodian-registered vessel, carrying fifteen North Korean Scud missiles in December 2002. These weapons, according to US intelligence sources, were en route to a third party via Yemen, but turned out to be part of a legitimate arms sale to the Yemeni government. Nevertheless, the message was clear: Washington was watching Yemen's actions very closely.

Yemen and America have since co-operated closely on the issue of maritime security, with Washington stepping up its assistance, Commander CJT-HOA, US Marine Corps Major General John F. Sattler, visited Yemen in February 2003 to discuss countering infiltration and smuggling with Brigadier Ali Rasa, head of Yemen's Coast Guard. The US provided technical support for the Yemeni Coast Guard, helping establish the General Authority Coastguard (GAC) and is assisting with the training of Yemeni Coast Guard officers. On 11 August 2003 the Yemeni prime minister, Abdul Qader Ba-Jamal, and commander of the Yemeni Navy, Ruis Abdullah Majoor, met a US naval delegation.

In theory, from bases on Perim Island and Socotra Island, the Yemeni Navy should be able to monitor the Red Sea, Gulf of Aden and Arabian Sea quite effectively. Nonetheless, the US Navy remains concerned by the smuggling of arms and personnel across the Gulf of Aden. Possible Saudi complicity in the movement of al-Qaeda operatives may be highlighted by the fact CJTF-HOA is not working directly with the Royal Saudi Navy.

In reality, the Yemeni Navy has no blue water capability and can do little to patrol even the Gulf of Aden. Only one of its two, twenty-year-old, Soviet-built missile corvettes are operable, and this was in poor condition; similarly, only one of its three missile boats was seaworthy. Likewise, its three Chinese-built Hunan class missile boats are also in a state of disrepair.

Meanwhile, the CIA also had their attention on Yemen. The agency's task was to scour the country for those responsible for the *Cole* bombing. Following the Coalition invasion of Afghanistan, there was good reason to believe that bin Laden might have returned to the land of his forefathers and taken sanctuary in Yemen (although his family was from Yemen, Osama bin Laden was born in Riyadh in 1957). Some thought that perhaps bin Laden had escaped along the drug-smuggling trails through eastern Iran, on through Baluchistan in Pakistan to the port of Gwador. He could then have boarded a *dhow* to cross the Arabian Sea to Oman and then to Yemen.

To that end, in mid-November 2002, it emerged that the British SAS Special Forces had shifted their hunt from the Afghan-Pakistani border to the Hadhra Maug, the lawless tribal region of the south-east Yemen, where bin Laden's father was born.[11] This area would have gladly provided refuge, as the tribesmen are reportedly extremely loyal to the bin Laden clan, hostile to westerners, and were involved in the *Cole* attack. However, as with all leads on the whereabouts of the world's most wanted terrorist, it proved a dead end.

Operated possibly from Djibouti, on 3 November 2002, an MQ-1 Predator UAV launched a Hellfire into a car, killing Qaed Senyan al-Harthi, also known as Abu Ali, the al-Qaeda leader thought to be responsible for the *Cole*. This attack took place in Yemen's northern province of Marib, about 160 kilometres (100 miles) east of the capital Sana'a.[12]

In this instance, Predator was used as a weapon of last resort as Harthi – who had been on the run for years – was thought to be planning more attacks on Western interests. Yemeni government forces had tried to arrest him at al-Hosun, a tribal village in Marib, in December 2001. In the gun battle that followed, eighteen Yemeni soldiers and three villagers died and Harthi escaped. This was the first occasion such a UAV capability was used outside a war zone, and some viewed it as an illegal act under international law. A US citizen, Ahmed Hijazi, was also killed in the attack and this was the first time the US government had killed an American in a country it was considered to be at peace with. Neither the CIA, nor President Bush would comment publicly on the controversy over the method of al-Harthi's destruction and the CIA did not use Predator in such a way again outside Afghanistan – until the killing of al-Yemeni in Pakistan. Perhaps in retaliation, on 30 December 2002, Islamists killed three Americans and wounded a fourth in a hospital in Jibla.

In the meantime, in early 2003, the Yemeni government arrested Fawaz Yahya al-Rabeei, after the FBI issued an alert based on intelligence gathered from members of al-Qaeda and the Taliban held by the US at Guantanamo Bay. It transpired that al-Rabeei and others were suspected of planning attacks on US targets in Yemen.

After years of neglect, the US Congress designated Yemen a front-line state in the war on terror and the US State Department placed a high priority on Yemen's internal security because of its closeness to Somalia, Saudi Arabia and the other Gulf states. Between 2002 and 2006 Yemen received $55.5 million in US military aid.

It seems Washington has been publicly satisfied by Yemen's actions, for it has praised the Yemeni government's efforts in combating international terrorism. In particular, Yemen has been working hard with its immediate neighbours Eritrea, Ethiopia and Sudan to enhance security in the Horn of Africa and the Red Sea. The Yemeni Minister of Transport also claimed, at the end of July 2003, that insurers had dropped the premium increase for vessels entering Yemeni ports, particularly after the tightening of security in Aden Port. Even so, while the Yemeni government is keen to please the US and its neighbours, the country is likely to be a security problem for some time to come.

This was highlighted by the north-western Saada insurgency in June 2004, when dissident cleric, Hussein Badreddin al-Houthi, head of the Shia Zaidiyyah sect, launched an uprising against President Saleh's government. The Shia Houthis also objected to Yemen's alliance with America. Three months into the rising, Yemeni security forces killed al-Houthi.[13] The government claimed that the Houthi Shabab al-Mumineen sect wanted to overthrow it and implement Shariah religious law. It also accused Iran of supporting the insurgency.

Terrorism in Yemen is greatly aggravated by its internal arms trade, run from the weapons market at Souq al-Talh and Ma'rib. Although the latter was closed six months before the al-Houthi rebellion, al-Houthi was able to arm his supporters via the various arms markets throughout the country. Not surprisingly, Souq al-Talh was closed down in the spring of 2004, as a result of the revolt. However, his supporters were still obtaining arms from the market in March 2005. Yemen is recognised as the principal arms supplier to the Somali warlords and is the main source of weapons in the Bakara arms market. This means that Yemen is likely to be a ready source of arms for militants, including al-Qaeda, for some time to come.

During March and April 2005, over 200 people were killed in a resurgence of fighting between government forces and supporters of the slain cleric. In March 2006, the Yemeni government freed more than 600 captured Shia fighters. This did little to placate the insurgents, who, on 28 January 2007, attacked multiple government installations, killing six soldiers and injuring twenty more.[14]

In response, that February, the government launched a major counter-offensive involving 30,000 troops. By the middle of the month, almost 200 members of the security forces and over 100 rebels had been killed in the fighting.[15] Also, some 77,000 refugees were displaced by the conflict. Although a cease-fire was agreed in June 2007, and the rebel leaders went into exile, violence continued.

With about 40 per cent unemployment, Yemen remains the poorest of the Arab states. To make matters worse, by 2007, the UN was reporting 84,000 mainly Somali refugees in Yemen, while the Yemeni government claimed the figure was nearer 300,000. They often sail from Basaso, in Somalia's Puntland, and land at Bir'Ali, which is a largely ungoverned part of Yemen. Ultimately though, Yemen has its own motives for wanting Somalia to remain destabilised. For example, the Socotra Islands, off the Somali coast, may have oil, and with Somalia weak, it will not be able to challenge the ownership of the islands.

After the fall of the Islamic Courts in Somalia, there was concern that the Islamists would be pushed into Yemen. Sheikh Sharif did arrive in Yemen but he was not a free guest and subsequently went to Eritrea. Also, the rebellion in northern Yemen distracted the government from the Somali problem. Rebel leader, Abdel Malik al-Houthi, accepted President Saleh's peace terms in August 2008, but this was widely viewed by both sides as simply an opportunity to rearm. Demonstrations in southern Yemen also put a strain on the republic.

During the summer of 2009, three weeks of renewed fighting between government forces and Shia rebels in Saada province displaced 35,000 people. The government rejected offers of a truce by the Houthis.

The fear is that Yemen's Jihadi networks are expanding as the terrorists are slowly squeezed out of Iraq and Saudi Arabia. Instability in Yemen could then spread from northern Kenya, through Somalia and the Gulf of Aden to Saudi Arabia.

Chapter 7

Bosnia: Trouble with 'Ragheads'

In the early 1990s Yugoslavia was like a scene from Frederick Forsyth's novel *Dogs of War*, as the competing factions sought to tear the country apart, assisted by some very unsavoury outsiders. Prior to that, it had been a Cold War backwater; having rejected Moscow and the Warsaw Pact, Yugoslavia and neighbouring Albania held little or no interest for NATO.

The country had been cobbled together from the uneasy remains of the Austro-Hungarian and Ottoman Empires. Following the Second World War it was clenched by the iron grip of President Josip Broz Tito, until his death in 1980, whereupon the ethnic and religious patchwork that was Serbia, Slovenia, Croatia, Bosnia-Herzegovina, Montenegro and Macedonia slowly but surely fell apart.

To safeguard Yugoslavia's neutrality, the powerful Yugoslav People's Army, or JNA, fielded Europe's fourth-largest Army. It was dominated by Orthodox Christian Serbs, who made up 42 per cent of the manpower, followed by the Croats who contributed 14.2 per cent and Montenegrins with 9.4 per cent. The Slovenes, Macedonians and Bosnians only provided small numbers of recruits.[1] Open conflict first broke out in June–July 1991, with the Slovenian War of independence. This was quickly followed by the equally brief Croat-Serb War of 1991–92.

The JNA, despite its military muscle, was humiliated in Slovenia, signalling to all the other republics keen to be free of Belgrade just how easily independence could be achieved. It was an initial lesson that was not lost on the Muslim Bosnians or Bosniaks and Kosovars. But the Serbs also learned from the humbling experience and were determined not to make the same mistakes in Bosnia.

Following the Croatian War, things remained relatively calm until rival Croat, Muslim and Serb forces sought to parcel up Bosnia-Herzegovina. NATO intervened in the summer of 1992 but it would be three long years before it made any noticeable impact on the sectarian conflict. Disastrously for Bosnia, there was no real way that the country could be effectively partitioned, as it consisted of seven distinct ethnic areas, with three predominantly Muslim zones (including the cities of Bihac, Sarajevo and Gorazde), divided by two predominantly Serb areas with two Croat enclaves to the north and south centred on Lvino and Bosanski Brod. It also meant that the republics of Croatia and Serbia were inevitably drawn into the conflict.

Around the world, Muslims watched in dismay as Bosnia–Herzegovina tore itself to bloody shreds. In 1992–93, when the Bosnia Army was called up from the republic's old territorial forces, it had a theoretical strength of 150,000 men, but in reality the figure was nearer 45,000. Its ranks included Croats, Bosniaks and Serbs, and together they struggled to hold off the JNA and local Serbian militias. To confuse matters, there were also separate Bosnian Croat militias numbering some 50,000 and Serb forces numbering 67,000.[2] There were clear echoes of Lebanon a decade earlier.

The European Union and the US recognised Bosnia's independence on 7 April 1992. Just ten days later, a foretaste of the fate of Bosnia's Muslim population occurred at Bosanski Samac. A quarter of the population were Muslim, a quarter Croat and the rest Serb. Italian journalist Riccardo Orizio recorded:

> Bands of Serb paramilitaries armed with machine-guns, bandannas round their heads and the carefree expressions of boys on a day's hike, occupied the town, proclaiming it a 'Serbian municipality'. Prising it away from Bosnia and putting it under the jurisdiction of the [Serb] Republika Srpska, the artificially created mono-ethnic state under the leadership of Radovan Karadzic and crucially backed by the Yugoslav federal army, meaning by [Serb President Slobodan] Milosevic.[3]

The Serbs herded 17,000 Muslims and Croats into the nearby hills with many ending up at the 'Mita Trifunovic' elementary school, where they were tortured, raped and murdered. When the war ended there were just 300 Muslims and 100 Croats still living in Bosanski Samac. The international community was appalled by such barbarity.

In the spring of 1992, under international pressure, Belgrade ordered some 14,000 troops out of Bosnia. Despite strong denials, before leaving, they handed the bulk of their weaponry to the local Bosnian Serb militias and paramilitary forces. At the same time, up to 5,000 local Serbs took control of most of the hills surrounding the Bosnian capital Sarajevo. All Bosnian counter-attacks were easily beaten off and the city was besieged, trapping 350,000 civilians. The Bosnian garrison in Sarajevo, in the winter of 1992, comprised less than 3,000 territorial guards. The only piece of high ground they managed to recapture was Hill 850 at Buc. The presence of 1,000 UN peacekeepers at Sarajevo airport did little to alleviate the daily suffering of the population.

In order to help the Muslim-led Bosnian government, the Clinton adminis-tration courted the moderate Muslim states such as Brunei, Malaysia, Pakistan, Saudi Arabia and Turkey for support. Ironically, what they could offer and achieve was limited in comparison to America's long-standing enemy – Iran. Washington decided to dance with the devil: rather than keep the Islamists out of Bosnia, it decided to let them in. First, though, President Clinton had to indulge in some pretty half-hearted diplomatic window-dressing.

To try to offset criticism over the presence of Islamist radicals in Bosnia, Washington asked the Muslim states, particularly Turkey and Malaysia, to provide peacekeepers. This was, in part, to avoid the possible radicalisation of the Bosnian Army, but also to detract those critics who felt that America and Europe were not doing enough to protect the Bosniaks from the Serbs. It was agreed that Muslim peacekeepers would be provided by Bangladesh, Egypt, Indonesia, Jordan, Malaysia, Pakistan, Tunisia and Turkey. At the same time, Washington embarked on a parallel clandestine policy to arm Bosnia.

In April 1994, President Clinton green-lighted weapons shipments from Iran and other Muslim countries to the Muslim-led Bosnian government, which were supplied via Croatia. This was in complete contravention of the UN arms embargo against all combatants in former Yugoslavia. This decision was based on a misconception of the aims of President Izetbegovic's regime in Sarajevo. In addition, it was in direct violation of advice given by James Woolsey, the then Director of the CIA, about not developing close links with the Islamists. His fears were confirmed when the CIA sent its first station chief to Sarajevo to liaise with the Bosnians – he found himself targeted by the Iranians and had to be withdrawn.

Ironically, the Iranian connection was well in place before Clinton's decision – in fact, even before the war broke out in April 1992 and, therefore, before the Clinton administration was in office. US Intelligence and Security Congressional hearings show what a complete shambles America's policy towards Iranian support for Bosnia really was. This is borne out in particular by the testimonies of Charles Redman, who served as Washington's principal negotiator in Bosnia, and Peter Galbraith, who served as the US ambassador to Croatia.

President Izetbegovic first visited Tehran in May 1991 and in March the following year, Iran was the first Muslim country to recognise Bosnia's independence. Tehran saw an opportunity to gain a foothold in Europe and Iranian weapons, as well arms from other Muslim countries, flowed into Bosnia starting from 1992. In February of 1993, the Organisation of Islamic Countries, led by Iran and Turkey, appealed to the UN to remove the arms embargo on Bosnia. Arms brought by Iran and Turkey, using Saudi money, were delivered at night. The Croatians demanded a transit tax of up to 50 per cent of the weapons being supplied. Those delivered during the spring of 1995 soon turned up in the demilitarised enclave of Srebrenica.[4]

Iran clearly saw Bosnia offering the same possibilities as Lebanon, and by 1993 there were up to 500 Iranian Revolutionary Guards and other military and intelligence personnel in Bosnia, supporting the Bosnian Army. Clinton's acquiescence gave the seal of approval for the Iranian Revolutionary Guard (who had helped humiliate America in the Lebanon) and Iranian intelligence but also thousands of former Mujahideen.[5]

NATO was always desperate for intelligence on the foreign fighters, especially the Iranians, but due to the Clinton administration's duplicity was kept selectively in the dark. The general consensus among military intelligence circles seemed to be that they were a 'bunch of ragheads', who constituted little or no threat. One former UK National Intelligence Officer, based in Sarajevo, remarked: 'In hindsight we were like mushrooms, kept in the dark while the Americans got on with it. Again, with hindsight, this was just as well, as there would have been an almighty diplomatic row.'[6]

A subsequent Dutch investigation made it clear that the UK's Defence Intelligence Staff was only too well aware of Washington's clandestine arms supplies to the Bosnian Army:

> According to a British intelligence official, the DIS never made an issue of them, so as not to further damage the sensitive relationship with the US services. An internal DIS analysis concluded that the arms were delivered via 'a different network', and that the entire operation was probably led by the NSC [National Security Council]. It was stressed that the CIA and DIA were not involved in the Black Flights to Tuzla. Incidentally, the DIS received a direct order from the British government not to investigate this affair. This was not permitted for the simple reason that the matter was too sensitive in the framework of American-British relations.[7]

The DIS also gained knowledge of these secret supplies via the German military intelligence service and the BND or *Bundesnachrichtendienst*, as some of the flights were via Frankfurt (although no American-German agreement existed for the clandestine flights to the Bosnians).[8]

The Third World Relief Agency (TWRA), which had connections with bin Laden and Sheikh Omar Abdel Rahman (convicted for the 1993 World Trade Center bombing) quickly became involved in this arms pipeline to Bosnia. Headed by Elfatih Hassanein (a personal friend of President Izetbegovic), TWRA first attempted to smuggle 130 tons of weapons from Sudan to Bosnia via Slovenia in violation of the arms embargo in 1992.

In the meantime, during the autumn of 1992, the Serbs overran 70 per cent of Bosnia's territory and all that remained were a few beleaguered Muslim enclaves. In the west of the country, 400,000 people (90 per cent of whom were Bosniaks) were trapped in the Bihac pocket, in a zone 60km long and 50km deep; they were defended by just 5,000 fighters from Bosnia's 5th Corps (the 2nd, 3rd and 4th Corps were trapped in the middle of the republic). A tenuous humanitarian lifeline was kept open by French UN forces. To the south-east, 100,000 people were besieged at Gorazde, suffering 2,000 dead. After failing to take the town, the Serbs set about Srebrenica to the north-east.

To the Muslim world, NATO's greatest failing was to safeguard the Bihac pocket and the enclaves of Gorazde, Srebrenica and Zepa in eastern Bosnia from the Serbs. In Srebrenica alone, 25,000 people almost starved to death. When Major General Philippe-Morillon, the French commander of the UN Protection Force's Bosnia command, finally got into the city, he found the people living in 'near mediaeval conditions'.[9]

Horrified by events at Srebrenica, Clinton instigated Operation Provide Promise – a humanitarian air drop to the enclaves on 28 February 1993 – which ran until August 1994, by which time almost 3,000 sorties had been flown.[10] In the eyes of the Muslim world it was too little too late and begged the question why had the situation been allowed to reach crisis point before the West intervened to save Europe's Muslims?

While the EU and US dithered, the Islamists took matters into their own hands. As in any war, the foreign Islamist fighters had mixed motives. Some of the Arab fighters were believed to want Bosnia-Herzegovina reduced to a narrow ethnic strip from Mostar to Tuzla, including Sarajevo, which could become an Islamic state in the heart of Europe.

According to the International Criminal Tribunal for the Former Yugoslavia, Mujahideen under a bin Laden lieutenant, Abu Sulaiman al-Makki, began arriving from Saudi Arabia in the summer of 1992 (he was later a planner in the attack on the USS *Cole*). Al-Qaeda cells were also established in Bosnia in early 1990s by Ayman al-Zawahiri, bin Laden's right-hand man. The Bosnian government encouraged this relationship – for example, in 1993, the Bosnian embassy in Vienna issued bin Laden with a Bosnian passport and one of the 9/11 suicide hijackers also had a Bosnian passport.

Yet again, Western intelligence was watching the wrong threat: sources did indeed indicate that limited numbers of Iranian Revolutionary Guard had flown from the Lebanon to assist, which had understandably set alarm bells ringing around Whitehall, as, in the wake of the Iran-Iraq War, Tehran was still seen as regional enemy number one. This perception skewed the fact that hundreds, if not thousands, of Afghan veterans had been making their way to Bosnia to help their fellow Muslims resist Serbian encroachments. No one was greatly interested in this – after all, the Iranians were the problem. Former White House terrorist advisor, Richard Clarke, noted:

> What we saw unfold in Bosnia was a guidebook to the bin Laden network, though we didn't recognise it as such at the time. Beginning in 1992, Arabs who had been former Afghan Mujahideen began to arrive. With them came the arrangers, the moneymen, logisticians,

and 'charities'. As they had done in Afghanistan the Arabs created their own brigade, allegedly part of the Bosnian army but operating on its own.[11]

Initially, the Mujahideen were subordinated to the 7th Muslim Brigade, created in November 1992. The foreign Jihadists were then gathered into a special Bosnian Army formation known as the el-Mujahed, under Abu Abdel Aziz 'Barbaros', who was a senior al-Qaeda recruiter. Also known as Abdelrahman al-Dosari, born in Saudi Arabia in 1942, he was an Afghan veteran who gained the nickname 'Hown' because of his reputation gained from using Soviet-built Hound missiles. With his HQ at the Mehurici camp outside of Travnik in central Bosnia, he was military commander of all the Saudi and Afghani Mujahideen in Bosnia.[12]

El-Mujahed – the Battalion of Holy Warriors or the Kateebat al-Mujahideen – officially came into being on 13 August 1993, on the explicit orders of President Izetbegovic. This force, allegedly 10,000 strong, was placed under the Bosnian 3rd Corps and acted as its shock troops. It gained a notorious reputation for torturing and beheading 200 Bosnian Croat and Bosnian Serb civilians and prisoners of war. Iranian fighters were also reportedly serving in the Bihac area and elsewhere during 1993. Another unit was reportedly raised from Albanian Kosovars and Albanians, known as the Handzar division, reputedly up to 6,000 strong, which acted as a guard for Izetbegovic.[13]

Inevitably, the presence of the Mujahideen and other Islamists resulted in the Islamisation of the Bosnian Army. Before 1996 there were three main Mujahideen units serving with the Bosnians, two of which were deployed in the American peacekeeping zone. These consisted of the 7th Muslim Liberation Brigade (under the Bosnian 3rd Corps) at Zenica, and the 9th Muslim Brigade (under 2nd Corps) at Travnik. The 4th Muslim Liberation Brigade (under 4th Corps) was in the French zone at Konjic. Colonel Amir Kubra, commander of the 7th Brigade, and General Enver Hadzihasanovic, commander of 3rd Corps, were subsequently charged with war crimes.

Propaganda aside, estimates for the total number of Mujahideen in Bosnia in 1994 ranged from 400 to 4,000. The following year the UN put the figure at no more than 1,500 fighters. Certainly the Bosnian Army considered them of limited military value. Ultimately, Izetbegovic saw the presence of these Jihadists as the price he had to pay to secure funds from the wealthy Gulf states.

British Islamists fought in Bosnia. London-based Egyptian cleric, Abu Hamza al-Masri, told a British court in January 2006 that he had served in Bosnia. He also claimed to have advised Algerian fighters in Bosnia. After the Dayton Accords he travelled to London, where he urged his followers to go to Albania and Kosovo to support the Islamic cause.[14] It emerged that Hamza's followers had been trained in Wales in the late 1990s by former British soldiers who had served in Bosnia.[15]

The federation of Bosnia and Herzegovina was created in March 1994, with the aim of uniting the mainly Bosniak, pre-war republic government, with those areas held by the Bosnian Croats. Arriving to take command of the UN Protection Force, General Michael Rose took an instant dislike to the Bosnian vice president, Ejup Ganic. He recalled that he was 'Ruthless, without once demonstrating to me during my time in Bosnia, a shred of human decency.'[16]

Ganic, a Sanjak Muslim by birth, was also in charge of Bosnian military operations. General Rose observed disparagingly: 'This arrangement enabled President Izetbegovic to distance himself from some of the more unacceptable things that happened under his regime.' It was Ganic's task to drag the US and NATO into the conflict on the side of Bosnia by portraying it as the victim state. Ganic did not hide his desire that Muslims from Bosnia, Sanjak Kosovo and Albania should form one country: 'I regarded him as a contemptible individual,' concluded General Rose.[17] Meanwhile, General Wesley Clark, Director Strategic Plans and Policies on the US Joint Staff, observed:

> The immediate problem was centred around the Bosnian town of Gorazde, located near the border with Serbia. Muslim defenders were under attack in what had become house-to-house fighting, with Serb artillery positioned on the high ground overlooking the Drina river and firing into the town.[18]

Unfortunately, those troops from UNPROFOR trapped in the city were unable to halt the fighting. General Clark noted a fact regarding the Bosnian Muslims that was not lost on the wider Islamic world: 'in military terms they were the most poorly equipped and had been the chief victims of the fighting thus far'.[19] Quickly investigating, using NATO airpower to stop the Serb attacks on Gorazde, he found himself entangled in the legal niceties of the so-called rules of engagement, which constrained such peacekeeping operations. The escalating use of NATO airpower would be a slow and tortuous process over the coming years. The overall prognosis was not good. According to General Clark:

> The Muslims had barely managed to retain most of the capital of Sarajevo but it was surrounded and cut off by Serb forces. In several places east of the capital, large civilian populations of Bosnian Muslims were similarly encircled.[20]

The sense of moral outrage over this situation echoed from Riyadh to Tehran. By this stage, the Serbs had a stranglehold on Sarajevo, with up to 12,000 troops, 50 tanks, 300 artillery pieces and mortars, lots of anti-aircraft guns and man-portable surface-to-air missiles. Serb artillery encircling the city at Bjevave, Vogosca, Iiidza and Dobrinja enabled them to dominate the old town, the old JNA barracks and, importantly, the international airport.

Throughout the 1990s overhead imagery or IMINT was used in a wide variety of roles, from battle damage assessment to confirming the scale of Serbian ethnic cleansing and the extent of the sieges of Bihac, Gorazde and Sarajevo. A major imaging task now took place to locate the Serbs' SA-2 and SA-6 surface-to-air missiles. NATO methodically plotted all the fixed SA-2 sites in and around Bosnia; the mobile SA-6 was another matter. NATO also dedicated at least one reconnaissance aircraft over Bosnia, constantly scanning for vehicle movements, but top of the surveillance priorities was the feared SA-6.

The Royal Navy's Sea Harrier FRS1s were tasked with photographing all locatable SA-6 sites to determine if they were active.[21] In particular, photos were taken of batteries at Bihac, Tuzla, Sarajevo (they also picked up tanks, armoured personnel carriers and artillery south of the latter) and Banja Luka, which to all the world looked like deadly crop circles. Although the pilots could not make out any detail during the passes, this was for the photographic interpreters to worry about later. The subsequent loss of a Harrier made the SA-6 sites a very public issue.[22]

Bosniak Gorazde was considered a strategic prize by the Bosnian Serbs, due to its closeness to the Serbian border and because of the threat posed by it remaining in Muslim hands. Under General Ratko Mladic, Bosnian Serb troops, supported by tanks and artillery, renewed their offensive against the beleaguered city on 16 April 1994. At this point, London decided to covertly assist the Bosnian Muslim forces. An SAS tactical air control party was inserted and called in NATO air strikes on Serb tanks and artillery. They also instructed the Muslims on weapon handling – though it has to be pointed out, only after the Serbs shelled the SAS team.

The day the Bosnian Serb offensive opened, Lieutenant Nick Richardson, flying a Harrier, was shot down over Gorazde by Bosnian Serb missiles that he had been photographing. Once on the ground he later remembered:

> The only thing that really registered was the insignia on the shoulder of his combat jacket, which I recognised as BiH–Bosnian Army. To my enormous relief, there was no doubt I'd been found by Muslims not by the Serbs [...] The frightening thing was this: even if the Navy did know I was safely on the ground, I couldn't begin to see what they or anyone else could do about it. I was 125km inland and holed up with a tiny pocket of Muslim resistance fighters who could give in to the advancing Serbs at any moment. There was little chance of a helicopter rescue package – the threat density was too great.[23]

The friendly Bosniaks guided him to the UK Liaison officers in Gorazde (the SAS team that had moved into the city on General Rose's orders to monitor Muslim resistance and the Serb advance). Despite the presence of up to 20,000 Serb troops in the surrounding hills, he was later rescued by helicopter.

By mid-1994 the Bosnian Serb Army numbered around 80,000 men, nullifying the Bosnian Army's previous advantage in manpower. This enabled the Serbs to tighten their grip on Bihac. They wanted the city because it linked Serb-held territory in Bosnia and Croatia. The Croatians understandably sought to prevent this by launching their own offensive. The fighting was confused by the presence of 5,000 renegade Muslim fighters under Fikret Abdic near Velika Kladusa.

Once Gorazde was relieved by UN forces, the Serbs turned on Bihac and Srebrenica. In the latter, General Mladic's Bosnian Serb Army murdered 7,000 Muslims, and as news leaked out, a shock wave passed round the international community. In response to this, NATO airpower was finally unleashed on the Serbs: this, coupled to the Croat offensive, forced Mladic to the negotiating table.

General Rose had 24,000 peacekeepers from sixteen countries deployed in Bosnia by December 1994. Despite the best efforts of the UNPROFOR to prevent ethnic cleansing, it was too late to stop 40,000 Muslims and 30,000 Croats from being driven from the Bosnian Serb areas. But the Serbs were not the only perpetrators of ethnic cleansing: as a result of the Dayton Agreement, 250,000 Serbs were removed from the Krajina areas of Croatia and western Bosnia.

General Rose lamented the failure of the UN safe-haven policy; the UN Security Resolutions failed to authorise the peacekeepers to defend or protect them, instead authorising 'deterrence'. The fact that the Bosniak forces used the safe areas as bases from which to attack the Bosnian Serbs further complicated matters. The failure to explicitly demarcate the safe areas also hampered UNPROFOR in its mission. When General Rose attempted to get the Bihac safe area defined, the Bosnian government representative to the UN opposed this on the grounds that the whole of Bosnia should be a safe area.

The Dayton Agreement, signed in November 1995, recognised two autonomous bodies within the weak but sovereign union. It granted the Serbs their own autonomous entity, the Republika Srpska, which, with a Bosnian-Croat Federation, would exist under a tripartite presidency representing all the ethnic groups. Inevitably, this meant that Srpska would remain dominated by the Serb Orthodox Church, while it was only a matter of time before the Bosniak Islamic community asserted itself in Sarajevo. It was soon apparent that the goal of creating a joint army from the Bosniak Army of Bosnia and Herzegovina and the Croatian Defence Council was going to be no easy task. It was not until 1997 that a joint command headquarters was formed.

Around 20,000 US troops were despatched to Bosnia in late 1995 by Clinton as part of the NATO-led Implementation Force or IFOR. By the summer of 1996 Bosnia was reasonably peaceful and at the end of that year IFOR handed over to a new NATO command called the Stabilisation Force or SFOR. Shortly after, elections were held bringing peace – up to 250,000 people had died during the conflict.

Washington now belatedly sought to head off the Islamists. One of the stipulations of Dayton was that all foreign fighters were required to leave, as their services were no longer required. In particular, this was an attempt to get rid of the Iranian training camps. Some 200 Iranian Revolutionary Guards reportedly ended up in northern Bosnia, acting as military advisors and commanders. But the Bosnian government did not completely sever its intelligence links with Iran until the end of 1996. To reinforce this move, the Deputy Minister of Defence, Hasan Cengic, was dismissed, opening the way for $100 million worth of US weapons for the Bosnian Muslim and Bosnian Croat armies. Nevertheless, an undisclosed number of Islamists who served with the Bosnian Army were granted Bosnian passports and married local women. The Bosnian authorities did not finally start evicting them until July 2000, after the police raided Bocinja near Maglaj in central Bosnia.[24]

Expunging the Islamist influence, however, was not that easy. In Sarajevo the increasing power of the Islamic community was all too evident from the growing number of mosques and increasing numbers of young women wearing headscarves. In the spring of 2002, Bosnian authorities raided several Islamic organisations and closed the al-Haramain Islamic Foundation (banned in Kenya since the 1998 US embassy bombing), the Global Relief Foundation and Bosanska Idealna Futura – a branch of the US-based Benevolence International Foundation. The latter's head, Enaam Arnout, a Bosnian passport holder, is in US custody for funding al-Qaeda, Chechen rebels and various Bosnian groups. The raid uncovered 'The Golden Chain' – a list of twenty wealthy donors and their recipients.

Mira Milosevic – also known as 'The Red Witch' (wife of former Serbian President Milosevic) – was outraged at the West's duplicity, claiming:

> As for the arms, the Serbs of Bosnia and Croatia used the arms left behind by the Yugoslav federal army before the various republics declared independence. But if they are going to investigate who supplied the Serbs with arms then they should also investigate who was supplying them to the Croats and Muslims. Why do you Westerners never ask yourselves about that? There were three peoples at war, not only one. Why don't they say that Osama bin Laden armed the Muslims of Kosovo? And why don't they say that this Albanian

leader [...] Ibrahim Rugova – admitted that in 1998 there were Islamic guerrilla training camps in Kosovo?[25]

Ironically, it did all come out, thanks to the Dutch inquiry into the Srebrenica massacre, published in 2002. An entire volume was devoted to Washington's clandestine activities. It proved beyond a doubt the Clinton administration's full complicity with radical Islamic groups in Bosnia.[26]

There is no hiding the fact that US support for Saudi and Iranian activities in Bosnia ultimately encouraged the Mujahideen to expand their Holy War from Afghanistan into Bosnia and then across Europe. The Clinton administration knew that al-Qaeda-backed forces were secretly infiltrating into Bosnia via Croatia but did nothing. The Croatian capital, Zagreb, became the hub for Washington's efforts to prop up the Bosnian government, during which process the Americans made a pact with the devil. The blowback from Bosnia would result in 9/11. There were reports that al-Qaeda veterans from the Bosnian civil war were involved in the insurgency in Iraq as part of the Islamic Army in Iraq.

The remaining problem facing the uneasy alliance that is Bosnia-Herzegovina is: what happens if Croatia and Serbia join the European Union? Bosnian Croats hold Croatian passports and Bosnian Serbs have Serbian passports, meaning they could become EU citizens. If that happens, then the Muslim Bosniaks will be excluded, leaving a disaffected Muslim state in the heart of the EU. Although Bosnia has remained peaceful since 1995, if not handled properly, this issue could re-ignite the sectarian bloodshed.

Chapter 8

Algeria: Sacred Frustration

The growing impact of the scattering of international Jihadists from Afghanistan began to become really apparent by the summer of 1997. The British media was regularly showing image after image of the carnage being wrought in Algeria, much of it inflicted on helpless villagers rather than the insurgents. Whole communities were herded together and butchered. But this was viewed simply as an internal security problem for the Algerians – a bloody legacy of their French colonial past. No thought was given to the wider impact of the Afghantsi diaspora. Nobody seemed to grasp the bigger picture or the implications of the men returning to Algeria, Pakistan, Saudi Arabia and Yemen, or for that matter, the Central Asian states.

'To be honest,' said a British defence source in Algiers at the time, 'we think the security forces are as much to blame; they are deliberately trying to discredit the insurgents by covertly conducting these brutal killings.'[1] He went on to explain that, until the Algerian security forces caught or killed all the Algerian Afghantsi, then they were fighting a losing battle. These guys were trained, experienced and used to mountain warfare.

The Algerian *Groupe Salafiste pour la Prédication et le Combat* or Salafist Group for Call and Combat (GSPC) is known to have links with al-Qaeda. Hassan Hattab, its leader in the wake of 9/11, issued a threat, saying the GSPC would strike American and European interests if they attacked Muslim countries or attempted to interfere with their networks in Belgium, France, the UK and the US. Unsurprisingly, the group was subsequently designated a foreign terrorist organisation by Washington. Although the group itself has not targeted western interests, its members have been closely involved in al-Qaeda attacks.

The arrest, in Spain, in 2001, of Mohammad Bensakhria, reportedly a GSPC leader and al-Qaeda's senior representative in Europe, made it clear that there was a very close link between the two organisations. This was driven home when Nabil Sahraoui, a GSPC leader, issued a public statement on 11 September 2003 saying: 'We strongly and fully support Osama bin Laden's Jihad against the heretic America,' claiming the group was under the control of al-Qaeda and Mullah Omar.[2]

The complicity of the GSPC and the *Groupement Islamique Armé* (GIA) in international terrorism is not in doubt. At Guantanamo Bay, Cuba, America held twenty-four Algerian terrorist suspects (six of whom were handed over by the Bosnian authorities after a plot to bomb the US and UK embassies in Sarajevo). Additionally, it is believed that about 700 Algerian volunteers received weapons training in Iraqi camps before the Coalition invasion of Iraq.

Despite this, Algeria became one of NATO's newest allies, and on the surface, relations looked rosy after NATO naval visits to the capital, Algiers. NATO has been courting the Algerian government and Algerian Navy as part of the effort to foster greater counter-terrorism co-operation amongst the nations bordering the Mediterranean. This started in 2001, when the American destroyer, USS *Mitscher*, and submarine, USS *Norfolk*, called on Algiers to conduct anti-submarine warfare exercises.

President Abdelaziz Bouteflika made the very first visit by an Algerian Head of State to the Alliance's Brussels HQ in December 2001. NATO's standing Mediterranean naval force made a port call to Algiers the following year and Bouteflika visited Brussels again. The Algerian Navy sent an observer (for the first time) to NATO's bi-annual maritime exercise, Co-operative Engagement, in September 2003. All this was designed to head off Algeria's home-grown Islamists, who by now were operating throughout Europe.

The Algerian government and some international intelligence agencies confirm that GSPC has teamed up with al-Qaeda to launch attacks abroad. In late 2002, the Algerian authorities reported they had killed a Yemeni al-Qaeda operative who had been meeting GSPC representatives inside Algeria. The worry was that they were planning a USS *Cole*-type attack. An Algerian al-Qaeda cell operating in Canada planned to blow up a number of North American airports at the turn of the millennium, but the explosives were seized crossing over into America. More recent threats against the Strait of Gibraltar, emanating from neighbouring Morocco, have more than highlighted the very clear and present danger posed by North African Jihadists.

Algeria's Islamist violence was born of its French colonial past.[3] Although the National Liberation Front lost the war of independence it still won the peace, as France became sickened of almost two decades of continual warfare. In 1962, when Algeria finally gained independence, 145,000 European colonists and 15,000 colonial troops were re-settled in France. The FLN then meted out a bloody revenge on 100,000 men, women and children left behind, whom it considered collaborators.[4]

Sadly, from then on, Algeria was effectively a one-party state under the FLN, backed by the *Armée Nationale Populaire* (ANP) and was not to know peace. The failure of Socialism to deliver anything nearing social and economic equality led inexorably to the rise of Islam as a political force. It was not until after the Algiers riots of 1988, which left 500 dead, that President Chadli Bendjedid finally opened the way to multi-party politics. The *Front Islamique du Salut* (FIS) was determined to create an Islamic state and its success the following year in municipal elections ensured that it became the main political force in the country.

The appeal of an overtly Islamic party was easy to see: militant Algerian students wanted an end to the preference for the French language, while Algeria's unemployed youth saw the FIS as an alternative to the FLN, which was responsible for bloodily repressing the riots. Ali Belhaj, one of the co-founders of the FIS, boasted: 'When we are in power there will be no more elections because God will be ruling.'[5] The governing elite became even more alarmed when the FIS won the first round of the parliamentary elections in December 1991. The military stepped in, deposed Bendjedid, Ali Belhaj was imprisoned for twelve years and the FIS banned – all in the name of safeguarding democracy. But the military fooled no one – their key aim was to maintain the status quo. This led to a decade of bloody civil war.

The FIS message appealed to those Algerians who had fought in Afghanistan alongside the Mujahideen. Unsurprisingly, in the wake of the coup, it was these veterans who were in the forefront of the armed opposition, most notably as members of the al-Takfir wa-l Hijra, which had links to the Kabul Mosque at Belcourt in Algiers. Also to emerge was the *Mouvement Islamique Armé* (MIA), under Emir (Commander) Abdelkader Chébouti, the Kataeb el Qods (Jerusalem Brigades) and Algerian Hezbollah.

These groups came into being due to differences of opinion concerning the strategies employed by the FIS – not surprisingly, the former preferred armed struggle to the ballot box. With the FIS outlawed there was no shortage of willing recruits for the MIA, which rapidly launched guerrilla operations against the Algerian security forces. In turn Algerian Hezbollah was created to challenge the MIA's dominance of the Jihad. Known as 'the Afghans', the Takfir wa-l Hijra group in November 1991 carried out a brutal attack on the frontier post of Guemmar on the Tunisian border. The prime minister, Ahmed Ghozali, saw the militants as little better than Nazis commenting: 'Once he came to power Hitler burned the Reichstag. We have had the Guemmar events where Algerians have been killed, slaughtered.'[6]

It has been claimed that Algerians made up a third of all foreign combatants during the war in Afghanistan and were among the first recruits to bin Laden's camps in Sudan in the early 1990s. At least 2,800 Algerians are assessed to have fought or trained in Afghanistan, making them the third-largest contributor of manpower to al-Qaeda's cause after the Saudis and Yemenis. However, those Algerian groups, such as 'the Afghans', who had started their Jihad too early, were killed or arrested during 1992 and 1993. Only the MIA managed to escape reasonably intact.

Many were dismayed that the ANP was not prepared to come to terms with the FIS, despite its inability to contain the growing violence. Islamist contempt had been confined to the FLN, but it was now extended to the Algerian armed forces, making a power share almost impossible. Naively FIS supporters believed that the 2,000 MIA Mujahideen would be more effective than the ANP and anticipated a swift victory. In the meantime, some of the communes of Greater Algiers found themselves the scene of urban guerrilla warfare.

Crucially, in 1993, two new Islamist factions emerged: the *Groupement Islamique Armé* (GIA) and the *Mouvement pour l'Etate Islamique* (MEI). The GIA appeared because Abdelhak Layada, an MIA commander, challenged Chébouti's leadership of the Jihad, while Saïd Makhloufi set up the MEI because he disagreed about military strategy. It was GIA fighters who had fought in Afghanistan who are believed to have maintained a loose relationship with al-Qaeda. Bin Laden allegedly appointed Abu Qatada, an al-Qaeda theologian and propagandist, as the GIA's spiritual advisor.

Once the GIA was on the scene they easily outnumbered the MIA and by 1993 were some 22,000 strong. The guerrilla forces peaked at about 40,000 the following year, thanks to the addition of the *Armée Islamique du Salut* fighters. After the 1995 presidential elections, the various factions saw a decline in their numbers and, in all, hardcore fighters totalled about 10,000 (AIS 4,000, GIA 2,000–3,000 with the MEI and MIA accounting for the rest).[7]

By February 1993, the FIS was openly calling its fighters Mujahideen or holy warriors in the style of the Islamic militants in Afghanistan and Iran. Following a car bomb attack on the Algerian Minister of Defence, the FIS issued a statement saying: 'This is a clear warning from the Mujahideen to the tyrants who openly fight God and his Prophet.'[8] The FIS, reportedly on Iranian advice, targeted foreigners in order to bring international pressure to bear on the government. However, most of these kidnaps and murders were carried out by the GIA, which rapidly gained notoriety.

The government's military response was to set up a 15,000-strong counter-insurgency corps, which went into action in April 1993, reasserting control over the known FIS strongholds in the Greater Algiers communes of Baraki, Chararba and Les Eucalyptus. The net result was that the FIS completely abandoned any political struggle, leaving the military commanders or 'emirs' in the ascendancy. Militants of the former FIS formed a fourth rebel group known as the *Armée Islamique du Salut* or AIS in July 1994.

The government's anti-guerrilla corps by 1995 was some 60,000 strong. It was run by the *Coordination de la Sécurité due Territoire* or Territorial Security Coordination Office, which was given overall control of the security forces' anti-terrorist campaign. Until 1994 the anti-terrorist corps' efforts were mainly directed at the cities, in particular Algiers, with the intention of driving the Islamists into the mountains. A reign of terror followed with both the GIA and government paramilitary forces blamed for atrocities inflicted upon the civilian population. Between February 1992 and September 1995, around 30,000 people were killed.

Once the pro-FIS areas were under military occupation, the MIA found itself trapped in the Blida Atlas region, the mountainous area close to Algiers. The approaches to Carrefour des Quatre Saisons at Les Eucalyptus, on the road to Emir Chébouti's village of Larbaa, became a key strategic area. Chébouti found himself dubbed the 'Lion of the Mountains'.

The security forces successfully attacked a GIA congress in the mountains south of Ain Defla in late 1995, and in ten days of fighting killed anything from 650 to 1,500 militants. Notably, there were reports of Afghan, Iranian and Sudanese volunteers being among the militants, although no evidence was produced.[9]

The unending brutality of the GIA towards Algerian civilians, including women and children, resulted in the organisation fracturing in 1998. A new Algerian Jihadist group appeared in the form of the GSPC, under Hassan Hattab, a former GIA commander. He stated he would confine his attacks to the security forces and government targets. Al-Qaeda allegedly funded his defection after it was also sickened by the GIA's civilian massacres, which were viewed as counter-productive.

Abdelaziz Bouteflika, a former FLN leader, was elected president on 15 April 1999, amid promises of bringing an end to the bloodshed. When he granted amnesty for Islamic militants, the GSPC was one of the few groups not to take up his offer. Some 2,400 fighters from the AIS and another 1,500 from other factions laid down their arms in 2000. In total, some 6,000 Islamist insurgents surrendered, but several groups – including the GSPC and elements of the GIA– rejected the offer, labelling AIS members as enemies of Islam. This left an estimated 300 GSPC fighters aiming to topple the Algerian government, create an Islamic state, and attack Western interests in the region.

The Algerian intelligence and security services, having honed their skills, were able to ensure that after 2002, the GSPC suffered some major setbacks. The Algerian Army publicly acknowledged killing over 15,000 Islamist fighters by 2003, claiming that there were only 1,000 in total still active. Around 150,000 civilians are also thought to have died. Nabil Sahraoui, Hattab's successor after he disappeared in mid-2003, was killed in June 2004 and replaced by Abu Musab Abdelouadoud. Similarly, the GIA was reduced to just thirty members, following a successful ANP operation in late 2004. These successes, however, were to have ramifications for Europe.

The GSPC splintered, with Abdelouadoud commanding the cells operating in northern Algeria, while Mokhtar Belmokhtar was in charge of the *Groupe Salafist Libre* or Free Salafist Group (GSL), operating in southern Algeria. The latter first made its mark by kidnapping thirty-two European tourists in February 2003. Neighbouring Mauritania claims Mauritanians have been trained in GSPC camps to fight in Afghanistan, Chechnya, Iraq and Palestine. Attempts by the Mauritanian government, participating in the US Trans-Sahara

Counter-terrorist Initiative, to clamp down on the GSPC, led to revenge attacks by the GSL.

On 4 June 2005, in a night attack on the Mauritanian town of Lemgheiti (in the border zone with Algeria and Mali), 150 GSPC fighters killed fifteen Mauritanian troops and wounded another seventeen. This attack was supported by members of 'The Scions of Tariq' (an eighth-century commander who attacked Spain) and 'The Sons of Uqba bin Nafi' (the seventh-century conqueror of North Africa).[10]

Many Algerians felt that the world ignored the tragedy that had now almost played out in their country. France (with a population of 2 million Algerians) and the rest of Europe were soon to pay the price for ignoring Algeria's agony. The first indications that the GIA had ambitions to operate out of the country occurred in 1994, when Algerians attempted unsuccessfully to crash a hijacked Air France jet into the Eiffel Tower. Parisians were rattled by news stories of the enemy within. The following year, a GIA cell conducted bomb attacks on the Paris subway. They then planned to attack the 1998 World Cup in France, but fortunately French counter-terrorist operations were so successful that they effectively removed the GIA from European soil.

By 2003 it was apparent Algerian Jihad was again spreading across Europe, when four Algerians – Aeroubi Beandali, Salim Boukhari, Lamine Maroni and Fouhad Sabour – were convicted of planning to blow up the Christmas market in front of Strasbourg cathedral. The prosecution claimed they had trained in al-Qaeda camps in Afghanistan, though produced no evidence. In 2000 their terror cell had filmed the centre of Strasbourg and the accompanying video commentary stated: 'You are all doomed to rot in Hell. May God will it.' Three of the men had lived in Britain before moving to Frankfurt and Sabour had been involved in the bombing of the Paris metro and a TGV railway line near Lille.[11] Indeed, the group's progression to 'out of Algeria' operations made it potentially the most dangerous terrorist organisation within the al-Qaeda network at that time. It was evident by this stage that Algeria had eclipsed Afghanistan as a base for Jihadist operations. Algeria gained the dubious accolade of being dubbed the staging post for World Terror.

At home it was claimed that, after the protracted campaign, Islamic terrorists in Algeria only numbered several hundred rather than thousands. In October 2004 Libya handed over a senior figure from the GSPC group to the Algerian authorities, and in June the Algerian Army killed a number of GSPC leaders. By 2005 there were thought to be just 500–800 Islamic militants still active in Algeria.[12] This was, in part, due to many militants having left for Europe and Africa. Despite these successes, there can be no denying that Algerian Islamists still present a danger to the Mediterranean.

Indeed, Italy became a base of operations for the GSPC to target Europe and the US. Lounici Dhamel was arrested in 2004 and along with twelve other

Algerians convicted of supplying logistical support (weapons and fake documents) two years earlier. Italian counter-terrorist forces arrested five Algerian
nationals in late 2005 on suspicion of planning such operations. One of them,
Yamine Bohrama – was believed to be head of the GSPC Salerno cell with links
to others cells in Brescia, Milan and Naples. Subsequently, Mohamed Larbi
of the Brescia cell and Khaled Serai of the Naples cell were also arrested.
According to Italian Interior Minister, Giuseppe Pisanu, these two were intending to conduct attacks to surpass 9/11.

The arrests highlighted the connections between Algerian Jihadists in Italy
and other Salafist groups operating in Europe. The Italian police investigated
links between Algerian Jihadists in Belgium, France, Germany, the Netherlands,
Switzerland and the UK. Connections were also found to exist with the Takfir
organisation and Mujahideen in Bosnia.

Many of the operatives were first-generation immigrants (recruiting large
numbers of Moroccans, Syrians and Tunisians), who, while they did not have
any stake in the Algerian conflict, were interested in international Jihad. Many
were motivated by outrage over America's involvement in Iraq. A study released
by the Saudi National Security Assessment Project in March 2006, found that
North Africans constituted around 30 per cent of the foreign fighters in Iraq,
with 22 per cent from Algeria. While the US felt these estimates a little high, it
did not dispute that the Algerians and Salafist groups have played key roles in
the Iraqi insurgency.[13]

In the meantime, the insurgency war continued in Algeria. During its height
in the mid-1990s, the capital was disrupted by car bombs killing hundreds of
civilians. There were bomb blasts in Algiers in August and November 2001 and
January and March 2002. In May 2004 an Algerian naval captain was killed
while on leave south-east of Algiers: a stark warning about aiding NATO.

Perhaps appropriately, in September 2003, Algiers played host to a two-day
international conference on combating terrorism, with representatives from
twenty-two countries (ten of them from the West). During the last two weeks
of September 2003, security forces killed 150 GSPC fighters, but despite these
losses the movement continues to attract fresh recruits. Security forces attacked
Islamist guerrillas near Anaba, 370 miles east of Algiers, in June 2006, killing
nineteen, including the regional leader. The following year, Islamists attempted
to assassinate President Bouteflika at Batna. The attacker triggered his bomb
prematurely, killing twenty-two people and wounding another 107.[14]

Constructive dialogue is one thing, but in some circles, NATO's courtship
of Algeria seemed to defy logic. Amid the whole of North Africa, the country
stands out as the pre-eminent haven for militant Islamic groups and as such
constitutes a serious threat to the security of Europe and the sea lanes of the
Mediterranean. This may seem harsh for a country torn by civil strife, which
has claimed thousands of lives, but the fact remains Algeria is host to a cadre of

Fundamentalists still bent on Jihad – against not only the Algerian government but the international community.

Ultimately, if the GSPC closely aligned itself to al-Qaeda, as Ayman al-Zawahiri did with his Egyptian Jihad, it could propel it further into the forefront of Islamic terrorism. At the same time, it may distract it from its national struggle, thereby playing into the hands of the Algerian security forces. North Africa's gain is Europe's loss under such circumstances.

Chapter 9

Chechnya: Moscow's Running Sore

Western intelligence watched the collapse of the Soviet Union with a sense of professional pleasure: after all, it signalled the demise of the misnamed Cold War. Although Moscow largely abandoned its Central Asian states, Russian troops remained to help keep Islamic militants at bay. The loss of the Baltic States and especially the Transcaucasus proved far more traumatic. Moscow drew a line in the sand: while the Soviet Union had been allowed to crumble, it decided that the integrity of its successor – the Russian Federation – should be maintained at all costs. There were some ninety ethnic and religious areas within the Federation, which, if allowed greater autonomy or indeed independence, would spell the end of Moscow's remaining power.

Throughout the Transcaucasus the Muslim states were restive: Muslim Azerbaijan feuded with Christian Armenia, while Christian Georgia struggled with the Muslim Ossetians. Then came revolts in Chechnya and Dagestan. The fall-out from Soviet involvement in Afghanistan soon came home to roost. Just as the Taliban were emerging as a unifying force in Afghanistan, so the tiny Muslim enclave of Chechnya – numbering little more than 1.2 million people – sought to throw off Russia's rule. It declared independence in 1991 under President Dzhokhar Dudayev (a former Soviet Air Force general).

Russian President, Boris Yeltsin, tolerated the secessionist movement in Chechnya, as he had much more pressing matters to deal with. This led Dudayev to believe that Chechnya could walk away but Moscow wanted to retain Chechen oil. Meanwhile, Russian intelligence knew that Chechnya was a mafia hotbed and a centre for drugs and arms smuggling.

In November 1994, the Russian Army – supporting pro-Moscow Chechen forces – rolled into the Chechen capital, Grozny, heralding the so-called First Chechen War. To many in the Muslim world, this looked like Afghanistan all over again. Dudayev's forces resisted with surprising vigour, knocking out 120 tanks and, more importantly, capturing Russian troops, forcing Yeltsin to acknowledge complicity in this military action against the tiny Muslim enclave. It was as if everything learned in Afghanistan the hard way had been forgotten.

Yeltsin decided to play for all or nothing, and instructed both sides in Chechnya to lay down their arms by 15 December 1994 or the Russian military would use overwhelming force to end the civil war. The irony that he had, in fact, fuelled the conflict, was not lost on the rest of the world. To Islam, it was yet more proof of the West's seeming indifference to the suffering of Muslims, no matter where they were in the world.

Dudayev, perhaps hoping for the support of the international community, did not respond, and Grozny was fated to become another Stalingrad. Some 40,000 Russian troops massed on Chechnya's borders, while fighter-bombers attacked military bases and the airport in Grozny. Yeltsin, having tried a show of force once again, demanded the protagonists lay down their arms. Instead, facing a common enemy, the Chechens decided to fight together. General Aslan Maskhadov, the Chechen Chief of Staff, declared: 'The North Caucasus will become another Afghanistan for Russia.'[1]

Although the Chechen resistance was fortified by religion, this was not a clear-cut war of Muslim versus Christian – it was a war of Chechen versus Russian. At the start, after years of Soviet rule, many Chechens were not practising Muslims – Dudayev and Maskhadov, both ex-Soviet officers, were completely westernised. But as the war progressed, the sense of Muslim identity became much more pronounced, especially once outside help began to pour in.

Yeltsin, realising that the Chechens were preparing to fight, pre-empted his own deadline by four days and 75,000 Russian troops once again rolled into Chechnya: 40,000 of them heading for the capital. Dudayev still refused to bend to Moscow's will. To get to Chechnya, the Russian Army first had to fight its way through Ingushetia, the locals – again, a Muslim people – sided with the Chechens.

For the initial attack, the Russians mustered about 24,000 troops supported by 80 tanks and 200 armoured personnel carriers. Reinforcements were en route, which would boost the force to an overwhelming 38,000 men, 230 tanks and 450 armoured personnel carriers, but the Russian generals would not wait, as they wanted quick results. All the Soviet Army's years of experience in Afghanistan seemed to count for nothing in Chechnya. Instead of using elite units, raw conscripts were thrown into the fight with very little idea of what they were doing, or indeed why they were there in the first place. Journalist, Sebastian Smith, who covered the conflict for Agence France-Presse, recorded:

> When war broke out that winter, the Russian Army was expected to put a quick end to this people's rag-tag revolt. Instead, Chechen fighters gave the Russians a horrific mauling from the first day, worse, many said, than the Soviet experience in Afghanistan. The Russian response – bombing Grozny, a city of 400,000 people, to the ground, then doing the same thing to village after village – was sick beyond comprehension.[2]

By the 16th, the Russians had lost seven tanks on the main highway into Chechnya and the following day their attack on Sleptsovskaya was beaten off.

In late December, the Russians moved to cut Grozny off from the east by severing the road to Argun. Then Khankala – the airfield on the eastern outskirts of Grozny – was attacked on 29 December and the Russians fought the forces of Shamil Basayev. They were now at the very approaches of the city centre.

Western intelligence watched with some amusement as events unfolded – first Afghanistan and now this! Throughout the Cold War, NATO had greatly feared the Soviet Army's ability to overrun Western Europe. Now, just four years after the demise of the Soviet Union, the Russian Army could not even suppress tiny Chechnya.

The Russian assault into Grozny turned into a complete shambles. The north-western sector of the city around the airfield was held by around 2,000 Chechen fighters, with another 5,000 holding the central area around the railway station and presidential compound. 'They have planes and tanks,' said one 38-year-old guerrilla, 'and all we've got is Allah and the RPG [rocket-propelled grenade]. But we know what we are fighting for.'[3] Russian tanks got lost in the streets, were knocked out and the crews massacred. The infantry, refusing to leave their armoured personnel carriers, suffered a similar fate. The assault broke down within the first twenty-four hours and the Chechens remained in control of the presidential compound. The Russians were slaughtered – losing up to 2,000 dead and 3,000 wounded. It was a bloodbath, showing what a few Muslim insurgents could achieve against a former superpower. In particular, the Russian 131st Brigade – deployed from the Adygei capital Maikop – ceased to be an effective fighting unit after its mauling at the railway station. Likewise, the 1,000-strong 81st Motor Rifle Regiment was cut to pieces, losing half its manpower killed, wounded or captured.

Most of the blame fell on General Pavel Grachev, an Afghanistan veteran, who should have known better than to drive his troops into the heart of a well-defended city. By mid-January 1995 the Russians were in Grozny, but were driven out of the city centre by determined Chechen fighters who were both outnumbered and outgunned. It was clear that the city would have to be cleared house by house.

Moscow now found it was fighting its first televised war. The tail end of Soviet involvement in Afghanistan had attracted adverse home media coverage because of the mounting casualty toll, but on the whole, the general public had little idea how the war was going. Moscow's crude attempts to manipulate the media in Chechnya soon unravelled in the face of international reporting, which had little sympathy for the Russian Army or its plight.

While the Muslim world only saw images of the suffering of civilians in Grozny, the Russian Army fell apart. Corruption and incompetence reared its ugly head as the logistical supply chain failed. Russian journalist and former Afghan veteran, Oleg Blotsky, witnessed things first hand:

> The conditions of life for the soldiers in Chechnya were dreadful. In Afghanistan we were issued with special rations of canned meat, condensed milk, biscuits, tea and canned heat for cooking. All that I saw Russian soldiers eating in Chechnya was pearl barley and watery stew.[4]

On top of this, the Russians lacked clean drinking water, sleeping bags and fresh underwear. In a fury, Yeltsin instructed the Russian military to bring hostilities to a halt by 9 May 1995 – the 50th anniversary of the end of the Second World War in Europe.

Once Grozny had fallen, the rebels launched a series of raids, mounting a brutal guerrilla campaign, inflicting heavy casualties on the demoralised Russians and turning Russian public opinion against the war. By this stage, Moscow was admitting to 1,146 dead (unofficial sources put it as high as 4,000), 5,000 wounded and 400 missing in action. Moscow claimed to have killed 7,000 Chechen fighters – an unlikely figure, as this was more men than the Chechens had in the field.

Moscow's public relations campaign continued to come off the rails. The Russian military stormed into the village of Samashki on 7 April 1995, suffering forty-nine casualties and killing 120 Chechens, most, if not all, of whom were civilians. By this stage, Colonel-General Anatoli Kulikov was claiming the Russian Army controlled 80 per cent of Chechnya but this was complete nonsense. Peace negotiations were soon derailed and Maskhadov's men were soon taking up arms again. The Russians renewed their efforts to subdue the Chechens on 10 January 1996, when they flatted the eastern Chechen town of Novogroznenshy using artillery and helicopter gunships. The two sides finally agreed a peace deal in August, agreeing to defer the thorny issue of Chechnya's status for five years. The Russians withdrew from the republic and elections were held with Aslan Maskhadov, the former rebel chief of staff, becoming president. Chechnya spiralled into anarchy.

It was now that an international Islamist dimension to the Chechen conflict became apparent. This was brought home when four British telecommunications engineers were kidnapped in Grozny in October 1998. Their severed heads were found two months later – the beheadings were thought to have been in response to a bungled rescue attempt by President Maskhadov's anti-terrorist squad. A Chechen witness later claimed they had been killed at the request of Osama bin Laden.[5] It transpired that the Chechens had been radicalised over the last four years.

Unrest spread when a Chechen-based group of militant Jihadists mounted a major raid into the neighbouring Russian Federation republic of Dagestan in August 1999, with the intention of setting up an independent Islamic state there. Within weeks they had been driven back into Chechnya. But this was just a taste of things to come, for the Jihadists had decided to expand the conflict even further afield. The following month, a wave of devastating bomb blasts in Moscow and across Russia left 300 dead. In retaliation, the Russian Air Force began to strike suspected Islamic militant camps in Chechnya.

Few realised quite what an impact Chechnya had made on the wider Islamic community. Foreign fighters who went to Chechnya were reportedly inspired to do so after seeing television images of Chechens wearing Islamic headbands. There is a large Chechen expatriate population scattered across Iraq, Jordan, Turkey and Syria. Most were assimilated but in the case of Jordan there remains a distinctive Chechen community, numbering just under 10,000.

After it declared independence, numbers of Jordanian Chechens travelled to the land of their forefathers. Notable among them was Afghanistan veteran Sheikh Ali Fathi al-Shishani. Fathi watched Moscow's response to Chechen aspirations with growing hatred and in 1993 formed a Salafi Islamic Jamaat or 'Assembly', recruiting indigenous Chechens and Jordanian Chechens. After the outbreak of the First Chechen War, he began to assist in the recruitment of Arab fighters from Afghanistan, including Emir Khattab or Samir Salih Abdallah al-Suwaylim. According to author and investigative journalist, Adam Robinson:

> From 1994, the al-Qaeda network began ferrying men from its bases in Afghanistan through neighbouring Turkmenistan, across the Caspian Sea, landing in Dagestan and then travelling overland into Chechnya. The return journey was taken by many of Dudayev's men, who would be trained in guerrilla warfare tactics at al-Qaeda bases in Afghanistan.[6]

As a young man, Khattab had fought in Afghanistan against the Soviets in the late 1980s, and then took part in the Tajik civil war in 1992. Khattab has been described as being a friend of fellow Saudi, Osama bin Laden. Yet he always denied any connection, pointing out that he was only seventeen when he arrived in Afghanistan in 1987. There is, however, some evidence to suggest that they were in contact during the 1990s and early 2000s. Certainly there may have been some rivalry between the two, especially as Khattab's prestige rose following his involvement in the Chechen struggle.

In terms of strategy, though, the two men were very different. Bin Laden was obsessed with attacking the 'far' enemy, namely Israel and America, which formed, in his eyes, a Judeo-Christian alliance. Khattab's Jihad – as in the case of Bosnia and elsewhere – was much more localised, restricting his attacks to within the Russian Federation. He arrived in Chechnya in February 1995 with just eight men but had another ninety follow him.[7] Khattab's most famous military exploit in Chechnya was the ambush of a Russian armoured column in the central foothills on the road to Shatoi in April 1996. It was a classic

Afghanistan-style mountain ambush and from a force of just under 200 Russian troops, seventy-three were killed.

Ayman al-Zawahiri took a close interest in Chechnya. In 1998, before Egyptian Islamic Jihad merged with al-Qaeda, he travelled there on a fact-finding mission. His vision was clear:

> If the Chechens and other Caucasus Mujahideen reach the shores of the oil-rich Caspian, the only thing that will separate them from Afghanistan will be the neutral state of Turkmenistan. This will form a mujahid belt to the south of Russia ...[8]

A logistical network stretching from Afghanistan and the Middle East via Azerbaijan, Georgia and Turkey was soon to develop. Fathi chose Baku, the Azerbaijani capital, as the hub for his travel and finance network. He and Khattab were not slow in harnessing global multi media as a recruiting tool by disseminating Chechen rebel films via video and compact disc.

The Arab fighters soon found an ally in Chechen warlord Shamil Basayev. This was important, as the fiercely independent Chechens were very wary of outsiders. This meant that Khattab and his commanders (including his first deputy Abu Bakr Aqeedah, Aqeedah's successor Hakim al-Medani, Abu Jafar al-Yemeni, Yaqub al-Ghamidi and his then deputy Abu Walid al-Ghamidi) were incorporated into the rebel Chechen high command.

According to Aslan Maskhadov, about eighty Middle Eastern Arabs joined the struggle against the Russians during the first war, alongside them were also North Africans and Turks. It has been claimed that, in total, up to 2,000 al-Qaeda fighters flocked to Chechnya.[9] Their numbers were initially too few to make any impact on the fighting on the ground, but, as in the case of Bosnia, they were highly useful in their ability to attract foreign financing to buy arms and explosives.

It was not long before reports of Arab and Turkish fighters in Chechnya began to emerge. A key figure was Abu Hafs (a Jordanian with Saudi nationality), who, reportedly, was Osama bin Laden's envoy to Chechnya, having replaced Abu al-Walid. In 1995–96 Abu Hafs, who fought alongside Emir Khattab and Abu al-Walid in the early 1990s, accompanied them to Chechnya. There he initially served as a military trainer at Khattab's camp near Sergen-Urt and married a Chechen woman. After Khattab's death, al-Walid instructed Abu Hafs to take command of the foreign fighters. He was appointed Commander of Arab Ansar in Chechnya and may have been a member of the Military Shoura Council of Chechnya. At this stage he took another Chechen wife, the widow of Arab fighter Abu Jafar, killed in 2001.[10]

Khattab established training camps that offered not only military training but also religious indoctrination. He wanted an Islamic republic in Chechnya and once this was established he hoped to liberate all the neighbouring Muslim territories. Indeed, it was Khattab and Shamil Basayev who launched the abortive raid into Dagestan. He was assassinated in 2002, having never made any threats against the United States. But Chechnya, after decades of Russian rule, was largely a secular society and the foreign fighters' Islamic message was not altogether welcome.

After the Chechen victory in 1996, President Maskhadov found himself faced by a military religious alliance demanding the imposition of Shariah law. This was duly set up under the guidance of Sheikh Abu Omar al-Sayf. It also received guidance from a young Jordanian-Chechen called Abdurakhman, who succeed Fathi as head of the Islamic Jamaat after his death in 1997. By now, Khattab was too powerful to oppose, but Maskhadov, fearful for his position, expelled Abdurakhman, two of his Arab deputies and Bagautdin Magomedov, a Dagestani Islamist.

While Russian sources paint a seductive image of Arab fighters streaming into Chechnya, they have to be treated with caution, as Moscow had every reason to inflate the impact and connections of these volunteers. For example, they claim that Khattab was Jordanian and that his real name was Habib Abdul-Rahman, whereas, in reality, he was a Saudi by the name of Samir Salih Abdallah al-Suwaylim. There were also unsubstantiated claims that Abu Hafs had operated in the former Soviet republic of Georgia.[11]

According to Moscow, the main source of *naemniky* or mercenaries fighting in Chechnya was Turkey: 'It was an open secret,' says Sebastian Smith, 'that the Chechens had supporters in Turkey. Chechen separatist officials were sheltered and even able to set up offices in Istanbul.'[12]

Indeed, Russian security forces did come across dead Jihadists bearing Turkish passports. A Turkish Jamaat 'Osmanly' or 'Ottoman' platoon, under Amir Muhtar, is believed to have served within the Arab-dominated International Islamic Brigade.

Moscow produced a list of twenty-four Turkish fighters killed in Chechnya between 1999–2004 and Russian units reported fighting groups of Turks up to forty strong.[13] The first Turkish volunteers fought in Chechnya during 1995–96 and some were killed in the battles for Grozny. One such Turkish Jihadist, by the name of Ali Yaman, was captured alive in the Chechen village of Gekhi-Chu. Another, Shaheed Baila al-Qaiseri – a veteran of Bosnia and Kosovo – arrived in Chechnya in August 1999 and took part in the Dagestan operations in Botlikh. In response to the latest Russian invasion, he took part in the fighting in Argun and then Grozny, where he was wounded in February 2000. At the village of Katyr Yurt, the house in which he was sheltering was hit by a Russian rocket attack and he was subsequently killed at Shami Yurt.

Links existed between Chechnya and the Taliban. Zelimkhan Yandarbiyev, a Chechen ideologist, led a delegation to the Afghan city of Kandahar in January 2000. The Taliban formally recognised Chechnya as an independent Muslim state. Although Yandarbiyev denied any military relationship, a training camp was reported near Kandahar. Foreign fighters were difficult to assimilate due to language problems, so the Chechen tried to restrict volunteers to those with military experience. To that end, a Moroccan called Gahak acted as Khattab's representative in Afghanistan and screened potential recruits. However, after 9/11 and the invasions of Afghanistan and Iraq, it meant that 'would-be' volunteers were diverted there rather than being sent to Chechnya. The fall-out from 9/11 also meant that funding from the Gulf States began to dry up. Following Khattab's death there was a notable shift in policy by foreign fighters in Chechnya. Abu Walid and Abu Hafs al-Urdani began to promote attacks on American interests.

It was claimed that Iran was secretly training Chechen rebels at the Iranian Revolutionary Guards' Imam Ali camp near Tajris Square in Tehran in 2005. They were allegedly undergoing ideological and political indoctrination with the *mullahs* at Qom.[14] It was believed that Iran's hard-line President Mahmoud Ahmadinejad had sanctioned this in order to put pressure on Moscow and ensure its continued support for Iran's nuclear programme in the face of UN opposition.

In 1999 the new and little-known (outside intelligence circles) Russian president, Vladimir Putin, pledged to subdue troublesome Chechnya once and for all. While his military commanders promised a swift victory, a radical wing of the Chechen guerrilla movement brought the war to the very heart of Russia. Through 4–16 September 1999 Chechen militants waged what was dubbed the 'Russian apartment bombing' campaign in Moscow, which left almost 300 dead and over 1,000 injured. This and the Dagestan War led to the Second Chechen War.

Moscow was now swift to exploit the war on terror for its own ends. Putin laid the blame for the terrorist attacks at the feet of Khattab, Abu Umar and the Arab Jihadists. It was alleged that the campaign was planned at 'Caucasus' in Shatoy and 'Taliban' in Avtury – Khattab's guerrilla training camps in Chechnya. Certainly, most of the participants were not ethnic Chechens. Many of those involved were rounded up and arrested in Azerbaijan, Georgia and Kazakhstan, others were killed by security forces in Chechnya and Ingushetia. Some argued that the FSB, Russia's intelligence service, had orchestrated these bombings in order to justify invading Chechnya once more.

About 90,000 Russian troops struck on 30 September 1999 and by mid-December had encircled Grozny once again. Exhausted Chechen rebels with-drew from the city in early February 2000, after weeks of bitter street-fighting and Russian bombardment. Moscow's casualties were estimated to have been as high as 3,000. Chechen losses are unknown. Once more it was a hollow victory for Moscow, as journalist Sebastian Smith observed:

Large-scale combat in the second war ended in 2000 after the capture of Grozny and the scattering of thousands of poorly supplied rebels to the mountain villages. Yet, as happened in Iraq after President George Bush's famous declaration of an end to major operations, the war was only entering the first of numerous new phases. Each of these has been more opaque than the last, reaching the point today when few in Russia or even Chechnya can fully define what the conflict is about anymore.[15]

Despite the apparent pacification of Grozny, the fighting continued up in the mountains, with the Russians using artillery, helicopter gunships and fighter-bombers to keep the rebels at arms length. Aslan Maskhadov, veteran guerrilla leader and Chechnya's only freely elected president, continued to resist until his death in March 2005. On the plains the Chechens resorted to small-scale ambushes, intent on making life a misery for the Russian Army. In Grozny, a pro-Russian administration was set up under turncoat Akmad Kadyrov. He had served under Maskhadov but swapped sides in October 1999, having handed the town of Gudmermes over to the Russian Army.

Despite the presence of Moscow's 'peacekeepers', Chechnya remained a base for Jihadist attacks into neighbouring Muslim areas, further undermining Russia's hold on the troubled Caucasus. In October 2002, Chechen guerrillas carried out the Moscow theatre siege, during which 130 hostages were killed. The following year there was a spate of suicide bombs in Moscow.

International observers refused to attend the elections in 2003, when Kadyrov (backed by a private army of 7,000 former rebels) was Moscow's preferred candidate. Chechnya, having voted overwhelmingly to remain part of the Russian Federation, remained host to at least 50,000 Russian troops, who were dying at a rate of five to twelve a week.[16] President Kadyrov – universally hated – was assassinated in the summer of 2004 and replaced by Alu Alkhanov, another Moscow loyalist. He was endorsed by Magomed Khambiyev, who had served as the defence minister of the separatists' unofficial government since 1999. He had surrendered in March 2004 and Moscow claimed that this showed its peace plan was working. However, waiting in the wings was Kadyrov's son, Ramzan, with a private army of 4,000 men.[17]

Islamic militants were held responsible for blowing up the Moscow metro in February 2004 in an attack that caused over 170 casualties. Putin was quick to accuse Chechnya's deposed president and secessionist leader Maskhadov. At a press conference in response to the bombing, Putin declared: 'Russia does not negotiate with terrorists, it annihilates them.'[18] He went on to describe terrorism as the plague of the twenty-first century, which the world must unite to defeat.

A group calling itself the Islambouli Brigades, supporting Muslim Chechens, claimed responsibility for a follow-up attack on the Moscow metro in August

2004. Putin alleged that the bombs that brought down two passenger aircraft proved a link with international terrorism:

> If a terrorist organisation has taken responsibility for this and that group has links to al-Qaeda, then that confirms the ties between certain forces active in Chechnya and international terrorism.[19]

Over 100 Islamic militants attacked the city of Nazran in the republic of Ingushetia in June 2004, leaving ninety dead and 120 wounded. The world's attention was then caught, on 1 September 2004, when Chechen militants occupied a school in Beslan in North Ossetia. A bloodbath followed, as Russian security forces bungled their attempts to rescue the trapped schoolchildren, leaving around 350 people dead. Radical Chechen guerrilla leader, Shamil Basayev, later claimed responsibility. Moscow also tried to link al-Qaeda to the attack.[20]

The next year, a similar raid, conducted by 200 guerrillas, was carried out against Nalchik, the capital of the Muslim republic of Kabardino-Balkaria. Reportedly, forty-nine people were killed including twenty-five militants. The rebels included forces of the Caucasus Front and the Kabardino-Balkarian Yarmuk (Islamic Brigade).[21]

While Arab military intervention during the 1994–96 Chechen war had very little impact, it was Khattab who fanned the flames of war again in 1999 by organising the invasion of Dagestan. It is assessed that, around 100–200 foreign Jihadists fought alongside some 1,200 Chechen rebels, who were led by Arab commanders or Emirs, such as Khattab, Abu Walid (who was killed in 2004) and Abu Hafs.[22] Indeed, the greatest impact was not on the battlefield but on the religious and financial fronts. It also meant that President Putin was able to link the war in Chechnya with part of the greater struggle against global terrorism. It is doubted that more than 500 combatants have passed through Chechnya, but ultimately this is a sufficient cadre to cause problems elsewhere.

The real tragedy, like Bosnia, was the suffering inflicted on ordinary people. Grozny – once home to 450,000 Chechens but with a current population of perhaps 150,000 – has been devastated, and over 100,000 Chechen killed at a cost of around 20,000 Russian soldiers. During the Second World War, Grozny had been spared destruction. The German Army had failed to break through to the city, its key objective in the North Caucasus, stalling about 70 miles away.

Sebastian Smith, seeking to discover how the Chechnya conflict had affected its tiny neighbours, all of whom had experienced similar treatment at Russian hands over the centuries, found:

> Whichever autonomous republic you are in – from Dagestan, to Kabardino-Balkaria or Adygei – the scene is the same. The map says

you are on the southern border of the Russian Federation, but this is in theory. In fact, you left Russia long ago and you have now entered the ancient, enduring and tragic world of Allah's mountains.[23]

It seems global Jihad helped erode the last vestige of the Tsarist empire in the Caucasus.

Chapter 10

Kosovo: a Missed Opportunity

Strange as it may seem, Albania was crucial to the development of al-Qaeda in Europe. By the late 1990s, the terrorist organisation was well established there. Bin Laden saw the conflict in neighbouring Yugoslavia as Europe's Afghanistan and fed Arab militants through Albania to fight alongside the Bosniaks against the Serbs. He then supported Albanian separatists in Kosovo, fighting the Serbs. Also, by the late 1990s, there were some 4,000 Arab militants in Italy, many of them having come by sea via Albania.

Osama bin Laden even visited Albania in the mid-1990s as part of an official Saudi delegation (despite the fact he was supposed to be persona non grata with the Saudi government at the time), where he offered to finance construction and healthcare schemes. He allegedly befriended the head of the Albanian Secret Service, who subsequently allowed Islamic militants and terrorist-linked charity front organisations to flourish there. In intelligence circles, Albania has long been assessed as a source of friction in the Balkans, most recently because of its support for Albanian separatists in the troubled Serbian province of Kosovo. In 2000 it was reported that bin Laden had been training a group of 500 Mujahideen near the Albanian towns of Podgrade and Korce in Kosovo. It was also alleged that 2,000 fighters were to wage a campaign in southern Serbia.[1]

Similarly, Italy became a stopover point for Muslim extremists en route to the Balkans to take part in Jihad. Arriving by boat, they took sanctuary in the northern Italian city of Bologna. According to Italian intelligence sources, one local airline was dubbed 'Jihad Air' because of cheap tickets offered to Islamic fighters heading for former Yugoslavia. Furthermore, according to British intelligence, veterans of the Afghanistan and Bosnia conflicts living in Bologna pledged support for bin Laden's cause.

Just as NATO's SFOR assumed responsibility for Bosnia, Albania, to the south, collapsed into chaos. Rioting broke out in Tirana and Americans and Europeans were instructed to leave the country. This aggravated the situation in Kosovo, where there were long-standing tensions between ethnic Muslim Albanians and the minority Serb ruling elite. This led to NATO forces intervening in Kosovo in June 1999. Author and foreign correspondent Christian Jennings astutely observes:

The bombing campaign and subsequent military occupation of Kosovo by NATO and the UN in 1999 was something of a turning point, intended to rectify the mistakes made in Somalia, Rwanda and Bosnia. Having learned in Bosnia and across Africa that operating under a frustratingly limited UN Security Council mandate was often a recipe for lack of military progress, or at worst disaster ...[2]

Tiny Kosovo, like Albania and Bosnia, is a stronghold of the Islamic faith in the Balkans, left high and dry by the long-gone Ottoman Empire. The Serbs had been defeated by the Muslim Ottoman Turks in 1389 at the Battle of Kosovo Polje (Field of Blackbirds) and ever since, Kosovo has been seen as the Serbs spiritual and historical homeland. The Ottomans ruled it until 1912, when Serbia reclaimed the land. To the bitterness of the inhabitants, Kosovo was re-colonised by the Serbs, who treated the Muslim ethnic Albanians as religious and racial inferiors. It was not until the mid-1970s that Kosovo was granted autonomy under the Yugoslav constitution.

Ethnic Albanians – some 2 million of them – make up 90 per cent of the population, meaning that tensions with the Serb minority were inevitably going to boil over. Aspirations for full independence resulted in the Kosovo Liberation Army (KLA or *Ushtria Clirimtare e Kosove* – UCK) carrying out bomb attacks on the Serbs in 1996. American intelligence agents subsequently admitted they helped to train the KLA before NATO's bombing of Yugoslavia.[3] In the Kosovan heartland of the Drenica Valley, by mid-1998, a guerrilla war had broken out, with the KLA launching hit-and-run attacks on Serb villages and security forces. The Serbian reaction was predictable, with bloody reprisals against Albanian villages known to be harbouring the KLA.

Neighbouring Albania's armed forces – long trapped in a Cold War time capsule – were incapable of intervening openly in Kosovo. In the mid-1990s the Albanian Ministry of Defence drafted 'Force Objective 2010', which was designed to revise its armed forces, in particular the air force, with the aim of reducing manpower and phasing out obsolete equipment.[4] Waging a counter-insurgency campaign was not at the top of its priorities.

The KLA was variously portrayed as a bunch of opportunist criminals or unsavoury terrorists with support from al-Qaeda, Iran and the Taliban. Its stated political aim of creating a Greater Albania from territories belonging to Serbia, Macedonia and Greece certainly had a wide appeal within the Muslim world. Once again, it had the romantic image of an oppressed Muslim minority struggling for freedom. In contrast, the Clinton administration declared it a terrorist organisation. Former DEA agent and author Michael Levine had a dim view of the KLA:

> We were arming and equipping the worst elements of the Mujahideen
> in Afghanistan – drug traffickers, arms smugglers, anti-American

terrorists [...] same thing with the KLA, which is tied in with every known Middle and Far Eastern drug cartel. Interpol, Europol, and nearly every European intelligence and counter-narcotics agency has files open on drug syndicates that lead right to the KLA, and right to Albanian gangs in this country.[5]

It was even reported that the KLA was not really indigenous to Kosovo – certainly, its leadership seemed to be drawn from northern Albania (controlled by former President Sali Berisha and his Tropjoe clans as well as various Kosovo groups) and the Albanian diaspora living in Germany and Switzerland.[6] Michael Radu, in warning about the KLA's credentials, wrote:

The KLA has in fact never shown regard for democracy. When the Kosovo Democratic League of Ibrahim Rugova – the only democratically elected Kosovo Albanian leader ever – tried to establish its own armed branch (the Armed Force of the Kosovo Republic [FARK] with bases in Albania, the KLA promptly killed its leader. Nor did the KLA have any qualms about murdering Rugova's collaborators, whom it accused of the 'crime' of moderation.[7]

Serb troops massacred twenty-three members of Adem Jashari's family in March 1998. He was a prominent KLA leader from the village of Prekaz, in the heart of the Drenica Valley.[8] By committing such human rights atrocities and creating a humanitarian crisis, the Serbs drove the KLA into the arms of NATO: 'The KLA concentrated its operations in populated areas,' says Michael Radu, 'confident that the typically brutal Serbian forces, especially the irregular paramilitary groups, would eventually retaliate against civilians.'

By late March 1999, the British SAS were operating alongside the KLA. However, the team working with Ramush Haradinaj's Dukagjin Brigade in the west of Kosovo, bordering Montenegro, found them to be slippery customers. Rivalry between other units, led by Tahir Zemaj and commander Qorri, greatly hampered co-ordination efforts and led to the SAS being compromised on a number of occasions.[9]

Predictably, the actions of the Serb security forces resulted in hundreds of thousands of Kosovo Albanians being driven into neighbouring Albania and Macedonia. In response, NATO began to conduct air strikes to force the Serbian military out of Kosovo. Just four days after NATO began bombing, on 24 March 1999, the Scorpions – a special Serbian police unit under Slobodan Medic – massacred eighteen ethnic Albanians at Podujevo.[10]

It seemed inevitable that Kosovo and Albania would become fertile ground for Mujahideen Islamists. By late 1998, a joint CIA-Albanian intelligence operation uncovered the presence of foreign fighters from at least half a dozen

Middle Eastern countries, crossing into Kosovo from safe havens in Albania.[11] Washington, having learned its lesson in Bosnia, was swift to ask the KLA to distance themselves from the Jihadist groups.

In response, the KLA – clearly seeing NATO as a more powerful ally – agreed to refuse help from foreign Mujahideen and refrain from using terror tactics against the Serbs outside Kosovo. It also promised not to incite fellow ethnic Albanians in neighbouring Macedonia. This undertaking was obviously bought at a price, most likely weapons and training for the KLA.

The KLA claimed that their struggle against the Serbs was a national struggle, not a religious one. Indeed, around a quarter of the KLA were reportedly Roman Catholics. Even so, the KLA's cause still attracted Muslim extremists from far afield, as Fatos Klosi, Director of the Albanian intelligence service, commented in the late 1990s: 'We have information about three or four groups, there are Egyptians, Saudi Arabians, Algerians, Tunisians and Sudanese.'[12]

There were also reports of Iranian fighters, some of whom had come from Bosnia.[13] Likewise, it was claimed that bin Laden signed a secret agreement with Iran to facilitate Iranian Revolutionary Guard support for the KLA.[14] The aim was to make the region their main base for militant activity in Europe, though activities seemed to have been confined to the Bosnian town of Zenica.

There is evidence that fanatical Islamic fighters from Afghanistan, Algeria, Egypt, Chechnya, Iran and other countries were included into the command structures of KLA in Kosovo and Metohija. In May, through late June 1998, a combined unit of Mujahideen, known as Abu Bekir Sidik, under Ekrem Avdi of Kosovska Mitrovica, was operating in the Drenica area. It was equipped with automatic rifles of Yugoslav, Chinese and Russian manufacture, as well as sniper rifles, 40mm grenade launchers, RPGs, light and heavy machine guns, hand grenades and other weapons. Arms were procured by organisations in Zenica called the 'Islamic Balkan Center' and 'Active Islamic Youth'. The unit numbered 115 fighters, of whom about forty were foreign nationals (ten from Saudi Arabia, two from Egypt, four from Albania, four from the UK, with the rest from Bosnia and Macedonia). A large number of the Albanians returned home to Kosovo and Macedonia after the unit was disbanded, while some tried to enter Albania. According to Serbian intelligence sources:

> The presence of radical Islam in Kosovo and Macedonia is illustrated by the fact that in 1995 Osama bin Laden visited Albania as a guest of Sali Berisha, who was the president of Albania at the time, when bases for the logistic and financial support to the al-Qaeda organisation were set up, with cells in Kosovo and Macedonia. In addition to bin Laden, the meeting was attended by Bashkim Gazideda, former head of secret police of Albania, Hashim Thaqi and Ramush Haradinaj.

On the occasion, Bashkim Gazideda was elected into a group of al-Qaeda leaders for the Balkan region.

This was supported by US intelligence. Senator Pat Roberts, Chairman of the Senate Security Commission, stated that they had evidence of a connection between the KLA and bin Laden, as well as KLA involvement in the illicit drugs trade.

Likewise, intelligence circles in Albania confirmed the strong presence of bin Laden's network, as well as the existence of plans for attacks on American citizens and facilities. The same sources confirmed the presence of four Jihad groups (from Algeria, Egypt, Tunisia, Saudi Arabia and Sudan) in northern Albania and their participation in the conflicts in Kosovo and Macedonia as part of the KLA's forces.[15]

For the KLA, ultimately, the presence of Islamist fighters in Kosovo and Albania was a public relations disaster. For Serbian President Milosevic it was a propaganda coup, enabling him to portray the fighting in Kosovo as a holy war in which the Serbs were acting as a bulwark against Jihad in Europe.

Having endured three months of NATO air strikes, the Serbian Army withdrew from Kosovo in June 1999 and KLA political leader Hashim Thaqi signed a demilitarisation agreement with NATO. The 9,000-strong KLA, under their commander-in-chief, Agim Ceku, having fought a sixteen-month guerrilla campaign, agreed with British General Mike Jackson to peacefully disarm and disband. The KLA had claimed, by the summer of 1998, to have 30,000 men under arms.

The UN proposed raising a new civil defence force incorporating the KLA. This was to be composed of an honour guard, security force, small rapid reaction unit and a helicopter unit.[16] While bringing the KLA in from the field proved a great success, General Jackson had a struggle on his hands avoiding its subsequent resurrection as the army of Kosovo. Initially, Ceku wanted the proposed protection corps called the Kosovo Army Corps. Eventually, he and Thaqi – after much heated debate and the intervention of General Wesley Clark – settled for the Kosovo Protection Corps.

While it was intended that this uniformed Kosovo Corps would be 3,000–5,000 strong, only 200 were to be armed, in order to avoid Serbian claims that this was, indeed, the basis for a Kosovar national army.[17] Undoubtedly, the KLA – which still wanted full independence – saw it as such, so it was vital that the disarmament was completed on schedule (19 September 1999). Moscow was also understandably against reconstituting the KLA under another name. Hashim Thaqi kept his word and became Kosovo's prime minister in subsequent elections. Slobodan Milosevic lamented, while in a Belgrade prison in June 2001:

Western intelligence agencies created the Kosovo Liberation Army [...] and when we defeated those terrorists in 1998, they threatened us with bombs. There was no humanitarian or civilian catastrophe. They invented the Racak massacre as an excuse to bomb us [forty-five ethnic Albanians were massacred at Racak in southern Kosovo in January 1999].[18]

The idea of a Muslim ethnic Albanian homeland encompassing Pristina (Kosovo), Tetovo (Macedonia) and Tirana (Albania) did not go away. By 2003 guerrillas of the Albanian National Army (known as AKSh – Armata Kombëtare Shqiptare) were trying to incite their cousins in Albania, Greece, Kosovo, Macedonia and Serbia and Montenegro. Its mode of operation was to attack Serbian Army outposts in southern Serbia, although it began to make its presence felt elsewhere, notably in northern Kosovo and along the Macedonian border with Kosovo. Despite the 2001 accord with the KLA, once again, Albanian separatists who envisaged a Greater Albania encompassing Kosovo and Macedonia, caused ill-ease in the region's capitals.

In Macedonia, about 150 Mujahideen from Saudi Arabia, Afghanistan, Bosnia and Herzegovina and Turkey – as well as volunteers from Albania, Kosovo and Macedonia who had previously lived and trained in other Arabian countries – supported the activities of the KLA. Daut Haradinaj and Sedula Morati (a member of the Ismet Jashari unit that operated in the regions of Kumanovo and Lipkovo) organised the movement of the Mujaheedin into Macedonia.

In February, AKSh blew up a courthouse in Struga, Macedonia, followed, in April, by a bridge in northern Albania. AKSh was active in Kosovo and in the Presevo Valley in southern Serbia, which has a substantial ethnic Albanian population. In response, the United Nations Mission in Kosovo, UNMIK, declared the AKSh a terrorist organisation. This was followed by the arrest of Gafurr Adili, AKSh's political leader, by the Albanian authorities.

AKSh claimed that it was launching these latter attacks in support of Macedonia's Albanians, stating:

The fighting in Macedonia confirms that the multi-ethnic state is false. Macedonia's government cannot accept that Albanians have equal rights. It was waiting for an excuse to use violence.[19]

In reality, this campaign was launched in response to the Macedonian police's efforts to shut down AKSh smuggling activities. The core of the fighters, under Avdil Jakupi (also known as 'Chakala'), was thought to number no more than seventy cigarette smugglers. A British Army brigadier, advising the

Macedonian military, described the AKSh as 'criminals flying a political flag of convenience in the hope of finding legitimacy'.[20]

While it was claimed AKSh were little more than smugglers resisting Macedonian attempts to close them down, there was well-founded concern that the Macedonian authorities might overreact and cause a rod for their own backs. Indeed, the Albanians' Democratic Union for Integration (DUI – formerly the KLA) warned it would withdraw from Macedonia's Slav-led coalition government if the Macedonian police killed any Albanian civilians. The European Union agreed to send a 200-strong police mission to supplement the 400 troops despatched at the beginning of 2003. During the presidential elections in 2004, two of the candidates were former ethnic Albanian rebel commanders – Gezim Ostreni and Zudi Xhelili.

Kosovo was never fertile ground for Jihad: its people looked to NATO to save them from the Serbs, not militant Islamists. By mid-2002 the Saudis had largely washed their hands of the Kosovars: 'The Muslims here behave like Christians,' grumbled al-Hadi, in charge of the Saudi Joint Relief Committee, 'they have accepted living in Europe. I think in ten years it will be worse [. . .] We will not stay.'[21] It was clear that Saudi Wahhabi-driven Jihad had failed in Kosovo.

The CIA insisted that the 'Albanian Returnees' – a Saudi network – be deported from Albania to Egypt. This was following the arrest of Sabri Ibrahim al-Attar, a member of the Egyptian terrorist Islamic Group or Gamaa al-Islamiyya. He had been recruited in Saudi Arabia in the early 1990s by former Mujahideen and sent to Afghanistan via Yemen and Pakistan. In Afghanistan he had been involved with the al-Qaeda network. In 1996 he went to Bosnia but moved to Albania, following implementation of the Dayton Agreement that all foreign fighters leave.

When the United Arab Emirates undertook to build fifty new mosques, Naim Maloku – a former KLA commander – made it clear that Kosovo did not need them: what it wanted was jobs. Similarly, Saudi insensitivities, when restoring old Kosovo mosques, were not appreciated. At the Hadum mosque at Gjakova, the UN had to ban the Saudis after they started tearing up centuries-old gravestones – presumably in the name of modernity.

Ethnic resentment in Kosovo ever remains a source of friction. The worst trouble in Kosovo since 1999 occurred in March 2004, when 17,000 NATO peacekeepers were caught off guard by ethnic violence in the northern town of Kosovska Mitrovica. Around 300 people were injured and there were at least six fatalities. With the death toll rising to twenty and fighting spreading to Obilic east of the capital Pristina and Lipljan in eastern Kosovo, NATO sent in an extra 1,000 troops.[22] 'We have had similar attacks to these in Kosovo before,' said UN spokesman, Derek Chappell, 'but the fact that these attacks took place at the same time, all over Kosovo, does make me think they were orchestrated by the same extreme groups.' [23]

The fear that Kosovo might be partitioned led to concern that the KLA might reform to resist such a move. Indeed, the anarchy in Kosovo gave shadowy extremists the opportunity to settle old scores. Among the dead were two American UNMIK corrections officers, killed at the Mitrovica detention centre. The following month Albanian president, Alfred Moisu, visited Pristina – the first official visit ever by an Albanian head of state to UN-administered Kosovo. [24]

In the face of international airports being placed under ever closer security post 9/11, it is much easier for terrorist operatives to cross the Adriatic by boat to Italy than fly and then move northward. Under the provision of the UN's Counter-terrorist Committee, Albania has a clear responsibility to deny al-Qaeda safe haven. The route between the southern Albanian port of Vlora and the Italian port of Brindisi remains a security risk. At a distance of 65km, the crossing takes just two hours, through what is a very busy waterway. The Albanian, Italian and Greek Navies have found themselves constantly rescuing stranded refugees in this area. The concern is that al-Qaeda terrorists are also utilising this route to get into southern Europe. Al-Qaeda has a track record of using impoverished states as operating bases – just look at Afghanistan, Somalia and Yemen. Albania's lax immigration controls and rampant corruption have made it the perfect European base for al-Qaeda.

While NATO's maritime counter-terrorist Operation Active Endeavour encompasses the whole of the Mediterranean, the Albanian Navy found itself fighting an unequal struggle, trying to stem the flow of terrorists, drugs and illegal refugees across the Adriatic into Italy. Muslim Albania is Europe's pauper and many of its people are desperate to seek better lives elsewhere in Western Europe. Operating out of just five naval bases, the Albanian Navy has about thirty patrol craft, though few are seaworthy.

The Italian Navy, based at Brindisi and Ancona, is much better placed to patrol the Adriatic. Albanian and Italian naval vessels of Group 28 (Italian Military Marine) have been jointly patrolling against illegal trafficking in Albanian territorial waters, operating out of the Albanian port of Durres. In fact, the situation is such that the Italians are permanently stationed at Durres, in order to deter people smuggling. To the south, the Albanian Navy also co-operates closely with the Greek Navy, which has provided uniforms, diver training and ship recovery facilities. America is not blind to the threat posed by human trafficking and has also been developing naval relations with Albania.

Italy's efforts to stamp out militants have not been altogether successful. By the late 1990s, according to Italian security sources, there were some 4,000 Arab militants in the country, many having come by sea via Albania. This culminated in Operation Sphinx, designed to decapitate the various organisations, and resulting in the arrest of a dozen men. Italy fears Albanian organised crime is taking over on both sides of the Adriatic. To compound matters, Italy also has problems with illegal immigrants from North Africa, which provides al-Qaeda with another route into Europe.

Chapter 11

Lebanon: Cradle of Terror

Once dubbed 'the playground of the Mediterranean and the jewel of the Middle East', Beirut's legacy to the region has been terrorism and drugs. Iran and Syria hold the key to peace with Israel, through their Lebanese-based terrorist proxies, particularly Hezbollah. Lebanon stands out not only because of Hezbollah's links with Tehran, but also because its ports and banks are major transit points for the various Palestinian terrorist organisations and the international drug cartels. The conflict in Lebanon caused Sunni Islamists, including al-Qaeda, to reconcile their dislike for Shiite Muslims – indeed, al-Qaeda's leadership has always expressed a rather ambiguous view on Muslim sectarian violence.

Hezbollah partly funds itself through the international drugs trade and Lebanon has long been a major transit route for home-grown and Asian drugs. Lebanon's Bekaa Valley was once the site of major opium and cannabis cultivation. In the early 1990s, Lebanese and Syrian forces halted this but subsequently, Lebanon transformed from a producer to a regional hub for trafficking. According to the UN Office for Drug Control and Crime Prevention, there are allegations that Lebanese government officials have been involved in drug trafficking.[1]

Washington has categorised Hezbollah's leadership as 'Specially Designated Terrorists', intent on disrupting the Middle East Peace Process (MEPP). The UK's response was to add Hezbollah to the list of proscribed organisations under its Terrorism Act 2000. Hezbollah, whose stronghold is at Baalbek in the Bekaa Valley, clearly co-operates not only with other international terrorists but also organised crime. The International Financial Action Task Force added Lebanon to its Non-Cooperative Countries and Territories, meaning Lebanon was in violation of the UN convention for the suppression of terrorist financing. America, in particular, was disappointed in Lebanon's failure to shut down Hezbollah's finances.

While the Lebanese government tightened port security in Beirut, Sidon, Tyre and Tripoli, clamping down on terrorist finances was much harder, as Hezbollah has gone into mainstream politics and conducts reconstruction and charity work among Lebanon's impoverished Shia community. Palestinian terror group Hamas also distributes funds among Palestinian refugees. It took Lebanon a lot of hard work to divest itself of the NCCT status after the

government instigated money-laundering legislation and established a Special Investigation Commission.

While Hezbollah achieved its aim of forcing the Israeli Defence Force from southern Lebanon in May 2000, it has since helped Palestinian groups, such as Hamas and Palestinian Islamic Jihad (PIJ), use similar guerrilla tactics against the IDF in the West Bank and Gaza. Beirut was once a haven for the Palestinian Liberation Organisation (PLO) and other opposition groups, but most returned to the 'occupied territories' and Jordan after the Israeli invasion of southern Lebanon.

Hezbollah's reach is much broader than its immediate neighbour, with cells in Bahrain and Saudi Arabia – the latter probably involved in bombings in Saudi. Around the world there are large communities of Lebanese expatriates, mainly in South America, but also in West Africa, Canada, the US and Europe. These extended family ties are often mentioned in connection with smuggling networks, particularly with regard to continued trafficking of cocaine from Latin America.

Hezbollah has a truly global reach, with a presence in Paraguay at Ciudad del Este (on the joint border area with Argentina and Brazil), which is notorious for illegal weapons trafficking and drug money-laundering. From there, Hezbollah launched attacks against Jewish targets in Argentina. US Central Command or CENTCOM assesses that such groups operate in the islands of Trinidad and Tobago, and Margarita off Venezuela and Colombia.

While, traditionally, Hezbollah has not constituted a threat to British interests in Cyprus, terrorists are known to use it as a transit point for personnel and drugs. In particular, they found it easy to land at Famagusta or any of the small ports on the eastern end of the island in the Turkish zone. Maritime enforcement is lax, as the Cypriot National Guard and 'Turkish Republic of Northern Cyprus' maritime wings are both very small.

The best way for Hezbollah to infiltrate arms to Hamas and PIJ is down the Lebanese coast, and traditionally has had a strong presence in both West Beirut and Tyre. The Lebanese Navy, based at Beirut, Juniye and Tripoli (equipped with little more than a dozen patrol boats), is almost non-existent. Likewise, it is easier to dodge the Israeli Navy, operating out of Haifa and Ashdod, than pass through Israel's northern security zone.

While most terrorism in Lebanon and Israel is home grown, foreign Jihadists have gained a foothold in the region, following al-Qaeda's decision to expand its presence there. By 2007 the Jihadi networks were stepping up their efforts to strengthen their position in the country as a staging post for attacks not only on foreign targets in Lebanon, but also against Israel. Notably, the hotspots for the Jihadists are the Palestinian camps at Ein el-Hilweh, near Sidon, and Nahr al-Bared, near Tripoli. According to Israeli government sources, Ein el-Hilweh

– which is not under Lebanese government control – is associated with the Fath al-Islam, Usbat al-Ansar and Jund al-Sham Jihadi groups.[2]

Al-Qaeda is purported to have launched attacks in Lebanon at Osama bin Laden's behest. Additionally, Abu Musab al-Zarqawi's 'al-Qaeda in Iraq' claimed responsibility for a rocket attack on Israel, launched from southern Lebanon on 27 December 2005. Al-Zarqawi issued an audio tape in which he said bin Laden had ordered the attack, and it was believed there were up to 100 Salafi Jihadists in the country.[3]

Al-Qaeda and the Salafist movement increased their presence in Lebanon following the assassination of former Lebanese prime minister, Rafik Hariri, in order to capitalise on the upheaval. However, it was felt highly unlikely that the Salafi Jihadists would form an alliance with Hezbollah in southern Lebanon, as the Salafists have an intense dislike for the Shia. In response to the growing threat, Lebanon's security forces were quick to act, and in early 2006 the government charged thirteen al-Qaeda suspects (consisting of seven Syrians, three Lebanese, one Saudi, one Jordanian with Lebanese nationality and a Palestinian) with terrorist offences.[4]

Neighbouring Syria has always regarded Lebanon as part of Greater Syria and has constantly sought to manipulate Lebanese politics. Lebanon achieved independence from France in 1943, but just five years later, with the creation of the State of Israel, 400,000 Palestinian refugees moved north from Israel and crossed into southern Lebanon. For twenty years they lived in squalid poverty, in refugee camps, dreaming of an independent state of Palestine. In 1968 Beirut became the headquarters of the Palestinian Liberation Organisation (PLO), the umbrella organisation for the different political factions dedicated to the overthrow of Israel. The PLO set up bases in southern Lebanon to carry out cross-border operations. Largely unwillingly, the Lebanese were dragged into the Arab-Israeli conflict.

Lebanon was then split along factional lines during the civil war in the mid-1970s, which resulted in 80,000 deaths. The PLO was unable to keep out of this internecine warfare and was soon fighting Lebanese Christian militias. At the height of the fighting, Syria despatched the Saiqa (Syrian-sponsored PLO faction) and the Palestinian Liberation Army to fight alongside the Muslim forces. In turn, the Christians supported the Syrian-Lebanese peace plan but the PLO refused to co-operate.

Syria sent in 40,000 troops, sanctioned by the Arab League, to help the Christians and prevent the PLO establishing a state within Lebanon capable of resisting Syrian aspirations. The Syrians consolidated their positions in Beirut and the Bekaa Valley. After the 1979 Camp David accord between Israel and Egypt, Syria's relations with the PLO improved and the Syrians withdrew from the coast. Despite this, by 1981, Syria still controlled two-thirds of Lebanon and refused to leave.

Israel's primary concern in helping the Lebanese Christians was to secure its northern border against frequent PLO incursions. With the PLO operating from havens in Lebanon, it was clear that Israel and Syria were likely to come to blows over the prostrate country. Sure enough, in 1982, Israel launched Operation Peace for Galilee, invading southern Lebanon along a 63-mile front.[5] While this was intended to force the 15,000-strong PLO out, it was inevitable that confrontation with the Syrians – deployed in the Bekaa, Beirut, the Shouf mountains and along the Beirut-Damascus Highway – would occur.

Israel was able to act largely with impunity because it had secured its southern flank with Egypt in 1979, thanks to the Treaty of Washington. This was the same year that the Iranian Revolution had stirred up a hornet's nest in the Gulf, precipitating the Iran-Iraq War. Egyptian president, Anwar Sadat, was already at odds with Syria and Libya over his reconciliation with Israel and this, coupled with his support for Iraq, culminated in his assassination in 1981, leaving Egypt with a growing Islamist problem.

The PLO was besieged in Beirut until early August 1982, when it finally agreed to quit the city: some 14,398 Palestinian fighters and Syrian soldiers withdrew. Syrian Army losses are believed to have totalled up to 1,200 dead, approximately 3,000 wounded, 296 prisoners, as well as almost 500 armoured vehicles destroyed and captured. The PLO lost 1,500 dead, an unknown number of wounded and, more importantly, their entire infrastructure (including their archives). Operation Peace for Galilee cost the Israelis 368 dead and 2,383 wounded in just six weeks of fighting.

Over two days in mid-September 1982, Lebanese Christian militia ran amok in the Sabra and Shatila refugee camps, which were under Israeli control. The death toll has been much disputed over the years, but at least 800 civilians were murdered. The Muslim world – already furious at the Israeli invasion – was in uproar over these events, which fuelled renewed hatred for the Israelis. This overshadowed the Damour and Karantina massacres in the mid-1970s and generated anti-Western feeling over the failure to punish Israel. It was now that Lebanese Hezbollah emerged to resist the Israelis. Drawing support from the poverty-stricken Shia population, it took its inspiration from the teachings of Ayatollah Khomeini and the Iranian Revolution.

That year, the Iranian Revolutionary Guard established themselves in the Bekaa Valley (though were never seen near the front) and by 1984 reportedly numbered 600 men.[6] They did, however, assist in orchestrating Jihad against the Western Multinational peacekeeping force, culminating in the bomb attacks on the US embassy and US Marine Corps HQ in Beirut on 23 October 1983,[7] helping drive the Western powers out. This left Lebanon partly occupied by Syria and in a state of anarchy, ripe for the establishment of an Islamic republic. The Jihad-al-Islami (The Islamic Holy War), a Shiite terrorist group with links to Iran and Syria, based in the Bekaa Valley, claimed responsibility for both attacks.[8] Significantly, it portrayed Western – in particular, American – impotence in the Middle East.

Iran also supported a Revolutionary Guard in Afghanistan known as Sepha-e-Pasdara, which favoured union with Iran. The group numbered about 3,000 Shia Hazaras, who received the bulk of Iranian support from the mid-1980s.[9] Most of the Mujahideen groups based in Peshawar were Sunni. Similarly, Hezbollah also had limited supporters in Afghanistan.[10]

Although Israel won the battle, within two years Israeli casualties had almost doubled and by 1984 they had suffered 600 dead. The number of wounded rose to 3,600 – proportionally, much higher than those suffered by the US in Vietnam. The indigenous Shia Muslim Lebanese slowly turned on the Israeli Defence Force, once it was apparent that it was not going to withdraw after ousting the Palestinians. Israel wanted to put safeguards in place to ensure that the PLO could not return. This saddled the Israelis with a security zone in southern Lebanon, which was to be a political and military headache for almost twenty years. The IDF finally withdrew from southern Lebanon in May 2000.

Despite the PLO being ejected from southern Lebanon and Beirut, the country was not to enjoy peace. The various factions – pawns of the Iranians, Israelis and Syrians – became ever more radicalised and Islamist. During 1983, as well as supporting dissident PLO forces against Arafat, Syria provided the Druze militia with artillery and tanks.[11] The following year, just as Washington was withdrawing its 1,600 marines (part of a multinational peacekeeping force), the Lebanese Army collapsed in the face of attacks by the Druze and Shia Amal militias. The Lebanese Army had about 25,000 men, but 10,000 Muslim troops refused to leave their barracks and the Druze easily destroyed the 2,000-strong Fourth Brigade.[12]

The international community – particularly the Americans and French who had been so badly mauled in Beirut – abandoned peace-keeping efforts and left Lebanon to tear itself apart once more. The ferocity and complexity of this sectarian violence greatly increased between Lebanese Christians, Shia, Sunnis and Palestinians. The Muslim world looked on in dismay as the Sunni and Shia set about each other. Lebanon became wracked by acts of terrorism and open warfare. Tens of thousands of Palestinian refugees were left stranded in camps in northern Lebanon, and around 8,000 were east of Sidon. The Ein el-Hilweh and Mieh Mieh camps were strongholds of the PLO, while the city itself was controlled by a Lebanese Sunni militia called the Popular Liberation Army. South of Beirut, at Tyre, in the Rashidiyeh camp, were another 17,000 refugees.

The 'War of the Camps' started after Yasser Arafat's Fatah, the military wing of the PLO, joined the peace process. The Syrian-backed Amal militia, which previously had enjoyed good relations with the Palestinians, was alarmed at the prospect of a resurgent PLO, so moved against the refugees. The PLA ended up forming a buffer between the Palestinian and Amal positions at Sidon, while Amal also besieged Rashidiyeh. Fatah found itself not only at war with the Syrians and Amal, but also the pro-Syrian Palestine Struggle Front. Way to the south, the Christian Lebanon Army, defending the security zone established by the Israelis, came under increasing attack from the Iranian-backed Shia Hezbollah.

Palestinian fighters conducted their largest offensive since the Israeli invasion when they overran Shia-controlled villages east of Sidon in 1986. This was an attempt to lift the siege of Rashidiyeh.[13] Amal did not end the 'War of the Camps' until early 1988, by which time it had left 2,500 dead and caused deep enmity among the Arab states, which accused it of killing Palestinians.[14] It also distracted the world's attention from Israeli treatment of the Palestinians in the West Bank and Gaza.

Syria's support for the Islamic militants came unstuck. Pro-Iranian Hezbollah drove the more moderate Syrian-backed Amal out of the Shia slums in Beirut, and Syrian President Assad was faced with the prospect of intervening, as a total victory by the Islamic militants would have threatened Syria's hold on Lebanon.[15] The presence of 25,000 Syrian troops was, in part, to prevent Hezbollah and Iran turning Lebanon into an Islamic Republic.

Assad sought a political settlement, rather than fall out with long-term strategic ally Iran. He had also been attempting to shed Syria's image as a sponsor of terrorism. Nevertheless, Amal and Hezbollah then spent over a year fighting each other and did not sign a peace agreement until early 1989.[16] They both agreed that they would share southern Lebanon, from which to launch attacks on Israel. Also by this stage, for the first time, the PLO was calling for a ceasefire with Israel in southern Lebanon. Nonetheless, Hezbollah and Hamas attacks continued against southern Lebanon and northern Israel throughout the 1990s, resulting in regular Israeli air strikes in retaliation.

By now, Iranian-backed Hezbollah had replaced the PLO. It demonstrated that the IDF was not invincible, after successfully seizing the Tel Dabsha outpost in the southern security zone in 1994. By the late 1990s there were still several hundred Iranian Revolutionary Guards in the Bekaa, co-ordinating Iran's assistance, which amounted to $100 million a year and weapons transited through Damascus.

The PLO's Fatah, which renounced terrorism in 1988, became the political power behind the Palestinian Authority – Israel's best hope of peace. The Authority was accused of taking insufficient steps to curtail the activities of Hezbollah-backed Hamas and PIJ. It is no coincidence that a renewal of the Palestinian uprising began in September 2000, just three months after the Israeli withdrawal from southern Lebanon. Since then, according to IDF figures, Israel has endured over 18,000 terrorist incidents.

Also, during Operation Iraqi Freedom, US intelligence had indications that extremists from Hezbollah and PIJ infiltrated Iraq. Worryingly, Hezbollah has the ability to derail the MEPP and America's much vaunted Middle East Road Map. It also remains a much wider international threat. Hezbollah expert, Professor Judith Harik, observed that:

> Hezbollah also connects with other Islamic Fundamentalist groups as well as secular Arabs and Muslims in its efforts to fan the flames of the Palestinian revolt, which it believes will inevitably lead to the destruction of the 'Zionist infidels' and the return of all Palestinians to their homeland.[17]

Following the Palestinian Intifada in Gaza during 2001, the last thing Israel wanted was the opening of another front in the north against Hezbollah. To that end, the Bush administration leant on the Lebanese government to cripple Hezbollah by threatening sanctions. In the meantime in late March 2002, Israeli prime minister, Ariel Sharon, conducted Operation Protective Shield against Palestinian terrorist organisations in the Occupied West Bank territories.

Since 2004, according to Israeli intelligence sources, Hezbollah has spent $10 million a year supporting Palestinian terrorist activity against Israel. Those most closely affiliated with Hezbollah are Fatah's Tanzim and Palestinian Islamic Jihad.[18] Tension mounted after the Islamic Resistance Movement or Hamas electoral victory in the Palestinian legislative elections in January 2006, defeating Fatah and the Palestinian Authority.

While Hezbollah continued to fire rockets into northern Israel, Hamas escalated its attacks from the Gaza strip. In 2008 alone they fired over 3,000 rockets and mortar bombs into southern Israel.[19] In response, Israel launched Operation Cast Lead, invading Gaza on 27 December 2008, in an effort to destroy Hamas' infrastructure once and for all. Although all Israeli troops had withdrawn by 21 January 2009, the rocket attacks continued.[20]

Iran and Syria have no real desire to see Israel achieve peace with its neighbours, which leaves Hezbollah as a thorn not only in Lebanon and Israel's sides but also a threat to the Middle East Peace Process. America's continued support for Israel will also always be a cause of grievance in the Muslim world.

Chapter 12

The Mahdi and the Pharaohs

Sudan has long been considered a sleepy backwater overshadowed by its neighbours, Egypt and Ethiopia. Even during the Cold War, Moscow and Washington showed little inclination to meddle in the Sudanese civil war – they had far more interest in the Horn of Africa and the Suez Canal. Nevertheless, Sudan played a central role in the evolution and development of militant Islam, providing Osama bin Laden with sanctuary after he fell out with the Saudi royal family. Washington listed Sudan as a state sponsor of terrorism back in the early 1990s, accusing it of harbouring members of al-Qaeda, the Abu Nidal Organisation, Egyptian Islamic Jihad, Hamas, Hezbollah, Jamaat al-Islamiyya and Palestinian Islamic Jihad.

Following the attacks on the US embassies in East Africa, America launched cruise missile attacks on the al-Shifa pharmaceutical factory in Khartoum on 20 August 1998, because of its alleged production of chemical weapons and links to al-Qaeda. At the same time, the US also hit al-Qaeda camps in Afghanistan, where bin Laden had moved following his May 1996 expulsion from Sudan.

Afterwards, Khartoum showed a new willingness to co-operate with counter-terrorism measures by signing the International Convention for the Suppression of Financing of Terrorism. The following year, it ratified the International Convention for the Suppression of Terrorist Bombing, which prompted the UN Security Council to lift its terrorism-related sanctions in 2001. Sudan ratified the African Union's Convention on the Prevention and Combating of Terrorism in 2003, and the Sudanese government also signed additional counter-terrorism agreements with Algeria, Yemen and Ethiopia.

The Sudanese authorities raided a suspected terrorist training camp in Kurdufan State, in May 2003, arresting more than a dozen extremists and seizing illegal weapons. Four months later, a Sudanese court convicted a Syrian engineer and two Sudanese nationals of training a group of Saudis, Palestinians, and others to carry out attacks in Iraq, Eritrea, Sudan and Israel. Three years later, the US State Department said Sudan had become a strong partner in the war on terror. Despite this, Sudan remains firmly on the US list of state sponsors because it continues to support Palestinian Hamas. In addition, in 2006, after Washington proposed to send a peace-keeping force to war-torn Darfur, bin Laden released a tape urging his followers to go to Sudan to fight

UN troops. Similar messages were repeated the following year by Ayman al-Zawahiri and again by bin Laden himself.

Sudan has a very long history of Islamic militancy, dating back to the Mahdi revolt in the 1880s, which took control of Sudan from Britain and Egypt. The Mahdists embroiled Egypt, Eritrea and Ethiopia in a series of wars. Britain's strategic interest in Egypt – due to the Suez Canal – inevitably meant that it came into conflict with Mohammed Ahmed Ibn al-Sayyid Abdullah, who had proclaimed himself the 'Mahdi'.[1] He was a Summaniya Dervish or Muslim friar vowed to poverty and austerity, whose followers he simply referred to as 'Ansars' or supporters. British troops knew them as Dervishes or 'Fuzzy Wuzzies'.

British forces took control of Sudan from the Mahdists in the late 1890s and until independence in 1956 Britain ruled the country as two entities – the Muslim north and the Christian south. The two halves came to blows just before and after independence, sparking a civil war that dragged on until 1972. General Jaafar Nimeiry seized power in Khartoum in 1969 and three years later the Addis Ababa Agreement brought peace with the Anya Nya or Snake Poison guerrillas.

In the north, Sudan found itself split by the Ansar or Muslim Mahdists on the right and Sudanese Communist Party (the largest and best organised in Africa) on the left. The pro-Egyptian Khatmiya religious group also opposed the Ansar. On the extreme right, fanatical Islamic traditionalists took shape as the implacably anti-Communist 'Muslim Brotherhood', which eventually became the Sudanese National Islamic Front. Nimeiry quickly shifted his base support from the Communists to the Muslim Brotherhood and clamped down on the Communists. Following an assassination attempt, he then attacked Imam al-Mahdi's Ansar stronghold on Aba Island, on the White Nile. Supporting fighter-bombers flown by Egyptian pilots helped massacre some 3,000 Ansar civilians.[2] However, the power of the Ansar remained far from broken and al-Mahdi's nephew, Sadiq al-Mahdi, became leader.

The imposition of Islamic Shariah law in 1983, and Nimeiry ignoring the Christian south's autonomy, saw war break out again with the Sudanese People's Liberation Army. In Khartoum clashes flared between the Muslim Brotherhood and the Communists. It was also discovered that the Brotherhood was plotting against the government. Nimeiry was ousted and succeeded by Sadiq al-Mahdi, but the civil war dragged on, costing £570,000 a day and claiming 250,000 lives.[3] Khartoum was saddled with $12 billion in foreign debt and inflation running at 90 per cent. Also, 20,000 people were facing starvation in Sudan's western province of Darfur.

While some elements of Shariah had been implemented by Nimeiry's regime, al-Mahdi sought to impose it fully, much to the alarm of the southern Sudanese, thereby stifling any chance of peace.[4] In fact, he had pledged to abolish it, but his hands were tied by the National Islamic Front run by his brother-in-law, Dr Hassan al-Turabi. In the north, the Fundamentalist NIF emerged as an alternative to the Khatmiya and Mahdiya, which had dominated Sudanese politics for 100 years. The NIF was able to put 750,000 people onto the streets bearing placards, 'Shariah: it came with the people and with the people it will stay.'[5]

The ill-equipped, 54,000-strong, Sudanese Army struggled to contain the 50,000 fighters of the SPLA in the upper Nile, Baha el-Ghazal and Equatorial provinces. Military operations were a disaster for Khartoum. Some 2,000 Sudanese troops abandoned lonely government outposts and fled into Uganda; another 6,000 were trapped by the rebels in the southern city of Juba, where 300,000 people faced starvation.[6]

The military felt forced to intervene, and on 30 June 1989, Lieutenant-General Omar al-Bashir, supported by the NIF, seized power in Khartoum. The latter's aggressively Islamic stance soon brought it to loggerheads with its immediate neighbours, reducing Sudan to a troublesome pariah. Under al-Turabi's influence, Sudan became the most militant and Fundamentalist Sunni Islamic state in the world. Former US president, Jimmy Carter, and the presidents of Egypt, Kenya, Tunisia and Uganda, all visited Khartoum in a vain effort to get al-Bashir to adopt more moderated policies, but to no avail.

Militant al-Mahdi established links with Libya and began buying guns from the Iranians – moves that resulted in Egypt and Saudi Arabia cutting aid. Iran established a Sudanese Hezbollah in Khartoum to help export Islamic revolution throughout Africa. Al-Mahdi also offered support to the Palestinian group Hamas and the rebel *Front Islamique du Salut* in Algeria. In addition, al-Mahdi despatched weapon shipments to opposition groups in Algeria, Egypt, Eritrea, Ethiopia, Somalia, Uganda and Zaire.

After the 1991 Gulf War, bin Laden moved to Khartoum, as a guest of al-Turabi, from where he continued to aggravate the House of Saud. Although he moved to Sudan with up to 1,000 followers, he kept open his recruiting offices and guest houses in Pakistan, as well as his bases in Afghanistan, including the al-Farooq, Darunta, Khalden, Khalid ibn Walid and Jihad Wal training camps.

Fed up with his activities in 1994, Saudi King Fahd demanded the Sudanese surrender bin Laden's passport. When Egyptian Islamic Jihad, operating from Sudan, tried to kill the Egyptian president, Hosni Mubarak, the following year, the Sudanese government realised that it was host to a growing hornets' nest. As Egypt was an American ally, Washington joined Cairo to pressure Khartoum to expel bin Laden. Sudan offered to give him up to Saudi Arabia, but the Saudis did not want him home, causing trouble. Eventually, in May 1996, he returned to Afghanistan and the embrace of the Taliban.

e architects of the rise of militant Islam: Osama bin Laden, leader of al-Qaeda and Ayman Zawahiri, former leader of Egyptian Islamic Jihad. Despite the $25 million bounty, both men oided capture following 9/11.

Looking like Iraqi Feyadeen, these fighters are actually Palestinian Liberation Organisation commandos. Saudi Arabia sought to radicalise the PLO, as it did the Afghan Mujahideen. In turn, Iran helped radicalise Lebanese Hezbollah and Palestinian Hamas.

Beirut, the cradle of terror that spawned the PLO, Hezbollah and Hamas. In 82 Israel outraged the Arab orld by occupying southern banon and driving the PLO from the city.

The Soviet invasion of Afghanistan in December 1979 sparked off an unforeseen chain of events th
fuelled the global rise of militant Islam. Holy War was declared on the Soviet armed forces.

Pakistan's tribal areas became a haven for the Afghan
Mujahideen and their foreign backers following
Moscow's military intervention in Kabul.

About 35,000 Islamic militants from over forty Muslim
states poured into Afghanistan to fight Jihad against the
Soviets. In total, over 100,000 radicals were exposed to
the teaching of Jihad in Afghanistan and Pakistan.

The official view of Moscow's involvement in Afghanistan: in reality the ten-year intervention cost 50,000 Soviet casualties. It also helped bring the Soviet Union to its knees.

Ultimately, the rag-tag armies of the Mujahideen, with the backing of America, Pakistan and Saudi Arabia, humiliated the Soviet armed forces.

Osama bin Laden was incensed when US troops were sent to defend Saudi Arabia in 1991, despite assurances that they would leave once Kuwait was liberated. This proved a hollow promise.

Following the withdrawal from Afghanistan, the Soviet Union's waning military power and ailing economy heralded its demise. This coincided with Jihadists moving from Afghanistan into Central Asia.

A knocked-out Soviet armoured personnel carrier on the streets of Baku. Moscow's treatment of the Soviet Muslim republics in the Transcaucasus and Central Asia also fuelled militant Islam.

Algeria was one of the first countries to experience 'blowback' from Afghanistan. The security forces' bitter struggles with Algerian militants drove the latter into Europe, thereby spreading Jihad.

eft) President Bouteflika sought to contain the Islamist movement inspired by Algerian Afghan *eterans during the late 1990s, with little help from the international community.

ight) In the wake of the collapse of the Soviet Union, the tiny Islamic republic of Chechnya, under *esident Dudayev, sought to break away from Moscow. The Russian military response resulted in *eign Islamists flocking to support the beleaguered Chechens during two bloody wars.

e international Muslim community was appalled by the destruction wrought on the city of *ozny* and triggered a terrorist campaign against Moscow.

The failure of the West to save the Muslims of Bihac, Gorazde, Sarajevo and Srebrenica saw Jihadists flocking to the aid of the Bosniaks.

Bosnians welcome Turkish peace-keepers. The Clinton administration sought to distract attention from its secret military support for the Bosniaks via Iran by publicly courting the moderate Muslim states.

Russian peace-keepers searching for Kosovo Liberation Army weapons. Kosovo proved less receptive to the Islamists than Bosnia: the KLA sided with NATO

ming the Taliban was never a problem as, by the 1990s, both Afghanistan and Pakistan were vash with weapons courtesy of the CIA.

amic militants first made their presence felt in Saudi Arabia with the bombing of Khobar Towers 1996: it would take another seven years for things to get really out of hand.

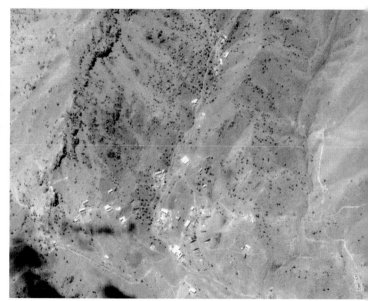

Zhawar Kili terrorist camp in Afghanistan, just prior to Washington's retaliatory missile strikes in 1998, following attacks on the US embassies in East Africa.

Washington also attacked the El-Shifa pharmaceutical plant in Khartoum in 1998. During the 1990s, Sudan became the world's most militant and fundamentalist Sunni state, offering support to numerous Islamic militant movements including al-Qaeda.

The American Predator unmanned aerial vehicle, armed with Hellfire missiles, was being developed by the CIA and USAF to hunt bin Laden just before 9/11.

Mujahideen veteran, Ahmad Shah Massoud, was instrumental in resisting the rise of the Taliban. Al-Qaeda agents assassinated him just two days before 9/11.

Manhattan's skyline showing the Twin Towers of New York's World Trade Center, visible in the upper left.

That fateful moment on 9/11. Osama bin Laden was immediately named prime suspect for the attacks.

The damage to the Pentagon is clearly visible on the lower right, following the 9/11 airliner attacks.

After 9/11, Taliban tribal leaders offered to surrender Osama bin Laden to Saudi Arabia only if America produced evidence of his complicity.

Ousting the Taliban was achieved quickly, but tracking down bin Laden in the mountains of Afghanistan and Pakistan proved a fruitless exercise in the winter of 2001–2002.

The destruction of the caves at Tora Bora, where the Taliban and al-Qaeda made a half-hearted last stand to cover bin Laden's escape. Instead of concentrating on Afghanistan, America lashed out at Iraq.

A French Army reconnaissance vehicle patrolling the streets of Kabul in support of ISAF in January 2002. Controlling the provinces proved far more difficult.

British troops hunting Taliban and al-Qaeda fighters in the spring of 2002.

A German armoured personnel carrier guarding Kabul airport in the summer of 2003. German and other NATO forces soon came under fatal attack by a resurgent Taliban, which had regrouped in Pakistan.

Following the collapse of Iraq's regular armed forces in early 2003, the irregular Feyadeen Saddam resistance soon took to the streets.

By mid-2003 the Coalition in Iraq was facing a growing insurgency, with Jihadists flowing over the Syrian border to join Abu Musab al-Zarqawi's 'al-Qaeda in Iraq'. Its tactics were brutal and uncompromising.

US troops were forced to wrestle back control of a number of Iraqi cities from al-Qaeda-inspired militants in 2004, including Fallujah.

Iraqi soldiers being trained by American and British instructors. The future of Iraq ultimately rests with its armed forces.

Pakistan's North West Frontier was the scene of the great game between the British and Russian empires. Following the Soviet invasion of Afghanistan and the rise of the Taliban, Pakistan's western provinces became so destabilised as to threaten the very fabric of the country.

Backing the Taliban and Kashmiri separatist groups fighting India has come back to haunt Pakistan.

Despite support from NATO the Afghan National Army struggled to assert its authority or contain the resurgent Taliban across Afghanistan.

Some argue that Washington's invasion of Iraq created a new generation of Islamic terrorists who will seek revenge on the US homeland.

As well as hosting Egyptian Islamic Jihad, Sudan gave sanctuary to the Eritrean Islamic Jihad Movement, led by Khalil Mohammed Amer. This organisation's predecessors emerged in the mid-1970s, having split from the Eritrean Liberation Front, which had been fighting for independence from Ethiopia. In 1988, the various Sudanese-backed Islamic groups, including the Jabhat Tahrir al-Iritriyya al-Islamiyya al-Wataniyya (the National Eritrean Islamic Liberation Front), al-Intifada al-Islamiyya (Islamic Awakening) and the Munzamat al-Ruwwad al-Muslimin al-Iritria (the Organisation of Eritrean Pioneer Muslims), merged to form the EIJM. It is also variously known as the Abu Suhail Organisation, the Eritrean Islamic Reform Movement, the Eritrean Islamic Salvation Movement and the Eritrean Islamic Party for Justice and development.

Following Eritrean independence in 1993, the EIJM opposed the new ELF government under President Isaias Aferweki. A militant faction emerged, under a former Afghan veteran, Shaykh Abu Suhail, who is believed to have had links with al-Qaeda. However, Eritrea and the EIJM have little to offer the wider global Islamist movement. From Khartoum, the EIJM only operates in western Eritrea, attacking government, rather than Western, targets. Its most notable attacks occurred in 2003 and 2006.

Similarly, during the mid-1980s, Khartoum turned a blind eye to the presence of Ugandan opposition movements, such as the Ugandan National Liberation Army and the People's Democratic Movement, operating from southern Sudan. Guns were readily available along the border with Sudan and Kenya, where up to 20,000 Ugandan rebels lurked.[7] Sudan also allowed 2,000 Libyan troops to operate against neighbouring Chad from its soil, though Khartoum finally asked them to leave in April 1987, following Libya's defeat in Chad.[8]

Khartoum did not sign a peace agreement with the Christian south until January 2005, which granted it autonomy for six years, to be followed by a referendum on independence. In the meantime, war broke out in Darfur, with government-backed militias going on the rampage in an effort to stamp out the Sudanese Liberation Movement. Attempts at a peace settlement come to nothing, leaving the problem festering.

The West's – particularly Britain's – interest in Egypt became irreversible once that vital strategic waterway, the Suez Canal, opened in 1869, greatly shortening the sailing distance to India. Once it had turned away from its military love affair with Moscow, Egyptian stability became a cause for concern. The issue of security has always been a key worry for the Suez Canal Authority. The threat of the Canal being closed for any length of time is something that haunts the Egyptian government. It is one of Egypt's main sources of foreign currency, bringing in up to $2 billion annually. It was closed in 1956 and again in 1967 by military action. In fact, following the 1967 Arab-Israeli War, it was closed for eight long years.

The wellspring of many Islamist groups is the Muslim Brotherhood, founded in Egypt in 1928 by Hassan al-Banna, with the ideological aim of creating a true Islamic society, where all institutions – including the government – obey strict Islamic principles. Although it disavowed violence and denies any links with militant groups, it was banned in Egypt in 1954. And yet, although the group is illegal, it is tolerated because of its non-violent stance. The Egyptian media has even declared the Muslim Brotherhood a possible moderate Islamic opposition party – not the rather sinister group that it is usually (and historically) depicted.

Cairo faces not only the risk of anti-US sentiment but also Islamic terrorism from indigenous groups, such as al-Jihad and the Islamic Group (both offshoots of the Muslim Brotherhood), whose senior leadership are also members of al-Qaeda. Both groups are proscribed under the UK's 2000 Terrorism Act. The Islamic Group has a non-terrorist arm that runs social welfare programmes in Cairo, Alexandria and southern Egypt. Al-Jihad specialises almost exclusively in assassinations. The country suffered from Islamic-inspired violence in the early 1990s in Upper Egypt, though by the late 1990s the government had curtailed it.

As with many Muslim countries, the British Foreign Office warns of the danger of 'indiscriminate' terrorist attack and there is a latent anti-Western terrorist threat still in Egypt. The Islamic Group is assessed to have a few cells still operating in Egypt, Sudan, the UK and Yemen, supported by funds from Osama bin Laden, Iran and Islamic charities. Additionally, according to the UN's International Maritime Organisation (IMO), multi-million dollar cargoes are at risk of being stolen in the eastern Mediterranean by an organised criminal group. NATO's Operation Active Endeavour continues to be vigilant in the Mediterranean. According to the al-Jazeera news agency, on 3 June 2004, Turkish authorities impounded a Ukrainian ship bound for Egypt after it was found to be carrying two containers of undeclared weapons. Egypt is also a co-operative participant of NATO's Mediterranean Dialogue Programme.

Egyptian Islamic militancy first came to a head in 1981, when al-Jihad assassinated President Sadat. While the Egyptian government rounded up the perpetrators, once in prison they formed the basis of what was later to become Egyptian Islamic Jihad and al-Gama'a al-Islamiyya or the Islamic Group. Among the Cairo militants was Ayman al-Zawahiri. The Islamic Group was formed from militant students after the Muslim Brotherhood renounced violence. Their spiritual leader, Omar Abdel-Rahman, was implicated in the 1993 World Trade Center Bombing and is serving life imprisonment in America.

While four of Sadat's killers were condemned to death, the others – once they had served their brief prison sentences – fled to Afghanistan and Pakistan to join the Mujahideen. Egyptian Islamic Jihad was born in Peshawar and although it paid lip service to Abud al-Zumur – a former Egyptian intelligence officer and plotter who was still in prison – Sayyed Imam al-Sharif headed it. In Afghanistan the Egyptians soon gained influence with bin Laden and moved to sideline his mentor, Abdullah Azzam, who had been a driving force behind galvanising foreign support for the Afghan Mujahideen. Al-Zawahiri took control of EIJ in 1991.

Back in Egypt, the government scored a major intelligence coup against the militants, when their membership director was caught with the entire computerised membership database. In one fell swoop, al-Jihad lost some 800 members. In retaliation, in August 1993, Islamists targeted the Egyptian Interior Minister, who was championing the crackdown. The suicide bomber killed himself but not the minister. The adoption of suicide tactics was thought to be as a result of contact with Hezbollah, as al-Zawahiri supporter, Ali Mohamed, had been sent to Lebanon for training.

In November 1993, the group then made an attempt on the Egyptian prime minister. The terrorists missed their target and blew up a girls' school, injuring twenty-one and killing a pupil. This, coupled with al-Gama'a al-Islamiyya's ongoing campaign, which would leave 1,300 dead, resulted in 280 members of Egyptian Islamic Jihad being rounded up. In Sudan they fell out with the government and bin Laden and al-Zawahiri and the others were ordered out. In Afghanistan, the Egyptians had little choice but to get further into bed with al-Qaeda.

Still the Islamists assaulted the Egyptian government. Under the command of Mustafa Hamza, EIJ, in league with al-Gama'a al-Islamiyya and Sudanese intelligence, tried to murder the Egyptian president, Hosni Mubarak, during a conference of the Organisation of African Unity, in Ethiopia, in June 1995. Fortunately for Mubarak, the attackers' rocket-propelled grenade failed to launch and the president escaped unharmed in his bullet-proof limousine. In Pakistan, as a foretaste of the al-Qaeda bombings of the US embassies in East Africa, on 19 November 1995, the Egyptian embassy in Islamabad was blown up, killing sixteen and injuring sixty.

The Islamic Group's terror campaign through the 1990s greatly harmed Egypt's economy, particularly tourism. The Egyptian government's response was a repressive clampdown that involved the arrest of 20,000 Islamists. The Non-violence Initiative brokered in July 1997 resulted in 2,000 being released. Islamic Jihad sought to derail the initiative, enlisting the Islamic Group's leaders, Mustafa Hamza and Rifai Ahmed Taha, who were exiled in Afghanistan.

Most shockingly, Islamists attacked tourists at the Temple of Hatshepsut (Deir el-Bahri) on 17 November 1997, slaying fifty-eight plus four Egyptians, in a forty-five-minute massacre. Average Egyptians were horrified by this wanton bloodlust, and the tourist industry all but collapsed overnight, losing Egypt millions of dollars. The Egyptian people completely rejected Jihadi terrorism, while government repression and violation of human rights became even harsher, as it sought to keep the lid on the Islamists.

By the late 1990s, al-Jihad was dwindling and in June 2001 it merged with al-Qaeda to form Qaeda al-Jihad. Three years later, the network merged with Jordanian militant Abu Mus'ab al Zarqawi's Iraq-based group, which became Qa'idat al-Jihad fi Bilad al Rafidayn or 'al-Qaeda in the Land of Two Rivers'. The Egyptian Islamic Group renounced violence in 2003 and in response the government released 1,000 prisoners. A similar number were released three years later. A split in the organisation's leadership was signalled on 5 August 2006, when al-Zawahiri announced a new alliance between al-Qaeda and the Islamic Group.

Egypt has continued to suffer from a spate of terrorist attacks against Western tourists, culminating in the bombing of the Mövenpick Hotel in Sharm el-Sheikh in the Sinai in July 2005, which left at least eighty-eight dead. This followed on from the bomb attacks that killed thirty-four people at the Hilton hotel in Taba, north of Sharm el-Sheikh. President Mubarak's response was unequivocal: 'This cowardly and criminal act, which is aimed at destabilising Egypt, will reinforce our determination to press the battle against terror through to its eradication.'[9] With around 8 million tourists visiting Egypt every year, the authorities took swift measures to tighten security: most notably in Sharm el-Sheikh traffic was banned from the town centre. One official said: 'We have to do everything in our power to reassure visitors that Egypt is safe and that there will be no repeat of 2005.'[10]

A British defence source in Cairo pointed out: 'Egypt has gone a long way to successfully suppressing any terrorist threat there may be within the country.' However, they caution that Suez, 'is a route vital to the strategic interests of a number of Western countries; as such it could be an attractive target to any terrorist organisation seeking to upset Egyptian stability'.[11]

Chapter 13

Middle East Sojourn: Saudi Arabia

Saudi Arabia, ruled by the royal House of Saud, enjoys significant international prestige because of its unique role within the Islamic faith and because of its vast oil wealth. Politically, though, it remains a feudal society, divided between those seeking greater liberalisation and those greater Islamic adherence. The country bears a degree of responsibility for the rise of militant Islam: despite claims of being a modern progressive state, it has pursued a dangerous dual-track policy.

Saudi Arabia's status plummeted after 9/11 (fifteen of the nineteen hijackers were Saudis). Tellingly, the US report on 9/11 removed most references to Saudi Arabia. Even before then, America was beginning to tire of its troublesome and, some might argue, ungrateful, ally. In the mid-1990s, Saudi nationals bombed a US military facility in Riyadh, followed by the high-profile attack on Khobar Towers.

While Sunni-dominated Saudi Arabia encouraged Jihad in Afghanistan, it also sought to distance itself from such ideas, by condemning those who employed Islam to justify violence in the name of being holy warriors. In 1984, Abdullah Naseef, secretary general of the Muslim World League in Mecca, condemned terrorism:

> Islam condemns violence of any nature [. . .] it is unthinkable that any honest [Islamic] scholar would condone crimes against humanity, destruction of installations and terrorism against innocent people committed under the pretext of Jihad. Jihad was instituted to further the causes of justice, dignity and Koranic law through a formal declaration of war against forces bent on undermining these values and rights.[1]

He went on to add that militant Fundamentalist movements were 'abusers' of the faith. Britain and America – so reliant on Saudi oil, Saudi support in Afghanistan and in the midst of selling the kingdom billions of dollars worth of arms – preferred to believe this rather than the alternative. The West and Saudi Arabia created a rod for their own backs.

Behind the scenes, Riyadh developed a very specific agenda – one of keeping the West happy, while at the same time remaining at the forefront of the

Islamic World. The demands of Saudi Wahhabism made this a difficult task. In the West there was always an underlying consensus that the Saudis were spoilt hypocrites. They always seem to say one thing at home and do the reverse when abroad. On the one hand, they were the devoted custodians of the two holy places, while on the other, in Knightsbridge and 5th Avenue, they were rich playboys who did not want for anything. This attempt at having the best of both worlds was to come back and bite them, when al-Qaeda came home to roost in the mid-2000s.

Yasser Arafat, leader of the PLO, found himself discussing Jihad when he visited Riyadh in mid-January 1986, seeking funding. The Saudis kept the PLO financially afloat with a massive annual $20 million subsidy.[2] Arafat desperately needed more money because the PLO's various factions were scattered after their expulsion from Lebanon in 1982. While his HQ was in Tunisia, he had bases to maintain in Iraq, Jordan and North Yemen.

Arafat discovered the Saudis wanted to make the PLO more Islamic in outlook. It seemed that they intended to radicalise the PLO, as they were doing with the Mujahideen in Afghanistan, in the belief that this would make Arafat's organisation much more effective. Some saw this as playing with fire, in the light of Iran's Shia revolution being preached at Saudi's Shia minority. Saudi Arabia should have taken heed of the Islamic Jihad group in Egypt, which was trying to murder President Mubarak. During the 1980s Islamic Jihad made itself felt across Europe, like the Abu Nidal Organisation, but it was soon seeking regime change in Egypt.

Ironically, Arafat had brought this upon himself, for, in a speech made in Khartoum, on 15 October 1985, he had invoked Jihad, saying:

> The holy war and the armed struggle will escalate [...] I tell [President] Reagan and his agents in our Arab world that the will of the Arab nation is from the will of Allah. Therefore, the Arab nations will be victorious.[3]

Arafat's use of Jihad and reference to the will of Allah was tacit admission of the Islamisation of the PLO. This process, in fact, had started years before, and Arafat himself had been a member of the Muslim Brotherhood in Egypt, which initially preached Jihad. In hindsight, it seemed odd – in light of Arafat being Sunni and the PLO's numerous factions being ardently leftist – that he should adopt the Shia revolutionary model. It was now, however, that the Sunnis began to emulate Shia-style attacks, which they had virtually no hope of surviving.

Surprisingly, few Saudis flocked to the PLO cause, with most preferring to fight the Soviets rather than the Israelis. Arab countries that did provide volunteers included Egypt, Iraq, Jordan and Yemen, most of whom were employed in staff jobs within the PLO's command structure. Hundreds of fighters were also provided by Bangladesh and Pakistan, with smaller numbers from India and Sri Lanka.[4] While Saudi Arabia's military support for the various Arab-Israeli conflicts was small, its financial support was considerable, as was its funding of the PLO. In the past, Saudi Arabia also rendered financial and military assistance to Jordan, Lebanon, Morocco, Yemen, Pakistan, Somalia, Sudan, Syria, Turkey and Iraq.

In contrast, it is estimated that 10,000 Saudis served in Afghanistan – coupled to rising numbers of unemployed and a readily available stream of guns from Iraq and Yemen, this provided an ideal breeding ground for al-Qaeda. Upon returning to Saudi Arabia, Osama bin Laden created a welfare organisation for 4,000 veterans, forming a cadre for al-Qaeda. After the Iraqi invasion of Kuwait in 1990 he offered to lead the resistance: instead, Riyadh turned to Washington. Affronted by calling on the assistance of infidels, bin Laden fell out with the Saudi royal family and was declared persona non grata. Publicly, the country tried to distance itself from its unwanted son: the Saudi media even accused him of 'putting the whole Islamic nation on a butcher's block'.

It was not lost on the world that Saudi Arabia and UAE recognised the Taliban as the legitimate government of Afghanistan. Saudi backers also supplied money and arms to the Islamic Moment of Uzbekistan (IMU) via the Gulf. The Taliban and IMU were funded through drug money and the US Drug Enforcement Agency (DEA) was only too aware of these activities. A DEA official has commented: 'Through the taxation of illicit opium production, the Taliban were able to fund an infrastructure capable of supporting and protecting Osama bin Laden and the al-Qaeda organisation.'[5]

To avoid trouble at home, the Gulf States tried to buy off the radicals, allowing funding to reach them and permitting them to use their facilities. The Taliban, al-Qaeda and the IMU used their ports for a range of criminal activities, including drug-smuggling. The Emirate of Dubai, in particular, was identified by Western intelligence as a centre for extremist money-laundering and banking. The bin Laden family reportedly own large areas of property in Dubai. Additionally, the black sheep of the family, Osama bin Laden, is believed to have used banks – such as the Dubai Islamic Bank – to move funds about. The US government has since put pressure on UAE to prevent him doing so. Notably, though, Saudi Arabia and the UAE were not members of the International Financial Action Task Force (FATF), which has been helping curtail terrorist funding (though the Gulf Co-operation Council has corporate membership, which they are members of).

In fact, Dubai, rather than Peshawar or Karachi in Pakistan, became the main centre for arms and fund-raising for the Taliban and IMU during the late 1990s. Saudi intelligence turned a blind eye or actively acquiesced in such activity. While the Taliban was securing power in Afghanistan, Saudi funding, fuel and trucks were routed through Dubai's Port Rashid to Kandahar. Goods smuggled from Dubai helped make Mazar-e-Sharif in Afghanistan a key staging post for the massive smuggling trade between Pakistan, Central Asia and Iran. Additionally, electronic goods from Dubai, Sharjah and other Gulf ports are still smuggled into Pakistan by the Pakistani transport Mafia. In recent years, it has come to light that children have been smuggled from Pakistan to serve as camel jockeys in Dubai: the UAE's Federal Investigations Agency (FIA) has been implicated in facilitating this ugly trade.

The scale of the problem of drug-smuggling in the Gulf is considerable and goes all the way to the top. Certainly, if the FIA turns a blind eye to human trafficking then it almost certainly does the same with drugs. The UK has very good intelligence on who the chief culprits are, but is powerless because of the diplomatic and economic ramifications. An intelligence source confirmed that senior members of certain key Gulf States' governments are complicit in drug smuggling at the highest levels, but cannot act on this information because of the row that would ensure. In the meantime, all the Royal Navy and USN can do is chase the smugglers, while the backers remain at large.

According to the United Nations Office on Drugs and Crime, there 'appears' to be no significant transit trafficking through Saudi Arabia and there is no significant drug production reported in the country. Saudi is party to all three international drug control conventions. It also has bilateral co-operation agreements with Jordan, Syria and Turkey, and is hosting a US customs advisory team. In recent years, the DEA has been more concerned about the smuggling of drugs into the region for use as much as onward transit. In particular, the DEA has highlighted the smuggling of Fenethylline (an amphetamine-like drug) via Turkey into the Arabian Peninsula for recreational purposes.

Saudi Arabia's security has always been a priority because it holds the largest proven oil reserves in the world. Since the 1973 Arab-Israeli War, Saudi pre-eminence has increased, for while it lacks significant military strength, it has a leading OPEC role in oil pricing, production and embargoes. To counter regional threats, Riyadh embarked on one of the most expensive procurement programmes outside the superpowers.[6] In light of the Iran-Iraq war, defending Saudi's huge airspace became a top priority, as well as its vulnerable maritime lines of communication. The end of the Iran-Iraq War did not herald a halt to this regional arms build-up. Washington became Riyadh's single largest arms supplier, though the pro-Israeli lobby in the US Congress sought to derail this relationship. In the late 1980s, the pro-Israeli lobby forced Saudi to seek arms from Britain and France. The Anglo-Saudi deal of July 1988 sealed a long-term defence relationship with Britain, to the detriment of the US and France.

Also, Saudi Arabia sought to expand its paramilitary forces because of the threat of Fundamentalist subversion and Iranian-inspired riots at Mecca. Notably, the 1979 Grand Mosque Occupation in Mecca and pro-Iranian demonstrations in the eastern provinces required the deployment of 20,000 troops.

Only 5–10 per cent of Saudi's population are Shia, the rest are Sunni. This situation boiled over when Saudi police clashed with Iranian pilgrims in Mecca in July 1987.

Three years later, Osama bin Laden was outraged at the Iraqi invasion of Kuwait and sought to offer the services of his Afghan veterans to the House of Saud. He reasoned a Muslim army should defend his homeland and to that end he promised 10,000 Mujahideen, who, he claimed, would be more than a match for Saddam Hussein's Republican Guard.[7] Five days after the invasion bin Laden was incensed by the news that America would send troops to defend Saudi Arabia, despite reassurances by the Saudi government that the Americans would leave once Kuwait was liberated.

In response to the Kuwaiti crisis, the US instigated Operation Desert Shield, a massive multinational effort to defend Saudi Arabia. The Arab states of the Gulf Co-operation Council only deployed 10,000 men, though in the Gulf region they had 150,000 men and 800 tanks available. The largest Arab contingent came from Egypt, with 47,000 troops and Syria committed 19,000 men. In return for its support, Syria received $1 billion from Saudi Arabia.

Saudi Arabia, having for so long cultivated leading Islamists around the world, was dismayed at their response to Saddam Hussein's actions. Former British ambassador to Saudi Arabia, Sir Alan Munro recalled:

> Prominent among the targets of this Saudi attention were Abbas al Madani in Algeria, Rashid al Ghannouchi in Tunisia, Hassan al-Turabi in Sudan, and the most hard-line of the leaders among the Afghan Mujahideen, Gulbuddin Hekmatyar. Yet none of these made an effort to disguise an opportunistic support for Saddam Hussein in his confrontation over Kuwait. It was a chastening experience for Saudi Arabia.[8]

It also meant that, shortly, they would find bin Laden's message much more appealing than that of the House of Saud.

Saddam tried to invoke Jihad against the Coalition, calling it an infidel intrusion into the Islamic world. During the Iran-Iraq war, Saddam had gone from progressive Muslim to traditionalist and claimed lineage to the Prophet Mohammed. Few were convinced by such credentials, however, and all he got was verbal support from the Palestinian groups. When 400 leading Islamic figures met in Mecca, on 13 September 1990, they not only refused to recognise Saddam's call to Jihad, but also granted Kuwait the right to declare holy war against Iraq.[9] The month before, the Arab league had voted in Cairo to send troops to Saudi Arabia and demanded Iraq's withdrawal from Kuwait.

After the liberation of Kuwait by US military forces, bin Laden, as noted by Indian writer, M.J. Akbar:

went public with his resentment. He would make his accusations more explicitly later: the Saudi family had betrayed the Muslim people, befriended Christians and Jews, and were no longer fit custodians of the holy places. They would, he said, disperse and disappear like the Persian Royal family [Shah of Iran]. As for the Americans, he promised they would leave Saudi Arabia in coffins.[10]

For a long time, the view prevailed that, as long as the pro-Western House of Saud remained ensconced and popular, the strong US-Saudi defence tie would remain the cornerstone for safeguarding Western interests in the Gulf, but by 2003 Iraq offered Washington a possible alternative.

In the meantime, bin Laden's criticism of the Saudi government and the deployment of US troops there led to his expulsion from Saudi Arabia in 1992, the loss of Saudi citizenship, his bank accounts frozen, and his disinheritance from the bin Laden fortune. The US State Department estimated he stood to inherit up to $300 million, although this figure has been widely contested.[11] Bin Laden headed for Afghanistan via Pakistan. But Afghanistan was in the midst of an appalling civil war and the offer of sanctuary in Khartoum by Dr Hassan al-Turabi, the leader of the National Islamic Front, seemed a much better option. This would be a good place from which to conduct Jihad.

According to the US State Department: 'Saudi donors and unregulated charities have been a major source of financing to extremist and terrorist groups over the past twenty-five years.' Indeed, 9/11 poured oil on criticism that Saudi was involved in terrorism or was lax in acting against such groups.[12] Although Saudi Arabia recognised the PLO as the legitimate representative of the Palestinian people, there are unsubstantiated claims that the Saudis also supported its rival, Hamas (believed to constitute 50 per cent of its operating budget).[13]

Since 9/11, Saudi has said that it is committed to the fight against terrorist financing, especially once international terrorism had come home to roost. Indeed, the al-Qaeda-affiliated terrorist attacks in Saudi Arabia during 2003–6 focused the Saudis' efforts. It is impossible to quantify money passing through or originating from Saudi Arabia that ended up in terrorist hands. The Saudi banking system made it almost impossible to trace transfers – income records are not kept for tax purposes, and, in any event, most people operate on cash transactions. To further hamper the audit trail, *zakat* or Muslim charitable contributions are an obligation and make up one of the five 'pillars of Islam'. Such contributions are normally given anonymously.

The line between private and public donations to Islamic charities is often blurred. There have been allegations that the Saud family, numbering some 5,000, along with other senior officials, acted independently of the government. While progress has been made in combating terror funding, individuals in

Saudi Arabia and other Gulf states are known to have bankrolled the Sunni insurgency in Iraq.[14]

Washington views Riyadh's attempts to clamp down on al-Qaeda and other Fundamentalist groups as half-hearted, though Riyadh claims it agreed to end the handling of bin Laden's money by Saudi banks. Saudi Arabia also reportedly now monitors about 200 charities, which provide funding for Islamic projects abroad. In March 2002, in a raid on a Saudi-based charity in Sarajevo, Bosnia, FBI agents retrieved a handwritten list of twenty alleged al-Qaeda financers. Bin Laden referred to this group as 'the Golden Chain'.

The 9/11 Commission, while exonerating the Saudi government, did highlight that al-Qaeda had raised funds in Saudi Arabia. It also pointed out that charities such as the al-Haramain Islamic Foundation, which had significant Saudi sponsorship and links to the Royal family, 'may' have diverted funds to al-Qaeda. It also highlighted that al-Qaeda and bin Laden used the informal financial network supporting the Mujahideen in Afghanistan set up in the 1980s by senior Saudi and Gulf individuals. Al-Haramain was finally dissolved in late 2004.

Saudi Abdullah Duhajman, founder and head of the Islamic Balkan Center in Zenica, also sponsored the World Bureau for Islamic Call. The latter was founded for the mobilisation of Muslims for the global Jihad. During the conflict in Bosnia, Duhajman was reportedly involved with the Mujahideen el-Mujahed unit. He was also in touch with an Islamic terrorist organisation named the 'Muslim Brothers', and there are some indications of collaboration with bin Laden (some unconfirmed sources suggest that Abdullah Duhajman may be an alias for bin Laden himself).

To restore Saudi Arabia's position, King Fahd established the Saudi Non-governmental Commission on Relief and Charity Work Abroad in February 2004. This became the body through which all private Saudi donations for international distribution should flow. The following year, the Saudi Council of Ministers decided all charitable overseas contributions should go through the commission. There have also been concerns over the spread of radical Islam through Saudi-funded *madrassahs* or religious schools in Bangladesh, Bosnia-Herzegovina, Indonesia, Pakistan, Spain and even America teaching Saudi Wahhabism.

It is clear that terrorist attacks and internal security problems in Saudi Arabia forced the House of Saud to take even greater steps to curtail the financing of terrorism. This became something of an imperative following the 2003 attacks on residential and office compounds targeting the Saudi government and Westerners. By the summer of 2003, all American combat troops had left Saudi Arabia (having shifted to Qatar), thereby removing a major source of friction in the eyes of some Muslims.

In the face of the escalating terrorist problem in Saudi Arabia, and America scaling down its military presence, there is growing disquiet over Saudi Arabia's future stability. Notably, Washington's post 9/11 report omitted sections on Saudi Arabia, either because they indicated complicity or were considered too inflammatory. Since the destruction of New York's World Trade Center, Riyadh has been fighting a rearguard PR exercise, having spent over $30 million trying to rehabilitate itself with the American public. Behind the scenes, some think the days of the pro-Western Royal House of Saud are numbered.

In this context, there is growing concern about Riyadh's ability to safeguard the Red Sea and, indeed, what would happen to the Royal Saudi Navy (RSN) if the House of Saud should fall to a Fundamentalist revolution? By 2003, thanks to Saudi oil dollars, it has been transformed into a powerful fleet, sporting some of the best vessels money can buy, with some 13,500 personnel (including 3,000 marines). It appears the RSN has already begun to exhibit Fundamentalist tendencies. On 1 May 2003 a Saudi naval officer shot a US contractor four times at King Abdul Aziz naval base in the eastern city of al-Jubail. The victim later died of his wounds. Riyadh glossed over the incident by stating the attacker, who conveniently escaped, had been 'dressed' like an RSN officer.

Perhaps tellingly, during Operation Iraqi Freedom, the RSN did not join the Global Coalition Task Force (GCTF) in the Gulf or the Combined Joint Task Force-Horn of Africa (CJT-HOA) in the Arabian Sea. A belligerent Saudi Western Fleet, from its headquarters at Jeddah and naval bases at Haqi, al-Wajh and Yanbu, could severely disrupt the Red Sea. Any escalation of the troubles in Saudi Arabia could threaten not just international commerce transiting the Red Sea, but ultimately the Suez Canal and the Gulf of Suez. This threat has to be tempered by the fact the Saudi Red Sea Fleet has very limited operational capabilities.[15] In the Gulf, America has many allies among the Gulf Co-operation Council (GCC) states, enabling the US Fleet to remain on station. Keeping a permanent US naval presence in the Red Sea would be far more difficult.

Any threat from RSN anti-shipping missiles pales into insignificance compared to Saudi's Chinese-supplied nuclear-capable CSS-2 (DF-3) intermediate range ballistic missiles. The Saudis are assessed to have some forty missiles and ten launchers with a range of almost 3,000km – in the wrong hands, they could menace the whole of the Middle East. Although the Saudis only have the conventional version, they can carry a 2-megaton nuclear warhead. They are stored in blast-proof silos deep in the Rub al Khali desert, but after nearly twenty years, who knows what condition the missiles are in?

There have been regular allegations that Saudi al-Qaeda has nuclear aspirations. It has been claimed that bin Laden had discussions with Pakistani nuclear scientists and tried to obtain radioactive waste from Bulgaria. Washington also claims he has sought enriched uranium on various occasions. According to some US experts, the possibility of bin Laden's organisation obtaining finished nuclear weapons, components or design expertise cannot be ruled out.

Immediately following the shooting at King Abdul Aziz naval base, Saudi Arabia received a major wake-up call on 12 May 2003, when al-Qaeda launched a co-ordinated suicide bombing on three compounds in Riyadh housing foreigners, leaving thirty-five people dead (including nine bombers) and injuring 190.[16] In response, the Saudi authorities arrested 600 suspects and killed some of those on a list of twenty-nine most wanted. Nonetheless, the attacks escalated. Most notably, a car bomb killed eighteen in another bombing in Riyadh.

The most critical period of attacks commenced on 21 April 2004, when a suicide bomber attacked a Riyadh police headquarters. The following month, there were more attacks in Riyadh, and also at Yanbu and Khobar. The latter two attacks were particularly worrying, as these explicitly targeted Saudi's vital oil industry and resulted in the death of Westerners. The 'al-Qaeda Organisation in the Arabian Peninsula' claimed responsibility for the Khobar attack and issued a statement, saying: 'The heroic Mujahideen of the Jerusalem Squad were able, by the grace of God, to raid the locations of American companies [...] specialising in oil and exploration activities and which are plundering the Muslims' resources ...'[17]

Security experts reasoned that bin Laden's al-Qaeda was attempting to bring down the House of Saud by forcing Western companies to withdraw from the kingdom. Abdul Aziz al-Mugrin, the leader of al-Qaeda in Saudi Arabia, indeed called for urban guerrilla warfare, identifying those steps required to unseat the royal family. Fortunately, Saudi security forces managed to kill al-Mugrin in June 2004.[18] The following month they shot his successor, Saleh al-Oufi. He was then replaced by Saud bin Hamoud al-Otaibi, making him the organisation's fourth leader in a year.[19]

Also in June, al-Qaeda militants gunned down two BBC journalists in broad daylight in the streets of Riyadh. Reporter, Frank Gardner, while he escaped with his life, was left unable to walk. His cameraman, Simon Cumbers, was killed. Rather foolishly they had been filming in the Suweidi district – a well-known al-Qaeda neighbourhood.

By late August 2004 the Saudi government was claiming that it had defeated the terrorist threat: 'We are past the stage of terrorism. What you are seeing today is the liquidation of the last pockets and hunting for the remaining [terrorists],' said Crown Prince Abdullah.[20] This was evidently untrue, as al-Qaeda shot a British citizen on 15 September 2004 in the car park of a Riyadh shopping complex. Nevertheless, a Saudi terrorist financier admitted in March 2008 that al-Qaeda in Saudi Arabia had been defeated and urged all remaining Jihadists to take flight to Yemen.[21] However, just to prove they were still very much alive, in December 2008, al-Qaeda launched an audacious attack against the US consulate in Jeddah, killing at least five foreign workers.

The question remains whether al-Qaeda in Saudi Arabia will ever be placated by the American military withdrawal, or whether its true goal is to topple the House of Saud, which it sees as tainted by its long relationship with Washington. It is feared that Saudi Arabia is ultimately incapable of countering the anger and hatred towards the West caused by the invasion of Iraq and America's continued support for Israel in the Palestinian conflict. In part, the House of Saud brought this internal terrorist threat upon itself, thanks to its dual-track policy of courting the West and the Islamists at the same time.

Chapter 14

East Africa: War is Finally Declared

While Somalia and Yemen were clearly recognised as problems by the international community, few felt that sleepy Kenya and Tanzania would be fertile grounds for Islamist militants. Even fewer could have conceived that, as a result of its actions in these two countries, al-Qaeda would find itself at war with America. In the Horn of Africa, Osama bin Laden was known to have cultivated links with the Islamic Jihad movement in Eritrea, the Eritrea Kinama Movement and the Red Sea Democratic Organisation, based in Sudan.[1] These links were then extended to rebel groups in the Ogaden region in south-eastern Ethiopia and Somalia. Terrorism penetrated even further than this.

Unfortunately, to the south, Kenya's Muslim-populated islands provided a haven for some of the region's most wanted terrorists. For example, Pate (situated near the maritime border with Somalia) was, for a while, the refuge of Fazul Abdullah Mohammed – suspected of involvement in the US embassy bombings in Kenya and Tanzania in 1998, as well as the 2002 bombing of the Kikambala Paradise Hotel, and the failed missile attack on an Israeli airliner. US marines have since kept the village where he stayed – before escaping to Somalia – under surveillance.[2]

Fatefully, Islamists struck, killing and injuring 5,000 in East Africa. The simultaneous car bomb attacks took place on the US embassies in the capitals of Dar es Salaam and Nairobi on 7 August 1998. In Nairobi, about 212 people were killed and an estimated 4,000 injured; in Dar es Salaam at least eleven were killed and eighty-five wounded. These attacks were linked to local members of al-Qaeda, bringing bin Laden and his organisation to international attention for the first time.

In order to assist with Washington's counter-terrorism efforts in the region, the Kenyan government permitted America to base troops on Lamu Island, just 50 miles south of the Kenyan-Somali border. Washington immediately accepted, as this allowed it to bolster its military and intelligence presence along the troubled Somali and Ethiopian borders. It also hoped that this might help slow the spread of radical Islam southwards. Suspects for the embassy bombings (including Fazul Abdullah Mohammed, mentioned above) had all lived on Lamu. Due to the island's poverty, it was a fertile recruiting ground for disenchanted Muslim youth: 'We are not thirsty for the blood of Europeans,' declared the local Imam of Pani Mosque, Mahmud Ahmed Abdulkadir,

> but this is now a global village and we see what is happening in Iraq, in Afghanistan, in Chechnya. If these things continue, we will see the hatred of the West they have in Somalia come down to this place.[3]

To head off such sentiment on Lamu, US marines embarked on a rapid hearts-and-minds campaign, helping to refurbish local classrooms. Locals, however, were concerned that Washington was planning to establish a base on Manda island, which is adjacent to Lamu and Pate islands. The latter is a strategic location for US intelligence. It is watched closely because, from there, you can only go north to the unpoliced border with Somalia. Furthermore, some Imams were not happy about the presence of US forces on Lamu, claiming it was part of a scheme to counter Islamic influence and Swahili culture in the region: 'The Americans don't want to heal the wounds from terror attacks. They want to be at the bottom of a place they suspect of breeding terrorism,' claimed Ustadh Idarus Mwenye, the principal of the Swafaa Islamic College of Shia Muslims.[4]

After the embassy bombings, Saddam Hussein's son, Uday, praised bin Laden as an 'Arab and Islamic hero'.[5] At the time, according to US intelligence sources, some Taliban leaders were urging bin Laden to leave Afghanistan and go to Iraq. Such a prospect alarmed Washington, as it would place al-Qaeda at Saddam's disposal and make it almost impossible to find bin Laden. Bruce Riedel, of the US National Security Council, warned Sandy Berger, National Security Advisor, that Saddam Hussein wanted bin Laden in Baghdad so as to step up the hunt for him in Afghanistan before he escaped.[6] In the meantime, a Taliban court ruled that bin Laden was 'a man without sin' in regard to the attacks in Kenya and Tanzania.

In retaliation for the East Africa attacks, President Clinton launched a two-pronged missile strike against al-Qaeda targets in Afghanistan and Sudan on 20 August 1998. For Clinton, it was a useful diversion from the Monica Lewinsky sex scandal he had embroiled himself in, but controversy raged as to the validity of striking the El-Shifa pharmaceutical factory in Sudan. Nonetheless, these actions signalled that Washington would no longer tolerate the activities of Osama bin Laden. Clinton severed relations with the Taliban government in Afghanistan and pressured the Saudis to negotiate with the Taliban to hand bin Laden over.

Gary Berntsen of the CIA's Counter-terrorism Center (which was concentrating on Islamic Jihad and Hezbollah at the time, rather than al-Qaeda) knew that the experts felt the missile strikes were a waste of time:

When I met with Mike Scheuer, the career intelligence analyst who had led the CIA bin Laden group, a few days after the US reprisal attacks, he was pissed [...] He said categorically that the destruction of bin Laden and his forces in Afghanistan could be accomplished only with direct intervention of some type of force on the ground.[7]

The attacks in East Africa were the final straw, and in December 1998, the Director Central Intelligence signed a memorandum declaring: 'We are at war.' While war may have finally been declared on al-Qaeda, the change of administration in America greatly slowed its counter-terrorism plans in the run up to 9/11.

Richard Clarke, head of the Counter-terrorism Group within the US National Security Council, was convinced that, in the wake of the subsequent bombing of the USS *Cole*, bin Laden would next strike American soil. To that end, he was advocating dealing al-Qaeda a devastating blow in Afghanistan. However, when he presented his strategy to Sandy Berger on 20 December 2000, the Clinton administration only had a month to go before George W. Bush took over (after a much disputed electoral count in Florida). Berger rightly felt that Bush would want to find his feet first before initiating any military action in Afghanistan. Ironically, democracy got in the way of fighting terrorism.

In his defence, during January 2001, Berger scheduled ten threat briefings by his staff for his successor, Condoleezza Rice and her deputy, Stephen J. Hadley. Most notably, on 3 January, Clarke presented his plan to attack al-Qaeda: specifically, it called for air strikes and Special Forces operations inside Afghanistan. His policy was that Islamist terrorists should be forced to fight and die for the Taliban rather than be permitted to wage global attacks against US interests (this plan, of course, was not instigated until eleven months later, in response to 9/11).

This briefing was a wake-up call for Rice, because, like so many people, her view of terrorism was mired in the old concepts of state-sponsored terrorism perpetrated by the likes of Iran, Iraq and Libya – this threat, posed by transnational Jihad, as espoused by bin Laden and al-Qaeda, seemed totally new to her.[8] George Tenet, Director CIA, stated in February 2001: 'The threat from terrorism is real, it is immediate, and it is evolving.'[9] No one in the Bush administration seemed to be listening.

The US Defense Department, fatefully, was gunning for Iraq, and Clarke's warnings and proposals fell by the wayside until it was too late. Saddam Hussein was the villain, not Osama bin Laden: he was seen as the bigger threat to Middle East stability. We will never know if President Bush had implemented Clarke's proposals, whether it would have been sufficient to stop 9/11.

It is notable that, when Bush's new administration replaced Clinton's, Secretary of State Colin Powell told officials in the US State Department to no longer use the term peace process when it came to the Israelis and Palestinians. It seemed that President Bush saw al-Qaeda, Saddam Hussein, the Arab-Israeli conflict and bringing democracy to the Middle East as inexorably linked. To the Bush administration's way of thinking, an American victory in Iraq would inevitably result in an Arab-Israeli settlement as a by-product. In reality, it beggared common sense linking the Israeli-Palestinian question with regime change in Baghdad.

In the meantime, in East Africa, it was not until May 2001 that four men were convicted for being involved in the embassy bombings. They were: Khalfan Khamis Mohamed (a 27-year-old Tanzanian), Mohamed Rashid Daoud al-Owhali (a 23-year-old Saudi), Wadih el Hafe (a 40-year-old Lebanese-born US citizen, who was accused of conspiracy), and Mohamed Sadeek Odeh (a 35-year-old Jordanian, accused of helping to plan the Kenyan bombing).

On the eve of 9/11, George Tenet, Director of the CIA, warned the US Senate Select Committee on Intelligence of the continued threat posed by global terrorism:

> Never in my experience, Mr Chairman, has American intelligence had to deal with such a dynamic set of concerns affecting such a broad range of US interests. Never have we had to deal with such a high quotient of uncertainty. With so many things on our plate, it is important always to establish priorities. For me, the highest priority must invariably be on those things that threaten the lives of Americans or the physical security of the United States. With that in mind, let me turn first to the challenges posed by international terrorism. We have made considerable progress on terrorism against US interests and facilities, Mr Chairman, but it persists.[10]

These were prophetic words indeed.

Post 9/11, many see Africa as an irredeemable basket-case, its countries stricken by civil conflict, despotic governments and crushing poverty. All of which are ideal breeding grounds for terrorists. In 2003, Marine General James L. Jones, Commander of US European Command (EUCOM), declared Africa the new front line on global terror. While the North African states of Algeria, Tunisia, Libya and Morocco were seen by EUCOM as the greatest terrorist threat, the failed states to the south were also a concern: 'You don't want to be reactive in about five years to some really serious problems,' warned General Jones.[11]

Across Africa and in its littoral waters, Washington has sought to improve bilateral ties in order to deny Islamic terrorists a safe haven, and to head off attacks on its interests in the region. This took shape in a sustained hearts-and-minds campaign, as well as counter-terrorism training and joint naval and military exercises. However, the scale of the task remains vast and the list of African countries touched by militant Islam is long.

The US Navy maintains a presence off the Horn of Africa, and there was talk of establishing a base in West Africa. Clearly, most prominent of Washington's efforts in East Africa is the presence of the Combined Joint Task Force-Horn of Africa (CJTF-HOA), stationed in Djibouti. According to Marine Major General Timothy Ghormley, who commanded CJTF-HOA, it comprises 800 personnel from all branches of the services and operates throughout Kenya, Sudan, Eritrea, Djibouti, Yemen and Ethiopia. In particular, from Djibouti, it can monitor terrorist activity in Yemen and Somalia, as well as liaising with the maritime component Combined Task Force 150 (CTF 150), patrolling the Arabian Sea, which was established at the beginning of the campaign against the Taliban and comprises warships from Germany, France, Pakistan, Canada, the UK and the US.[12]

While Washington's counter-terrorism strategy for Africa may be broad, its budget is not. According to the US State Department, the East Africa Counter-terrorism Initiative (EACTI) earmarked only $100 million, to improving police and judicial counter-terrorist capabilities in Djibouti, Eritrea, Ethiopia, Kenya, Uganda and Tanzania. The focus is primarily on military training for border and coastal security. Kenya, Uganda and Tanzania also aimed to set up a common intelligence and information network to monitor terrorism activities in the region.

Seven long years after the embassy bombings, senior regional military, police, immigration and customs officials met in Nairobi in September 2005 to devise a strategy to tackle the problem. In response, the US National Defence University honoured Kenya's National Security Intelligence Service chief, Brigadier General Wilson Boinett, for his achievements.

The US marines regularly stop off at Mombasa, and points north, for the training exercises, since they were first held in 1999, following the embassy bombings. In 2004 about 1,500 marines participated in exercises off Lamu Island's shores. They established a presence on both Lamu and Pate from where they can support the Kenyan Navy, conducting searches of local *dhows*. Members of the 13th US Marine Expeditionary Unit have also conducted hearts-and-minds work in the area.

Marines conduct regular exercises from Manda Bay Naval Station, which lies close to Lamu and Pate. The size of their presence caused some alarm, leading to a statement by the US embassy in Nairobi to the effect that there were only twenty-five US personnel temporarily staying at the Manda and not 400, as had been previously reported by the media. Locals have suspected that the Americans were planning to establish a marine base there. Across a narrow navigable channel from Manda is Lamu's Magogoni Naval Base, which was refurbished at great expense. Rumour has it that Washington footed the bill.

The Kenyan government always denied any plans to hand Manda over to the US Marines.

Neighbouring Tanzania has also been doing its bit. In early 2004 Tanzania launched a port security campaign for its international seaports, Dar es Salaam, Tanga, Mtwara and Zanzibar. This was driven by the International Maritime Organisation's (IMO) International Ship and Port Facility Security (ISPS) code. IMO inspectors toured Tanzania's ports and were not greatly impressed: overall, security measures were far from internationally accepted standards.

In North and West Africa, the Pentagon has been training and equipping the forces of Algeria, Chad, Mali, Mauritania, Niger, Senegal, Nigeria, Morocco, Tunisia and possibly a rehabilitated Libya. In particular, Washington's greatest fear is that the al-Qaeda-linked Salafist Group for Preaching and Combat, which has been losing ground in Algeria, might regroup in Niger. In turn, Niger's authorities fear the GSPC could encourage the Tuareg tribesmen to revolt once more.

About 1,000 US troops spread across the region in 2005 for a major exercise laying the groundwork for the Trans-Sahara Counter-terrorism Initiative (TSCTI). During three weeks of initial training, members of the US military worked alongside soldiers in Chad – the world's fifth-poorest country and, according to the anti-corruption group, Transparency International, the third most corrupt. Also, during the year, American forces conducted exercises throughout the Trans-Saharan region, concentrating on ground and air operations, as well as human rights training. Countries involved included Chad, Mauritania, Mali and Senegal.

Washington acknowledges its work in the region as far from done. The West African coast is of increasing strategic importance. The Gulf of Guinea supplies the US with 15 per cent of its oil – a figure projected to rise to 25 per cent by 2015. Nigeria is America's fifth largest source of foreign oil; additionally, one-third of America's imported oil arrives in Liberian-flagged tankers. Oil has been discovered in large quantities off the coast of Gambia.

Washington has stepped up its diplomatic/military ties with West Africa. Colin Powell, US Secretary of State, visited Angola and Gabon in 2002, in the first trip by such a high-ranking American official. The following year, President George W. Bush visited Senegal, Nigeria, Botswana, Uganda and South Africa. In early 2004, General Charles F. Wald, Deputy Commander EUCOM, toured Angola, Nigeria, Tunisia, Algeria, Ghana, South Africa and Gabon. Afterwards, top-ranking military officials from Chad, Mali, Mauritania, Morocco, Niger, Senegal and Tunisia visited EUCOM: 'Every place I go in Africa, where we talk about the war on terrorism, there is a resonance and an agreement that we have something in common,' observed General Wald.[13]

In February 2004, Washington signed a pact with Liberia, allowing American forces to board and search any Liberian-registered foreign ship suspected of carrying weapons of mass destruction. The Liberian Bureau of Maritime Affairs does not have a good track record, particularly with regard to granting Liberian flags of convenience to all and sundry (Liberia is the world's second largest shipping registry after Panama). All this was part of a wider trend by America to head off terrorism on the African continent, spearheaded by the TSCTI. Apart from terrorism, poor regional law enforcement means that smuggling and piracy remain an issue. The presidents of Ghana and Senegal have pressed Western leaders to implement the Africa Action Plan. The G8 envisaged training and equipping some 50,000 soldiers for peace-keeping operations in Africa. In the meantime, EUCOM and the US Navy are considering increasing their footprint in the region with possible deep-water port facilities at Sao Tome and Principe.

Washington's financial commitment to its counter-terrorism effort in Africa remains modest, despite the huge scale of the problem. Some analysts even argue that America's military presence, albeit temporary, may end up exacerbating the situation by alienating poor Muslims in countries such as Kenya. Meanwhile, the USN and Coalition partners have worked hard to ensure there is not a repeat of the USS *Cole* attack in the waters off Africa.

Chapter 15

Punishing the Taliban

Eleven days after 9/11, Washington stated Osama bin Laden was responsible and issued a five-point ultimatum to the Taliban, which called for the handing over of all al-Qaeda leaders, the immediate closure of Afghan terrorist training camps, subsequent inspection of those sites, surrender of all terrorists to appropriate authorities, and the release of imprisoned foreign nationals. The following day the Taliban rejected these demands on the grounds they had no evidence linking bin Laden with the attacks in America.[1]

In protest, Saudi Arabia and the United Arab Emirates withdrew their recognition of the Taliban government, leaving only Pakistan with diplomatic ties. The Taliban did begin to waver in the face of the US military build-up and offered to put bin Laden on trial if Washington provided evidence of his complicity with 9/11.[2] America, however, after six years of al-Qaeda attacks, wanted bin Laden – it was all or nothing.

In pursuit of punishing those responsible for 9/11, Washington decided to dust off Richard Clarke's plans to use air power and Special Forces to assist the Afghan Northern Alliance to oust the Taliban and destroy al-Qaeda's presence once and for all. The feeling was that most of the opposition factions were untrustworthy, particularly those originally based in Iran. Ironically, in northern Afghanistan, General Rashid Dostum's Uzbek militia, which at one time had formed the Afghan Army's Northern Command and had fought alongside the Soviets, was now considered a possible ally against the Taliban.[3]

In retribution for continuing to harbour Osama bin Laden and his al-Qaeda network, Washington launched air strikes, using US Navy (USN) and strategic air assets, as well as ship- and submarine-launched Tomahawk Land Attack Missiles (TLAMs), to destroy terrorist-related facilities, the Taliban's military infrastructure and their field forces. The end game for the air campaign was the complete rout of the Taliban and the creation of a broad-based successor government under UN auspices to meet the needs of all Afghanistan's ethnic groups. Otherwise drugs, war and terrorism would remain a way of life for another twenty years.

In light of its victories over the Northern Alliance and previous experience against the Soviets, the Taliban was not expected to be a pushover. The Afghan economy was already in ruins well before the air campaign started, as the continuing civil war had prevented any recovery. Under the Taliban, taxation had ceased, foreign investment dried up and inflation was rampant. The situation was exacerbated in 1998 when Saudi Arabia withdrew essential financial support for the Taliban regime in response to its harbouring bin Laden. By then, he was wanted for the attacks on US interests in Kenya, Saudi Arabia, Tanzania and Yemen.

Behind the scenes, bin Laden and Mullah Omar confidently expected to defeat the Americans as they had done the Russians ten years before, through a combination of guerrilla warfare and inhospitable geography. Indeed, Afghanistan was not like Bosnia, Serbia or Kosovo: the country was not a target-rich environment. For policy-makers either side of the Atlantic, finding military targets that provided strategic leverage against the Taliban and al-Qaeda proved near impossible.

A major intelligence gap was the strength of the Taliban's ground and air forces, and the whereabouts of the terrorist training camps. The Taliban Army was a mishmash of loose groupings fleshed out with foreign fighters from such organisations as the IMU. Taliban ground forces were variously estimated by British defence sources at about 25,000 during the late 1990s.[4] American sources assessed the Taliban to number double that, while the Northern Alliance had up to 15,000 men.[5]

After the Russian withdrawal, Afghanistan descended into chaos and major weapon-system supplies ceased. It is almost impossible to get a consensus on the Taliban and Northern Alliance's armoured vehicle holdings. However, it would be fair to say that, at the time of the American-led offensive, the Taliban had roughly 300 tanks, mostly old Soviet-built T-55s and some T-62s, perhaps several hundred tracked armoured personnel carriers (APCs), 500 wheeled APCs and some scout cars.[6] The serviceability of all these vehicles was poor and it is doubtful that even half were operational. Certainly, the Taliban did not operate any sizeable armoured units.

The fact that it failed to move almost 100 vehicles from the Kandahar depot before the air attacks commenced indicates that most of them were just broken-down old scrap. Similarly, the failure to disperse the 300–odd vehicles at Pol-e-Charkhi before the bombing shows they were also already junk. At both locations, air strikes needlessly flattened the vast vehicle storage sheds.[7] Taliban mobile rocket launchers included some Soviet BM-21 and BM-14, while there were probably no more than a handful of mobile surface-to-surface missile launchers of the Scud and FROG-7 variety.

Importantly, the Taliban had little that could threaten the US Air Force and RAF – at best, they had some ancient Blowpipe, Stinger and SA-7 man-portable surface-to-air missiles and some mobile SA-13 missiles mounted on the ancient tracked MT-LB armoured vehicle chassis, which, in NATO parlance, was known as the Gopher.[8] The Taliban were thought to have few, if any, of the latter operational, though at least one had been photographed on a Taliban airfield. This was certainly one Gopher that would go to ground in the face of American Suppression of Enemy Air Defenses strikes.

The Taliban Air Force, such as it was, had an unknown number of ancient MiG-21 and Su-17/22 in its inventory. Since its foundation, the TAF had been quite active, flying over 150 sorties during the Taloqan campaign. However, with the loss of Bagram air base in 1998, the TAF was forced to destroy or disable many of its aircraft during its retreat from the Shomali plain. Against the Coalition, the TAF initially fielded about eight MiG-21, eight Su-22, four L-39 light jets and a few Mi-8/17 helicopters. Most were destroyed on the ground in the opening minutes of the air attacks. Satellite imagery of the key airfields at Kabul, Kandahar, Herat and Mazar-e-Sharif showed them to be defended with ancient anti-aircraft artillery, which could be easily dealt with.

US Central Command at McDill AFB, Florida, directed Operation Enduring Freedom. USN tactical assets deployed to the region included F-14 Tomcat and F/A-18E/F Super Hornet fighter-bombers and global assets included B-1, B-2 and B-52 strategic bombers. The US was not able to conduct any regional land-based fighter missions using F-16s, as, crucially, Saudi Arabia and Pakistan refused to allow any attacks to be conducted from their soil. Pakistan's government, with its Pashtun population – brothers of the Pashtun Taliban – had to walk a precarious diplomatic tightrope. Domestically, abandoning its one-time ally was a difficult and deeply unpopular decision, which was to have far-reaching consequences.

While the air campaign was designed to punish the Taliban for fostering global and regional Jihadists, the intention was that the attacks would also flush out the terrorists, making it easier to target them. To that end, a broad range of targets were struck in order to confuse the Taliban and the al-Qaeda leadership. Washington played its cards close to its chest and London was not privy to the target listing. Such was the lack of liaison, it meant that British intelligence officers were reading about American air strikes on a day-to-day basis in the newspapers before they were debriefed. American air attacks were also a cover for US Special Forces operating on the ground, which sought to capitalise on the chaos.

Uzbekistan – keen to see the Islamic Movement of Uzbekistan crushed once and for all – allowed US Special Forces to operate from its K2 air base, on the proviso American air strikes target the IMU. It is quite possible that the Uzbeks themselves conducted covert operations into Afghanistan against known militants. Uzbek commandos would have blended in much more easily than CIA field agents and US Rangers. At the time, Uzbekistan's poor democratic credentials made it an ally of convenience, rather than one of choice – under the circumstances, it seemed better to ignore the unwelcome truth that Uzbekistan was using the attack on the Taliban as an opportunity to deal with Uzbek political opposition movements.

American air attacks opened on 7 October 2001, with B-1B and B-52H bombers flying from the island of Diego Garcia in the Indian Ocean and B-2As flying from Whitman Air Force Base Missouri. The latter flew on to Diego Garcia after a record forty-four hours in the air and six air-to-air refuellings. Carrier-based strike aircraft operating from the USS *Carl Vinson* and *Enterprise* joined the heavy bombers and some fifty Tomahawks were also launched. Around thirty targets were hit that first day.

The UK's contribution, although small, was significant compared with that of other nations. The Royal Navy fired two batches of TLAMs, and the RAF contributed several hundred reconnaissance and tanker refuelling flights in support of US raids. France's contribution consisted of reconnaissance sorties and an intelligence-gathering ship. Italy volunteered tactical reconnaissance, air-to-air refuelling, transport aircraft and a naval group. Turkey announced it would send Special Forces to train the Northern Alliance, but did not take part in the actual fighting.

In the opening attacks at least 50 per cent of the targets hit were terrorist-related. These included training camps, stores, safe houses and mountain hide-outs used by Chechens, Kashmiris, Pakistanis, Saudis, Tajiks, Uzbeks, Uighurs and Yemeni Islamists. Notably, the bulk of the terrorist facilities bombed were mainly in the Kabul, Kandahar and Jalalabad areas and belonged to al-Qaeda and the IMU. In particular, Kandahar and Jalalabad remained the favoured targets, as this was where Osama bin Laden and his cronies were most likely to have gone to ground. Kandahar was the stronghold of bin Laden's one-time ally, Taliban leader, Mullah Omar.

According to Indian intelligence, in total there were thought to be some 120 terrorist training camps in Afghanistan and an unspecified number in Pakistan (many of which had been used to train the Taliban).[9] Key among the Afghan ones were al-Farouq (which trained four 9/11 hijackers), Khalden (where at least three of the 1993 WTC bombers and three 9/11 hijackers had trained), Tarnak Farms (bin Laden's HQ) and Zhawar Kili al-Badr (which actually covered four separate sites). Russian information supplied to the UN indicated that fifty-five of them belonged to al-Qaeda. But many were not permanent and moved regularly, in order to avoid unwanted attention. In the case of Tarnak Farms, near Kandahar, bin Laden moved there from Najim Jihad outside Jalalabad after the Northern Alliance threatened to overrun the city.

Estimates vary widely when it comes to the number of militants who passed through the camps. According to the US Counter-terrorism Center, between 1996 and 2001, up to 20,000 trained in Afghanistan. However, Senator Bob Graham, citing CIA sources, claimed it could have been as high as 120,000. Among them were allegedly some 4,000 British citizens. Mullah Mohammed Khaksar, the Taliban's former Deputy Interior Minister, claimed 3,500 men alone passed through Rishkhor, a sprawling complex 10 miles south of Kabul.

The US Department of Defense released declassified imagery of the air strikes on airfields at Kandahar, Herat and Mazar-e-Sharif, vehicle depots at Kandahar and Pol-e-Charkhi, Herat army barracks and a Kabul radio station, to name but a few. As well as attacking terrorist bases and the Taliban's infrastructure, Coalition assets also struck vulnerable dispersal areas – for example, catching exposed Taliban armour in the hills outside Herat. The key achievement of the air attacks was the swift acquisition of air superiority, through the destruction of the Taliban's rudimentary air force, air defences and early warning systems. In total, about 250 Taliban targets suffered air strikes, with the USAF's strategic bombers comprising less than 10 per cent of the force dropping about 50 per cent of the bombs.

Crucially, apart from the crippling air strikes against the Taliban's field forces, which aided the Northern Alliance to rapidly seize Kabul and Mazar-e-Sharif, the regime was able to shrug off most of the early attacks. Initially, the strikes did not greatly affect the Taliban's basic infrastructure or ability to wage war against the Northern Alliance, only its ability to resist Coalition air attack. The Northern Alliance had little in the way of meaningful air assets that posed a threat to the Taliban air defences. Until the concentrated attacks on the Taliban's field forces, the degradation of the Taliban's communications was the greatest hindrance to their conduct of the war.

The US Special Forces raids on 19 October against a command-and-control facility and an airfield near Kandahar illustrated the Coalition's freedom of operations on the ground. However, it was B-52 carpet-bombing, coupled with Taliban defections and withdrawals that produced dramatic results and hastened the end of organised resistance. By the end of October, air strikes began to shift away from high-profile urban targets towards Taliban front-line positions.

Heavy strikes, including B-52 carpet-bombing, were conducted on 31 October, against Taliban forces near Bagram, 45km north of Kabul. Lasting several hours, they were the most intense attacks on Taliban front-line positions since the air campaign opened. The following day, the strategic Taliban garrison at Kala Ata, guarding the approaches to Taloqan, was bombed. The raids lasted for over four hours and windows were allegedly broken up to 20km away. Attacks also continued in the Kandahar and Mazar-e-Sharif areas. Within a week of this intense bombing the Taliban crumbled – first at Mazar-e-Sharif, then Kabul and Jalalabad, their forces in headlong retreat towards Omar's stronghold at Kandahar.

In just a few days, in early November, the Taliban lost control of much of the country in the face of the Northern Alliance's ground offensive. The dramatic collapse of their ground forces was due to a combination of the air attacks, sizeable Taliban defections and an unprecedented level of co-operation between rival anti-Taliban factions. The Northern Alliance quickly gained control of most of the non-Pashtun cities north of a line extending from Herat in the west to Kabul in the east. By the end of the month, with the disintegration of the Taliban field forces, the focus of the air campaign switched to Kandahar and Tora Bora near Jalalabad in eastern Afghanistan.

The world watched in awe as US air power first chewed up the Taliban's air force, its air defences and then its armour during Operation Enduring Freedom. Although, in the wake of 9/11, America rapidly came to the decision that it wanted the Taliban government and al-Qaeda terrorists destroyed, it did not want to do it at the cost of thousands of US troops on the ground. The solution was to use six-man Close Air Support (CAS) Special Forces A-Teams, operating alongside the Taliban's nemesis, the Northern Alliance.[10] These Special Forces, equipped with laser designators, would pinpoint enemy targets for immediate US air strikes.

Just twelve days after the air campaign opened, America began to secretly insert its CAS teams. The six men of Tiger 01 were infiltrated into northern Afghanistan on 19 October 2001 by two MH-53J Pavelow helicopters of the 160th Special Operations Aviation Regiment. In the next few days, liaising with General Fahim's opposition forces, they were involved in efforts to capture Bagram airfield 45km north of Kabul. This they found defended by some fifty armoured vehicles, including tanks, armoured personnel carriers and ZSU-23 Shilka self-propelled Anti Aircraft Artillery (AAA).

Six hours of air strikes, called in by Tiger 01 against the Taliban forces near Bagram, obliterated everything. Tiger 02 helped General Dostrum capture Mazar-e-Sharif on 9 November, seizing the vital airfield and opening the supply route to Uzbekistan. The team called in strikes directing US Marine Corps FA/-18 fighter-bombers and AC-130 Spectre gunships to silence the deadly ZSU-23–4 and T-55s, accounting for at least fifty vehicles. During the attack on Kabul three days later, Tiger 01 accounted for twenty-nine tanks plus numerous vehicles and artillery pieces. By the 14th it was all over – Kabul had fallen to the Northern Alliance.

Tiger 03, directed to help capture the city of Kunduz, destroyed fifty tanks, APCs, AAA and artillery. Texas 11 helped General Daoud's forces liberate Taloqan, the Northern Alliance's former HQ and capture Kunduz. On 17 November, Texas 11 called in air strikes that claimed fifteen armoured vehicles and four trucks. Between 14–29 November, battle-damage assessment included sixteen armoured vehicles, fifty-one lorries and five anti-aircraft guns. Texas 12, assigned to Hamid Karzai (future president), at the town of Tarin Kowt, north of Kandahar, stopped a Taliban counter-attack involving over eighty vehicles, including armoured cars – between thirty-five and forty-five of these were destroyed.

These results seemed outstanding, and it appeared as if the Special Forces alone had accounted for the Taliban's armour. However, a former Green Beret cautioned the author:

> Special Forces teams in general are rather poor. The A-teams are
> barely okay, but B and C teams absolutely suck. The Special Forces
> reserve teams are even worse. There are always some excellent troops
> around, but don't believe half that bullshit that is spread around by a
> desperate public affairs department of the military.[11]

Nevertheless, within three months of the air campaign commencing, the
Taliban government collapsed. Osama bin Laden and al-Qaeda suffered notable
losses, particularly at Mazar-e-Sharif and Konduz. The Taliban troops trapped
in Konduz surrendered, abandoning some 2,000–5,000 foreign supporters
to flee or capitulate. After the fall of Kabul, the Taliban retired to prepared
positions in and around Kandahar, their spiritual heartland.

Kandahar surrendered to opposition forces on 7 December 2001 without a
fight. Al-Qaeda fighters, trapped by the peaks and valleys of the 15,400-foot
White Mountains, lost most of their heavy equipment. They had nothing with
which to shoot back at their enemy's exposed tanks perched on the foothills.
Opposition forces proceeded to pound the mountains with artillery, mortars,
rockets and Russian-supplied T-62 tanks. In the clear blue skies, American
B-52s disgorged their heavy munitions in a continuing effort to smash the
caves. To the defenders of Tora Bora, it must have seemed as if the American
and opposition forces were trying to pulverise the very rock itself. The enemy
scattered and it was soon all over bar the shouting. Clear up parties found
heavy weapons, including one or two tanks, actually inside some of the caves.

Despite the success of the CAS teams, the use of Special Forces in
Afghanistan has come in for some criticism. The former Green Beret told the
author that:

> All special operations troops depend too much on technology and
> aerial support [...] The entire campaigns in Afghanistan and Iraq are
> flawed. Heavy-handed and misuse of special operations troops – thus
> no relationships with locals and no real intelligence.[12]

He was right. In reality, prior to the arrival of the American Special Forces,
much of the Taliban's armour had already been smashed at the Afghan storage
depots and barracks. Nonetheless, the combination of these teams and US
air power sealed the fate of the Taliban's tanks. The whereabouts of Osama
bin Laden and other senior al-Qaeda members was another matter.

Although scattered to the four winds, the Taliban was far from a spent force
and would soon be reinvigorated by foreign Jihadists. Just as the term 'New
al-Qaeda' came into use, so did 'New Taliban'. US forces redeploying to
Afghanistan from Iraq found that, far from quiet peace-keeping duties, they
were immediately embroiled in fierce battles with pro-Taliban forces. According to Army Brigadier General James G. Champion, Deputy Commander

Combined Joint Task Force 76, operating in small groups to avoid major engagements with Coalition forces, the Taliban became increasingly ruthless and continued to disrupt reconstruction work. The UN envoy to Afghanistan also noted insurgents loyal to the former Taliban becoming increasingly violent.

In the face of a resurgent Taliban, US military units were obliged to conduct operations to deny them sanctuary and freedom of movement. In the mountains of Zabul province, US paratroopers found themselves involved in battles for Gazek Kula and Miana Shin – both Taliban strongholds. What was surprising American troops was that the Taliban were standing and fighting, even in the face of overwhelming US air power. In one instance, they fought through seven hours of air strikes. Similarly, the International Security Assistance Force (ISAF), based around Kabul, noted a marked increase in attacks.

This resurgence, in the wake of the largely peaceful Afghan elections, was blamed on Pakistan's *madrassahs*, which allegedly were turning out new recruits to fill the Taliban's depleted ranks. Certainly, US forces on the ground blamed President Musharraf for not doing enough to seal the porous border with Afghanistan. Musharraf claimed he would expel all foreigners from the *madrassahs* and quoted a figure of 1,400, which seemed suspiciously low, considering there are 16,000 such schools in Pakistan. The general consensus was that, while American troops continued to kill the Taliban rank and file, its leadership remained safe to plan its next outrages from inside Pakistan, using fresh recruits.

The new Afghan National Army (ANA) remained very much a junior party in the war against the Taliban compared to American and ISAF forces, which were drawn from some thirty-seven nations. NATO assumed control of ISAF in 2003 and it was planned that the ANA would total 70,000 men by 2007, allowing foreign forces to withdraw. According to Brigadier General Champion, the ANA was initially to take on the main responsibility for combating terrorist activity in Oruzgan province.

ISAF expanded its area of responsibility from Kabul to encompass the country's southern and eastern provinces in 2006. This meant bringing the 12,000 US and other Coalition forces in the region under NATO control. It gave ISAF responsibility for the whole of Afghanistan, with around 40,000 troops. The upshot of this was greater integration in the south with the US-led Operation Enduring Freedom. However, the two operations continued to be directed separately, the rationale being that ISAF had a stabilisation and security mission, while OEF was overtly counter-terrorism.

The HQ of NATO's Allied Rapid Reaction Corps, under British direction, took control of ISAF in May 2006 for a nine-month period. This coincided with ISAF's move south and the arrival of additional British troops in Helmand province for three years. Taliban activities soon made it clear that British numbers and equipment were insufficient to contain the threat. This forced the British Ministry of Defence to hurriedly procure more armoured vehicles for deployment in Afghanistan during the first half of 2007. British troop numbers rose to 7,800 with a view to maintaining them at that level until 2009. While numerous countries have provided contingents for peace-keeping in Afghanistan, the only notable numbers beyond the UK and US were 3,460 men from Germany, 2,800 from Canada and 2,200 from the Netherlands. By early 2009 there were 56,420 foreign troops in Afghanistan, of which 24,900 were American and 8,300 were British. The Afghan National Army totalled 79,300, though the Afghan government and UN agreed in September 2008 to boost the ANA to 122,000 troops by 2011.

The Taliban remained far from defeated and continued to attract Jihadists. Seven years after the liberation of Kabul there were assessed to be around 10,000 Taliban, of whom about 3,000 were full-time fighters. Up to 10 per cent of them were foreign combatants.[13] These foreign volunteers were coming from various Arab countries (Egypt, Libya and Saudi Arabia), Chechnya, China, Kazakhstan, Pakistan, Siberia and Turkey. There was a horrible sense of déjà vu, echoing Iraq and Bosnia. Afghanistan had again become the scene of a Jihad, as foreign fighters sought to oust an unwanted Western military presence.

According to US Brigadier General Rodney Anderson:

> The Arabs, the Russians, the Chechens, the Central Asians that have been involved in the fighting, they bring, what I call, a force multiplier capability to the insurgency. And that is, they provide increased ability to kill Afghan and NATO forces through suicide attacks [...] These foreigners increase the ability of local Taliban to fight ...[14]

In Russia amongst the ranks of the old Soviet–Afghan war veterans there was a very real sense of sympathy for their Western counterparts, trapped in a seemingly unending struggle with the Taliban.

In the meantime, the Hazaras like the Tajiks had welcomed the Coalition. Persecuted by the mainly Sunni Pashtun Taliban for their Shia faith, this had culminated in the 2001 Yakawlang massacre. The Hazaras' Eastern Council fought in support of the Northern Alliance against the Taliban. In particular they played a key role in the attempt to trap bin Laden at Tora Bora.

Chapter 16

Tora Bora: Afghanistan Revisited

Within three months of the Coalition air campaign commencing, the Taliban had completely collapsed. As political correspondent John Kampfner observed:

> For the Americans the 'eureka' moment came as journalists and alliance soldiers combed through al-Qaeda safe houses, documents and computer records revealing that bin Laden's network had been trying to acquire weapons of mass destruction. The assumption, which they struggled to prove, was that they had been looking to Iraq for supplies.[1]

Remnants of the Taliban armed forces and al-Qaeda fighters – perhaps over 1,000 strong – withdrew on the Tora Bora stronghold, high in the Spin Ghar or White Mountains. Their intention was to conduct hit-and-run attacks or make a last stand. This defensive complex lays south of the city of Jalalabad and west of the famous Khyber Pass, linking Afghanistan with neighbouring Pakistan. Consisting of miles of interconnecting caves and tunnels, it was built by the Mujahideen twenty years earlier, when they carved Tora Bora into the side of Ghree Khil Mountain with American and Pakistani sponsorship during the Soviet occupation.

While American air strikes continued, British and American Special Forces focused on their search for bin Laden and Mullah Omar. They concentrated on suspected terrorist strongholds, particularly Tora Bora, where Osama was believed to be hiding following the fall of Kandahar and Jalalabad.[2] There were conflicting reports regarding his movements. Initially, it was thought that US Special Forces had tracked him down to Maruf, 80 miles east of Kandahar in southern Afghanistan.[3] The reports proved false.

Other sightings put him east of Kabul at the city of Jalalabad. Babrak Khan, a Jalalabad resident who worked as a guard at an Arab base during the 1990s, said:

> I saw Osama in the sixth or seventh truck and behind him were from 100 to 200 vehicles. At the end of the convoy were five armoured vehicles. Arabs from across the city were gathering here, coming from all directions.[4]

It was claimed bin Laden had helped the city's former governor strike a deal with city elders so they could take control until the formation of an interim government. Having done that he escaped to Tora Bora.

While the Tora Bora region was heavily bombed, Afghan opposition forces under the Eastern Council started to advance into the area. These troops blocked off all escape routes prior to launching a major offensive on the region, following the fall of Kandahar. In the meantime, Mohammad Omar and 500 of his supporters were thought to be besieged in the rugged mountains of northern Helmand.

Tora Bora had first seen action in mid-1981 when a Soviet-led offensive caused widespread destruction, but failed to yield a result against the Mujahideen. The Soviets heavily bombed the stronghold but could not root out the resistance fighters. Now the Russians dusted off their old maps and gave them to the Coalition. The stronghold was believed to be well provisioned with weapons and food, which could allow bin Laden and his supporters to withstand a lengthy siege. Russian advice to the Coalition was that Tora Bora would prove impregnable if the defenders resisted to the last.

It was anticipated that Tora Bora would be protected by minefields, ingenious booby-traps and defended by Islamic fanatics prepared to resist to the death. Washington stated that it would not deploy its 500 marines on standby at Kandahar, but leave it to its Special Forces and the Eastern Council to clear the caves. On the Pakistani side of the border, Pakistan's military kept the Khyber and Bati passes closed to try to prevent any terrorists slipping through un-detected and up into the unruly North West Frontier Province.

For the first time, Pakistan moved its army into the Terah Valley area, following reports that Arab suspects may sneak into the tribal territory via Spin Ghar to escape the intense US bombing of the Tora Bora caves. Up to 2,000 al-Qaeda fighters were thought to have fled towards Pakistan. Islamabad stationed 50,000 men on the Afghan frontier, of whom 8,000 regular and para-military troops were tasked to stop Taliban and al-Qaeda fighters crossing the border.

Almost the entire American strike force – ten long-range bombers, a dozen tactical jets and four or five gunships – pounded one complex near Tora Bora over the space of a few days. The bombing proved successful, with the death of many al-Qaeda Arabs, including twelve senior personnel in early December. A BLU-82 Daisy Cutter – or Big Blue – bomb was dropped on a cave near Tora Bora on 9 December.[5] It was hoped the massive pressure wave cause by the blast would kill suspected al-Qaeda leadership in the cave. The BLU-82 had already been used three times against Taliban and al-Qaeda front lines, but this was the first time it was used against their mountain stronghold.

Senior military commander in the eastern region, Haji Mohammad Zaman (leading the Eastern Council opposition forces), began the laborious task of clearing the Tora Bora Valley, before advancing on the stronghold itself. First, Zaman's troops had to capture the village of Tora Bora and other surrounding hamlets, then clear the Tora Bora forest. A bitter battle was expected and for the first week the cautious advance was met with some resistance. The Eastern Council's efforts were sluggish because co-ordination between the various forces was poor. Nevertheless, al-Qaeda and the Taliban were slowly driven back, higher up into the mountains.

After two weeks of constant US bombing, the defenders commenced radio negotiations on possible terms. They wanted to surrender to the UN, to avoid being handed over to the Americans, but the US would not countenance it. The talks ended and the opposition forces requested the US halt its attacks.

The main Coalition ground offensive started late on 13 December. The Council forces then advanced on the caves still held by Arab al-Qaeda fighters. The mountain paths were narrow and those caves undetected by the bombers were difficult to locate. During the second week of December, in the face of varying degrees of resistance, the Eastern Council captured most of al-Qaeda's remaining positions.

The core of the defenders were thought to number 300, of whom 150 were Arabs, seventy-five Chechens, and the rest Uzbek, Tajik and Afghans. Other estimates, however, put the number of defenders as high as 1,000. Bodies of men posted in machine-gun posts along the ridges were found scattered around the scorched remains of their weapons. The first caves captured revealed evidence of desperate attempts to escape the bombing. Strewn with documents, equipment, ammunition, bloodied rags and weapons, their walls were blackened from fire. Those al-Qaeda fighters not killed had fled without time to plant the feared booby-traps.

Eastern Council troops then entered secret hideaways in the Malawa Valley for the first time. The ceilings were made from rock, walls several feet thick, built from tree-trunks packed with stone and dirt. British and US Special Forces came under machine-gun and mortar fire as they advanced up the rocky slopes. They then fought fierce battles with the survivors for control of the area. With Eastern Council forces pushing their way from the north and Pakistani forces blocking the border to the south, the al-Qaeda fighters could only flee east or west over the mountains or fight their way out.

Gary Berntsen, a key CIA commander involved in the fight against the Taliban around Kabul and the drive on Tora Bora, noted:

> Bin Laden split his force in two. One group, numbering 135 men, headed east into Pakistan [...] A number of al-Qaeda detainees later confirmed that bin Laden escaped with another group of 200 Saudis and Yemenis by a more difficult eastern route over difficult snow-covered passes into the Pashtun tribal area of Parachinar, Pakistan.[6]

On the 16th, Zaman announced that his forces had taken Spin Ghar at 0900 without any resistance. They came across fifty al-Qaeda dead and captured an Arab fighter. Zaman claimed to have captured 80 per cent of the mountain and by the evening it was all over, with the capture of thirty-five al-Qaeda fighters and the discovery of about 200 dead. The al-Qaeda suicide squads did not materialise. Despite exhortations to fight to the last, many of the dispirited defenders were buried by the bombardment, surrendered, or just slipped away, hoping to escape into Pakistan.

Nonetheless, Eastern Council commanders described the final battle as brutal, leaving the slopes of Tora Bora strewn with the bodies of al-Qaeda fighters. In the aftermath, Pakistan arrested at least 350 al-Qaeda members, including more than 300 Arab nationals (mainly Saudis, Sudanese, Egyptians, Jordanians and Yemenis). Most were transferred to the US detention facility, Camp Rhino, at Kandahar.

The battle for al-Qaeda's Tora Bora stronghold resulted in the loss of some 300 defenders, including Chechens, Pakistanis and Saudis. Two-thirds were killed, the rest taken prisoner. Akram Lahori, of the Lashkar-i-Jhangvi movement, was killed during the fighting in Tora Bora, while his chief, Riaz Basra, was captured in Kandahar. The motley collection of prisoners displayed after Tora Bora included a mix of Arabs, Uzbeks and South Asians. Many were shipped off to Cuba. Ibn al-Shaikh al-Libi, who ran Khalden – the largest training camp in Afghanistan – was taken while trying to flee the fighting.[7] Among those captured by the Eastern Council's fighters was Mohamed Akram, who claimed to have been bin Laden's chef and who gave a good account of his boss's escape from Tora Bora. Bin Laden's driver, Salim Ahmed Hamadan, was also taken.[8]

By mid-December, al-Qaeda's supporters had been almost completely driven from the White Mountains. The speed of the victory came as a surprise to everyone. Zaman Gamsharik, the Eastern Council's defence chief in eastern Afghanistan, announced on 16 December 2001: 'This is the last day of al-Qaeda in Afghanistan. We have done our duty: we have cleansed our land of all al-Qaeda.'[9] US Defense Secretary Donald Rumsfeld, visiting US forces at Bagram near Kabul, told them: 'The World Trade Center is still burning as we sit here. They are still bringing bodies out. Fortunately, the caves and tunnels at Tora Bora are also burning.'[10] However, despite the victory at Tora Bora, bin Laden – perpetrator of the attacks on New York – had escaped capture. Phil Smucker, an American reporter who covered the battle for Tora Bora, says:

> Bin Laden's great Houdini act had been almost predictable. Though some optimistic analysts and military minds had hoped that bin Laden would fight to his death in Tora Bora, the strategic thinking behind

his flight became apparent a few weeks later when a London Arabic-language newspaper published a treatise titled 'Knights under the Prophet's Banner: Meditations on the Jihadist Movement', written by his top lieutenant, Dr Ayman al-Zawahiri. It declared that when faced with certain military defeat, 'the movement must pull out as many personnel as possible to the safety of a shelter' to continue the fight at another time and place.[11]

In Afghanistan, the battle at Tora Bora proved not so much a dramatic last stand but more of a desperate rearguard action to distract the Coalition while the Taliban and al-Qaeda leadership fled. Bin Laden's supporters, trapped in Tora Bora, proved not to be a resilient guerrilla army, as expected, but demoralised terrorists, whose plans for global mayhem had gone awry. The number of foreigners remaining in the mountains was thought to be between 2,000–5,000; but scattered, cold and hungry, they were not deemed a threat. By the end of the war, the new Afghan government was holding about 7,000 prisoners. Around 100 of these were handed over to the US for further interrogation and a further 900 were identified as being of potential interest to the US.

All that remained after Tora Bora was to mop up and local opposition forces scoured the caves for clues to the whereabouts of Osama bin Laden. US forces examined abandoned cave complexes in the Tora Bora region, where some believed he had been hiding, but by early January 2002 the US had publicly given up chasing him to focus on capturing his remaining supporters. About 350 Taliban and al-Qaeda prisoners were in US custody, some of whom were reportedly held at the US naval base at Guantanamo Bay, Cuba (it was anticipated that up to 2,000 would be transferred there).

US air strikes continued against regrouping Taliban/al-Qaeda forces and their facilities in eastern Afghanistan. These were concentrated in Paktia province against Zhawar Kili terrorist training camp – site of the Soviet-backed offensive in 1987. According to the US, on 28 December, they bombed a walled compound and bunker associated with the Taliban and al-Qaeda leadership. The media subsequently claimed the attack killed up to 100 innocent civilians.

Despite three attacks on the complex over a four-day period by US aircraft, surviving al-Qaeda leaders repeatedly tried to regroup at a warren of caves and bunkers. One strike on Zhawar Kili hit tanks and artillery, but it was feared the terrorists remained. On 6 January 2002, strikes on Khost and the Zhawar Kili training camp were among 118 sorties flown by US air assets over Afghanistan. In one week, 250 bombs were dropped on Zhawar Kili alone.

Sustained raids were conducted on both Zhawar Kili and anti-aircraft defences near the town of Khost. The US feared that Zhawar Kili was going to be another Tora Bora. General Richard Myers of the US Joint Chiefs of Staff said: 'We have found this complex to be very, very extensive. It covers a large area. When we ask people how large they often describe it as huge.'[12] The camp was composed of three separate training areas and two cave complexes. US marines and Special Forces moved into the areas after the initial wave of strikes by B-1 and B-52 bombers and carrier-based fighters. They then piled up unexploded ammunition and heavy weapons, which were destroyed by a second series of attacks.

Mopping-up operations continued well into the New Year, with the Coalition determined not to repeat the mistakes of the battle for Tora Bora. The next area to be subject to a search-and-destroy mission was the Shah-i-Kot Valley (also the scene of heavy fighting against the Soviet Army in 1987). Some 29km south of Gardez in eastern Afghanistan, up to 600 al-Qaeda terrorists and 1,500 Taliban troops under Saifur Rahman were reportedly ensconced in a system of bunkers and caves in the Arma Mountains. Most worryingly, Rahman had reportedly brought in heavy weapons, including Stinger anti-aircraft missiles, from Tora Bora. On the road to Shah-i-Kot, south-west from Tora Bora, in early January 2002, reporters discovered a party of al-Qaeda fighters who said: 'The enemies of Islam have broken our backbone, our people are abandoning us and we have dispersed like orphans into the valleys.'[13]

The local defenders, while expecting attack from the Coalition, did not anticipate it happening so soon. In late February 2002 their strongholds were softened up by fighter-bombers, using 3,500 precision-guided munitions, B-52H bombers dropping over 250 bombs and Hercules gunships spraying the area in gunfire. Then, on 2 March 2002, Operation Anaconda launched 1,200 US troops and 1,000 new Afghan government troops under General Zia Lodin against Shah-i-Kot, supported by an armada of warplanes.

The key to the operation was to prevent al-Qaeda forces from escaping into Pakistan, so heliborne assault troops were used to block the escape routes. However, Anaconda proved to be one of the bloodiest battles for US troops after they stirred up a hornets' nest. The column pushing up the valley road came under intense rocket and mortar fire and stalled, while one of the heliborne forces was accidentally landed in the midst of al-Qaeda defensive positions and suffered twenty-eight wounded. In another incident, two US helicopters were lost to ground fire. Air power proved crucial in helping clear the valley, though a further 1,000 Afghan government soldiers with armoured personnel carriers and tanks had to be called in. Few al-Qaeda dead were found and the enemy were either buried under the mountains or once again escaped.

Following Tora Bora and Anaconda, the American Special Forces conducted Operation Full Throttle on 14 June 2002, in the foothills of the Spin Ghar Mountains. This was in response to the Taliban regrouping north of Kandahar. Although Mullah Omar and bin Laden had gone to ground, these forces were thought to be under Mullah Akhtar Mohammed Osmani and Mullah Barader.

In particular, Osmani – formerly the Taliban's 2nd Corps commander – had assumed the role of acting Taliban military chief in November 2001. Full Throttle was followed by Operation Anvil, which succeeded in capturing Osmani, but he subsequently escaped to Pakistan.[14]

In response to 9/11, Operation Enduring Freedom brought the Taliban government to its knees, ending five years of hated rule and scattered al-Qaeda. Also, in a worldwide clamp-down, some 500 terrorist suspects were arrested. Al-Qaeda suffered notable leadership losses in Afghanistan, though it was unclear whether its international supporters depended upon their survival in Afghanistan to function, thereby leaving a residual international threat. Encouraged by the swift resolution in Afghanistan, many countries with long-standing terrorist problems made fresh attempts to address them and there was a greater level of support for the Middle East Peace Process. At the same time, the US developed a broader anti-terrorist strategy, focusing on al-Qaeda links and networks in such countries as the Philippines, Somalia, Uzbekistan and Yemen. The international community had finally woken up to the fact that it was at war with militant Islam, requiring an unprecedented level of co-operation.

Chapter 17

Saddam's Terrorists

Washington claimed that one of its main reasons for attacking Iraq was because of Saddam Hussein's links with al-Qaeda and international terrorism. This rationale was based on alleged contact between al-Qaeda and Iraqi intelligence in Afghanistan, Pakistan and Sudan during the early 1990s. Critics argue that these meetings never happened. The Bush administration also cited the presence of Ansar al-Islam (The Partisans of Islam) in northern Iraq, which had links with Baghdad, might have been involved in 9/11, and subsequently evolved into 'al-Qaeda in Iraq'.

Certainly, throughout the 1970s and 1980s, Iraq, Iran and Libya – as well as providing facilities for Palestinian and other terrorist groups – also sent their own agents abroad to carry out acts of terrorism. While Iran and Libya gained high-profile reputations as state sponsors of terrorism, Saddam Hussein quietly outstripped the others in employing terrorism against his own population. Perhaps a little ironically, it was an Iraqi agent who masterminded the seizure of the Iranian embassy in London by Iranian Arabs in 1980. Domestically, Saddam had to contend with the Iraqi Shia al-Dawa al-Islamia (Islamic Call Party), which sought to end his regime and some of the sheikdoms in the Gulf.

Even so, many within the CIA felt an invasion of Iraq was a completely unnecessary distraction from the war on terrorism: 'A lot of people went to George [Tenet, CIA Director] to tell him that Iraq would hurt the war on terrorism, but I never heard him express an opinion about war in Iraq,' recalled one Tenet aide. 'He would just come back from the White House and say they are going to do it.'[1] It seemed the invasion was inevitable. Indeed, the CIA had known that an attack on Saddam was at the top of President Bush's agenda since 2002. If anything, Bush viewed 9/11 as an unwanted distraction: while Clinton had grappled unsuccessfully with al-Qaeda, Bush was not gunning for bin Laden at all – it was Saddam Hussein who was in his sights.

Following 9/11, there was strong scepticism in London regarding any possible Iraqi complicity. Prime Minister Blair had urged President Bush to focus on Afghanistan, al-Qaeda and the Taliban to the exclusion of all else. In turn, Blair had been reassured that Iraq would have to wait until another day. There was nothing to suggest that during their get-together in September 2001, Blair and Bush agreed to attack Iraq after Afghanistan. However, by 2002 it was clear that the hawks in Washington and the Pentagon were intent on war with Iraq, even if it meant sidelining the CIA – and everyone else, for that matter.

Sir Christopher Meyer, then Britain's ambassador to the US, saw the failure by Washington to get full UN backing for the invasion as something of an own goal, as it bore all the hallmarks of a grudge:

> A more united Security Council would have been of inestimable value for rebuilding Iraq. The case for going through the UN was always as strong for the post war period as for the war itself. UN backing would have done much to defuse the notion of a Christian crusade against the Arabs and Islam – and the argument about whether Iraq belonged to the 'war on terror' or was something quite separate.[2]

Behind the scenes, Western intelligence agencies actually deduced that Saddam had rebuffed bin Laden's approaches. A report based on over half a million captured Iraqi documents prepared for the US Joint Forces Command by the Institute for Defence Analyses found that during the early to mid-1990s, Saddam had supported Egyptian Islamic Jihad (which merged with al-Qaeda in 1998), but found no direct collaboration between Saddam Hussein's regime and al-Qaeda.[3] It is likely that, despite Saddam's dislike for America, he saw little gain in an alliance with bin Laden.

Britain's controversial role in supporting America's rationale for war was to produce a dossier that stated Saddam Hussein still possessed weapons of mass destruction and that this was an immediate threat to Western interests. This provided no evidence of a link between bin Laden and Saddam, or indeed, any evidence for Iraq supporting terrorism, which was the fundamental reason for invading Iraq. In the dossier, Blair said: 'I am in no doubt that the threat is serious and current, that he has made progress on WMD, and that he has to be stopped.'[4] These weapons, it was claimed, could be deployed within forty-five minutes: this was later to be discredited for being derived from single-source intelligence.

Ultimately, none of this mattered. Once Washington had set its course there was no turning back, regardless of the detractors within the UN, or indeed, the shaky support of Tony Blair. On 5 February 2003, US Secretary of State Colin Powell, briefing the UN Security Council, stated:

> Going back to the early and mid-1990s, when bin Laden was based in Sudan, an al-Qaeda source tells us that Saddam and bin Laden reached an understanding that al-Qaeda would no longer support activities against Baghdad ...[5]

Such a statement proved nothing.

Farouk Hijazi, a high-ranking Iraq intelligence officer (who was Saddam's ambassador to Turkey), met bin Laden in Kandahar in July 1998.[6] The purpose of this contact was not clear, but it was speculated that bin Laden was seeking sanctuary if the Taliban should ask him to leave, or that Saddam – impressed by his exploits in East Africa – was offering him a base. Washington also claimed contact between lead 9/11 hijacker Mohammad Atta and Iraqi intelligence during meetings with Ahmad Samir al-Ani (Iraq intelligence chief in Prague) in 1999 and 2001, based on information provided by the Czechs. The FBI and CIA eventually concluded that, on the basis of Atta's movements in the US in April 2001, that these meetings never actually took place (after al-Ani was captured by invading US forces in 2003, he confirmed this).[7]

Ansar al-Islam came into being in the late 1990s, when it split from the Islamic Movement of Iraqi Kurdistan. Both groups were initially entirely Kurdish – it was not until after the Coalition's invasion of Afghanistan that concerns were raised that al-Qaeda Arabs had joined Ansar. At its strongest, around 600 al-Qaeda fighters were reported at the Ansar enclave near Khurmal.[8] Notably, the commander of the Arab contingent was Abu Musab al-Zarqawi, a Jordanian who had fought in Afghanistan, though his links with bin Laden are not clear. Nonetheless, he was connected with alleged al-Qaeda plots in Jordan in the 1990s and early 2000s. America's worst suspicions about Ansar al-Islam were confirmed after its remaining fighters fled into Iran in 2003, only to filter back, and their spiritual leader, Mullah Mustapha Krieka, exiled in Norway, likened Ansar's operations to al-Qaeda and the Taliban.

Before al-Zarqawi's arrival, Iraq's greatest terrorist protégé was Palestinian Sabri al-Banna, alias Abu Nidal. He was once as feared as Osama bin Laden, though he was a secular left-wing terrorist, not an Islamist. In 1958 he had gone to live in Saudi Arabia but was expelled for being anti-monarchist. In Iraq he began his real terrorist career by forming 'Black June', which broke with the PLO in 1972. He owed complete allegiance to Iraq for the next eight years, mainly attacking Jordanian and Syrian interests. He broke briefly with Iraq in 1981, opening an office in Syria, but soon mended his fences with Baghdad.

Nidal was the founder of the PLO splinter group Fatah – The Revolutionary Council or the Abu Nidal Organisation – and at the height of his operations, conducted throughout Europe in the 1980s, he was considered the world's most dangerous terrorist. In the mid-1980s he orchestrated attacks on Rome's and Vienna's international airports. It was his attempt to kill the Israeli ambassador to London in 1982, at the behest of Baghdad, which partly prompted Israel's invasion of southern Lebanon.

Saddam Hussein expelled Abu Nidal in 1983, believing Syria was going to use Nidal to assassinate him. Having completely fallen out with the PLO, he sought refuge in Libya – but he did not come cheaply, as Colonel Gaddafi bought his organisation as a going concern for an annual subsidy of $12 million.[9]

The Libyans were not known for their radicalism and Gaddafi wanted holy warriors in the Shia Muslim mould. Abu Nidal agreed, which was bad news for Europe. In mid-August 2002, Nidal was killed when Iraqi intelligence tried to arrest him in Baghdad for allegedly conspiring against Saddam again.[10]

More importantly, Baghdad gave shelter to al-Zarqawi (formerly Ahmad Faadil al-Khalailah), considered second only to Osama bin Laden in terms of the threat he posed to the West.[11] He travelled to Afghanistan to fight the Soviets but by the time he arrived they had withdrawn. While there, he allegedly had a dream in which he saw a sword with the word Jihad written on it falling from the sky. He returned to Jordan in 1992 and was arrested for planning acts of terrorism and was not released until seven years later under a general amnesty. He then went to Pakistan and in June 2000 crossed into Taliban-run Afghanistan. It was at this point that he changed his name, which translates as 'Imposer from Zarqa'.

After being wounded in the leg during the Coalition invasion of Afghanistan, he crossed Iran to reach Iraq. Before leaving, al-Zarqawi was snubbed by bin Laden, who refused to admit him into al-Qaeda's ruling council. It is claimed that he escaped at the expense of the Iraqi government and that Saddam refused to extradite him to Jordan, despite King Hussein being a one-time ally during the Iran-Iraq war. Al-Zarqawi is believed to have travelled through Syria, Lebanon and Jordan before settling in the Iraqi Kurdish region bordering Iran, held by Ansar al-Islam in the summer of 2002.

After the Ansar enclave was overrun in the late spring of 2003 by Kurdish troops supported by US Special Forces, al-Zarqawi fled into north-western Iraq to the Sunni triangle. Gathering his followers, he dubbed them Tawhid wal Jihad (Monotheism and Holy War). It is believed al-Zarqawi was supported by Saddam's old intelligence and security services and he based himself in the city of Fallujah, west of Baghdad.

Meanwhile, Washington pressed on with its unfinished business with Saddam. American armour, taking part in Operation Thunder Run, entered Baghdad on 5 April 2003, heralding the end of Saddam's regime. The Iraqi capital was always seen as the centre of gravity, which is why Coalition strategy utilised blitzkrieg tactics, slicing through Iraqi defences and pressing on regardless. US marines and three British brigades were pitched at Basra, while the US 3rd Infantry Division headed for Karbala and the 1st Marine Division for Nasiriyah and Najaf, with Baghdad as the ultimate goal. Elements of the US 101st Airborne Division were also assigned to secure Najaf and defend the long lines of communication.

In an attempt to stave off the American advance, those Republican Guard Divisions around Baghdad (Hammurabi was dug in to the south-west, al-Nida the south-east and Nebuchadnezzar to the north) moved to engage them. They did little good. Saddam Hussein's supposedly elite Guard were attacked by US aircraft for the first time on 25 March 2003. By the time the Americans had reached Baghdad they were claiming to have destroyed most of Iraq's 2,500-strong tank force. The Special Republican Guard and the Adnan Republican Guard Division were expected to make a last stand at Tikrit, Saddam's home town, but after seven days of bombing the Americans brushed aside the 2,500 defenders. US marine armoured vehicles entered Tikrit on 13 April: Saddam's rule lay in tatters.

Initially, the Iraqi insurgency was largely home-grown. Saddam and his intelligence services had always planned to wage a terror campaign against any occupiers from the very start. After the 1998 Desert Fox bombing campaign against Saddam, he sought to set up a guerrilla army that would oppose any occupation and form the core of a new underground government. It consisted of three elements: the first and most notable was the Mujahideen, consisting of Iraqis from outside the ruling Ba'ath party and Islamic volunteers who had seen service in Afghanistan and Chechnya, with a strength of about 6,000. Then there was the al-Ansar (the supporters) and al-Muhajiroun, both of which drew on party members.[12]

Money not militant Islam was what Saddam proposed to use as the driving force behind his planned underground opposition to the Coalition. His intelligence services were behind the Fedayeen Saddam militia or 'men of sacrifice', which provided the initial opposition once the Iraqi armed forces had collapsed. The Fedayeen were offering $100 to anyone prepared to fire a rocket-propelled grenade at American troops, with a $5,000 bounty on every US soldier killed. Saddam's son Uday had originally commanded the 30,000-strong Fedayeen Saddam in the mid-1990s, as an instrument with which to crush political dissent.

Across Iraq, following the invasion, looting soon turned into organised attacks and the anarchy turned into insurgency in the Sunni central region. Most of the militants were Iraqis who had offered the most resistance to the invasion in March and April – namely the Fedayeen, though they were soon to be reinforced with Islamists from other countries, who made the most of Iraq's poorly-guarded borders. The insurgency had all the hallmarks of the Palestinian Intifada, hit-and-run gunmen, car bombs and suicide bombers. It was particularly intense for the American forces in the Baghdad area, known as the Sunni triangle.

Both Saddam's sons Uday and Qusay were killed after being discovered in a safe house in Mosul, on 29 June 2003, by Task Force 20. But this success was short-lived: Iraq's cities spiralled into anarchy and it took eight months to track down Saddam Hussein. For a while it was beginning to look like Osama bin Laden all over again. How could the most powerful nation on the face of the planet be incapable of tracking down the world's two most wanted men?

Finally, on 13 December 2003, Task Force 121 and elements of the US 4th Infantry Division ran Saddam to ground.

In the meantime, the multinational 'peace-keeping' force divided Iraq into six geographical regions (North, North Central, Western, Baghdad, Centre South and South East). Each area was assigned a multinational division, though none of these were anywhere near divisional strength. Multinational Division (South East) was created in mid-2003 and placed under British command. Multinational Division (Centre South) became operational that year but maintaining international troop commitments proved a major headache for Washington.

Under British command, the Multinational Division (South East) comprised over 13,000 soldiers (from the UK, Italy, Australia, Japan, Denmark, the Czech Republic, Lithuania, Norway, Portugal, the US, Norway and Romania) supported by the local Iraqi 10th Division, numbering about 9,000. These forces were responsible for the ongoing security operations in south-eastern Iraq, including the cities of Basra and An Nasiriyah (the British finally withdrew from Iraq in 2009).

Within two years the insurgency was all but unmanageable. The city of Haditha proved a constant thorn in the US military's side, as it sits astride the main highway from Syria, forming part of a network of towns in Anbar province used by Iraqi insurgents. By 2005 there was growing concern that the insurgents were becoming ever more sophisticated and were receiving help from Iran, Hezbollah in the Lebanon and Syria. In British military circles the view was that the insurgents were more sophisticated than the IRA.

On 1 August 2005, a marine foot patrol lost six dead after being ambushed outside Haditha, while another marine was blown up by a car bomb. In total, fourteen US marines died when their amphibious assault vehicle struck a triple-stacked anti-tank mine on 3 August near Haditha, creating an 8-foot-wide and 4-foot-deep crater. The blast was so powerful that it flipped the vehicle, killing its occupants instantly. Also that day, a marine assigned to 2nd Marine Division was killed in action by small-arms fire during combat operations in Ramadi, about 60 miles west of Baghdad. A suicide car bomber killed a marine from the 2nd Marine Division on 6 August near Amiriyah. (To date, the American military has suffered over 4,300 deaths and 31,000 casualties in Iraq.)

American troops, spearheaded by the marines and supported by Iraqi security forces, seized the initiative in a series of ongoing counter-terrorism operations throughout Iraq. During mid-July 2005 Operation Hard Knock saw marines alongside Iraqi troops search a wired-off sector of Fallujah for weapons and insurgents. The following month, Operation Quick Strike was designed to interdict and disrupt terrorist operations in western Iraq, near the cities of Haditha, Haqliniyah, and Barwanah. According to the marines, intelligence gathered by Coalition forces confirmed that terrorists were operating in these cities and in surrounding areas. As well as seizing various arms caches, they also destroyed car bombs while conducting cordon-and-searches in Haqliniyah. In Baghdad, Operation Lightning was designed to establish security in the Iraqi capital.

By mid-2007 there were 181,519 troops in Iraq, the vast bulk being American, numbering 140,000. The marines and other Coalition forces looked forward to 2010, when Iraq's security forces were to take over the burden of the security operations. Iraqi security forces had about 175,000 members, with 105 battalions of soldiers and police. Eighty per cent of the units were fighting alongside American forces, but the units were not yet able to operate independently. The plan was to have over a quarter of a million Iraqis under arms ready for the US withdrawal.

In the meantime, Iraq became a new breeding ground for international Islamists waging Jihad. The Coalition found themselves sitting on a Sunni hornets' nest stirred up by 'al-Qaeda in Iraq' led by the brutal 'Imposer from Zarqa'. Saddam had been punished, but at what cost? Once again, militant Islam was incensed by the actions of the Christian West.

Chapter 18

Unwelcome Aftermath: International Jihad

In the wake of 9/11 and the invasions of Afghanistan and Iraq, the popular perception was that militant Islam went global like some sort of fast-spreading virus. In fact, what happened was that many existing militant Muslim organisations simply sought to identify with al-Qaeda's creed. In 2003, the Director of the British Security Service (MI5), Eliza Manningham-Butler observed:

> al-Qaeda does not have the rigid structures of other terrorist groups, instead their strength is drawn from alliances, affiliations and networks forged in the terrorist training camps of Afghanistan and the conflicts of Algeria, Bosnia and Chechnya.[1]

Only now were such links being explicitly acknowledged.

By late 2004 it was estimated that, globally, up to 70,000 terrorists remained at large and that some 3,500 al-Qaeda members and affiliated supporters had been killed or captured.[2] According to the US State Department, by the third anniversary of 9/11 over 3,400 terrorist suspects had been seized in over eighty countries.[3] Many were being held in various foreign prisons around the world, the most notorious being Abu Ghraib in Iraq and Guantanamo Bay, Cuba.

Having rallied to the cause after 9/11, the international community was doing all it could to eradicate the worldwide scourge. The UN's Terrorism Prevention Branch helped 150 countries develop their counter-terrorism strategies, while direct assistance was provided to 114 of them between January 2003 and December 2007.[4] Also, US Congressional analyst Raphael Perl notes in Washington:

> The administration's response to the September 11, 2001 events was swift, wide ranging, and decisive. After administration officials attributed responsibility for the attack to Osama bin Laden and the al-Qaeda organisation, there was an announced policy shift from deterrence to pre-emption, generally referred to as the 'Bush Doctrine'.[5]

This was initially to prove all but useless, as al-Qaeda's reach continued to be global. For example, there was to be no escape from the activities of the Islamists for the moderate Muslim states of North Africa. There was a Moroccan link to 9/11. Zacarias Moussaoui, a 37-year-old French citizen of Moroccan origin, pleaded guilty in April 2005 to conspiring with the nineteen men who carried out the suicidal hijacking attacks on New York and Washington. He has sometimes been referred to as the twentieth hijacker, after suggestions that he would have taken part had he not been arrested three weeks earlier on immigration charges after behaving suspiciously at a flight school.

In mid-2002, the Moroccan Secret Service unmasked an al-Qaeda plot to attack American and British warships in the Mediterranean. Acting on intelligence gained from al-Qaeda suspects held by the US in Guantanamo Bay, three Saudis were kept under surveillance before being apprehended. There was a clear issue of maritime security because in September 2002, a USN Battle Group held a bilateral exercise with the Royal Moroccan Navy and Royal Moroccan Air Force.

The warship plotters were finally put on trial at the end of 2002, along with seven Moroccans also accused of being part of an al-Qaeda plot. The three Saudis were allegedly planning to obtain small speedboats, pack them with explosives and use them for suicide attacks against warships crossing the narrow Strait of Gibraltar. The Saudis received ten-year prison sentences in February 2003 – prosecutors had requested the death penalty. Adel al-Rafiki, alias Abu Hafs, a radical preacher who distributed Osama bin Laden tapes following 9/11 (and who served the Taliban in Afghanistan as a military medic), was also jailed when NATO intelligence services implicated him in the plan to blow up US warships. Foiling the plot was heralded as a major success in defeating attempts by al-Qaeda to recruit in Morocco and open a new terror campaign – others were not so sure.

Indeed, many hoped that this would be the end of the affair, then an attack of unprecedented ferocity shook Morocco's image as a tranquil haven immune from the violence besetting much of the Arab world. In five attacks on Western and Jewish targets (a Spanish restaurant, the Belgian consulate, a Jewish community centre, cemetery and a hotel) in Casablanca, forty-four people – including twelve suspected suicide bombers – were killed on 16 May 2003. The Moroccan government blamed the attacks on indigenous groups such as the banned Salafia Jihadia (SJ – Holy War of the Prophets) and Atakfir Wal Hijra (Exile and Redemption). But it also claimed they were linked to international extremists, notably al-Qaeda. However, an unknown group, al-Saiqa (Thunderbolt), claimed responsibility, stating its intention had been to target Moroccan and American intelligence agents. There is no evidence that al-Qaeda was involved, but synchronised suicide attacks are al-Qaeda trademarks.

In response, the Moroccan parliament passed a controversial anti-terrorism law. Over 1,000 people were arrested, some 700 of whom were charged with direct or indirect involvement – at least fourteen received death penalties and another thirty-nine received sentences varying from six to twenty years. Among those arrested was a French national, head of a key SJ cell in Tangiers, who had received weapons training in Afghanistan and Turkey. He allegedly planned to wage Jihad in Morocco. A British detainee, Perry Jensen, claimed he had been trained in Chechnya and Afghanistan. However, Perry and Abdelatif Merroun (who has Moroccan and British nationality) were acquitted of belonging to SJ at the High Court in Fez.

Strategically situated at the junction of the Atlantic and Mediterranean, Morocco has EU membership aspirations, but there is scant support for the proposal. The EU estimates that £2 billion worth of Moroccan cannabis helps fund terrorism. While Morocco used to turn a blind eye, the fact that proceeds have been aiding terrorists brought Western pressure on the Moroccan government. Human rights are also a source of contention. In mid-2003 the Paris-based media rights organisation, Reporters Sans Frontières, condemned 'regular interference' in the press by the intelligence services, as well as a prohibitive press law, effectively limiting free speech.

According to Tunisian sources there is no real appeal in Tunisia for militant Islam, despite the fact that Moroccans and Tunisians fought in Afghanistan against the Soviets.[6] Like Egypt and Morocco, Tunisia does not want any activity that could be detrimental to the vital tourist trade. Alarmingly, on 11 April 2002, Islamists blew up a Tunisian synagogue on the island of Djerba, killing fourteen German tourists.[7] Al-Qaeda official Sulaiman Abu Ghaith said his organisation took responsibility for the attack. In February 2008, militants kidnapped two Austrian tourists in southern Tunisia. An al-Qaeda spokesman named Salah Abou-Mohammad said:

> The Mujahideen have previously warned and alerted that the apostate Tunisian state cannot and will not be able to protect you [Western tourists], and the hands of the Mujahideen can reach you wherever you are on Tunisia soil.[8]

In Marrakech, sources claimed the Moroccan security services had a good handle on the handful of known local Islamists, and that the government was determined nothing should harm its lucrative tourist trade.[9] And yet, even though Morocco has experience of counter-insurgency warfare – after its long struggle against Polisario in the Western Sahara – these proved hollow words, in light of the activities of SJ and others.

In West Africa, Nigeria has been wracked by the activities of the Nigerian Taliban or Boko Haram, based in and around the northern city of Maidugiri. The Boko Haram sought the imposition of full Shariah law in northern Nigeria, culminating in violence during the summer of 2009. Boko Haram, which translates as, 'Western education is a sin', first emerged in 2004, opposed to the secular government. Although there is no evidence of links to the Afghan/

Pakistani Taliban, they are believed to have been inspired – like so many groups
– by Afghan radicals and veterans.

*

In the wake of the invasion of Iraq, the level of violence in Indian-administered
Kashmir dropped, largely because Pakistan feared that the US might turn its
attention on Islamabad, regardless of Pakistan's support for the global fight
against terrorism. Since then the militants have stepped up their bomb attacks
in Kashmir, including the capital, Srinagar. India continues to counter Islamic
militants attempting to cross the Line of Control between Pakistan/Pakistani
Kashmir and Indian Kashmir. By late 2003, Indian intelligence indicated that
1,600 militants, including twenty suicide squads, were preparing to cross.
According to the Indian Army, Pakistan uses shelling as a way of distracting
Indian troops while militants cross the Line of Control.

Islamic militancy in the Indian-administered half of Kashmir started as
an indigenous popular uprising, but now it has a heavy Pakistani slant to it.
India claims the Pakistan-backed separatist organisations Jaish-e-Mohammed
and Lashkar-e-Tayyiba were responsible for the audacious attack on Delhi's
parliament building on 13 December 2002. However, in late September 2003,
Yasin Malik, head of the separatist Kashmiri group, the Jammu Kashmir
Liberation Front (JKLF), was acquitted of receiving funds from Pakistan by
an Indian anti-terrorism court.

*

In South East Asia, on 12 October 2002, in the tourist district of Kuta on
the Indonesian island of Bali, Indonesian terrorists struck. The attack was the
deadliest act of terrorism in the history of Indonesia, killing 202 people – 164 of
whom were foreign nationals and the remainder Indonesian citizens. A further
209 were injured. The attackers were from Jemaah Islamiah (JI), an organisation linked to al-Qaeda. After this bombing, Indonesia became the focal point
for the global war against terrorism in the Asia-Pacific region. JI's main aim
is the establishment of Islamic governments across the region, followed by
the formation of a unified South East Asian Islamic state. Other Indonesian
extremist groups include the Darul Islam, Islamic Defenders' Front (FPI) and
Laskar Jihad.

The arrest of almost 100 JI members and the imprisonment of the group's
spiritual leader, Abu Bakar Ba'asyir, for plotting to overthrow the Jakarta
government is unlikely to cripple the organisation. Its network is believed to
cover not only Indonesia, but also Malaysia, the Philippines, Singapore and
Thailand. Smaller cells may also operate in Cambodia, Vietnam, and even
Australia.

Attacks continued in Indonesia, most notably with the Marriott Hotel bombing in Jakarta in August 2003 – again, the work of JI. Indonesia's Chief of Police
stated that he expected more attacks and Washington feared JI could target US

officials or facilities. Instead they struck Bali again, when a series of suicide-bomb attacks occurred on 1 October 2005. Bombs exploded at two sites in Jimbaran and Kuta, both in south Bali. Twenty people were murdered and 129 people injured by three bombers, who killed themselves in the attacks.

*

Al-Qaeda-inspired attacks also spread across Europe. More than sixty people were killed by a series of suicide bombings in Istanbul in November 2003, which the authorities linked to al-Qaeda – suspected al-Qaeda suicide bombers blew up trucks packed with explosives at the British consulate and London-based HSBC Bank, killing at least twenty-seven people and wounding nearly 450. In Madrid, on 11 March 2004 (three days before Spain's general elections), there was a series of co-ordinated bombings against the commuter train system, killing 191 and wounding 2,050. The official investigation determined the attacks were directed by an al-Qaeda-inspired terrorist cell. It is the only Islamist terrorist act in the history of Europe where non-Muslims collaborated with Muslims.

In 2003, terrorists planned to hijack an aircraft from eastern Europe and fly it into Heathrow airport. An intelligence tip-off ensured that armoured vehicles and troops were sent to protect Heathrow and the plot was thwarted.[10] Then, on 7 July 2005, the so-called '7/7 bombings' saw a series of co-ordinated terrorist bomb blasts hit London's public transport system during the morning rush hour, killing fifty-two people.

*

Just four years after 9/11 the US State Department, drawing on data provided by the National Counter-terrorism Center (NCTC), was reporting that radical Jihadists were becoming more widespread, diffuse and increasingly deadly, as well as being inspired by al-Qaeda. According to NCTC figures, in 2005 around 40,000 people were killed or wounded by terrorists, compared to 9,300 in 2004 and 4,271 in 2003. Terror attacks peaked at 11,111 in 2005, up from 208 in 2003.

President Bush signed the Intelligence Reform and Terrorism Prevention Act on 17 December 2004, creating the post of Director of National Intelligence (separate from the CIA Director) to serve as the president's senior intelligence guru, overseeing both America's domestic and foreign intelligence activities. The NCTC was also set up to co-ordinate counter-terrorism activities across all government agencies. It reportedly holds over 325,000 terrorist-related records.[11]

US tools to combat international terrorism included constructive engagement (though some have been sceptical – former CIA Director James Woolsey's view was that 'they want to blow up the table and everyone who is sitting at the table'),[12] diplomacy, economic sanctions, economic inducements, covert action, law enforcement co-operation and what many see as the preferred option, military force, better known as the 'big stick'. America continues to list Iran as a state sponsor of terrorism and yet praises Libya, Saudi Arabia and Sudan for anti-terrorism efforts.

Some argue there is no such thing as a global war on terror, that it is an artificial construct allowing Western democracies to erode civil liberties and Developing World regimes to clamp down on political opponents. However, the most recent collated figures produced by the US NCTC show that between 2006 and 2007 there was a 9 per cent increase in deaths due to terrorism and a 15 per cent increase in the number injured. Fortunately, due to a slackening of the insurgency in Iraq, attacks decreased by 18 per cent during 2008 with deaths dropping by 30 per cent. This equates to over 14,500 terrorist attacks during 2007, which caused 67,000 casualties (22,000 of which were fatalities). The majority of these, however, were accounted for by the insurgency in Iraq.[13] During 2008 there were 11,800 attacks, resulting in 50,000 casualties.[14]

For Washington, countering terrorism on US soil is an almost impossible task. For example, in 2008 it was estimated that there were 11.6 million illegal immigrants living in America[15] and that same year 175 million foreign nationals (including tourists and business travellers) were granted temporary entry into the US.[16] Between 2000 and 2008 the illegal population of America increased by 3.1 million, representing a net annual increase of 390,000 people. Keeping track of such numbers is almost impossible, regardless of the resources devoted to the task.

Every country around the world faces a similar problem. For example, there are, on average, some 8.4 million passenger arrivals through Australian international airports each year, of which some 5 million are not Australian citizens.[17] The only figures available for the number of illegal immigrants living in the UK were published in 2005 and cover 2001. According to the Home Office they totalled 430,000 people – helpfully, the British government has not researched numbers since.[18] Monitoring the 'enemy within' becomes a fruitless task under such conditions.

Partly in response to the fall-out from 9/11, the UK established the Joint Terrorism Analysis Centre (JTAC).[19] Although the delay in arresting, repatriating or extraditing Muslim extremists, such as Abu Hamza, seems frustrating, all the time that these individuals remain at liberty it means that the Security Service (MI5), Secret Intelligence Service (MI6), GCHQ Cheltenham, the Defence Intelligence Staff (DIS) and JTAC can continue to exploit their contacts. As soon as an individual is arrested, any source of intelligence inevitably dries up.

In terms of tracking terrorism in the UK, the Terrorism Act 2000 is the primary piece of legislation. It came into force in response to the changing threat from international terrorism, and replaced the previous temporary anti-terrorism legislation that dealt primarily with Northern Ireland. It made it illegal for proscribed terrorist groups to operate in the UK and extended the list to cover extremist Muslim terrorist groups such as al-Qaeda.[20]

Police officers were given greater powers to help prevent and investigate terrorism, including: wider stop and search; the power to detain suspects after arrest for up to twenty-eight days (periods of more than two days must be approved by a magistrate).[21] The government also launched a Commission on Integration and Cohesion to look at how communities in England tackle tensions and extremism.[22] Since this initiative, the British Security Services have continued to unmask various Islamic plots in the UK. Following 7/7, community-led working groups were set up under the banner of 'Preventing Extremism Together' to develop practical recommendations for tackling the problem.[23]

Young Jihadists, especially the 'lone wolves', remain largely undeterred by such measures. Furthermore, international intelligence co-ordination evidently remains deficient in light of the 2009 'Christmas Bomber' slipping through the intelligence net – despite all the warnings. In this instance America was swift to blame Britain for its own failings.

Chapter 19

Where's bin Laden?

What of Islamist mastermind Osama bin Laden: did he escape his Tora Bora lair in Afghanistan? US Senator, Bob Graham, head of the Senate's Intelligence Committee, is convinced he is still alive. Recorded references he has made to America's subsequent actions in Iraq indicate that he may well be. As America prepared to mark the second anniversary of 9/11, the first new footage of bin Laden seen in more than a year was broadcast by the Qatar-based TV channel, al-Jazeera, on 10 September 2003. The video footage, also featuring Ayman al-Zawahiri, has no dialogue, but al-Jazeera also aired two audio recordings purportedly of the pair praising 9/11 and encouraging attacks on US troops. American intelligence assesses the video to be authentic but is unable to date it. Al-Jazeera claims the recording was probably made in April or early May 2003. Most agree it was certainly shot in Afghanistan or Pakistan, indicating that bin Laden had not fled far.

This was followed on 28 September 2003 by a message broadcast by two Arabic TV stations from al-Zawahiri, accusing General Musharraf of Pakistan of betraying Islam and calling on Muslims to topple him. Pakistani security forces continued to co-operate closely with US efforts to track down bin Laden and al-Qaeda supporters along the Afghan border where they may be hiding. This no doubt sparked the threat.

Within three years of the fall of the Taliban, the war on terror in Afghanistan was gathering momentum. Elements of the US Special Forces Task Force 121 (TF-121), which captured Saddam Hussein, relocated from Iraq to Afghanistan in February 2004 to hunt bin Laden.[1] The irony is that the 5th Special Forces Group, which made up TF-121, were originally re-deployed from their pursuit of bin Laden prior to the invasion of Iraq. While the unsuccessful hunt for bin Laden continued during the war in Iraq, the Pentagon acknowledged that co-ordination problems with its plethora of Special Forces led to the creation of TF-121.

TF-121, along with their British counterparts in the Special Boat Service (SBS) and Special Air Service (SAS), supported by the Royal Navy off Pakistan, stepped up their efforts. In theory, TF-121 (which incorporated the earlier Task Force Dagger, TF-20, TF-5 and probably elements of Combined Joint Task Force-7) should have been re-designated after its move. Confidence had been running high in Washington that this force was close to capturing bin Laden. In 2003, a US forces spokesman announced: 'We have a variety of intelligence, and we're sure we're going to catch Osama bin Laden and Mullah Omar this year.'[2]

Furthermore, US officials admitted that the Delta–SEAL Task Force might be used inside Pakistan if detailed intelligence emerged on bin Laden's whereabouts. Such intelligence was gained at the end of February 2004, when the son of Ayman al-Zawahiri was captured by Pakistani security forces in South Waziristan. He was swiftly interrogated by Pakistan's ISI and the CIA. Additionally, in early March, the Zaklikhael tribesmen of Waziristan agreed to help the 70,000 Pakistani troops deployed to hunt out al-Qaeda militants.

On the other side of the border, at Salerno base near Khost, 1,600 US troops, including the Delta–SEAL TF, were poised for an all-out effort to find bin Laden. Throughout February 2004 the 1st Battalion, 501st Parachute Infantry Regiment, operating out of Salerno, conducted search-and-destroy sweeps in the area, hunting former Taliban leaders.

The two-month American-led operation in Afghanistan – Mountain Blizzard – ended in mid-March 2004. It was part of a continuing series of operations in south-eastern Afghanistan designed to root out al-Qaeda and destroy its infrastructure.[3] Mountain Blizzard was then followed by a hammer and anvil operation involving US Special Forces from TF 121 supported by 100 SAS and 10,000 US troops.[4] The grandly-named Operation Mountain Storm was intended to trap al-Qaeda/Taliban remnants against some 12,000 Pakistani troops across the border.

Pakistan's co-operation in the hunt for bin Laden and Mullah Omar remained vital, particularly in the North West Frontier Province and Federally-Administered Tribal Areas adjacent to Afghanistan. Pakistan's strategic coastal province of Baluchistan and the landlocked North West Frontier Province were the original secret breeding grounds of the Taliban and this legacy continues to plague the Pakistani authorities to this day. While all attention was focused on Pakistan's lawless North West Frontier Province, way to the south, the Baluchi insurgency remains largely forgotten. Its porous borders with Afghanistan mean that al-Qaeda and the Taliban have been able to pass back and forth with little hindrance in this area.

The security of Pakistan's nuclear programme also remains a concern. There have been regular indications that al-Qaeda has nuclear aspirations. It has been claimed that bin Laden held discussions with Pakistani nuclear scientists and tried to obtain radioactive waste from Bulgaria. Washington also claims he has sought enriched uranium. Alarmingly, according to some US experts, the possibility of bin Laden's organisation obtaining finished nuclear weapons, components or design expertise cannot be ruled out.

Eliza Manningham-Butler, Director of the Security Service, warned that renegade Pakistani scientists had provided Islamic militants with technical information on how to build a radiological 'dirty bomb'. In February 2004, Abdul Qadeer Khan, father of Pakistan's nuclear bomb, confessed to hawking Pakistan's nuclear secrets on the black market. Al-Qaeda had been prepared to spend over $1.5 million to get its hands on nuclear weaponry, but only ever got as far as building a crude radiological device in Herat in western Afghanistan.

Pakistan reportedly secretly agreed to allow both American and British forces to cross into its tribal areas in pursuit of al-Qaeda and Taliban fighters. Notably, America and Pakistan have denied that Washington will take a softer approach over Pakistan's nuclear proliferation in return for allowing US forces to operate on Pakistani soil. However, Pakistan turned a blind eye to such incursions in return for the $700 million the State Department promised to help support the war against terrorism. American intelligence assets, including U-2 spy planes and Predator UAVs, were deployed to 'assist' the Pakistani armed forces.

CIA covert Ops got more and more prominent on the Pakistani side of the border. US intelligence officials confirmed that a missile fired from a CIA guided-Predator killed a senior al-Qaeda operative in Pakistan on 13 May 2005. Although the CIA refuses to confirm or deny operational details, bomb-maker Haitham al-Yemeni had been under close surveillance in case he provided a lead on the whereabouts of Osama bin Laden. After the capture, in north-west Pakistan, of Abu Faraj al-Libbi, bin Laden's third in command, American and Pakistani authorities were concerned al-Yemeni would go to ground, so decided to act. Contrary to US statements, Pakistan denied al-Yemeni was killed on its soil.

The deployment of Predator to Pakistan was not new. President Musharraf admitted that CIA agents and technical experts were based in his country, and in early 2004 Predator UAVs assisted Pakistani armed forces conducting extensive security operations in South Waziristan. This was in concert with Operation Mountain Storm. Subsequently, a well-known pro-Taliban tribal leader, Nek Mohammad, and five of his companions were killed in Waziristan, on 17 June 2004, by a laser-guided missile that probably came from a Predator.[5] Mohammad had been using his satellite phone just before the missile struck and locals say they saw a drone overhead. Shortly after his death, Predator was reported patrolling near Shkin on the Afghan side of the Waziristan border. The CIA remains tight-lipped about any role in Mohammad's death.

Nek Mohammad fought with the Taliban against the Northern Alliance during the late 1990s and then ran a conduit for fleeing foreign fighters after the US invasion of Afghanistan in 2001. In the wake of America's Operation Anaconda, he assisted Arab and Central Asian fighters driven from Paktia province. When the Pakistani forces launched their operations in South Waziristan he was sheltering the leader of the IMU, Tahir Yuldashev. Ironically, dissident IMU members are believed to have betrayed al-Yemeni to the CIA.

In early 2004, hopes had been high that Osama bin Laden or Ayman al-Zawahiri would be killed or captured in Waziristan. They proved elusive quarry. Unfortunately, several years earlier, a news report alerted bin Laden and his supporters to the fact that their mobile phones were being monitored by the National Security Agency. The CIA, FBI and the Pentagon had relied on such telephone intercepts, as well as informants, to pinpoint bin Laden.

Since the invasion of Afghanistan, the remnants of al-Qaeda and the former Taliban regime operate out of the Federally Administered Tribal Areas (FATA) in north-western Pakistan, particularly the North and South Waziristan agencies, while to the south they have a foothold in Baluchistan province. The first major counter-insurgency operation and the Pakistani Army's first-ever attack against al-Qaeda was conducted on 22 June 2002, at Azam Warsak, South Waziristan. The mission was flawed because of local sympathy for the Taliban and foreign fighters, fostered by resentment towards America following the US-led invasion of Afghanistan.

Afterwards, the Pakistani military pledged to consult tribal leaders before further action was taken, and that responsibility would rest with the local tribes to take measures against the foreign fighters. Nonetheless, on 2 October 2003, with support from twelve helicopter gunships, 2,500 commandos were air-dropped into the village of Baghar, near Angor Ada. According to local sources, some of the helicopters flew from the US air base at Machdad Kot in Afghanistan. This operation did little to help foster relations with the local tribes. Pakistani security forces' attacks against foreign militants reached a crescendo in 2004, when they fought a vicious campaign in Waziristan. On 24 February 2004, the Pakistani Army launched an operation against the Mehsood and Wazir tribes. Reportedly, US helicopters helped oversee this mission. Khalid, the son of al-Zawahiri, was captured in South Waziristan and interrogated by the ISI and the CIA.[6]

In a prelude to America's spring offensive in neighbouring Afghanistan, Pakistani troops, supported by helicopter gunships, fixed-wing aircraft and artillery, deployed into three towns in South Waziristan. A new offensive centred on Wana, involving the elite commandos of the Special Services Group (SSG) of the Pakistani Army, commenced on 16 March 2004 with the usual mixed results.

The day before, top al-Qaeda and Taliban leaders, including al-Qaeda commander Abdullah Ahmed Abdullah (alias Abu Mohammed), al-Qaeda special training cell operative Qari Rashi Maqtoom, Taliban commander Abdul Bari Sayyaf, Afghan veteran Jalaluddin Haqani and IMU commander Tahir Yuldashev (also allegedly number ten in al-Qaeda), gathered at Kalosha. However, by the time the offensive commenced they had fled (apart from Yuldashev), probably acting on a tip-off.

The operation met stiff resistance by up to 400 al-Qaeda fighters, including Afghans, Arabs, Chechens, Chinese Uighurs and Uzbeks, and Pakistani officials concluded they must be defending a high value target. Initially, it was claimed they had trapped Ayman al-Zawahiri and this was reinforced by a CIA assessment, which had identified South Waziristan as his most likely hiding place in late 2003.[7] However, Pakistan subsequently revised its assessment to say the man was Yuldashev.[8]

In an effort to prevent al-Qaeda fleeing by sea, the Pakistani government agreed to allow Coalition warships to patrol its territorial waters. When the Taliban were ousted from Afghanistan, al-Qaeda militants were able to escape to Yemen and the Horn of Africa. President Musharraf also committed the Pakistani Navy to join the seven-nation Royal Navy-led task force patrolling the Arabian Sea. Musharraf's agreement came after talks in Islamabad with Admiral Sir Alan West, First Sea Lord and Chief of the Naval Staff. However, some American forces operating in Afghanistan remained sceptical about Pakistani efforts to seal the porous border.

Musharraf wrote in his memoirs in 2006 that he was clearly annoyed by allegations that he and Pakistan had not done enough in the war on terror. He was also irked at being treated as a hired help:

> We have captured 689 and handed 369 to the United States. We have earned bounties totalling millions of dollars. Those who habitually accuse us of 'not doing enough' in the war on terror should simply ask the CIA how much prize money it has paid to the government of Pakistan.[9]

By the end of March 2004, Pakistan claimed its forces had wounded Yuldashev, though apparently failed to capture him, killed an al-Qaeda intelligence chief along with sixty-three guerrillas and captured another 100. The wounding of Yuldashev led to a backlash in Uzbekistan. There were bomb attacks and gun battles in the streets of the Uzbek capital, Tashkent, while Uzbek Special Forces stormed a terrorist safe house north of the president's residence.

According to Peshawar Corps Commander, Lieutenant General Safdar Hussain, by March 2005 the Pakistani military had carried out almost fifty military operations throughout South Waziristan alone. The Pakistani military attempted to shift the foreign fighters from the Pashtun areas of Baluchistan, to the Waziristan area of the FATA, to join the existing remnants of al-Qaeda, the IMU, the Jundullah (Army of Allah) and elements of the International Islamic Front. The Pakistani Army agreed to suspend operations in return for assurance that the fighters would only operate in Afghanistan. Pakistani troops deployed on counter-terrorism duties in Waziristan, including their Cobra helicopters, were then redeployed to Baluchistan to commence offensive operations against the nationalist Baluchistan Liberation Army (BLA).

Despite these efforts by the end of 2005, al-Qaeda and the Taliban had switched from using Baluchistan as a logistical hub to an operational base. To complicate matters, north-west Baluchistan's border city of Chaman became a stronghold for the Laskar-i-Jhangvi, a Pakistani Sunni group that has attacked Pakistani Shias. The Jundullah, which had suspended its operations in Karachi, resumed them on 2 March 2006, with a suicide bomb directed at a US consulate car.

The Pakistani Army's greatest success was eliminating al-Qaeda's operational commander. Abu Hamza Rabia, believed to be one of al-Qaeda's top five, was killed along with four other militants on 22 December 2005, after a Pakistani Cobra fired rockets into a house in Mirali in North Waziristan (a CIA Predator using Hellfire missiles has also been credited with the kill). The attack, acting on US intelligence, caused bomb-making materials to explode. However, confirmation of the deaths was hampered by removal of the bodies by al-Qaeda fighters. Rabia reportedly replaced Abu Faraj al-Libbi as operational chief, after he was captured in May 2005. Rabia's death weakened al-Qaeda's ability to launch attacks from the Afghan/Pakistani border region. This was at least the second attempt to kill him, as he was targeted by an American Predator attack on 5 November 2005.

Acting on intelligence (allegedly from the Afghan side of the border), the Pakistani Army struck a training camp for foreign fighters, which included a sizeable ammunition dump, on 1 March 2006. It had been under intelligence surveillance after a raid some weeks previously triggered a militant attack on a Frontier Corps outpost and other installations. According to Pakistani Army spokesman, Major-General Shaukat Sultan, at the beginning troops from a Special Operations Task Force (SOTF), backed by helicopter gunships, attacked Islamic militants at Saidgai some 15km north of Miran Shah in North Waziristan. The gunships blasted a small compound consisting of eight houses before the ground forces moved in for the kill. During the heavy fighting, which involved up to fourteen helicopters, forty-five militants were killed, while the army suffered one fatality and ten wounded, including one of the Cobra pilots. The helicopters also reportedly fired on several vehicles trying to break out of the area, killing a Chechen rebel leader.[10]

Major-General Sultan noted that most of the dead troublemakers had come from Central Asian or Arab countries. According to the Arab media channel, al-Jazeera, the Pakistani Army responded after the fighters had infiltrated Pakistan, following a raid inside neighbouring Afghanistan's Khost province. According to local tribal sources, the militants had kidnapped nine Pakistani soldiers.

This operation came in the wake of Afghanistan's accusations that the Pakistani government was not doing enough to control the lawless border and that ousted Taliban and al-Qaeda forces were using Pakistani soil from which to launch attacks. Afghan authorities passed the Pakistanis a list of 150 named militants (including bin Laden and al-Zawahiri), who are allegedly hiding in Pakistan, but claim no action has been taken. In January 2006 bin Laden was reportedly hiding in Zhob, Baluchistan, but escaped while the authorities dithered. Afghan President Hamid Karzai has claimed that former Taliban leader, Mullah Omar, is also hiding in Baluchistan.

When Pakistan gained independence the Sunni Baluchis were forcibly incorporated, leading to two rebellions in 1958 and 1962, as well as a guerrilla war between 1973–77. The clampdown, triggered by an attempt on President Musharraf's life on 14 December 2005, during a visit to Quetta, resulted in hundreds of deaths and thousands of arrests. Reportedly, some six Pakistani Army Brigades, plus paramilitary forces numbering some 25,000 men were struggling to contain the BLA, consisting of the Bugti clan and other assorted tribals, in the Kohlu Mountains. They keep holding the main gas pipeline hostage. Previous governments had paid the ransom in the form of 'royalties', but the current government refused and was rewarded with an insurgency masquerading as a bid for greater resources and autonomy. Allegedly, weapons are smuggled into Baluchistan from Afghanistan to feed the insurgency. Musharraf claimed that India has also been assisting the Baluchi insurgents, smuggling in weapons via the long and porous Rajahstan border.

Despite the ongoing use of American-supplied hardware, the US State Department has ruled that the Baluchi conflict is an internal matter. The worry is that the insurgency could foster ethnic unrest in the neighbouring Sindh province. Furthermore, the bulk of Pakistan's natural resources, such as gas, oil, uranium and copper, are located in Baluchistan and the province's strategic importance has grown since China started building a major port at Gwadar.

In the fighting in the frontier provinces during early 2006, Pakistan suffered more than it would care to admit. Pakistan has made considerable sacrifices to try to cut off the terrorists using its soil as a base for attacks in Afghanistan and Pakistan itself. To cut cross-border infiltration, the Pakistani government has proposed a fence along the Durand Line – whether this will happen remains to be seen.

Both Pakistan and India have their own indigenous terrorist problems, stemming from their volatile dispute over divided Kashmir. The Harakat ul-Mujahidin (HUM) is a Pakistan-based Islamic militant group seeking to end Indian control of the Muslim-inhabited parts of Kashmir. It is believed to comprise militant Islamist Pakistanis, Kashmiris and Arab veterans of the Afghan war against the Soviets. Other groups include the HUM splinter faction Jaish-e-Mohammed (JEM or Army of Mohammed) and Lashkar-e-Tayyiba (Army of the Righteous). HUM and JEM are believed to be aligned with al-Qaeda. Under pressure from Washington, Pakistan banned these organisations and froze their assets.

Pakistan remains plagued by two types of terrorism. First, sectarian strife between Shia and Sunni. The main groups are Shia Tehrik-e-Jaffria Pakistan and the breakaway faction, Sipah-e-Mohammad (Army of Mohammad), pitted against the Sunni or Deobandi Sipah-e-Sahaba Pakistan (Army of the Companions of the Prophet, Pakistan) and Lashkar-e-Jhangvi (Army of God). Second, Jihadist strife prosecuted by numerous groups used by the Pakistani government prior to 9/11 as a strategic weapon in the struggles in Afghanistan and Kashmir. Worryingly for the authorities, the distinction between the sectarian and Jihadist groups has become increasingly blurred. Lashkar-e-Tayyiba is believed to have been involved in the December 2001 attack on New Delhi's Parliament, the 2006 Mumbai train bombings, and the February 2007 blast on a train running between India and Pakistan.

While the war on terror had reasonable success against the Taliban and al-Qaeda leadership, bin Laden and his senior entourage remained elusive. Senior al-Qaeda leader, Abu Zubaydah, was captured in March 2002 in Pakistan. He was seized in a Lashkar-e-Tayyiba safe house in Faisalabad, clearly indicating a link between the two organisations. The following March, the alleged mastermind behind 9/11, Khalid Sheikh Mohammed, and al-Qaeda's treasurer, Mustafa Ahmed al-Hawsawi, were also captured in Pakistan. In April 2006, Abdul Rahman al-Muhajir and Abu Bakr al-Suri, two of al-Qaeda's chief bomb-makers, were killed in Pakistan. Abu Laith al-Libi was eliminated in January 2008 and Abu Obaidah al-Masri, another senior commander, reportedly died of hepatitis in Pakistan in April 2008. Most, if not all, of those captured were passed to America.

It was claimed by Saudi intelligence sources that bin Laden had died of typhoid on 23 August 2006 in Pakistan. However, the Pakistani Home Minister Aftab Ahmed Sherpao dismissed these reports as totally baseless. Such rumours were fuelled by the fact that while he continued to issue audio tapes, bin Laden had not recorded any new video messages since late 2004 and the US presidential election. This contrasted sharply with the regular video broadcasts by al-Zawahiri. In fact, bin Laden did issue his first video tape in three years in September 2007.[11]

By 2009 CIA Director Michael Hayden assessed that bin Laden was probably hiding in the tribal area of north-west Pakistan. He also warned that al-Qaeda continued to grow in Africa and the Middle East, adding that progress has been made in curbing it in the Philippines, Indonesia, Saudi Arabia and Iraq. After bin Laden's apparent offer of a truce with America was rejected by Washington, he turned on the moderate Arab states and Israel. Earlier offers of a cessation of hostilities in Europe were likewise rejected.

An audio message emerged in March 2009, in which he accused the moderate Arab leaders of conspiring with the West against Muslims. In addition, he accused Israel of committing war crimes in the Gaza strip. Bin Laden called for a renewed Jihad to first conquer Iraq and then Jordan, which could be used as a route into the West Bank. In his previous audio message, in January 2009, he called for a holy war to stop the Israeli offensive against Gaza. He also criticised Sheikh Hassan Dahir Aweys, president of Somalia, calling for his overthrow.

Just two days after the 8th anniversary of 9/11, an audio message allegedly from bin Laden was released. In it a voice claimed the US president was powerless to halt the wars in Afghanistan and Iraq and went on to reiterate 9/11 was in part due to US support for Israel. This was followed by another audio tape, urging European nations to withdraw from Afghanistan. In a previous message, issued in June, he accused President Obama of stirring up Muslim hatred towards the US. All this seemed to indicate he was alive.

While the consensus is that bin Laden fled Tora Bora into Pakistan, reports also suggested he was hiding near the Afghan-Iranian border. Certainly, members of his family escaped westward to Iran. Some twenty-five senior al-Qaeda officials, including bin Laden's eldest son, Saad, and his brothers Mohammed and Othman, along with senior commander Saif al-Adel and spokesman Sulaiman Abu Ghaith, were given sanctuary there. Iran claimed they were under house arrest and would be put on trial but this did not happen and Adel was able to make a phone call from Iran in May 2003, ordering the Riyadh bombings.[12] Another of bin Laden's son's, Omar, sought sanctuary in Egypt, having unsuccessfully sought political asylum in Spain and the UK. After living in Egypt for a year he was sent to Qatar in November 2008.[13]

Former President Musharraf aptly summed up the failure to completely decapitate al-Qaeda:

> The key question that remains is, of course, the whereabouts of Osama bin Laden and Ayman al-Zawahiri. They could be in one of the tribal agencies, hiding with sympathetic locals. But they could just as well be on the Afghan side, enjoying the hospitality of Mullah Omar. Or they could, cleverly, be moving close to the border, alternating between Afghanistan and Pakistan, to confuse those looking for them.[14]

He went on to claim that al-Qaeda was shattered and stated: 'I can say with surety that in Pakistan we are winning the war against the terrorists.'[15] Whether you believed him was another matter – after all, he was the man who claimed that the Taliban was not operating in Pakistan.

While in Saudi Arabia the authorities drove the militants underground, in Pakistan they increasingly sought to accommodate them. This resulted in the followers of the Lal Masjid or Red Mosque imposing Shariah law in whole neighbourhoods of Islamabad. This was a direct challenge to the authority of Musharraf. This Talibanisation of the capital had far-reaching consequences for the rest of the country.

Ultimately, the legacy of the wars in Afghanistan has been the almost complete destabilisation of Pakistan's western border provinces. By 2009 the Pakistani Taliban were completely out of control. Once they had been the guardians of the Afghan Taliban and al-Qaeda, but the Pakistani Taliban have since developed their own political agenda – turning northern Pakistan into an Islamic state ruled through Shariah law.

Bajaur is one of the Pakistani tribal areas where the Taliban established themselves after they were ousted from Afghanistan. They set up camps at a number of locations, including Salarzai and Dasht. Senior Afghan Taliban leaders are also based in Baluchistan and Sindh provinces, from where they provide logistics for the Taliban's war against US and Nato forces in Afghanistan. Maulvi Faqir Mohammad, commander of the Taliban in Bajaur, controls almost 10,000 armed militants. Maulvi Omar, spokesman for the militant alliance Tehrik Taliban Pakistan (TTP), comes from Bajaur. Analysts felt the area might be the hiding place of bin Laden, al-Zawahiri and other top al-Qaeda leaders. A year-long military operation ended in Bajaur in early 2009 but a peace agreement collapsed and the Taliban was soon in control of most areas outside the regional capital, Khar.

Musharraf was forced to retract his claim by April 2009 when pro-Taliban forces took over a vast swathe of the North West Frontier Province and advanced to within 60 miles of Islamabad.[16] Over a million people were forced to flee their homes and it required a major Pakistani Army offensive to reassert control of the city of Mingora in the Swat Valley. The Pakistani security forces committed around 15,000 men against an estimated 5,000 militants. They claimed over 1,000 militants and fifty troops were killed during the offensive. By this stage, the military were saying that, no matter how many they killed, they could not win.

Following the Swat Valley offensive, Taliban leader, Baitullah Mehsud, was reported killed in a CIA missile strike in early August 2009 in South Waziristan. He had declared himself 'Ameer Sahib' (Mr Chief) of the Pakistani Taliban in 2007, gathering various factions together to make north-west Pakistan a stronghold of both the Taliban and al-Qaeda. Commanding up to 20,000 followers, his stated mission was to destroy the Pakistani state for its 'collaboration' with the West. Mehsud claimed responsibility for the assassination of President Asif Zardari's wife, Benazir Bhutto, on 27 December 2007.

Over an eighteen-month period, twenty al-Qaeda commanders were killed in the same manner (including Saad bin Laden, one of bin Laden's sons, al-Qaeda's chief in Pakistan, its director of external operations and its propaganda and financial heads) following an influx of operatives from Bangladesh, North Africa, Saudi Arabia, Somalia and Turkey.

Retribution for Mehsud's death was swift. In just ten days, during early October, his successor and former deputy, Hakimullah Mehsud, dispelled any illusions that the militants were in retreat. Hakimullah also alarmed neighbouring India when he summed up his objectives as: 'First stop, an Islamic state in Pakistan, second stop, attacks in India.' It was hoped that Baitullah's death would undermine the Pakistani Taliban's links with such groups as Jaish-e-Mohammed and Lashkar-e-Tayyiba, but this failed to happen.

Audaciously, Taliban fighters stormed the Pakistani Army's headquarters in Rawalpindi, while commando-style attacks were also conducted in Islamabad, Peshawar and Lahore. Half of the attackers in Rawalpindi were Punjabi militants from the group Harkat-ul-Jihad-al-Islami, showing an increasing level of co-operation among Pakistan's various militant factions.

A major three-pronged offensive was launched into South Waziristan in October 2009, targeting the Taliban towns of Ladha and Makeen. However, as this operation had been in preparation for at least six weeks, the Taliban and foreign fighters, including Arabs and Uzbeks, either retreated into the surrounding mountains or neighbouring Orakzai (one of Hakimullah's strongholds along with the tribal regions of Khyber and Kurram).

It appears Pakistan's war against the Pakistani Taliban, as with its other militant groups, may be unending.

Chapter 20

Syria: on the Brink

While Syria's presence in Lebanon was a constant source of friction with the Lebanese and Israeli governments, so was its hosting of militant Palestinian groups such as Hamas and Islamic Jihad. Despite pressure on the Syrian president, Bashr al-Assad, from Washington, following the fall of Saddam Hussein, the Syrians were still supporting at least seven organisations deemed undesirable by America. Both Hamas and PIJ, headed by Imad al-Alami and Abdallah Ramadan Shalah respectively, were running operations from offices in Damascus. Volunteers were being trained in Syrian camps to conduct attacks in the West Bank and Iraq – in particular, al-Alami was overseeing numerous suicide attacks in Israel.[1]

An Italian report in April 2003 claimed that Syria had become a hub for al-Zarqawi's operations in Iraq. Transcripts of wiretapped conversations among the arrested suspects and others paint a detailed picture of overseers in Syria co-ordinating the movement of recruits and money between Europe and Iraq.[2] In April 2004, Jordanian police uncovered an al-Qaeda cell, and most of the plotters had trained in Syria. The Syrian-Iraqi border was unmonitored for much of 2003, but in March 2004, the Coalition announced a $300-million scheme to double the number of Iraqi border police to around 18,000 men.

Nor was Washington slow to accuse Syria of allowing al-Qaeda and Iraqi Ba'athist militants to cross into Iraq to feed the insurgency. Nonetheless, by early July 2004, Syria had reportedly increased its assistance to the insurgents in Iraq and was providing safe passage for both Islamist and secular fighters. While Syria had promised to crack down on such activity, it was claimed Syrian intelligence was helping insurgents such as Abu Musab al-Zarqawi and his 'al-Qaeda in Iraq'. Fighters captured by American forces crossing the border, though mainly Syrian, also included Egyptians, Moroccans, Saudis, Sudanese and Yemenis.[3] This proved that Syria was not only offering training facilities but was also acting as a transit point for international Jihadists.

Ironically, hosting Islamist terror groups did not make Damascus immune from such attacks. Up to fifteen gunmen suspected of having al-Qaeda links conducted co-ordinated attacks in the city's diplomatic area in April 2004. Explosions and shooting occurred in the Mazzeh district, near the British ambassador's residence. In fact, the British embassy had been closed for weeks for fear of a repeat of the bombing of the British consulate in Istanbul.[4]

A Syrian citizen, Mohannad Almallah Dabas, was arrested in Spain in March 2005, on suspicion of involvement in the Madrid train bombings. A month earlier, two Syrians, Imad Eddin Barakat Yarkas and Ghasoub al Abrash Ghalyounnd, and a Moroccan, Driss Chelbi, were put on trial after being accused of aiding the 9/11 attacks.[5]

Syria's complicity with the insurgency in Iraq was hardly surprising. The country has a long track record of supporting various militias and terrorist organisations in Lebanon and Palestine throughout the 1980s, in particular the Palestine Liberation Army, the Palestine Liberation Front (Abu Nidal faction), George Habash's Popular Front for the Liberation of Palestine (a pro-Marxist group that became famous in the 1970s for a series of airliner hijackings) and the Druze militia. Cynically, the Syrians abandoned Yasser Arafat's PLO al-Fatah to its fate in the face of the Israeli invasion of Lebanon in 1982. Damascus then backed around 5,000 dissident Fatah forces under Abu Moussa (Musa) against Arafat's remaining 4,000 loyalists in Tripoli. Once they were ousted, Syria was left with a largely free hand in Lebanon.

Syrian-backed groups along with Iraqi, Kurdish and Lebanese terror cells, met in Libya in 1986 at the invitation of Colonel Gaddafi. Prominent members of the ruling Syrian Ba'ath Party also attended. At this meeting it was decided to escalate attacks against Israel and Western (principally American) targets. They also agreed to set up revolutionary suicide forces. While these left-leaning organisations were not Islamist, they were clearly adopting the suicide tactics of Revolutionary Shia Iran.

It also proved that Abu Nidal was working for the Libyans as well as the Syrians. Having been expelled from Iraq, as a result of protests from Washington, the Abu Nidal Organisation had been taken under the protection of the Syrians. President Assad permitted them to set up an HQ in Damascus, in what was described as a 'political and cultural centre'. Such co-operation was not welcomed by Egypt, Austria, Germany, Italy, Pakistan and Turkey – all victims of Abu Nidal's terror attacks in the mid-1980s. All this culminated in the UK and US breaking off diplomatic relations with Damascus and sanctions being imposed. Syria became enemy number one in terms of being a state sponsor of terrorism.

Therefore, long before the invasion of Iraq, Syria was vigilant – only too conscious of Western intelligence activities. During the 1990s American U2 spy planes were regularly flying out of RAF Akrotiri, Cyprus, on Olive Branch operations in support of UN inspection efforts in Iraq.[6] The aircraft transited Turkish airspace, but the Syrians were understandably suspicious that these activities were not just directed against Iraq. Nor was Syria blind to the fact that Western naval intelligence operations had been conducted off the Turkish coast. Similarly, the Americans flew special Black Hawk Ops out of Cyprus into Lebanon.

On top of this, nearby Cyprus is the biggest Western eavesdropping facility in the eastern Mediterranean. The fact that these facilities have been used in two campaigns against Iraq and Serbia will have done little to sway Syrian insecurities. Similar systems are deployed in Turkey, in and around Incirlik, again capable of collecting intelligence against Syria.[7] In the wake of Operation Iraqi Freedom, Syria was increasingly alarmed about US regional intentions. Although the Syrians were members of the Coalition against Iraq in 1991 and took part in Desert Storm, this has since done little to curry favour in the West. During the attack on Saddam Hussein, Washington warned Damascus not to intervene.

Washington even went as far as to publicly accuse Syria of providing the Iraqi Army with night-vision equipment and offering a safe haven for the Iraqi leadership. Syria had every reason to be concerned as a possessor of weapons of mass destruction and a haven for terrorist organisations – both of which are major US bugbears. America was looking for full Syrian compliance with the Middle East Peace Process, an end to its weapons of mass destruction programmes, and an end to its support for terrorism. The alternative, clearly, was the Iraqi option.

In April 2003, US Secretary of Defense, Donald Rumsfeld, began to up the ante, publicly stating Damascus had conducted chemical weapons tests over the previous year and a half. The following month, US Secretary of State, Colin Powell, was in Damascus, pressing Syria to close its anti-Israeli terrorist offices. Syria is assessed to have developed a chemical and biological weapons (CBW) capability, although it has consistently denied this, as well as reports that it is capable of installing chemical warheads in its surface-to-surface missiles. In 2002, Syria was reportedly seeking chemical precursors, as it remains dependent on foreign sources for key elements of its CW programme, including precursor chemicals and key production equipment.

Just as worrying, Syria has, for some time, been in talks with Russia about obtaining a nuclear reactor. In May 1999, Moscow agreed to provide at least one light water nuclear reactor, which would be subject to IAEA safeguards. Even so, Syria does not have the infrastructure or the financial resources to pursue an indigenous nuclear weapons programme.

Not surprisingly, Syria found itself the object of increasing disapproval. This reached a peak after the assassination of former Lebanese prime minister, Rafik Hariri, on 14 February 2005.[8] The Lebanese blamed Syrian intelligence and 'troops out' became the cry against Syria's military presence. At the time of Hariri's death there were some 5,000 Syrian troops in the hills overlooking the cities of Beirut and Tripoli, and another 10,000 stationed in the Bekaa Valley. Additionally, nothing went in and out of Lebanon's ports without Syrian intelligence knowing about it. Added to local protests, America, Britain,

France, Germany and even Egypt and Saudi Arabia all demanded that Syria end its twenty-nine-year presence.

Hezbollah – a long-time beneficiary of Iranian and Syrian support – brought 100,000 people out onto the streets of Beirut in favour of Syria.[9] It was fearful that an end to Syria's hegemony in Lebanon would stifle its military wing, Islamic Resistance, and force Lebanon from the Syrian-Iran axis towards a more pro-Western orientation, which might result in accommodation with Israel. Of all Lebanon's militant groups, Hezbollah remains the one capable of opening old wounds and re-igniting civil war. Islamic Resistance was believed to number some 300–400 full-time fighters with several thousand reservists.[10] To that end, everyone involved urged restraint.

Washington's mounting anti-Syrian sentiment, while part of its wider policy of fostering regional democracy, was undoubtedly more to do with a desire to punish Syria's support for terrorism, particularly in neighbouring Iraq, and for its alleged weapons of mass destruction programmes. US Secretary of State, Condoleezza Rice, made no bones about Washington's view: 'There's no doubt that Syria is a big problem. Syrian involvement in Lebanese affairs, has, of course, created a destabilised environment . . .'[11]

Israel had more reasons than most to get Syria out of Lebanon and Syrian/Iranian terror surrogates disarmed. At the time, the concern was that Israel would not sit on the sidelines, especially as the US claimed it had firm evidence that Syria was involved in the nightclub bombing in Tel Aviv. Indeed, the Israeli Air Force has never been shy about conducting punitive raids against terrorist bases inside Lebanon and Syria.

After the Israeli Defence Force withdrew from southern Lebanon in May 2000, it made it difficult for Syria to justify its continued presence. The Syrians were in violation of the 1989 Taif Accord, which ended Lebanon's civil war, under which they were supposed to leave within two years. In September 2004, the UN Security Council, fed up with the lack of progress, issued Resolution 1559, calling for the withdrawal of all remaining foreign forces in the Lebanon (i.e. the Syrians) and the disbanding of all militias (Hezbollah, Hamas and Islamic Jihad). Ironically, Syria was the only Arab member of the UN Security Council. Subsequently, the Syrians claimed they had redeployed 3,000 troops, but warned that a complete withdrawal could re-ignite the Lebanese civil war. After Syria engineered a change in Lebanon's constitution, allowing Syrian-backed President Lahoud to remain in power, Rafik Hariri called on them to implement the UN resolution and resigned as prime minister in October 2004.[12]

Even Walid Jumblatt, veteran Druze leader and former Syrian ally, pointedly called Lebanon the last satellite nation on the earth. In December 2004, the so-called Democratic Forum (including Christian and left wing groups and Jumblatt's Druze) denounced the interference of Syrian and Lebanese intelligence services, which had transformed Lebanon into a police state. After Hariri's assassination, Jumblatt said: 'There is no way to convince the Lebanese, not even a single one, that Syria's Mukhabarat hasn't murdered Hariri or is innocent of [spilling] his blood.'[13]

Afterwards, the offices of the Syrian Mukhabarat intelligence service were closed in Beirut and Syrian forces in the mountains moved. According to Lebanese press rumours, the Syrians approached the British embassy in Damascus, offering to reduce their forces in Lebanon to 3,000 (to protect Syrian anti-aircraft radars in the Bekaa Valley). Allegedly, Syria was politely informed the radars only needed 300 personnel.[14] Syria ended its twenty-nine-year military presence in the Lebanon by withdrawing its remaining 14,000 troops in 2005.

In the event of any Western military action against Syria, there was little its cash-strapped Navy could do to ward off assault from the Mediterranean. Syrian defence spending has always concentrated on its considerable ground and air forces.[15] It has been assessed that the Syrian armed forces would be unlikely to last more than a week. However, any future Western military action against Syria could result in a Syrian strike on Israel. According to satellite imagery, the operational alignment of Syria's Scud-C missiles are such that they are able to launch a surprise chemical attack.[16]

Nonetheless, if Iraq is any yardstick to go by, it seems unlikely that Syria would resort to such measures. Damascus knows that it must tread carefully in the diplomatic arena. Once the US had a foothold in Baghdad, Syria remained ill at ease along its eastern border with Iraq, for this gave Washington even greater intelligence-gathering opportunities. Washington found Syria co-operative in combating al-Qaeda. Damascus shared intelligence with the CIA and is known to have passed on the results of at least one interrogation – that of Mohammed Haydar Zammar, accused of having links with al-Qaeda.

When Libya dramatically renounced its weapons of mass destruction, following the lifting of UN sanctions in 2003, it raised the big question of whether this rehabilitation would open the door for the Libyans to join NATO's Mediterranean Dialogue Programme (MDP) and co-operate fully with NATO's counter-terrorist efforts. Libya does have an unsavoury track record of supporting terror groups, gun-running and attacking NATO territory. Libyan intelligence penetration of the tiny island of Malta was a cause for concern over the years, culminating in it being a transit point for one of the Pan Am 103 Lockerbie bombers in 1988.

Libya supported a broad range of militant Muslim groups, including the PLO. The alleged Libyan involvement in terror attacks in Europe in 1986 led to US military strikes against Tripoli. Also that year, a terrorist group with Libyan connections launched an unsuccessful seaborne attack against the British base on Cyprus. The Lockerbie bombing, seen as the final straw, resulted in

UN sanctions, including a ban on the sale of arms and other military equipment. Libya continued to obstruct the Lockerbie investigation and meddle in the affairs of its neighbours.

Libya did not formally take responsibility for Lockerbie until August 2003. Since then it announced its intention to dismantle its WMD programme. As part of the negotiations that led to the UN sanctions being lifted, Libyan intelligence provided Britain with detailed information about the 120 tonnes of weaponry and millions of pounds in funding supplied to the IRA. During the 1990s, Libya helped the IRA stockpile over a ton of Semtex explosive, 1,500 firearms and 1 million rounds of ammunition, all of it smuggled in by sea. The IRA and the Basque separatist group ETA also received training in Libya.

The Spanish prime minister visited Tripoli, the Libyan capital, in September 2003. Spanish officials pointed out Libya wanted to be seen as a country that had rejected terrorism, adding Tripoli has been co-operative with the UN Counter-terrorism Committee, and was quick to offer humanitarian aid to the US after 9/11. However, Spain has an economic agenda for easing Libya back into the international fold. In May 2003, Libya awarded Spanish companies contracts to explore for Libyan oil and gas.

Washington was not so conciliatory. Whereas many countries are the victims of unwanted terrorist activity, Libya, along with Iran and Syria, stands accused by the US State Department of being state sponsors of terrorism. Libya and Syria found themselves added to America's Axis of Evil list in 2003, though Libya emerged as America's public enemy number one during the 1980s. The US deputy ambassador to the UN, James Cunningham, noted the vote to lift sanctions, 'must not be misconstrued by Libya or by the world community as tacit US acceptance that the government of Libya has rehabilitated itself'.[17]

Nor are relations so cordial with Italy. The Italian government is sick of illegal immigrants arriving in Sicily by sea from Libya. North Africa and other Mediterranean states are to establish a single command authority to co-ordinate with Italian efforts under legislation nicknamed the 'anti landing decree'. Under this, the Italian Navy will be responsible for international waters, the coastguard rescue operations and the financial police will be granted powers to board suspect vessels and, where possible, send the boats back to the port of origin with the immigrants.

Although the connection between al-Qaeda and militant Islamic terrorist activity in Algeria, Morocco, Somalia and Yemen is well established, this is not the case in Libya. Also, it seems Libya has little in the way of ties with Hamas and Hezbollah, as it broke off diplomatic ties with the Lebanon in 2003. However, after the arrest of an American Muslim charity worker in October 2003, the FBI gained evidence that Libyan government charitable donations going to Syria might be helping bankroll al-Qaeda, Hamas and Islamic Jihad attacks on Coalition forces in Iraq. Gaddafi and bin Laden were far from soul mates. It is a little known fact that Gaddafi issued the first Interpol arrest warrant for bin Laden in March 1998.

The common thread with Libya and al-Qaeda was the Soviet Afghan war. For several thousand Libyans fought in Afghanistan, and in the early 1990s, Libyan Mujahideen had formed the Libyan Islamic Fighting Group, whose aim was to depose Gaddafi and create an Islamic state in Libya. Between 1996 and 1998 they had tried to assassinate Gaddafi on four occasions – ironically, the West's 'Master Terrorist' found himself on the receiving end of things. The events of 9/11 helped him redeem himself.

In the past, Gaddafi has taken a dim view of NATO's MDP. Just after it was established, he made his position more than clear:

> They are building bridgeheads to land NATO troops in North Africa, and they call it partnership for peace. This partnership is a word which, as far the revolutionaries are concerned, should be translated as bridgeheads to land NATO troops in the Arab world, from Palestine to the Maghreb.[18]

Libya remains surrounded by NATO allies, with Algeria and Tunisia to the west and Egypt to the east, and such remarks were seen as hollow rhetoric.

Chapter 21

Iraq: the New Breeding Ground

Disastrously for Iraq, while Washington had a very clear military strategy for bringing down Saddam Hussein, it exhibited an appalling lack of foresight when it came to overseeing the transition to a post-Saddam regime. As American political commentator, Kevin Phillips, notes:

> The supposed liberation of Iraq in 2003 unleashed guerrilla warfare and produced a massive anti-American surge in Islamic nations from North Africa to Indonesia. One side effect may have been to print recruiting posters for a generation of suicide bombers.[1]

The presence of foreign fighters was first confirmed when Iraqi Kurdish militia, supported by US Special Forces, overran the Ansar al-Islam base on 28 March 2003. Quite frankly it was a case of taking a sledgehammer to crack a nut, as the operation involved around 8,000 Peshmerga Kurdish guerrillas. Despite these overwhelming numbers, Ansar resisted at Dekon, Gulp and Vagorat, as the Coalition forces approached their base. The Kurds suffered seventy-five wounded and twenty-four dead in just forty-eight hours. Although the operation was a success, only a handful of Ansar fighters were captured alive, including a Syrian and a Palestinian. Among the dead were Arabs from Yemen, Qatar and the United Arab Emirates – there were also some from undisclosed European countries.[2] Captured documents showed links to Abu Sayyaf and Hamas.[3]

From the very beginning, the Iraqi insurgency in mid-2003 had a clear foreign-fighter element. The bombing of the UN HQ in Baghdad, on 19 August 2003, and the bombing of the Najaf mosque on 29 August 2003, resulted in the US concentrating on Jordanian commander Abu Musab al-Zarqawi and his foreign-fighter network. He formally pledged allegiance to bin Laden and joined al-Qaeda in 2004. His strategy for 'al-Qaeda in Iraq' was to provoke civil war between Iraq's Shia and Sunni populations in order to make the country ungovernable and drive the Americans out.

It was believed that those foreign fighters infiltrating Iraq had formed an alliance with former members of Saddam's intelligence services, known as the Jaish Mohammed or Army of the Prophet Mohammed. This was headed by a senior Saudi al-Qaeda officer based at Razaza, 30 miles from the town of

Ramadi. His support was derived from wealthy Saudis rather than the Saudi government itself.[4]

It was when al-Zarqawi arrived in Fallujah that the Iraqi insurgency began to gather momentum. The Americans came close to capturing him twice during 2003, but each time he escaped. His brutality was highlighted when he beheaded British engineer Kenneth Bigley in Fallujah in October 2004, an atrocity that, like many others, was posted on the Internet. Bigley was preceded by two American colleagues who suffered the same fate: in April and November 2004, US forces fought two major battles to pacify Fallujah – the first involved 2,000 troops who sought to eject insurgents, following the deaths of US personnel. At the same time, the Americans were battling for control of Ramadi, where about 300 insurgents had to be rooted out, most of whom were killed in the fighting. In early October 5,000 American and Iraqi troops were also obliged to clear up to 1,000 supporters of al-Zarqawi from the city of Samarra.

The presence of al-Zarqawi and his supporters in Fallujah was proving a major headache for the US military. While his centre of operations was based in the city, he was thought to have around 1,000 men – largely foreign fighters – in Iraq, particularly in Baghdad and Mosul. Initially, Fallujah had fallen under the influence of some 500 fighters, supported by around 2,000 part-time supporters. By the end of the year they had swelled to 3,000. It took the US marines nine days of street-fighting in November to drive them out, although only the local insurgents stayed on to fight. Ironically, as US troops were redeploying from Mosul to help at Fallujah, insurgents from Fallujah were filtering into Mosul. Remaining American forces in Mosul came under intense attack and the insurgents took control of two-thirds of the city. Iraqi and US reinforcements had to be rushed in to wrestle back control.

Unfortunately, at Fallujah, 200,000 people were displaced, 6,000 killed and thousands of buildings destroyed, including sixty mosques. Once again, al-Zarqawi eluded his captors. Also, the victory was short-lived, because, by September 2006, the whole of al-Anbar province was in insurgent hands, with the exception of Fallujah. It would be another two years before the city was placed under the control of the Iraqi government.

Al-Qaeda's intention was to isolate the US-backed Iraqi administration by cutting it off from the rest of the Arab world. To that end, it kidnapped the first Arab ambassador to post-war Iraq on 3 July 2005. The Egyptian ambassador designate, Ihab al-Sherif, was abducted and murdered. Attacks were also conducted against the envoys of Bahrain and Pakistan in Baghdad. Gory beheadings of Westerners and Iraqi officials soon began to count against al-Zarqawi and were seen as counter-productive by mainstream al-Qaeda. In mid-October 2005, the Americans released a letter from Ayman al-Zawahiri to al-Zarqawi, criticising him for his tactics. He warned that the battle against the 'crusaders' was being fought in the media. In particular, he questioned

Zarqawi's attacks on innocent Shia in Iraq and the 'slaughtering' of hostages: 'We are in a media battle in a race for the hearts and minds of the Umma (the followers of Islam),' wrote Zawahiri. He pointed out this was the only way Zarqawi could win in Iraq, arguing that no matter what al-Qaeda's capabilities, 'They will never equal one-thousandth of the capabilities in the Kingdom of Satan that is waging war on us.'[5]

In Zawahiri's mind, Iraq was just a stepping-stone:

> It has always been my belief that the victory of Islam will never take place until a Muslim state is established in the manner of the Prophet in the heart of the Islamic world, specifically the Levant, Egypt, and the neighbouring states of the peninsula and Iraq.[6]

By August 2005, insurgents were attacking British forces in the Amarah area with increasing sophistication. According to military sources, the predominantly Shia militants had received not only Iranian help, but also support from Syria and Hezbollah.[7] Because of Syria's long-standing support for Palestinian groups such as Hamas and Islamic Jihad, and Lebanon's Hezbollah, it became inevitable that Syria would be a conduit for Jihadists flowing into Iraq. The Lebanese group, Hezbollah, was also, reportedly, providing assistance in 2006.

According to US intelligence officials, up to 2,000 members of Moktada al-Sadr's Mahdi Army and other Shia militias received training in the Lebanon at the hands of Iranian-backed Hezbollah. Certainly, during the summer, a Mahdi commander had admitted to sending 300 fighters known as the Ali al-Hadi Brigade to Lebanon.[8] The Iranian Revolutionary Guard was also providing training for Iraqi Shia fighters in Iran, as well as providing logistical support. According to the British Defence Intelligence Staff, the Iraqi Badr Organisation retained 'strong links' with the Iranian Islamic Revolutionary Guard Corps, which funded, trained and armed the militia group, totalling up to 20,000 men.[9] It was also suspected that Libya was up to its old tricks by providing funding for Hamas and other Islamist attacks on Coalition forces in Iraq.[10]

Initially, US authorities seemed confused over whether al-Qaeda or al-Qaeda-inspired fighters were playing a key role in the growing insurgency. President Bush, in his 20 January 2004 State of the Union message, said: 'These killers, joined by foreign terrorists, are a serious, continuing danger.'[11] While the military agreed with US politicians that there was a foreign component to the post-Saddam insurgency, there were sharply differing views about how significant a part they were playing. After the arrest of suspected bin Laden aide, Hassan Ghul, in January 2004, Lieutenant-General Ricardo Sanchez, commander of US forces in Iraq, commented that the arrest 'is pretty strong proof that al-Qaeda is trying to gain a foothold here to continue their murderous campaigns'.[12] At the same time, he seemed to be contradicted by General John Abizaid, in charge of US Central Command, which directs operations in the Middle East: 'I am confident,' said Abizaid, 'that there is no flood of foreign fighters coming in [to Iraq].'[13]

At their height, the overall number of insurgents was put at about 5,000, of which up to 3,000 were estimated to be foreign fighters – clearly a significant proportion.[14] However, generals on the ground were reporting that only small numbers of prisoners were foreign fighters. Nonetheless, by late 2006 and early 2007 senior US officials considered 'al-Qaeda in Iraq' as the driving force behind the insurgency. Its membership was estimated to number anything from 5,000 to 10,000, making it the largest Sunni extremist group in Iraq. Also, up to eighty foreign fighters were infiltrating the border every month, of which some 40 per cent were Saudi.[15]

The rehabilitation of the Iraqi Army was a slow and painful process, tainted as it is by association with Saddam Hussein's appalling catalogue of human rights abuses. The Coalition faced a dilemma: it wanted to ensure that the Iraqi Army would never again be a threat to the Iraqi people or to Iraq's neighbours, so the Iraqi armed forces – seen as servants of Saddam – were demobilised and sent home. Not only did this cause mass unemployment and resentment, it meant that the security burden fell on the Coalition forces.

Nonetheless, like the phoenix rising from the ashes, a new Iraqi Army emerged to help fight the war on terror. Most notably, in mid-May 2006, the Iraqi 2nd Brigade of the 9th Mechanised Division assumed responsibility for security in the Taji area and the Iraqi 2nd Brigade, 5th Division, began independent operations in Diyala province. The Iraqi 7th Division also took responsibility for al-Anbar province. Notably, the 9th Mechanised is the only Iraqi armoured unit with tanks and armoured personnel carriers and was dubbed the 'jewel of Iraq' by military leaders.

After six months of training, in late February 2006, Iraqi tanks of the 9th Mechanised began operations in the streets of the Kadhamiya area of Baghdad. The following month, the 9th Mechanised, supporting the American 66th Armor Regiment, from the US 4th Infantry Division, conducted counter-insurgency operations near Halasba, shortly after an improvised explosive device attack on a convoy. On 7 September 2006, the Coalition formally handed operational control of the Iraqi armed forces (Navy, Air Force and Iraqi 8th Division) over to the Iraqi government. By mid-2007, Iraq security forces totalled 353,100, which encompassed the armed forces and police.

In the meantime, on 7 June 2006, the Coalition tracked al-Zarqawi to a safe house in Hibhib, near the city of Baqubah, and mortally wounded him in an air strike.[16] It was thought Abu Ayyub al-Masri might replace al-Zarqawi, but Islamist websites pledged allegiance to Abdul Rahman al-Iraqi, though the Americans believed they had killed him as well.[17] Bin Laden despatched an aide, Abd al-Hadi al-Iraqi to al-Masri, but he was captured before even reaching Iraq. Just twelve days after the death of al-Zarqawi, the Americans scored another success, capturing Abu Mumam (alias Hamed Jumaa Farid al-Saeedi or Abu Rana) near Baqubah. Information gleaned from him resulted in the capture of another twenty al-Qaeda members. This was followed by a series of Iraqi security operations resulting in forty-nine al-Qaeda fighters being killed and another 225 captured.[18]

In January 2007, President Bush instigated a counter-insurgency campaign, developed by General David Petraeus, which relied on a massive US troop surge in Iraq. These troops were used to target 'al-Qaeda in Iraq' sanctuaries with Operations Phantom Thunder, Phantom Strike, Iron Harvest and Iron Reaper. By early 2008, there were signs that al-Qaeda was withering, following a mass defection of Sunni supporters to the US military. Over 80,000 Sunnis then helped the local tribal group's Concerned Local Citizens militias to eject al-Qaeda from western and northern Iraq. In the Balad area, north of Baghdad, Abu-Tari (the emir of the al-Layin and al-Mashahdah sector) saw his force drop from 600 fighters to less than twenty.[19]

There were indications that al-Qaeda's leadership in Iraq was relocating to Pakistan. This suggested that al-Qaeda viewed Afghanistan as a better environment to launch attacks on American troops. But US intelligence officials cautioned against too great an optimism, as al-Qaeda had switched its attacks to the local militias.

Nonetheless, in June 2009, US combat troops withdrew from Iraq's towns and cities. This followed President Obama's announcement that US-led combat operations would cease by the summer of 2010, with a complete military withdrawal from Iraq by the end of 2011. It was time for the Iraqi armed forces to stand on their own and shoulder the burden of containing the insurgents.

While the Iraqi insurgency attracted foreign Jihadists, Washington was not blind to the possibility of a revenge attack on US soil. Before the Coalition invasion there were 50,000 Iraqis living in the States, many of them former Saddam supporters. America's border with Mexico, always a problem with economic migrants and refugees, provided a conduit for Iraqi terrorists. To coincide with the war in Iraq, Mexico implemented the 'Sentry Plan' – a major security crackdown along its borders. The results included two Iraqis and an American of Iraqi descent being arrested en route to California at Tijuana bus station. Mexico's national security agency also tipped off the CIA that they were looking for six Iraqi nationals with German passports, believed to be carrying 'toxic materials'.[20] According to Mexican media sources, five Iraqis with German papers were deported to America.[21]

This seems to have done little to deter Iraqis trying to enter the US via Mexico. In 2007, sixteen Iraqi nationals were caught illegally entering America, while another 178 crossed the border seeking asylum.[22] Although US intelligence sources say details and numbers of terrorists transiting the border remain classified, they do cite the example of Mahmoud Youssef Kourani, who entered the US via Tijuana with the aim of raising money for Hezbollah, in 2001. He had bribed a Mexican consulate official in Lebanon for a Mexican visa and was then smuggled over the US border in the trunk of a car.[23]

The quick fix anticipated for Iraq rapidly failed to materialise. In fact, Iraq, in the name of countering terrorism and the proliferation of weapons of mass destruction, soaked up vastly more resources than Afghanistan. Iraq became a breeding group for disaffected and demobbed Iraqi soldiers, policemen and intelligence operatives following the invasion. As Washington fed in more troops, so Iraq inadvertently became a magnet, attracting global Jihadists from far and wide.

Critics of the invasion contend that Saddam Hussein had no real links with al-Qaeda and that the invasion prompted al-Qaeda or pro al-Qaeda elements to move into Iraq to fight the US military. Washington's actions have created new al-Qaeda followers within Iraq and beyond. Certainly, the Sunni-Shia schism in Iraq ensured that the former provided new and fertile recruiting grounds for al-Qaeda. The more cynical argue that Washington overemphasised the al-Qaeda threat to bolster public support following the invasion, especially once US casualties began to mount. From the Pentagon's perspective, the invasion had the desired effect, in that it was always better to fight Islamists abroad rather than await further attacks on the US homeland. The long-term effects of this policy have yet to be truly understood.

Chapter 22

Holy Terror: the Rage of Islam

The concerted international campaign against al-Qaeda and its supporters has resulted in significant success. Nonetheless, despite its losses, the network remains in existence and has evolved. There remains a hardcore al-Qaeda, secondary groups inspired by al-Qaeda, and, lastly, affiliate groups or sub-contractors, such as 'al-Qaeda in Iraq' and the 'Ten Dollar Taliban'. Funda-mentally, eliminating support for the Taliban in the lawless north-western Pakistani enclaves is essential to stabilising Afghanistan and Pakistan, but is probably an impossible task. In Iraq, the war only went against al-Qaeda once the population was persuaded not to support it.

In hindsight, it seems the invasion of Iraq, in the name of the war on terror, was a mistake – Saddam's regime would probably have imploded anyway, after his death. Iraq has been so traumatised by an unending succession of conflict, like Afghanistan it is hard to see how it will ever recover. The long brutal reign of Saddam, the Iran-Iraq War, the Gulf War, the Shia Rising, the 2003 invasion and the subsequent civil war have all left their mark. Whether Iraq can completely throw off the allure of Islamic militancy remains to be seen, though in the long term, Afghanistan and Pakistan remain of greater concern. Both countries have uncertain futures.

What can we hope comes out of this blight on the close of the twentieth and opening of the twenty-first centuries? It would be reassuring to believe that al-Qaeda was an aberration, that having done much to harm the cultural and political achievements of Islam, it lost the terror war. But that is not the case: global Jihad is a culmination of the frustration born of a lack of understanding between Western and Islamic cultural and political ideals. Islamic militancy emerged from the Arab world's inability to solve – or even address – the creation of Israel from Palestine. At its most basic, in the eyes of some in the Muslim world, the Christian West sided with Zionism, and for that there can never be any accommodation. Al-Qaeda's true lineage is the PLO, Hezbollah and Hamas, as much as the Afghan Mujahideen – they showed the way to what is achievable with ultimate sacrifice.

While the late Yasser Arafat, one-time chairman of the PLO, has passed into the pages of history, Osama bin Laden has secured himself a much more prominent position in the world's collective psyche. After the terror outrages of the PLO and its successors are long forgotten, 9/11 will remain one of humanity's worst man-made catastrophies. The West paid the ultimate price for its ineptitude in reining in bin Laden and his followers. Some might claim that it was not for the want of trying, while others will argue that the West only really woke up to the danger after it was too late.

Inevitably, al-Qaeda – or the concept of al-Qaeda – will live on through some successor organisation or organisations, but whether they will be truly global is another matter. The environment in which terrorists now operate is vastly different to that of the 1990s and earlier. Ultimately, most militants have very localised goals and it is from this that we should take succour.

At the time of writing, the verdict on whether Osama bin Laden is still alive or indeed still constitutes a threat remains open. Living under the shadow of being the most hunted – and in some quarters, the most reviled individual in the world – must be a heavy burden for anyone. Nonetheless, we should not underestimate bin Laden or indeed his legacy – we have made that mistake once before and it allowed global Jihad to flourish for a time almost unchecked.

Should we wring our hands in despair at what has gone before? Of course not – hindsight is a seductively powerful tool, no matter how hard you try to wield it impartially. It seems a given that each generation is largely incapable of profiting from the mistakes of the past. Having learned the hard way, the world is now alert to global terrorism and will not tolerate it. The very fabric of society has had to evolve to counter this menace – most notably in terms of surveillance.

While Britain and America cannot be held solely responsible for the rise of Islamic militancy in Afghanistan, Bosnia, Iraq, Iran, Lebanon, Pakistan, Palestine, Sudan and Saudi Arabia, their policies did nothing to alleviate the situation. It remains my contention that their policies, deliberately or not, aggravated the situation at every turn and it is now civil society that has to pay the price.

MI5 has estimated that there are about 2,000 active terror supporters in the UK and claims that even schoolchildren have been recruited by al-Qaeda.[1] Therefore, there is a certain irony when the former head of MI5 accuses the government of the day of exploiting the public's fear of terrorism to restrict civil liberties,[2] or when the British Director of Public Prosecutions denies there is such a thing as a war on terror. In early 2009, the International Commission of Jurists reported that international law was being undermined and that the intelligence services enjoy immunity from human rights violations. They also accused the war on terror of repeating the same mistakes Britain had made in Northern Ireland, citing Abu Ghraib and Guantanamo Bay. Ultimately, the UK and US have set a bad example, for their counter-terrorism policies and legislation have given totalitarian regimes, such as Uzbekistan, a justifiable rationale for introducing repressive laws.

There can be no denying the war on terror has been invoked to weaken civil freedoms and has created an unwelcome sense of the enemy within. Our governments are complicit in this. Foreign policy decisions regarding the fate of faraway lands over the last two decades have led to the erosion of the rule of law, with prolonged detention without trial, the use of torture, violation of the Geneva Convention through the blurring of the term enemy combatants, the loss of privacy through the growth of the surveillance society (with the spread of CCTV and the obsession with national data-basing), restrictions on the freedom of speech through incitement and racial hatred legislation. Some might argue that it is better than the alternative.

The detention of terror suspects at Guantanamo Bay, Cuba, remains an undeniable blot on the war on terror. It has been claimed that fewer than a dozen detainees had any connection with terrorism.[3] Clive Stafford Smith, the Legal Director of Reprieve, the UK charity organisation, has struggled tirelessly over the years to get a fair hearing for those still held. By late 2006 over 450 prisoners had been released, indicating that well over half the original total were innocent.[4] About 300 remained, with a steady dribble of releases over the next few years.

One of the biggest headaches facing President Obama's administration is trying to ensure that some of the 800 men held at Guantanamo Bay over the years do not form the cadre of a new, even more embittered al-Qaeda. While I do not propose to examine the legitimacy or indeed veracity of the charges brought against those described as 'accidental warriors and unrepentant combatants'[5], there is clear evidence that some of those who have been released have taken up the cause once again. According to Pentagon sources, by early 2009, of the 520 prisoners released, over 10 per cent had turned to terrorist activity.[6]

Former Guantanamo Bay inmate, Mullah Abdul Kayum Sakir, released in 2008, reportedly operating from Pakistan, became involved in orchestrating attacks on NATO forces in Afghanistan. In particular, the hardcore of Yemeni prisoners is of concern: although many were released to a Yemeni government rehabilitation programme, three of the seven men involved in the attack on the US embassy in Yemen had been through this programme. A Kuwaiti from Guantanamo took part in a suicide attack against American troops in Iraq in early 2008.

It was revealed in 2009 that Guantanamo Bay inmates Khalid Sheikh Mohammed, long regarded as a senior al-Qaeda operative, and Ramzi Binal Shibh, Mustafa Ahmed al-Hawsawi, Ali Abd al-Aziz Ali and Walid Bin Attash, claimed to be the 9/11 Shura Council with responsibility for the attack.[7] Mohammed also admitted to taking part in thirty terror plots and claimed to have decapitated kidnapped US journalist Daniel Pearl in 2002 in Pakistan.

It is evident that the Islamists have evolved and adapted in the face of international counter-terrorism efforts. Algerian journalist, Mounir Boudjema, an expert on his country's Islamist groups, noted a significant change in the terrorists' modus operandi:

> The new generation is different from the pre-September 11 phenomenon. They have moved completely away from the mosque-based activities, which used to provide their environment, because they know that these are being watched.
>
> In the year running up to the March 11 attack in Madrid they have restructured, creating semi-autonomous groups with 'sleepers' who fought and trained in Afghanistan between 1996 and 2000, who can be activated at short notice.
>
> To this new generation Osama bin Laden is no more than a symbol, just as Che Guevara once was to a different revolutionary movement. The structure has gone from a vertical leadership to horizontal; it's very fluid.
>
> They are young with many years spent living in Europe, they blend in perfectly, they smoke and drink moderately. They raise no suspicions.[8]

Furthermore, there is a growing conviction that the global war against terrorism should be merged with the long-standing war on illegal narcotics – to some, they are the same beast. Alarmingly, almost 40 per cent of those groups designated a Foreign Terrorist Organisation by Washington have some connection with the illegal drugs trade. It is not surprising, then, that US policy-makers see narcotics-smuggling and terrorism as part of the same transnational threat to the US homeland.

As far as Washington is concerned, narco-terrorists and Islamic radical groups all practise the same business methods. In particular, the logistic cells in Colombia extend to the Middle East. The US military has identified Colombia as a flashpoint, and branded the three main rebel groups there: the Revolutionary Armed Forces of Colombia (FARC), the Army of National Liberation (ELN), and the United Self-Defense Forces, as common thugs. It is well known that these guerrilla armies are funded by illegal drug revenues (an estimated 90 per cent of all cocaine and 65 per cent of all heroin sold on America's streets comes from Colombia). It also appears that drug money financed IRA operatives to train FARC after the high-profile arrest of three Irishmen in Colombia.

The Latin American drug connection casts a wide global net. Islamic radical groups that support Hamas, Hezbollah, Islamiyya al-Gamat, are all active in Latin America. In the Lebanon, Hezbollah partly funds itself through drugs trafficking from Colombia and Turkey. Its presence in Paraguay raises further concerns about its involvement in the international drugs trade. The Taliban and al-Qaeda profited from Afghanistan's opium and heroin trade until America's invasion. Additionally, the IRA is long known to have nurtured international links with paramilitary organisations, including ETA in Spain and Palestinian groups, some of which have been involved in drugs. Certainly, in America, the ongoing war against terrorism has resulted in a greater degree of co-operation among the intelligence and law enforcement agencies. In terms of maritime interdiction, this has seen the US Navy and US Coastguard working ever more closely with the anti-drug agencies.

The West initially chose to ignore bin Laden at its peril; then, when it did decide to take action, it was too little too late, and he always escaped attempts to assassinate or capture him. A worrying problem with the legacy of Osama bin Laden is that, if in parts of the Muslim world he has achieved iconic status, this will be difficult to dispel, meaning that, to future generations, he may become a figure of inspiration. The late Mohammed Jamal Khalifa, bin Laden's brother-in-law, summed up charismatic Osama's elevation to global icon by pointing out that the West has turned him into 'the Nike stripe' of international Islamic terrorism.[9] If this proves to be the case, then militant Islam could become resurgent once more under his banner, despite the West's best efforts.

The UK's counter-terrorism strategy, known as 'Contest', has four main objectives: pursue, protect, prepare and prevent. It is unfortunate these were not in place sooner.[10] The end of the Cold War and the events of 9/11 have led many to conclude that the three disciplines of overhead imagery, human and signals intelligence need to be fundamentally reinvented. The collapse of the Soviet Union ended the massive military Soviet infrastructure, which could be readily observed by imagery. And 9/11 showed the intelligence world that it is now involved in a whole new ball game. In America, the intelligence community was placed under intense and unflattering scrutiny by the release of the 9/11 Congressional report. Damagingly, many of the failures highlighted were already well known.

Similarly, the British government's grasp on the cost of the intelligence war against the terrorists, publicly at least, seems weak, despite the shake-up of the UK's intelligence apparatus. Nick Harvey, Shadow Defence Secretary for the Liberal Democrats, questioned, in April 2009, how much Britain is spending on intelligence-gathering. The reply was far from encouraging. In response, he said:

> All these programmes mentioned are high-end procurement projects and not to have a handle on overall costs is impermissible – it also makes it very difficult to gauge long-term security costs when it comes to the war on terror and that is very worrying.[11]

It subsequently emerged that the UK was investing almost £130 million promoting counter-terrorism programmes around the world (principally in the Middle East, South and South East Asia and North and East Africa) over a four-year period (2008–2010). A million pounds was also allocated to support the Quilliam Foundation counter-extremism think-tank, founded by Maajid

Nawaz and Ed Husain, both former Hizb ut-Tahir militants. In a case of 'poachers turned gamekeepers', the latter have been working to help combat the rise of extremist ideology (notably in Pakistan, through engagement with university students). While this is a laudable, indeed a vital, initiative, arguably, it should have begun a decade earlier. Combating radicalised students and extremist ideology on university campuses in certain parts of the world will be an uphill struggle. Britain's domestic security bill is £3.5bn a year.

Many in Washington question whether they need so many expensive intelligence organisations. The answer lies in the fact that intelligence is a support function, and there are many competing interests who need such support. Additionally, the number of organisations, at least thirty, is driven by the broad diversity of their intelligence needs.[12] America has an intelligence application for just about everything. While total 'battle space' awareness/dominance is ultimately impossible, one can only marvel at the vast array of intelligence assets available to the American war fighter.

In America, the ongoing war against terrorism has resulted in a greater degree of co-operation between the intelligence and law enforcement agencies, particularly after the establishment of the Department of Homeland Security and State Department's Anti-terrorism Assistance Programme. Anti-terrorism legislation has been designed to facilitate greater sharing of intelligence between law enforcement agencies and the intelligence community. The American IC's Director of Central Intelligence (DCI) is also the Director of the CIA and Presidential Intelligence Advisor. The DCI's responsibilities are to guide and co-ordinate the entire community. Reporting to him is the National Intelligence Council, which interacts with the NSC.

The question that will haunt history is could the Clinton administration have done more to head off the rise of militant Islam under bin Laden before it got truly out of hand? Damningly, the 9/11 Commission concluded Clinton failed to take the threat of al-Qaeda seriously enough, and that the

> modest national effort to contain Serbia [...] between 1995 and 1999 [...] was orders of magnitude larger than that devoted to al-Qaeda [...] the most dangerous foreign enemy then threatening the United States.[13]

Crucially, Bill Clinton felt his legacy to America was turning around the US economy: in fact, it was failing to grasp that the biggest challenge of the twenty-first century was dealing with Islamist terrorism. While he appreciated the importance of the Middle East Peace Process and bringing the Israelis and Palestinians together, he ignored the bigger picture. The radicalisation of the PLO, Hamas and Hezbollah ultimately gained a wider global following once an organisation emerged that could articulate the goals of a burgeoning global Jihad – al-Qaeda filled that gap.

In the Balkans, at the cost of partition, Yugoslavia took a decade to ensure a shaky equilibrium and peace. It is hard to see how the tide of militant Islam will ever ebb while the issues facing Afghanistan, Iraq, Kashmir, Somalia and Palestine remain unresolved. To the Muslim world they are inextricably linked. The West has grappled with militant Islam for over three decades and the capture of bin Laden or Zawahiri is unlikely to end such a legacy.

Is there any solace we can take from the failure to curb the rise of global Jihad under the inspiration of Osama bin Laden? The answer is 'Yes' – because we have been in this position before. Writing in the late 1980s, Middle Eastern specialist, John Laffin, warned:

> Jihad – the holy war of Islam – is the greatest political-religious force of the late twentieth century and its commanders-in-chief are determined that by the year 2000 of the Christian era, Islam will have regained its 'rightful place' as the dominant world system.[14]

To date, they have yet to achieve this goal.

Epilogue

At the time of going to press the world's most wanted Islamists, Osama bin Laden, Ayman al-Zawahiri and Mullah Omar, still remain unaccounted for, almost a decade after the invasion of Afghanistan. They are probably dead or hiding in some remote and secure corner of north-east Afghanistan, north-west Pakistan, or even Yemen, where they are eking out their remaining days as international fugitives. Ultimately, their fate matters little, as no individual is greater than the organisation they helped create.

This is borne out by those who have gone before them. Ramzi Yousef failed to topple New York's World Trade Center and ended up in prison, but this did not stop a second much more deadly attack. In Afghanistan the Taliban's leadership has been killed, captured and scattered and yet the movement thrives. Abdul Rashid Ghazi, the radical leader from Islamabad's pro-Taliban Red Mosque is dead, as is the Pakistani Taliban leader, Baitullah Mehsud – though this has made little difference to the Islamists across Pakistan. Yasser Arafat is long dead, but Fatah lived on to wage war against its much more radical rival, Hamas, in the Palestinian territories. Sheikh Ahmed Yassin, the former leader of Hamas, is dead and yet Hamas survived to take power. Similarly, Hezbollah's founders are either dead (as in the case of Sheikh Abbas al-Musawi) or missing (as in the case of Sheikh Subhi al-Tufayli). Nonetheless, the organisation has thrived under Sayyid Hassan Nasrallah, in its struggle against Israel.

According to bin Laden's late brother-in-law, Mohammed Jamal Khalifa, it is the West who demonised Osama, turning him into an arch bogeyman that never really existed. Khalifa claimed bin Laden was incapable of organising anything and simply took the credit for Islamist exploits around the world. Charismatic but disorganised was how Khalifa characterised bin Laden. Osama was little more than a figurehead and Khalifa claimed bin Laden's military commander and other leaders were the real power behind the throne. While Khalifa may have been seeking to throw the hounds off the scent (he was gunned down in Madagascar in 2007), there is undoubtedly an element of truth in all this. On the basis of his background, it is hard to conceive of bin Laden as some puppet master or grand strategist.

The discontented Islamist cause will live on come what may. Certainly the political quagmire in Afghanistan and Pakistan will continue to cast a long shadow. Mullah Abdul Salam Zaeef, former Taliban ambassador to Pakistan and one-time Guantanamo Bay inmate, firmly believes that the resurgent Taliban is far more radical than the organisation he helped create. Some might argue that he has a conveniently short memory. He cites the use of suicide bombers as an al-Qaeda inspiration, not that of the old-school Taliban. What is clear is that drug money will continue to fund Afghanistan's renegade warlords and Pakistan's militant factions, as it has always done.

Afghanistan remains the world's largest illicit opium producer and this will continue to be a major obstacle for the reconstruction of the war-torn country. During the 1990s the Taliban were partly funded through heroin and opium trafficking and Operation Enduring Freedom sought to destroy all existing stocks. Renewed drug cultivation is helping to fund the resurgent Taliban – to the tune of $70 million in 2008. This will buy an awful lot of guns and explosives. Plus, the traffickers are sitting on considerable stockpiles due to over-supply. Organised crime, which comes with drug trafficking, also promotes corruption at the highest levels.

Washington has been spending $45 million a year trying to eradicate drug cultivation in Afghanistan through the United Nations Office on Drugs and Crime, as well as operations conducted under the auspices of Enduring Freedom. Working closely with the Afghan government, the UN has sought to develop the 'Opium Poppy Free Road Map'. This is a pipedream. The UN conducts crop surveillance, continuously monitoring poppy cultivation, price trends and the (half-hearted) eradication efforts led by the regional governors – this culminates in an annual survey, which in turn supposedly helps shape Afghan government policy. Despite these grand-sounding schemes, the poppy fields continue to flourish unabated.

Washington recognised that its crop eradication programme was a waste of time and money by mid-2009. All it had achieved was the alienation of local farmers. Targeting drug labs and distribution networks was hailed as the way ahead. The West cannot simply buy the farmers' opium to take it off the streets – wholesale value in 2008 stood at $3 billion, while the retail value was worth about $52 billion. Such an initiative would be impossible to fund. The UN, along with the Afghan Ministry for Counter Narcotics has sought to develop alternative livelihoods for local farmers – certainly, education and training remains the key to this slow process.

Elsewhere, largely ignored by the West, the war has been hotting up in the Arabian Peninsula. It seems the Islamists have found a new cause. Having driven al-Qaeda underground, Saudi Arabia found itself embroiled in the Shia Houthi insurgency at the end of 2009, as the rebellion spilled across the Saudi-Yemeni border. With up to 5,000 Houthis based in the mountainous border region, such clashes were perhaps inevitable. In a vain attempt to keep the Islamists out, Saudi Arabia's response was to erect a border fence. The Houthi militants accused the Saudis of permitting Yemeni security forces to attack them from Saudi territory. The Saudi Navy was also involved in efforts to stop the illegal flow of weapons from Eritrea into Yemen.

Following Houthi raids into the Jizan region, which resulted in Saudi military casualties, Saudi jets bombed Houthi strongholds (at al-Malahaid, Jabal al-Mamdud, al-Husama and al-Mujdaa) on the Yemeni side of the border. On the ground, Saudi army units and Special Forces moved to drive the Yemeni rebels from the Jabal al-Dood or Jabal Mudood mountain area. Among those captured in the fighting were Ethiopian and Somali fighters drawn to the Houthis' cause. The rebels denied any links with these foreign volunteers. The Saudi military did not have it all its own way, having lost prisoners and quantities of weaponry to the rebels. Despite pressure from the Saudi and Yemeni armed forces, the Houthis are likely to remain troublesome for both countries in the years to come. All Saudi Arabia has achieved is to incite the hatred of the Houthis, furthering Shia-Sunni rivalry in the region.

The Palestinian question is as intractable as ever and has created some strange bedfellows for the Israelis. Egypt became a major weapons-smuggling conduit for militants in the Gaza Strip and West Bank, via tunnels beneath the Gaza-Egyptian border. During 2005 anti-tank rocket-launchers, automatic rifles and ammunition were smuggled into Gaza. By the end of the following year this amounted to 20,000 assault rifles, 3,000 pistols and 6 million rounds of ammunition. The Egyptian authorities claimed the bulk of the arms was coming from Israel, intent on destabilising the Palestinians. However, the Arab world has its favoured Palestinian factions. As a result, Egypt suffered terror attacks in the Sinai, where the Bedouins profit from the smuggling.

Ironically, Israel found itself providing 3,000 rifles and 3 million rounds of ammunition in 2006 to its old enemy Fatah (former guerrilla wing of the PLO) to support their confrontation with Hamas, the ruling party in the Gaza Strip. Yasser Arafat would have been turning in his grave at this development. The leftist, anti-Israeli politics of the PLO are long dead and buried. Saudi Arabia got its own way with the radicalisation of the Palestinian cause, just as it had done with the Mujahideen in Afghanistan.

Closer to home there is no place for complacency. During a walkabout in the Muslim Bury Park area of Luton on 30 November 2009, Conservative peer Baroness Sayeeda Warsi (the shadow minister for community cohesion) was pelted with eggs. Under normal circumstances this would have been seen as a harmless expression of democratic protest, but the clearly hostile young Asian men responsible had two things on their minds – Afghanistan and Shariah law. This ugly incident showed that, despite the British government's social cohesion policies, British liberal democracy will never appeal to everyone.

Baroness Warsi, who has been described as the most powerful Muslim woman in the country, has been an outspoken critic of the intolerance of

Muslim hardliners. She has signalled the danger of allowing social and religious needs to become inextricably mixed. Religious dogma is no substitute for social aspirations and achievement. On the eve of a change of government in the UK, it was clear that any new administration would have its work cut out if the voices of moderation continued to be ignored – here and around the world.

Although the rise of militant Islam may be contained or indeed stalled in Afghanistan, Iraq, Somalia and Yemen, the disaffected 'lone wolves' continue to heed the call to global Jihad and remain a very real threat to international security.

Glossary of Militant Islamic Groups

Afghanistan
Afghan Hezbollah
Haqqani Network (HQN)
Harakat-i-Inquilabi-i-Islami (Islamic Revolutionary Movement)
Hezbi-i-Islami (Islamic Party of Younis Khalis)
Hezb-i-Islami (Islamic Party of Gulbuddin Hekmatyar)
Hezb-i-Islami Gulbuddin (successor to the above)
Ittehad-e-Islami (Islamic Alliance)
Jamiat-i-Islami (The Islamic Society)
Jebhe Milli Nejad (National Liberation Front)
Mohaz Melli Islami (National Islamic Front of Afghanistan)
al-Qaeda (The Base)
Quetta Shura Taliban (QST – successor to the above led by Mullah Omar)
Sazmar-i-Nasr (Organisation for Victory)
Sepha-e-Pasdara (or Sepah and Pasadran – Afghan Revolutionary Guard)
Shura-i-Inquilabi (Revolutionary Council)
Taliban (Students or 'one who is seeking') also known as the Taliban Militia (Students of Islamic Knowledge movement)

Albania
al-Qaeda

Algeria
Al Takfir wa-I Hijra
Algerian Hezbollah
Armée Islamique du Salut (AIS)
Groupe Salafiste Libre/Free Salafist Group (GSL)
Groupe Salafiste pour la Prédication et le Combat/Salafist Group for Call and Combat (GSPC)
Groupement Islamique Armé/Islamic Army Group (GIA)
Kataeb el Qods (Jerusalem Brigades)
Mouvement Islamique Armé (MIA)
Mouvement pour l'Etat Islamique (MEI)
al-Qaeda in the Islamic Maghreb (AQIM formerly the GSPC)

Azerbaijan
Islamic Party of Azerbaijan (IPA)
Jeyshullah (Army of God)
Nurcular

Bangladesh
Jagrata Muslim Janata Bangladesh (Awakened Muslim Masses of Bangladesh)
Jamaat-ul-Mujahideen

Bosnia
Iranian Revolutionary Guard
Kateebat al-Mujahideen (el-Mujahed – Battalion of Holy Warriors)

Chechnya
Arab Ansar
Islamic International Brigade
Jamaat Osmanly
Salafi Islamic Jamaat

China
East Turkestan Islamic Movement (ETIM)
East Turkestan Liberation Organisation (ETLO)

Egypt
Abdullah Azzam Brigades
Egyptian Islamic Jihad (EIJ)
Gamaa al-Islamiya (Islamic Group)
Ikhwan-ul-Muslimeen (Muslim Brotherhood – non-violent)
Islamic Group
al-Jihad

Eritrea
Eritrean Islamic Jihad Movement (EIJM)
Eritrean Kinama Movement

Ethiopia
al-Ittihad al-Islamiya (Islamic Unity – AIAI)

France
al-Qaeda
Salafist Group for Call and Combat (GSPC)

India/Kashmir
Al-Ummah (southern India)
Harakat ul-Mujahadin (HuM – based in Pakistan)
Harakat-ul Jihad Islami (Islamic Jihad Movement)
Hizb-ul-Mujahedin (Mujahedin Party)
Jaish-e-Mohammed (Army of Mohammed – JeM – based in Pakistan)
Lashkar-e-Tayyiba (Army of the Righteous – LeT – based in Pakistan)

Indonesia
Darul Islam
Islamic Defenders Front
Jemaah Islamiah (JI)
Laskar Jihad

Iraq
Ali al-Hadi Brigade
Ansar al-Islam (The Partisans of Islam)
Ansar al-Sunnah (Group of the Followers of Sunnah)
Jaish Mohammed (Army of the Prophet Mohammed)
Jama'at al-Tawid wal-Jihad (al-Qaeda in-Iraq)
Tawid wal Jihad (Monotheism and Holy War)

Italy
Salafist Group for Call and Combat (GSPC)

Kenya
al-Ittihad al-Islamiya (Islamic Unity – AIAI)
al-Qaeda

Kosovo
Abu Bekir Sidik
Kosovo Liberation Army (KLA or Ushtria Clirimtare e Kosove – UCK)

Kuwait
The Brigade of the Two Shrines
Martyr Abdul Aziz al-Murqrin Brigade
Mujahideen of Kuwait
Peninsula Lions Brigade
Shariah Falcons Squadron

Lebanon
Afwaj al-muqawamat al-lubnaniyya (Battalions of the Lebanese Resistance – Amal)
Asbat al-Ansar (Partisans' League)
Battalions of Ziad Jarrah
Hezbollah (Party of God)
Iranian Revolutionary Guard

Libya
Jama'a al-Islamiyyah al-Muqatilah (Libyan Islamic Fighting Group)

Macedonia
Albanian National Army (AKSh)
Ismet Jashari

Malaysia
Kumpulan Militan or Mujahideen Malaysia (KMM – Malaysian Militant Group)

Mali
al-Qaeda in the Islamic Maghreb (AQIM formerly the GSPC)

Mauritania
al-Qaeda in the Islamic Maghreb (AQIM formerly the GSPC)
The Scions of Tariq
The Sons of Uqba bin Nafi

Morocco
Atakfir Wal Hijra (Exile and Redemption)
Groupe Islamique Combattant Marocain (Moroccan Islamic Combatant Group)
Harakat al-Mujahedeen al-Maghrabia (Moroccan Mujahideen Movement)
al-Saiqa (Thunderbolt)
Salafia Jihadia (Holy War of the Prophets – SJ)

Niger
al-Qaeda in the Islamic Maghreb (AQIM formerly the GSPC)

Nigeria
Boko Haram al-Qaeda in the Islamic Maghreb (AQIM, formerly the GSPC)

Pakistan
Lashkar-e-Jhangvi (Army of God)
Sipah-e-Mohammad (Army of Mohammad)
Sipah-e-Sahaba Pakistan (Army of the Companions of the Prophet, Pakistan)
Tanzeem-e-Nifaz
Tehreek-e-Nafaz-e-Shariat-e-Mohammadi (Movement for the Enforcement of Islamic
    Law)
Tehrik-e-Jaffria Pakistan (Movement of the Followers of Shia of Pakistan)
Tehrik-i-Taliban Pakistan (Student Movement of Pakistan – TTP)

Palestine (West Bank & Gaza Strip)
al-Asqa Martyrs Brigade
Fath al-Islam
Harakat al-muqawamah al-Islamiyyah (Islamic resistance Movement – Hamas or Zeal)
Izz ad-Din al-Qassam Brigades (military wing of Hamas)
Jaish al-Islam (Army of Islam)
Jaish al-Umma (Army of the Nation)
Jund Ansar Allah (Soldiers of the Companions of God)
Jund al-Sham
Palestinian Islamic Jihad (PIJ)
Usbat al-Ansar

Former Leftwing and Nationalist Palestinian Groups superseded by Hamas and PIJ
Abu Nidal Organisation/Black June (ANO)
Arab Liberation Front (ALF)
Democratic Front for the Liberation of Palestine (DFLP)
Palestine Liberation Front (PLF)
Palestinian Liberation Organisation (PLO)/al-Fatah
Palestine Popular Struggle Front (PPSF)
Popular Front for the Liberation of Palestine (PFLP)
Popular Front for the Liberation of Palestine – General Command (PFLP-GC)

Philippines
Abu Sayyaf (Sword of God)
Moro Islamic Liberation Front (MILF)

Russia
Caucasus Front/Caucasus Caliphate Jihad
Islambouli Brigades
Kabardino-Balkarian Yarmuk (Islamic Brigade)
Special Purpose Islamic Regiment

Saudi Arabia
The Jerusalem Squad
al-Qaeda in the Arabian Peninsula

Somalia
al-Ittihad al-Islamiya (Islamic Unity – AIAI)
al-Qaeda
al-Shabaab
Islamic Courts Council (ICC)

Spain
al-Qaeda

Sudan
Ansar
Khatmiya
National Islamic Front (formerly the Sudanese Muslim Brotherhood, now the ruling
   party)
Sudanese Hezbollah

Tajikistan
Islamic Renaissance Group (IRP)
United Tajik Opposition (UTO)

Tanzania
al-Qaeda

Thailand
Gerakan Mujahideen Islam Pattani (GMIP)
Mujahideen Pattani Movement (BNP)
Pattani United Liberation Organization (PULO)

Tunisia
al-Qaeda

Turkey
al-Qaeda
Turkish Hezbollah

UK
Abu Hafs al-Masri Brigades
Secret Group of al-Qaeda of Jihad Organisation in Europe

US
al-Qaeda
al-Shabaab
Raleigh Jihad Group

Uzbekistan
Hizb-i-Islami Turkistan (Islamic Party of Turkistan)
Islam Lashkarlary (Fighters for Islam – Fergana Valley)
Islamic Movement of Uzbekistan (IMU)
Tauba (Repentance – Fergana Valley)

Yemen
Islamic Army of Aden (IAA)
al-Qaeda in the Arabian Peninsula

Notes and References

Preface

1. The Koran, verse 60, *al-Anfal*. (Spoils of War, Yusufali: 60,008)
2. For the purposes of counter-terrorism the term Western intelligence encompasses America's Central Intelligence Agency, Defense Intelligence Agency, Department of Homeland Security, Federal Bureau of Investigation and the National Security Agency; the UK's Joint Intelligence Committee, Joint Terrorism Analysis Centre, the Centre for the Protection of National Infrastructure, Security Service (MI5), Secret Intelligence Service (MI6) and Defence Intelligence Staff. (The author served with the latter for a decade and a half.) It was worth noting that America's intelligence and security community is simply vast. Its officially designated intelligence community (IC) has fourteen member organisations, but outside this there are at least another sixteen with intelligence interests. Most of America's intelligence agencies have specific roles, however in many instances there is a good degree of overlap both in terms of collection and analysis.
3. Al-Qaeda is a common Arab word and has a number of meanings: it is most often translated in the West as 'the base' but can also mean formula, maxim, methodology or pretext.
4. The term terrorism is broadly defined as politically motivated violence against non-combatant targets by a sub national group or clandestine agents; there is no universally accepted definition for international terrorism, although it is normally accepted that it involves the citizens or property of more than one country. See Raphael Perl, 'Defining terrorism, in International Terrorism: Threat, Policy, and Response', *CRS Report*, 3 January 2007.
5. Jihad means a 'great striving' in the name of Allah to bring the world under Islamic rule. Within the tenets of Islam there are two strands of Jihad; the greater Jihad is the struggle against evil within one's self, while the lesser Jihad is a secondary war against a direct threat to Islam. Global Islamists or Jihadists do not really distinguish between the two.
6. John Laffin, *Brassey's War Annual* 1, p. 60.

Chapter 1 – Killing bin Laden

1. In total the 9/11 attacks are estimated to have killed 2,976 people, some 2,752 at the WTC, 184 at the Pentagon and forty in Pennsylvania; fifteen hijackers were from Saudi Arabia, two from the UAE, one from Egypt and one from Lebanon.
2. US forces discovered a videotape recorded in November 2001 containing this statement by bin Laden made during a meeting with a Saudi supporter in Jalalabad, Afghanistan. Cited Peter L. Bergen, *The Osama bin Laden I know: An Oral History of al-Qaeda's Leader*, p. 283.

3. Bin Laden's complicity in 9/11 was confirmed by a videotape made in January 2000 obtained by the *Sunday Times*, this showed 9/11 hijackers Mohammed Atta and Ziad Jarrah at bin Laden's HQ at Tarnak Farms, near Kandahar airport, in Afghanistan. See Yosri Fouda 'Chilling Message of the 9/11 Pilots', *Sunday Times*, 1 October 2001.

4. Notably absent was the Chief of Defence Intelligence, head of the Defence Intelligence Staff. This supports Whitehall with vital all-source intelligence assessments and although it has a counter-terrorism role, traditionally it is seen as the poorer cousin by the rest of the British intelligence community. Its US counterpart is the Defense Intelligence Agency. Christopher Meyer, *DC Confidential*, p. 188.

5. Kuwaiti-born, British-educated Yousef was captured in Islamabad in early 1995 and extradited to the US and imprisoned in the Florence Correctional Unit, Colorado also known as Supermax. He and his co-conspirators demands were that the US stop all support to Israel and refrain from meddling in the Middle East. His WTC bombing killed six and injured another 1,042. After Yousef's capture bin Laden became the most wanted terrorist in the world. See Simon Reeve, *The New Jackals: Ramzi Yousef, Osama bin Laden and the future of terrorism*.

6. Author, 'Silent Killers', *Air Forces Monthly*, December 2005, p. 35.

7. Ahmed Rashid, *Taliban: the Story of the Afghan Warlords*, p. 134.

8. America's equivalent of GCHQ Cheltenham, which gathers signals intelligence.

9. James Risen, *State of War: The Secret History of the CIA and the Bush Administration*, pp. 183–184.

10. Ibid., p. 185.

11. Yosri Fouda and Nick Fielding 'CIA videos reveal the missed chances to kill bin Laden', *Sunday Times*, 4 September 2005, citing the al-Jazeera TV series *Blinking Red*.

12. Ibid.

13. Although the aptly named RQ-1 Predator UAV was not designed as a strike platform, the weaponised variant proved itself very versatile in the War on Terror. Since 9/11 armed UAVs are routinely employed to launch pre-emptive strikes on extremists.

14. Richard A. Clarke, *Against All Enemies: Inside America's War on Terror*, p. 220.

15. Ibid., p. 221.

16. George Tenet, 'The Predator', *Written Statement for the Record of the Director of Central Intelligence Before the National Commission on Terrorist Attacks Upon the United States*, 24 March 2004.

17. Ibid.

18. The target was not a terrorist, but a stationary tank. Initial trials were conducted employing the older AGM 114C Hellfire (analog guidance and control system); followed by the AGM 114K Hellfire II (digital guidance and control system). Its bunker-busting capabilities made it ideal for taking out terrorist sanctuaries in Afghanistan.

19. Armed Predator initially had an operational range of 400 miles, at 140mph, with a 24-hour mission time. Once America's air war against the Taliban commenced Global Hawk UAVs were also deployed over Afghanistan; although faster and with twice the range they were unarmed.

20. Tom Baldwin, 'Reports of bin Laden's death are dismissed as baseless', *The Times*, 25 September 2006.

21. Clarke, *Against All Enemies*, p. 231.

22. Tenet, 'The Predator'.
23. The CIA's Directorate of Operations, Special Activities Division, is responsible for armed MQ-1 Predator and MQ-9 Reaper covert ops, while USAF operates it in theatre.
24. Tenet, 'The Predator'.
25. Author, 'Silent Killers'.
26. Shaun Waterman, 'CIA too cautious in terrorist hunt, agency critics say', *Washington Times*, 28 February 2005.
27. Office of Inspector General, *Report on CIA Accountability With Respect to the 9/11 Attacks*, June 2005 (declassified August 2007).
28. Ibid., p. vii.
29. Ibid., p. xxi.
30. *9/11 Commission Report*, pp. 112–114, 130, 137–138, 140, 183.

Chapter 2 – Goodbye Afghanistan

1. Anthony R. Tucker, 'Armed Forces of the Afghan Conflict', *Jane's Soviet Intelligence Review*, March 1990, pp. 114–118.
2. Burchard Brentjes and Helga Brentjes, *Taliban: a Shadow over Afghanistan*, p. 113.
3. Tucker, 'Armed Forces of the Afghan Conflict'.
4. See Anthony Tucker, 'The Soviet Threat to the Middle East,' *Gulf Report*, June 1989.
5. Agence France-Presse (AFP), 9 January 1980 & Peter Kruzhin, 'The ethnic composition of Soviet Forces in Afghanistan', *RL 20/80, Radio Free Europe/Radio Liberty*, 11 January 1980.
6. Ibid.
7. Anthony R. Tucker, 'The Mujahideen Guerrilla War', *Survival Weaponry & Techniques*, February 1989, p. 67.
8. Ahmed Rashid, *Jihad: The Rise of Militant Islam in Central Asia*, p. 44.
9. Interview with author.
10. Jonathan Randall, *Osama: The Making of a Terrorist*, p. 76.
11. Interview with author.
12. *Kommunista Tadzhikistana*, 30 December 1987. According to Vladimir Petkel, the Russian Chairman of the local KGB, tens of Islamic leaders had been brought to trial in 1986–87, but the Soviet authorities did not want to draw public attention to the issue.
13. Alex Brummer, 'Stinger missiles snatched from Afghan rebels', *Guardian*, 15 October 1987. According to the Stockholm International Peace Research Institute, Iran obtained nine Stingers which were either captured or purchased by Iran from the Afghan Mujahideen, *SIPRI Yearbook 1988*, p. 191.
14. Anthony R. Tucker, 'The Soviet War Over Afghanistan', *Jane's Soviet Intelligence Review*, June 1989, p. 271.
15. Mark Tran, 'Kabul behind Pakistan blast', *Guardian*, 18 April 1988.
16. 'Kabul regains air supremacy as US halts Stinger supply', *The Times*, 24 January 1989.
17. Edward Gorman, 'Pakistan closes Mujahideen base: CIA aid to rebels may have trained foreign guerrillas', *The Times*, 5 April 1988.
18. Ibid.
19. Ibid.

20. By the late 1980s the Philippines had endured twenty years of insurgency warfare. The Communist New People's Army, which appeared on the northern island of Luzon in the late 1960s, and the Muslim Moro National Liberation Front, which emerged on the southern island of Mindanao in the early 1970s, plagued the country. In the late 1980s, the MNLF's Bangsa Moro Army numbered 15,000, while the breakaway Moro Islamic Liberation Front fielded about 2,900 fighters. These organisations were supported by Libya, Iran, Syria and the Organisation of Islamic Countries. Under the auspices of the OIC, the MNLF eventually withdrew its demand for full autonomy. See Anthony R. Tucker, 'Problems Remain in the Philippines', *Jane's Defence Weekly*, 22 July 1989 & Anthony R. Tucker, 'Counter-Insurgency in the Philippines', *Armed Forces*, August 1989.

21. The US includes Abu Sayyaf on its list of terrorist organisations because of its alleged links with al-Qaeda. US troops have been deployed to help their Philippine counterparts by providing training. However, the Philippines counter-terrorism efforts were discredited in mid-2003 when Abu Sayyaf members, Abdulmukim Edris and Omar Lasal, along with Fathur Rohman al-Ghozi, an Indonesian suspected of involvement in JI plots to plant bombs in Singapore and the Philippines escaped. Edris was eventually shot escaping re-capture.

22. Orchestrated by the Soviets to prove the Afghan Army's capabilities it involved 24,000 Afghan/Soviet troops, who were to relieve the 8,000-strong 25th Afghan Infantry Division and 2nd Frontier Brigade trapped in Khost by 9,000–20,000 Mujahideen. The Afghan Army did not break through until 30 December 1987 and then needed the assistance of Soviet paratroopers. See Anthony R. Tucker, 'Operation Magistral', *Jane's Intelligence Review*, October 1989.

23. Jonathan Steele, 'Kabul leader warns of another Iran', *Guardian*, 25 April 1988.

24. Zhores Medvedev, *Gorbachev*, p. 235.

Chapter 3 – The Mountains of Allah

1. Valeri Konovalov, 'Legacy of the Afghan War: Some Statistics', Report on the USSR, Vol.1 No. 14, *Radio Free Europe/Radio Liberty*, 7 April 1989, pp. 2–3.

2. Patrick Brogan, *World Conflicts*, p. 393.

3. Mikhail Gorbachev, *Perestroika*, p. 298.

4. Ibid., p. 297.

5. Medvedev, *Gorbachev*, p. 31.

6. Ibid.

7. By 1238 Georgia had fallen into bloody disunity and the following year became a Mongol vassal. The Mongols massacred the population of Ani, the ancient capital of Armenia. King Hayton of Little or Lesser Armenia hoped for a Mongol alliance against the forces of Islam and the Armenians achieved this against the Seljuks in 1254. This was a historic moment for it was one of the first occasions where Christian and Mongol acted in unison. Muslim Baghdad fell on 10 February 1258 and in a forty-day massacre 80,000 inhabitants were butchered. The Eastern Christians welcomed the Mongols as enemies of Islam and the Armenian king saw the advance against Syria as a crusade. In 1303 a Mongol-Armenian army was defeated at Marj as-Saffar, however the following year the Armenians defeated the Mamluks at Ayati. Christian Armenia was to struggle on for another 175 years.

8. Peter Balakian, *The Burning Tigris: The Armenian Genocide*, pp. 195–196. Sultan Abdul Hamid II, known as 'the bloody Sultan', who ruled the Ottoman Empire

from 1876–1908 was responsible for the killing of about 200,000 Armenians in 1894–96.

9. Ibid., p. 338.
10. Konovalov, 'Legacy of the Afghan War: Some Statistics', p. 1.
11. Rashid, *Jihad: The Rise of Militant Islam in Central Asia*, pp. 125–126.
12. Jeremy Page, 'Soviet "terrorist" soldier back from the grave', *The Times*, 28 September 2004.
13. Craig Murray, *Murder in Samarkand*, p. 26.
14. Ibid., p. 83.
15. Rashid, *Jihad*, p. 174.
16. Murray, *Murder in Samarkand*, p. 338.

Chapter 4 – Seekers of the Truth

1. Mahan Abedin, 'From Mujahid to Activist: An Interview with a Libyan Veteran of the Afghan Jihad', *Terrorism Monitor*, 24 March 2005 & Christopher Heffelfinger, *Unmasking Terror*, Vol II, pp. 142–158.
2. Ibid., p. 146.
3. Charles Stuart, 'Why is Kabul holding on', *Survival Weaponry and Techniques*, January 1991, p. 4.
4. Ibid.
5. John Laffin, *Holy War: Islam Fights*, p. 14.
6. Pervez Musharraf, *In the Line of Fire*, p. 209.
7. Interview with author.
8. President Sadat of Egypt announced his decision to deliver weapons, especially anti-tank and anti-aircraft missiles, to the Muslim rebels via Pakistan in the early 1980s. Crucially Egypt was producing the Soviet man-portable SA-7 surface-to-air missile and the Rocket Propelled Grenade or RPG-7: it was the latter type of weapon that brought down the US Black Hawk helicopter in Somalia in 1993. China also built both types of weapon that ended up in militants' hands.
9. Interview with author. To the layman there was no way of telling whether the Mujahideen' AK-47 look-alike assault rifle had been manufactured by Bulgaria (Bulgarian Arsenal AKKM), China (Norinco Type 56), Egypt (Maadi Misr), Poland (Lucznik Karabinek AKM), Romania (Romanian State Arsenal PM md.63/AIM), the Soviet Union (Tula or Izhevsk/Izhmash AKM) or Yugoslavia (Zastava M70). However, it was evident that the Mujahideen had received brand-new weapons when the likes of American author David Isby were photographed in Afghanistan brandishing a pristine Kalashnikov AKM 7.62mm assault rifle that had clearly come straight from the factory.
10. Osama bin Laden, 'The Declaration of Jihad on the Americans Occupying the Country of the Two Sacred Places', 23 August 1996.
11. World Islamic Front, 'Statement of Jihad against Jews and Crusaders', *al-Quds al-Arabi*, 28 February 1998. The Near East and Middle East were embroiled in 200 years of warfare. Between 1096–1254 there were seven major crusades, whilst between 1097–1299 there were over fifty major engagements and sieges, as well as countless smaller battles and skirmishes. The Crusaders' defeat at the Battle of Hattin fought in 1187 is one of the most famous turning points.
12. One of the few good things to come out of 9/11 was that the UN finally enacted numerous anti-terrorist measures, which had for so long languished for the want of majority endorsement by its members. The UN sought ratification of twelve

anti-terrorism conventions. The principal being the 1997 International Convention for the Suppression of Terrorist Bombing; 1998 Convention for the Suppression of Nuclear Terrorism sponsored by Russia; and the 1999 International Convention for the Suppression of the Financing of Terrorism. The most useful convention, sponsored by India, was the 2000 A Comprehensive Convention on Terrorism incorporating key elements from the existing anti-terrorism conventions into a single document. Nonetheless UNSCR 1373 also incorporated key elements from all the conventions, which meant they were legally binding on all members, whether the protocols and conventions have been ratified or not.

13. Statement by Director of Central Intelligence, George J. Tenet before the Senate Select Committee on Intelligence on the 'Worldwide Threat 2001: National Security in a Changing World' (as prepared for delivery), 7 February 2001, p. 11.
14. Phil Rees, *Dining with Terrorists: Meetings with the World's Most Wanted Militants*, p. 75.

Chapter 5 – Somalia: a Lesson in Victory

1. Thomas Ricks, 'Allies Step Up Somalia Watch', *Washington Post*, 4 January 2002.
2. Mark Urban, 'Soviet Intervention and the Ogaden Counter-Offensive', *Journal of the Royal United Services Institute*, June 1983.
3. Anthony R. Tucker, 'Conflict in the Horn of Africa', *Jane's Defence Weekly*, 17 December 1988 & Anthony R. Tucker, 'Ethiopia's Intractable Wars', *Armed Forces*, July 1989.
4. Marguerite Johnson, 'Genocide is the word for it', *Time*, 16 February 1989.
5. Angus Deming, 'Death and Fear in Mogadishu: Rebel insurgents close on the capital of Somalia', *Newsweek*, 14 January 1991.
6. Ted Dagne, 'The Horn of Africa: War and Humanitarian Crisis', CRS, 19 September 2000.
7. Richard Clutterbuck, *Terrorism in an unstable world*, p. 139.
8. Vernon Loeb, 'A Global Pan-Islamic Network', *Washington Post*, 23 April 1998.
9. Mark Fineman and Stephen Braun, 'Life Inside al-Qaeda: A Destructive Devotion', *Los Angeles Times*, 24 September 2001.
10. Nigel Hamilton, *Bill Clinton Mastering the Presidency*, p. 190.
11. Interview with author.
12. Hamilton, p. 191.
13. Ibid., p. 192.
14. Hamid Mir, interview with Osama bin Laden, Pakistan 18 March 1997, cited by Simon Reeve, *The New Jackals: Ramzi Yousef, Osama bin Laden and the future of terrorism*, p. 182.
15. Craig Timberg, 'Radicals Gain Edge in Somali Capital – Moderates Lose Key Positions in Islamic Militias', *Washington Post*, 4 July 2004.
16. 'Leader seeks Islamic rule', *The Times*, 27 June 2006.
17. Scott Baldauf and Mike Pflanz, 'US take hunt for al-Qaeda to Somalia', *Christian Science Monitor*, 10 January 2007.
18. Bill Roggio, 'Iran/Hezbollah connection to al-Qaeda, Somali terrorists fought with Hezbollah summer 2006', 21 January 2008 (www.newsgroups.derkeiler.com).
19. 'Somali gunmen use piracy ransoms to fund insurgency', Reuters, 25 August 2008.
20. 'Pirates fire rockets at French boat off Somalia', Reuters, 14 September 2008.
21. 'al-Qaeda Urges Somalis To Attack Ships', *World Watch*, CBS News, 16 April 2009.

22. Stephanie Hanson, 'al-Shabaab', *Backgrounder*, 27 February 2009.
23. Ibid.
24. Alex Spillius, 'US at risk of domestic Islamist terrorism, says FBI', *Daily Telegraph*, 14 March 2009.
25. Andrew Liepman, Deputy Director of Intelligence, National Counter-terrorism Center, Directorate of Intelligence, 'Violent Islamist Extremism: al-Shabaab Recruitment in America', Hearing before the Senate Homeland Security and Government Affairs Committee 11 March 2009.

Chapter 6 – Yemen: a Nest of Vipers

1. Anthony R. Tucker, 'Soviet Arms Supplies – A Strategic Lever?' *Jane's Soviet Intelligence Review*, August 1989.
2. Roy Eccleston, 'Bin Laden "driver" first at Cuba hearing', *The Times*, 25 August 2004.
3. The two men purchased the speedboat used in the attack. Al-Nashiri was believed to be the mastermind, but he was sentenced in absentia as he was in US custody. He was also believed to have been involved in the attacks on the US embassies in Kenya and Tanzania. See 'Two sentenced to death in Yemen for Attack on US warship', *The Times*, 30 September 2004.
4. Andrew McGregor, 'al-Qaeda Suspects on Trial in Yemen', *Terrorism Focus*, Volume III, Issue 4, 31 January 2006.
5. *9/11 Commission Report*, p. 195.
6. Bill Clinton Interview with Chris Wallace, Fox News, Sunday, 24 September 2006.
7. Sally Bedell Smith, *For the Love of Politics: The Clintons in the White House*, p. 434, citing the *New York Times*, 21 February 2007 & the *Washington Post*, 21 February 2007.
8. 'Yemen Rejects Some US Requests on Extremists', *Washington Post*, 25 September 2008.
9. Marie Colvin & Dipesh Gadher, 'Britain's Islamic Army', *Sunday Times*, 17 January 1998.
10. Michael Becket, 'Yemen Hostage Shootout', *Daily Telegraph*, 30 December 1998.
11. Christina Lamb, 'SAS joins hunt for bin Laden tracked down in Yemen', *Daily Telegraph*, 17 November 2002.
12. Craig Hoyle, 'Yemen drone strike: just the start?', *Jane's Defence Weekly*, 8 November 2008.
13. 'Yemeni forces kill rebel cleric', BBC News Online, 9 September 2004.
14. 'Shia gunmen kill Yemeni troops', BBC News Online, 28 January 2007.
15. 'More than 100 killed in five days of clashes between army and Shiite rebel clashes in Yemen, say officials', *International Herald Tribune*, 19 February 2007.

Chapter 7 – Bosnia: Trouble with 'Ragheads'

1. Eric Micheletti and Yves Debay, *War in the Balkans*, p. 24.
2. The International Institute for Strategic Studies, *The Military Balance 1992–1993*, p. 70.
3. Riccardo Orizio, *Talk of the Devil: Encounters with Seven Dictators*, p. 180.
4. Richard Aldrich, 'America used Islamists to arm Bosnian Muslims', *Guardian*, 22 April 2002.

5. Larry E. Craig, Chairman US Senate Republican Policy Committee, 'Clinton Approved Iranian Arms Transfers Help turn Bosnia into Militant Islamic Base', 16 January 1997, p. 5; also see 'How Bosnia's Muslims Dodged Arms embargo: Relief Agency Brokered Arms from nations' radical groups', *Washington Post*, 22 September 1996 & 'Saudis funded weapons for Bosnia, Official says: $300 million program had US stealth cooperation', *Washington Post*, 2 February 1996.
6. Interview with author.
7. Professor Cees Wiebes 'Srebrenica Report', Appendix II 'Intelligence and the war in Bosnia 1992–1995: The role of the intelligence and security services', Chapter 4 *Secret arms supplies and other covert actions*, Netherlands Institute for War Documentation (Amsterdam 2002).
8. Ibid.
9. During the first week of July 1995 Bosnian Serbs laid siege to the Srebrenica enclave under the protection of 600 Dutch peace-keepers. Bosniak fighters who had surrendered their weapons to the Dutch asked for them back – the request was refused. On 11 July 1995 Bosnian Serb commander Ratko Mladic and his forces entered Srebrenica and deported 23,000 women and children. Under shellfire 15,000 Bosniak fighters fled into the mountains; during the next five days 7,000 were reportedly killed. The UN DNA-assisted identification programme helped identify 12,518 individuals in Bosnia; of those 6,185 are Srebrenica victims.
10. Tim Ripley, *Conflict in the Balkans 1991–2000*, pp. 14–16.
11. Clarke, *Against All Enemies*, p. 137.
12. Carl Savich, 'al-Qaeda in Bosnia: Bosnian Muslim War Crimes Trial', *Serbianna*, 5 March 2009 (www.serbianna.com).
13. 'Albanians and Afghans fight for the heirs of Bosnia's SS past', *Daily Telegraph*, 29 December 1993.
14. Sean O'Neill, 'Abu Hamza "boasted of Bosnia action"', *The Times*, 17 January 2006.
15. Jamie Doward and Diane Taylor, 'Hamza "set up terror camps" with British ex-soldiers', *Observer*, 12 February 2006. Hamza was given seven years' imprisonment for soliciting murder and inciting racial hatred: it was claimed he was part of a global network that encompassed Afghanistan, Pakistan, Yemen, the UK and US.
16. General Sir Michael Rose, *Fighting For Peace: Bosnia 1994*, p. 26.
17. Ibid.
18. General Wesley K. Clark, *Waging Modern War Bosnia, Kosovo, and the Future of Combat*, p. 33.
19. Ibid.
20. Ibid.
21. According to Harrier pilot, Nick Richardson, the Fleet Air Arm had to fill the intelligence gap using the F-95 camera system. Accuracy depended on a crude sighting group chinagraphed on the inside of the canopy.
22. Also over former Yugoslavia the General Atomics RQ-1A Predator UAV came into its own, providing, for example, post-strike imagery. They were also instrumental in confirming to the World that the Serbs had withdrawn all their heavy equipment from the Sarajevo exclusion zone.
23. Nick Richardson, *No Escape Zone*, pp. 145 & 154.
24. Barry Schweid, 'CIA: Bosnia has broken military intelligence ties with Iran', Associated Press, 31 December 1996.
25. Orizio, *Talk of the Devil*, p. 189.

26. See Professor Cees Wiebes, 'Srebrenica Report', Appendix II, Chapter 4 *Secret arms supplies and other covert actions*, Netherlands Institute for War Documentation (Amsterdam 2002).

Chapter 8 – Algeria: Sacred Frustration

1. Interview with author.
2. Sara Daly, 'The Algerian Salafist Group for Call and Combat: A Dossier', *Terrorism Monitor*, Volume 3 Issue 5, 11 March 2005.
3. The bitter Algerian war of independence of 1954–62 cost the Algerian guerrillas in the region of 155,000 dead along with over 50,000 civilians. France and her colonial forces lost about 50,000 troops while 3,600 European civilians were killed or disappeared. At its peak the French Army had 400,000 troops in Algeria and succeeded in outfighting the Algerian Army of National Liberation.
4. See Martin Windrow, *The Algerian War 1954–62*.
5. David Sharrock, 'Algeria, staging post for the world of terror', *The Times*, 3 April 2004.
6. Interview with *La Libre Belgique*, 21 January 1992.
7. Luis Martinez, *The Algerian Civil War 1990–1998*, p. 215.
8. John Laffin, *The World in Conflict*, p. 18.
9. Ibid., p. 20.
10. Stephen Ulph, 'Algerian GSPC Launch Attack in Mauritania', *Terrorism Focus*, Volume 2 Issue II, 10 June 2005.
11. Roger Boyes, 'Algerians jailed for Christmas bomb plot', *The Times*, 11 March 2003.
12. Nissa Hammadi, 'Algerian National Security Agency Head interviewed on Terrorism, the Disappeared', *Algiers La Tribune*, 18 December 2004.
13. Craig Whitlock, 'al-Qaeda's Far-Reaching New Partner – Salafist Group finds limited appeal in its Native Algeria', *Washington Post Foreign Service*, 5 October 2005.
14. 'Insurgents killed', *The Times*, 27 June 2006 & 'Bomber kills 22 in attack on President', *The Times*, 18 September 2007.

Chapter 9 – Chechnya: Moscow's Running Sore

1. John Laffin, *The World in Conflict War*, p. 36.
2. Sebastian Smith, *Allah's Mountains: The Battle for Chechnya*, p. 3.
3. Ibid., p. 158.
4. Ibid., p. 37.
5. 'Chechen held over Britons' beheading', BBC News World Edition, 7 August 2002.
6. Adam Robinson, *Bin Laden: Behind the Mask of the Terrorist*, p. 176.
7. See Paul Tumelty, 'The Rise and Fall of Foreign Fighters in Chechnya', *Terrorism Monitor*, Volume 4 Issue 2, 31 January 2006.
8. Ibid.
9. Robinson, *Bin Laden ...* p. 176.
10. See Murad al Shishani, 'Abu Hafs and the future of Arab fighters in Chechnya', *Terrorism Monitor*, Volume 3 Issue 7, 7 April 2005.
11. Ibid.
12. Smith, *Allah's Mountains*, p. 216.

13. *Pravda*, 11 May 2004, also see Brian Williams & Feyza Altindag, 'Turkish Volunteers in Chechnya', *Terrorism Monitor*, Volume 3, Issue 7, 7 April 2005.
14. Con Coughlin, 'Tehran "secretly trains" Chechens to fight in Russia', *Sunday Telegraph*, 27 November 2005.
15. Smith, *Allah's Mountains*, pp. xx–xxi.
16. Clem Cecil, 'Chechens attack Moscow puppet's election "farce"', *The Times*, 4 October 2003.
17. Jeremy Page, '"Free" election, but Chechens are still too scared to vote', *The Times*, 26 November 2005.
18. Paul Quinn-Judge & Yuri Zarakhovich, 'Terror in the Dark: Putin blames Chechen rebels – one of the few forces in Russia still beyond his control – for Moscow attack', *Time*, 16 February 2004.
19. Damian Grammaticas, 'Moscow "suicide blast" kills 10', BBC News, 31 August 2004.
20. Nick Allen, '200 Chechen gunmen launch assault on city', *Daily Telegraph*, 14 October 2005.
21. Ibid.
22. See Brian Williams & Feyza Altindag, 'Turkish Volunteers in Chechnya'.
23. Smith, *Allah's Mountains*, p. 4.

Chapter 10 – Kosovo: a Missed Opportunity

1. See Patrick Goodenough, CNS London Bureau Chief, 'Nato Probes Claims that bin Laden is in Kosovo', 28 April 2000 & Gabriel Partos, 'Analysis: bin Laden and the Balkans', News.bbc.co.uk, 2 October 2001.
2. Christian Jennings, *Midnight in Some Burning Town*, p. 26.
3. Tom Walker & Aiden Laverty, 'CIA Aided Kosovo Guerrilla Army', *Sunday Times*, 12 March 2000.
4. 'Adriatic Phoenix: Albania looks west for air arm modernisation', *Aviation News*, August 2005.
5. Michael Levine, quoted in the *New American Magazine*, 24 May 1999.
6. Michael Radu, 'Don't Arm the KLA', Foreign Policy Research Institute, 6 April 1999 (see www.fpri.org).
7. Ibid.
8. Jennings, *Midnight in Some Burning Town*, p. 40.
9. Ibid., pp. 48–50.
10. Ian Traynor, 'Serb court jails paramilitary for massacre', *Guardian*, 18 March 2004.
11. Chris Stephen, 'US Tackles Islamic Militancy in Kosovo', *Scotsman*, 30 November 1998.
12. Ibid.
13. Steve Rodan, *The Jerusalem Post*, 14 September 1998.
14. Uzi Mahnaimi, 'Iranians move in', *Sunday Times*, 22 March 1998.
15. BIA Security Information Agency, 'Albanian terrorism and organised crime in Kosovo and Metohija', Belgrade, September 2003 (www.kosovo.net/albterrorism.html).
16. 'KLA future in the balance', BBC News Online, 7 September 1999.
17. Jon Leyne, 'Kosovo Corps – an army for Kosovo?' BBC News Online, 16 September 1999.
18. Dragisa Blanusca, 'The Inside Story', *Sunday Times Magazine*, 1 September 2002.

19. 'Kosovo and Macedonia: Fag-ends or freedom fighters?' *Economist*, 13 September 2003.

20. Ibid.

21. Stephen Schwartz, *The Two Faces of Islam: The House of Sau'd from Tradition to Terror*, p. 195.

22. Ian Traynor, 'Raging gun battle as ethnic violence erupts in Kosovo', *Guardian*, 18 March 2004 & Marcus Tanner, 'UN flounders as Kosovo plunges back into anarchy', *Independent*, 19 March 2004.

23. Jeta Xharra & Marcus Tanner, 'Burning churches, ruined homes and ethnic hatred. Are the Balkans set to explode again?' *Independent*, 19 March 2004.

24. 'Albanian President pays first official visit to UN-administered Kosovo', UN News Service, 22 April 2004 (UNNews@UN.org).

Chapter 11 – Lebanon: Cradle of Terror

1. The US government removed Lebanon and Syria from the list of major illicit drug-producing and drug-transit countries. However, according to the ODCCP there is evidence of transit trafficking of cocaine (mainly from Colombia), and heroin (from Turkey via Syria) and the existence of small laboratories, for processing of South West Asian opium into heroin and Colombian cocaine, in the remote side valleys of the Bekaa Valley, areas which are difficult to control. In early June 2003 the Lebanese Army conducted operations in the Britel area against an arms and drug-smuggling network.

2. 'Terrorism from Lebanon – 2007 update', Israeli Ministry of Foreign Affairs Press release, 5 June 2008.

3. Murad al-Shishani, 'al-Qaeda's Presence in Lebanon', *Terrorism Focus*, Volume III, Issue 4, 31 January 2006.

4. 'al-Qaeda Charges', *The Times*, 14 January 2006.

5. The Israeli invasion of southern Lebanon on 6 June 1982 involved 78,000 men and 1,240 tanks. Syria had 30,000 troops with 712 tanks deployed in the Bekaa Valley, the Shouf Mountains and around Beirut. Despite Israeli and Syrian forces having orders not to engage each other, they did between 8–11 June. See Z. Schiff & E. Ya'ari, *Israel's Lebanon War*, p. 168, J. Laffin, *The War of Desperation, Lebanon 1982–85*, pp. 33–37 and S. Katz, *Armies in the Lebanon, 1982–84*, p. 12.

6. Newsweek, 12 March 1984, also see A. Dornoch, 'Iran's Violent Diplomacy', *Survival*, Vol. XXX No. 3 (May/June 1982), p. 259.

7. Prior to that on 18 April 1983, a suicide bomb hit the US embassy in Beirut killing sixty-three people, including the CIA's entire Middle East Contingent.

8. Katz, *Armies in the Lebanon 1982–84*, pp. 34–35.

9. Mark Urban, *War in Afghanistan*, p. 243.

10. David C. Isby, *War in a Distant Country Afghanistan: Invasion and Resistance*, p. 102.

11. William E. Smith, 'Deeper into Lebanon', *Time*, 26 September 1983.

12. George J. Church, 'Failure of a Flawed Policy', *Time*, 27 February 1984.

13. Julie Flint, 'Palestinians capture Shi'ite villages', *Guardian*, 27 October 1986.

14. 'Shi'ite leader ends war of the camps in Lebanon', *Guardian*, 18 January 1988.

15. Scott MacLeod, 'The Battle for South Beirut', *Time*, 30 May 1988.

16. Jim Muir, 'Rival Lebanese Shia factions sign peace pact', *Financial Times*, 31 January 1989.

17. Judith Palmer Harik, *Hezbollah: The Changing Face of Terrorism*, p. 200.

18. 'Terrorism from Lebanon – 2007 update', Israeli Ministry of Foreign Affairs Press release, 5 June 2008.
19. 'The Hamas terror war against Israel', Israel Ministry of Foreign Affairs, June 2008.
20. 'Israel strikes back against Hamas terror infrastructure in Gaza', Israel Ministry of Foreign Affairs, 21 January 2009.

Chapter 12 – The Mahdi and the Pharaohs

1. Translates as the 'Guided One of the Prophet'.
2. Cecil Eprile, *War and Peace in the Sudan 1955–1972*, p. 130.
3. Tom Porteous, 'Khartoum reels from high costs of conflict', *Guardian*, 9 February 1988.
4. Eric Marsden, 'Sudan to revert to law of Islam', *Sunday Times*, 24 July 1988.
5. Tom Porteous, 'Sudan's disenchanted Muslims turn to fundamentalism', *Guardian*, 21 March 1988.
6. Ray Wilkinson, 'A Hellhole in the Sudan', *Newsweek*, 20 March 1989.
7. The Ugandan government was plagued by at least six guerrilla armies. See Anthony R. Tucker, 'Uganda's Cycle of Violence', *Armed Forces*, December 1989.
8. Gadaffi had 8,000 troops in northern Chad occupying the disputed Aouzou strip and backing Chadian opposition forces. See Anthony R. Tucker, 'The Toyota Army', *Armed Forces*, December 1988.
9. Hugh Miles, 'We heard a God almighty bang. Then another, and then another', *Sunday Telegraph*, 24 July 2005.
10. Interview with author.
11. Interview with author, see 'Suez attack could be Catastrophic', *Warships International Fleet Review*, August 2004.

Chapter 13 – Middle East Sojourn: Saudi Arabia

1. Robin Wright, *Sacred Rage*, pp. 162–163.
2. John Laffin, *Holy War: Islam Fights*, p. 211.
3. Ibid., p. 201.
4. Ze'ev Schiff & Ehud Ya'ari, *Israel's Lebanon War*, p. 134.
5. Author, 'Coalition aims to put al-Qaeda through Cold Turkey', *Warships International Fleet Review*, March 2004.
6. See Anthony R. Tucker, 'Saudi Arabia's Military Build-up', *Armed Forces*, February 1989, pp. 62–65.
7. M.J. Akbar, *The Shade of Swords: Jihad and the conflict between Islam and Christianity*, p. 208.
8. Alan Munro, *Arab Storm Politics and Diplomacy behind the Gulf war*, p. 144.
9. Bruce Watson et al, *Military Lessons of the Gulf War*, p. 49.
10. Akbar, *The Shade of Swords*, p. 208.
11. 'The Spider in the web', *Economist*, 22 September 2001.
12. Alfred Prados, 'Saudi Arabia: Current Issues and US Relations', CRS, 8 May 2006, p. 9.
13. See Christopher Blanchard & Alfred Prados. A.B., 'Saudi Arabia: Terrorist Financing Issues', CRS Report, 14 September 2007.
14. Ibid., p. 2.
15. Saudi's Eastern Fleet is based at Jubail on the Gulf with bases at Ad-Dammam, Ras al Mishab, Ras al Ghar and Jubail. At the latter US military personnel use

King Abdul Aziz naval base to train RSN officers. The Eastern Fleet is more capable than the Western: it regularly conducts exercises with the USN and has gained praise from its American counterparts.

16. 'Saudi Arabia wakes up to the reality of al-Qaeda', *Economist*, 17 May 2003
17. Syed Rashid Husain, 'Saudi gunmen hold sixty after rampage', *Sunday Times*, 30 May 2004.
18. Michael Theodoulou, 'Briton's murder refutes Saudi claims that terrorists defeated', *The Times*, 16 September 2004.
19. 'Saudi terror chief', *The Times*, 5 November 2004. Otaibi was already on the Saudis' most wanted list and therefore a marked man.
20. King Fahd died in 2005 after a long illness: he was succeeded by crown Prince Abdullah, de facto ruler for the previous ten years so it was business very much as usual for Saudi Arabia.
21. 'Why al-Qaeda in Yemen is wooing the Saudis', *Khaleej Times*, 10 May 2008.

Chapter 14 – East Africa: War is Finally Declared

1. Nick Fielding, 'Fertile ground for bin Laden's terror', *Sunday Times*, 1 December 2002.
2. Awadh Babo, 'Small Village with a reputation for Terrorism', *East African Standard*, 7 March 2004.
3. Mike Pflanz, 'Sleepy Kenyan island joins the front line', *Daily Telegraph*, 5 August 2005.
4. 'Marines Project Breathes new life into poor town', *East African Standard*, 7 March 2004.
5. 'How bad is the Senate Intelligence Report? Very bad', *Weekly Standard*, 25 September 2006.
6. *The 9/11 Commission Report*, p. 134.
7. Gary Berntsen & Raplh Pezzullo, *Jawbreaker*, p. 32.
8. Condoleezza Rice, 'Promoting the National Interest', *Foreign Affairs*, January/February 2000, also see Craig Unger, *House of Bush, House of Saud*, p. 221.
9. Statement by Director of Central Intelligence, George J. Tenet before the Senate Select Committee on Intelligence on the 'Worldwide Threat 2001: National Security in a Changing World', 7 February 2001, p. 1.
10. Ibid.
11. Author, 'US Marines are ordered back into West African turmoil', *Warships International Fleet Review*, October 2003.
12. Author, 'Africa's War on Terror off the radar screen?', *Warship International Fleet Review*, November 2005.
13. Author, 'US Marines are ordered back into West African turmoil'.

Chapter 15 – Punishing the Taliban

1. 'Taliban won't turn over bin Laden', CBSnews.com, 21 September 2001.
2. 'US rejects Taliban offer to try bin Laden', CNN.Com, 7 October 2001.
3. US Special Forces A-Team 595/ Tiger 02 were assigned to Dostum's forces to help him capture the strategic city of Mazar-e-Sharif on 10 November 2001. See Robin Moore, *Task Force Dagger: The Hunt for Bin Laden*, pp. 67–94.
4. The International Institute for Strategic Studies, The Military Balance 1996/97, p. 157.
5. CBSnews.com, 21 September 2001.

6. Author, 'Taliban Tanks', *Classic Military Vehicle*, February 2005.
7. Ibid.
8. Inventories of the Taliban's military equipment were largely useless, as much of it was junk. Unclassified sources estimated that by the late 1990s none of their SA-2 missile sites were operational and that only ten SA-3 sites were active.
9. Satinder Bindra, 'India identifies terrorist training camps', CNN.Com, 19 September 2001.
10. For more information on these operations see Moore, *Task Force Dagger*.
11. Interview with author.
12. Ibid.
13. David Rohde, 'Foreign Fighters of Harsher bent Bolster Taliban', Speigel Online, 30 October 2007.
14. Bill Rodgers, 'More Foreign Fighters Reported Aiding Taliban in Afghanistan', Voanews.com, 14 November 2007.

Chapter 16 – Tora Bora: Afghanistan Revisited

1. John Kampfner, *Blair's Wars*, p. 144.
2. Philip Smucker, 'Bin Laden "fled to hills" as Jalalabad fell', *Daily Telegraph*, 23 November 2001.
3. Alex Spillius, 'US forces said to have pinpointed bin Laden refuge', *Daily Telegraph*, 19 November 2001.
4. Smucker, 'Bin Laden "fled to hills" as Jalalabad fell'.
5. The 15,000–pound BLU-82 was developed in the late 1950s for clearing helicopter landing zones; it was previously deployed in Vietnam and the Gulf War.
6. Berntsen & Pezzullo, *Jawbreaker*, pp. 307–308.
7. Daniel McGory, 'CIA secretly holds 11 of bin Laden's lieutenants', *The Times*, 13 October 2004.
8. Hamadan served as bin Laden's driver and bodyguard for five years from 1996 and during his trial was implicated in the East Africa and *Cole* bombings. Roy Eccleston, 'Bin Laden driver first at Cuba hearing', *The Times*, 25 August 2004.
9. American Forces Press Service, 16 December 2001.
10. Ibid.
11. Philip Smucker, *al-Qaeda's Great Escape*, pp. 124–125.
12. US Defense Press Service, 16 December 2001.
13. Smucker, *al-Qaeda's Great Escape*, p. 146.
14. For more on this operation see Anonymous, *Hunting al-Qaeda*.

Chapter 17 – Saddam's Terrorists

1. James Risen, *State of War: The Secret History of the CIA and the Bush Administration*, p. 76.
2. Christopher Meyer, *DC Confidential*, p. 281.
3. Iraqi Perspectives Project, *Saddam and Terrorism: Emerging Insights from Captured Iraqi Documents* (www.fas.orga/irp/eprint/iraqi/index.html).
4. Lord Hutton, *Report of the Inquiry into the Circumstances Surrounding the Death of Dr David Kelly*, CMG, 28 January 2004, 'Chapter 1: The Government's Dossier on Weapons of Mass Destruction'.
5. US Secretary of State Address, the UN Security Council, transcript 5 February 2003.

6. *The 9/11 Commission Report*, p. 66, also see Randall, *Osama: The Making of a Terrorist*, p. 155.
7. Bill Gertz, 'September 11 Report Alludes to Iraq-al-Qaeda Meeting', *Washington Times*, 30 July 2003 & James Risen, 'Iraqi Agent Denies he met 9/11 Hijackers in Prague Before Attacks on the US', *New York Times*, 13 December 2003.
8. C.J. Chivers, 'Repulsing Attack By Islamic Militants, Iraqi Kurds Tell of Atrocities', *New York Times*, 6 December 2002.
9. John Laffin, *Holy War: Islam Fights*, p. 209.
10. Mohammed Najib, 'Abu Nidal murder trail leads directly to Iraq regime', Jane's Information Group, 23 August 2002 and Robert Fisk, 'Abu Nidal, notorious Palestinian mercenary, was a US Spy', *Independent*, 25 October 2008.
11. He was born Ahmad Faadil al-Khalailah in 1966 in Zarqa, north of Amman, the Jordanian capital. His family were originally Jordanian Bedouins and not Palestinians as sometimes stated.
12. Nick Fielding, 'Saddam set up resistance five years ago', *Sunday Times*, 21 September 2003.

Chapter 18 – Unwelcome Aftermath: International Jihad

1. Eliza Manningham-Butler, Director Security Service MI5, lecture transcript to the Royal United Services Institute 'The Oversight of Intelligence and Security', Conference, 17 June 2003.
2. This was according to Daniel Benjamin, former counter-terrorism advisor to President Clinton. Raymond Whitaker, 'A Chilling warning on a day of tears: 70,000 terrorists are at large', *Independent on Sunday*, 12 September 2004.
3. Daniel McGory, 'Ghost prisoners haunt terrorism hunt', *The Times*, 11 September 2004.
4. UN Office on Drugs and Crime, 'Delivering Counter-terrorism Assistance', p. 19.
5. Raphael Perl, 'International Terrorism: Threat, Policy, and Response', CRS, 3 January 2007, p. 1.
6. Interviews with author.
7. 'al-Qaeda claims Tunisian attack', BBC News Online, 23 June 2002.
8. 'al-Qaeda claims Austrian hostages', BBC News Online, 10 March 2008.
9. Interviews with author.
10. David Leppard, 'al-Qaeda's Heathrow jet plot revealed', *Sunday Times*, 9 October 2005.
11. Walter Pincus and Dan Eggen, '325,000 Names on Terrorism List: Rights Groups Say database May Include Innocent People', *Washington Post*, 15 February 2006.
12. See Testimony of James Woolsey before the Committee on National Security, US House of Representatives, 12 February 1998.
13. See National Counter-terrorism Center, *2007 Report on Terrorism*, 30 April 2008.
14. See National Counter-terrorism Center, *2008 Report on Terrorism*, 30 April 2009.
15. Randall Monger and Macreadie Barr, 'Nonimmigrant Admissions to the United States: 2008', *Annual Flow Report*, US Department of Homeland Security/Office of Immigration Statistics Policy Directorate, April 2009.
16. Michael Hoefer, Nancy Rytina and Bryan C. Baker, 'Estimates of the Unauthorised Immigrant Population residing in the United States: January 2008', *Population Estimates*, US Department of Homeland Security/Office of Immigration Statistics Policy Directorate, February 2009.

17. Philip Flood, *Report of the Inquiry into Australian Intelligence Agencies*, Australian Government, July 2004, 'Chapter 2: Australia's Intelligence Needs – Changing Global Needs', www.dcita.gov.au/cca.
18. Jo Woodbridge, *Sizing the unauthorised (illegal) migrant population in the United Kingdom in 2001*, Home Office Online Report 29/09.
19. This represents sixteen government departments, under the Director General of the Security Service. Four years later this was followed by the Centre for the Protection of National Infrastructure (created from the National Infrastructure Security Co-ordination Centre and a part of MI5, the National Security Advice Centre) which provides protective advice to government and businesses across the country. Both organisations also advise the Cabinet Office's Joint Intelligence Committee, the ultimate arbitrator of threat assessments to the British government.
20. In total forty-six organisations have been proscribed to date, see: http://security. homeoffice.gov.uk/legislation/current-legislation/terrorism-act-2000/proscribed-terrorist-groups.
21. This contains a comprehensive package of measures to ensure that the police, intelligence agencies and courts have the tools they require to tackle terrorism. The 2006 Act received Royal Assent on 30 March 2006 but was not a direct response to 7/7 as new terrorism legislation had already been planned. However, the government consulted with law enforcement and intelligence agencies, to make sure that their views were considered. This was followed by the Counter-Terrorism Act 2008.
22. The final report was published on 14 June 2007, see: http://www.integration andcohesion.org.uk/upload/assets/www.integrationandcohesion.org.uk/our_shared_ future.pdf. It offered four key principles to underpin a new understanding of integration and cohesion. The Commission found on average 79 per cent of people agreed that people of different backgrounds got on well and the level of agreement fell below 60 per cent in only ten out of 387 local areas.
23. The working groups published their report in November 2005. The report and the government's response are available on the Department for Communities and Local Government (DCLG) website, see: http://www.communities.gov.uk/ embedded_object.asp?id=1502016. DCLG are responsible for tackling dis-advantage in all communities, and for working in partnership with them to improve their capacity to fight extremism.

Chapter 19 – Where's bin Laden?

1. TF-121 included the elite US Navy SEALs (Sea, Air and Land) commandos and the US Army's elite Special Forces Operational Detachment – Delta (SFOD-D) or Delta Force, transported by the 160th Special Operations Aviation Regiment.
2. Author, 'US Navy SEALs & UK SBS Spearhead Coalition Hunt for Bin-Laden', *Warships International Fleet Review*, June 2004.
3. 'Coalition in Afghanistan Wraps up Mountain Blizzard', American Forces Press Service, 13 March 2004.
4. Michael Smith and Peter Foster, 'SAS joins hunt for Osama', *Daily Telegraph*, 20 March 2004.
5. Afzal Khan, 'Death of Tribal leader reveals tribal borderland may be sanctuary for Taliban, al-Qaeda Remnants', *Eurasia Daily Monitor*, Volume 1 Issue 36, 22 June 2004.

6. Massoud Ansari and Philip Sherwell, 'Hunt for bin Laden intensifies after top aide is captured', *Daily Telegraph*, 7 March 2004.
7. Andrew Buncombe and Jan McGirk, 'Pakistan in major battle to capture bin Laden's deputy', *Independent*, 19 March 2004.
8. 'Trapped al-Qaeda leader is Uzbek mullah', *Daily Telegraph*, 21 March 2004.
9. Pervez Musharraf, *In the Line of Fire*, p. 237.
10. Author & Usman Ansari unpublished report on the role of Pakistan's Army Aviation in the counter-insurgency war.
11. Richard Beeston and Zahid Hussain, 'Wanted: dyed and alive. Bin laden reappears – and he's had a make over', *The Times*, 8 September 2007.
12. Philip Sherwell, 'Tehran providing refuge for al-Qaeda terrorists', *Sunday Telegraph*, 6 November 2005.
13. Omar bin Laden hoped to come to the UK with his British wife but was refused entry. 'Bin Laden son flies to Spain for asylum', 4 November 2008, *Evening Standard* and 'Egypt says No to bin Laden's son', *Western Morning News*, 10 November 2008.
14. Musharraf, *In the Line of Fire*, p. 272.
15. Ibid., p. 273.
16. The Taliban took control of the Swat, Lower Dir, Shangla and Buner and had a presence in many of the NWFP's other districts. In addition the Taliban controlled North and South Waziristan. During the Raj British colonial forces fought numerous engagements in the North West Frontier, including the Swat Valley in 1897 that resulted in at least 2,000 dead tribesmen.

Chapter 20 – Syria: on the Brink

1. 'Hamas returns to Syrian base', *Sunday Times*, 21 September 2003.
2. 'Probe Links Syria, Terror Network', *Los Angeles Times*, 16 April 2004 and 'A Road to Ansar began in Italy: Wiretaps are said to show how al-Qaeda sought to create in northern Iraq a substitute for training camps in Afghanistan', *Los Angeles Times*, 28 April 2003.
3. Richard Beeston and James Hider, 'Terrorists cross Syrian border to join Iraqi rebels', *The Times*, 3 July 2004.
4. Anton La Guardia, 'al-Qaeda gunmen attack Syrian capital', *Daily Telegraph*, 28 April 2004.
5. 'Terror suspect', *The Times*, 19 March 2005 and 'Trio accused of terror attacks', *The Times*, 15 February 2005.
6. Author, 'US Airborne Spying', *Air Forces Monthly*, January 2004 and 'Goodbye U-2?', *AIR International*, September 2004.
7. Author, 'Malevolent in the Med?', *Warships International Fleet Review*, August 2003.
8. Nicholas Blanford, 'Former premier assassinated as the bombers return to Beirut', *The Times*, 15 February 2005.
9. Nicholas Blanford, 'Hezbollah fights back in war of words over Syrian influence', *The Times*, 9 March 2005.
10. Ibid.
11. Gerry J. Gilmore, 'Rice calls Syria "Big Problem" at Senate Hearing', US Defense Press Service, 16 February 2005.
12. Nicholas Blanford, 'Lebanese PM resigns over Syria's role', *The Times*, 21 October 2004.

13. Nicholas Blanford, 'Lebanese say spies, not troops are the problem', *The Times*, 8 March 2005.
14. Richard Beeston, 'Syrian regime fights for survival', *The Times*, 5 March 2005.
15. Designed primarily as a coastal defence force, the Syrian Navy numbers approximately 4,000 regular and 2,500 reserve officers and men. It only has a handful of frigates and three submarines, all of which according to Israeli sources are non-operational. The rest of the force consists of a plethora of patrol boats. Like the Iraqi Navy it could never resist a US Carrier Battle Group.
16. The Syrian Navy could deploy chemical weapons using its SS-N-3 cruise missiles, coastal defence SSC-1b Sepal and SS-C-3 shore-to-sea missiles. Indeed, the Syrians are believed to have converted some naval cruise missiles to use chemical warheads.
17. Author, 'Can the Libyan Leopard really change his spots?', *Warships International Fleet Review*, August 2004.
18. Ibid.

Chapter 21 – Iraq: the New Breeding Ground

1. Kevin Phillips, *American Dynasty*, p. 329.
2. Robin Moore, *Hunting Down Saddam*, p. 37.
3. Ibid.
4. Marie Colvin, 'Iraqi hit squads run by al-Qaeda terror leader', *Sunday Times*, 10 August 2003.
5. Jim Garamone, 'al-Qaeda Leader's Letter Questions Zarqawi Tactics', US Defense Press Service, 18 October 2005.
6. Ibid.
7. Thomas Harding, 'Iraqi insurgents learn deadly new tricks', *Daily Telegraph*, 4 August 2005.
8. Michael R. Gordon and Dexter Filkins, 'Hezbollah Said to Help Shiite Army in Iraq', *New York Times*, 28 November 2008.
9. Defence Intelligence Staff, *Armed Groups in Iraq*, dated 21 November, 2003, cited Edward T. Pound, 'The Iran Connection', USNews.com, 22 November 2004, www.papillonsartpalace.com/irCan.htm.
10. Abdurahman Alamoudi, a leading American Muslim activist was stopped at Heathrow airport in August 2003 en route to Syria carrying £240,000, which had come from the Libyan government. He was a supporter of Hamas and president of the American Muslim Foundation. The FBI claimed he was bankrolling Hamas-linked groups. See David Leppard, 'Libya funding terror in Iraq', *Sunday Times*, 2 November 2003.
11. President Bush, *State of the Union Message*, 20 January 2004, reported *New York Times*, 21 January 2004.
12. Megan Stack, 'US General sees al-Qaeda evidence in Iraq', *Los Angeles Times*, 30 January 2004.
13. Thom Shanker, 'US Commander surveys challenges in Iraq region', *New York Times*, 30 January 2004.
14. Raymond Bonner and Joel Brinkley, 'Latest attacks underscore differing intelligence estimates of strength of foreign guerrillas', *New York Times*, 28 October 2003.
15. See Kenneth Katzman, 'al-Qaeda in Iraq: An Assessment and Outside Links', CRS, 15 August 2008.

16. Al-Zarqawi was killed in an air strike by two American F-16 fighters using 5001b bombs.

17. Ned Parker, 'al-Zarqawi died after air strike as American medics tried to save him', *The Times*, 10 June 2006.

18. Sara Wood, 'al-Qaeda Leader Captured in June, US Spokesman Says', US Defense Press Service, 6 September 2006.

19. Martin Fletcher, 'al-Qaeda leaders admit: "We are in Crisis. There is panic and fear" ', The Times Online, 11 February 2008.

20. 'Iraqi terrorists head to US via Mexico?', WorldNetDaily.com, 22 March 2003.

21. Ibid.

22. 'Iraq terrorists caught along Mexican border', WorldNetDaily.com, 23 August 2007.

23. Ibid.

Chapter 22 – Holy Terror: the Rage of Islam

1. Robert Winnett, 'Britain "a soft touch for terrorists" ', Telegraph.co.uk, 17 February 2008.

2. Kim Sengupta, 'Terrorist threat "exploited to curb civil liberties" ', *The Independent*, 17 February 2009.

3. Clive Stafford Smith, *Bad Men: Guantanamo Bay and the Secret Prisons*, p. 164; Smith cites US Army linguist Eric Saar who was involved in the interrogations.

4. Ibid.

5. Kim Ghattas, 'Beginning of end for Guantanamo?', BBC News, Washington, 30 November 2008.

6. Frank Gardner, 'Guantanamo inmate joins Taliban', BBC News, 3 February 2009.

7. 'Five accused boast of 9/11 role', BBC News, 10 March 2009.

8. David Sharrock, 'Algeria, staging post for the world of terror', *The Times*, 3 April 2004.

9. Khalifa was killed in 2007 when twenty gunmen stormed his guesthouse in Madagascar. Bob Shepherd, *The Circuit*, p. 210.

10. *The National Security Strategy of the United Kingdom: Security in an interdependent world*, March 2008, p. 25.

11. Interview with author.

12. Washington's often competing intelligence organisations have taken considerable steps to dovetail their efforts. The IC works with the National Security Council (NSC) in the Executive Branch and with two Congressional Committees in the Legislative Branch (the House Permanent Select Committee on Intelligence (HPSCI) and the Senate Select Committee on Intelligence (SSCI)). Other governmental organisations also interact with the IC.

13. *9/11 Commission Report*, pp. 340, 351.

14. John Laffin, *Holy War*, p. 12.

Bibliography

Periodicals
Daily Telegraph
Economist
Financial Times
Guardian
Independent
International Chamber of Commerce Commercial Crime Services Weekly Piracy Report
Jamestown Foundation Terrorism Monitor
Jane's Defence Weekly
Los Angeles Times
Sunday Times
The Times
Washington Post
Washington Times
USA Today

Occasional Papers

Chatham House

Azzam, M., 'Al-Qaeda Five Years On: The Threat and the Challenges', *Briefing Paper*, MEP BP 06/02, September 2006.

Azzam, M., 'Al-Qaeda: the Misunderstood Wahhabi Connection and the Ideology of Violence', *Briefing Paper*, No. 1, February 2003.

Garraway, C., 'The War on Terror: Do the Rules Need Changing?' *Briefing Paper*, IL 06/02, September 2006.

Hill, G., 'Yemen: Fear of Failure', *Briefing Paper*, MEP BP 08/03, November 2008.

Jones, B.J. & Shaikh, F., 'Pakistan's Foreign Policy Under Musharraf: Between a Rock and a Hard Place', *Briefing Paper*, ASP BP 06/01, March 2006.

Middleton, Roger, 'Piracy in Somalia Threatening Global Trade, Feeding Locals Wars', *Briefing Paper*, AFP BO 08/02, October 2008.

Noetzel, T. & Scheipers, S., 'Coalition Warfare in Afghanistan: Burden-sharing or Disunity?' *Briefing Paper*, ASP/ISP BP 07/01, October 2007.

Pickerill, J., 'Islam, Politics and Security in the UK', *Briefing Paper*, ISP/NSC 07/01, October 2007.

Shehadi, N., 'Palestinian Refugees: The Regional Perspective', *Briefing Paper*, MENAP/PR BP 2009/02, April 2009.

Stansfield, G., 'Accepting Realities in Iraq', *Briefing Paper*, MEP BP 07/02, May 2007.

Congressional Research Service

Best, R.A., 'Intelligence Issues for Congress', *CRS Briefing for Congress*, 4 February 2002.

Blanchard, C.M. & Prados, A.B., 'Saudi Arabia: Terrorist Financing Issues', *CRS Briefing for Congress*, 14 September 2007.

Katzman, K., 'Al-Qaeda in Iraq: Assessment and Outside Links', *CRS Report for Congress*, 15 August 2008.

Katzman, K., 'Iraq: Post-Saddam Governance and Security', *CRS Report for Congress*, 10 January 2008.

Katzman, K., 'Al-Qaeda: Profile and Threat Assessment', *CRS Report for Congress*, 17 August 2005.

Katzman, K., 'Al-Qaeda: Profile and Threat Assessment', *CRS Report for Congress*, 10 February 2005.

Katzman, K., 'Iraq and al-Qaeda: Allies or Not?' *CRS Report for Congress*, 5 February 2004.

Katzman, K., 'Terrorism: Near Eastern Groups and State Sponsors 2001', *CRS Report for Congress*, 10 September 2001.

Lee, R., 'Terrorism, the Future, and US Foreign Policy', *CRS Issue Brief for Congress*, 31 January 2002.

Nichol. J., 'Uzbekistan's Closure of the Airbase at Karshi-Khanabad: Context and Implications', *CRS Report for Congress*, 7 October 2005.

Nichol. J., 'Central Asia's New States: Political Developments and Implications for US Interests', *CRS Issue Brief for Congress*, 5 March 2003.

Perl, R.F., 'International Terrorism: Threat, Policy, and Response', *CRS Briefing for Congress*, 3 January 2007.

Perl, R.F., 'Taliban and the Drug Trade', *CRS Report for Congress*, 5 October 2001.

Perl, R.F., 'National Commission on Terrorism Report: Background and Issues for Congress', *CRS Report for Congress*, 6 February 2001.

Prados, A.B., 'Saudi Arabia: Current Issues and US Relations', *CRS Issue Brief for Congress*, 8 May 2006.

Serafino, N.M., 'Peacekeeping and Related Stability Operations: Issues of US Military Involvement', *CRS Report for Congress*, 24 January 2007.

Sharp, J.M., et al, 'Lebanon: The Israel-Hamas-Hezbollah Conflict', *CRS Briefing for Congress*, 15 September 2006.

Woehrel, S., 'Bosnian Muslim-Croat Federation: Key to Peace in Bosnia?' *CRS Report for Congress*, 26 June 1998.

Council on Foreign Relations

Bajoria, J., 'Profile: Lashkar-e-Taiba (Army of the Pure)', *Backgrounder*, 2 December 2008.

Bajoria, J., 'Al-Qaeda', *Backgrounder*, 18 April 2008.

Bhattacharji, P., 'State Sponsors: Sudan', *Backgrounder*, 2 April 2008.

Fletcher, H., 'Egyptian Islamic Jihad', *Backgrounder*, 30 May 2008.

Fletcher, H., 'Jamaat al-Islamiyya', *Backgrounder*, 30 May 2008.

Fletcher, H., 'Palestinian Islamic Jihad', *Backgrounder*, 10 April 2008.

Hanson, S., 'Al-Shabaab', *Backgrounder*, 27 February 2009.

Kaplan, E., 'Somalia's High Stakes Power Struggle', *Backgrounder*, 7 August 2006.

Kaplan, E., 'Somalia's Transitional Government', *Backgrounder*, 12 May 2008.

Zissis, C., 'Terror Groups in India', *Backgrounder*, 27 November 2008.

'Hamas', *Backgrounder*, 7 January 2009.
'A Morphing al-Qaeda', *Daily Analysis*, 20 August 2008.
'Hezbollah Soldiers On', *Daily Analysis*, 13 August 2008.

House of Commons Library

Beale, E., Lunn, J., Taylor, C. & Youngs T., 'Pakistan's Political and Security Challenges', *Research Paper 07/68*, 13 September 2007.
Berman, G., 'The Cost of Military Operations in Iraq and Afghanistan', *Standard Note: SN/SG/3139*, 10 October 2007.
Broadbridge, 'Abu Hamza al-Masri', *Standard Note: SN/HA/2895*, 23 July 2008.
Jones, S., 'The UK Government's Decision to Proscribe the Military Wing of Hezbollah', *Standard Note: SN/IA/4791*, 10 July 2008.
Lunn, J., 'Interlocking Crises in the Horn of Africa', *Research Paper 08/86*, 25 November 2008.
Lunn, J., 'Kashmir: an Update', *Standard Note: SN/IA/4829*, 10 September 2008.
Smith, B., 'Morocco', *Standard Note: SN/IA/4402*, 24 July 2007.
Strickland, P., 'Intelligence Services and Security Agencies', *Standard Note: SN/HA/1132*, 4 February 2004.
Taylor, C., 'Coalition Forces in Iraq: Recent Developments', *Standard Note: SN/IA/4099*, 27 June 2007.
Taylor, C., 'International Security Assistance Force (ISAF) in Afghanistan: Recent Developments', *Standard Note: SN/IA/4143*, 17 October 2007.
Winstone, R. & Smith, B., 'Hizb ut-Tahrir and Proscribed Organisations', *Standard Note: SN/IA/3922*, 11 July 2007.
Youngs, T., 'International Terrorism and the Evolution of al-Qaeda', *Standard Note: SN/IA/3716*, 21 July 2005.
Youngs, T., 'Nagorno-Karabakh', *Standard Note: SN/IA/1743*, 20 January 2002.
Youngs, T., Bowers, P. & Oakes M., 'The Campaign Against International Terrorism: Prospects After the Fall of the Taliban', *Research Paper 01/112*, 11 December 2001.
Youngs, T., 'The Conflict in Chechnya', *Research Paper 00/14*, 7 February 2000.
House of Commons Defence Committee, *Defence White Paper 2003*, Fifth Report of Session 2003–04, Volume II: Oral and Written Evidence, 23 June 2004.
House of Commons Defence Committee, *Defence White Paper 2003*, Fifth Report of Session 2003–04, Volume I, 23 June 2004.
House of Commons Foreign Affairs Committee, *Foreign Policy Aspects of the War Against Terrorism*, Fourth Report of Session 2005–06, 21 June 2006.
House of Commons Foreign Affairs Committee, *Foreign Policy Aspects of the War Against Terrorism*, Second report from the Session 2003–2004, March 2004.
House of Commons Foreign Affairs Committee, *Foreign Policy Aspects of the War Against Terrorism*, Tenth Report of Session 2002–2003, 2003.
House of Commons Intelligence and Security Committee, Annual Report 2007–2008.
Ministry of Defence, *Operations in Iraq: Lessons for the Future*, December 2003.
Ministry of Defence, *Delivering Security in a Changing World Supporting Essays*, December 2003.
Ministry of Defence, *Kosovo: Lessons from the Crisis*, 2000.
National Audit Office, *Operation Telic – United Kingdom Military Operations in Iraq*, 11 December 2003.
UK Terrorism Act 2000/Prevention and Suppression of Terrorism Proscribed Organisations.

Other Published Sources

Akbar, M.J., *The Shade of Swords: Jihad and the Conflict Between Islam and Christianity* (London 2002).

Anonymous, *Hunting al-Qaeda* (St Paul, USA 2005).

Balakian, P., *The Burning Tigris: The Armenian Genocide* (London 2004).

Baxter, J. & Downing, M. (eds), *The Day That Shook the World: Understanding September 11th* (London 2001).

Ben-Ami, S., *Scars of War, Wounds of Peace: the Israeli-Arab Tragedy* (London 2005).

Benjamin, D. & Simon, S., *The Next Attack: the Globalisation of Jihad* (London 2005).

Bergen, P.L., *Holy War, Inc: Inside the Secret World of Osama bin Laden* (London 2002).

Bergen, P.L., *The Osama bin Laden I Know: an Oral History of al-Qaeda's Leader* (New York 2006).

Berntsen, G. & Pezzullo, R., *Jawbreaker: the Attack on bin Laden and al-Qaeda: a Personal Account by the CIA's Key Field Commander* (New York 2005).

Bodansky, Y., *Bin Laden: the Man Who Declared War on America* (New York 2001).

Bowen, J., *War Stories* (London 2006).

Brentjes, B. & Brentjes H., *Taliban: a Shadow Over Afghanistan* (Varanasi, India 2000).

Brogan, P., *World Conflicts: Why and Where They Are Happening* (London 1989).

Bryant, M. (ed.), *The Afghan Tragedy* (London 1987).

Buell, B., *Words to Deeds: a New International Agenda for Peace and Security – Oxfam's Ten-point Plan* (Oxfam International May 2002).

Burke, J., *On the Road to Kandahar: Travels Through Conflict in the Islamic World* (London 2007).

Burke, J., *Al-Qaeda: the True Story of Radical Islam* (London 2004).

Cabinet Office, *The National Security Strategy of the United Kingdom, Security in an interdependent world* (London, March 2008).

Campbell, A. & Stott, R. (eds) *The Blair Years: Extracts from the Alastair Campbell Diaries* (London 2007).

Chomsky, N., *Hegemony or Survival: America's Quest for Global Dominance* (London 2004).

Cincotta, H. & Price, A., *Afghanistan, the Struggle to Regain Freedom* (USA 1981).

Clark, V., *Allies for Armageddon: The Rise of Christian Zionism* (London 2007).

Clark, W., *Waging Modern War: Bosnia, Kosovo, and the Future of Combat* (Oxford 2001).

Clarke, R., *Against All Enemies: Inside America's War on Terror* (London 2004).

Clutterbuck, R., *Terrorism in an Unstable World* (London 1994).

Coll, S., *Ghost Wars: the Secret History of the CIA, Afghanistan and Bin Laden, From the Soviet Invasion to September 10, 2001* (London 2005).

Corbin, J., *Al-Qaeda: In Search of the Terror Network that Threatens the World* (London 2002).

Crille, G., *Charlie Wilson's War* (London 2007).

Duncan, A. & Opatowski, M., *Trouble Spots: the World Atlas of Strategic Information* (Stroud 2000).

Eprile, C., *War and Peace in the Sudan 1955–1972* (Newton Abbot 1974).

FATF, *Financial Action Task Force on Money laundering, Annual Report 2000–2001* (Paris 2001).

Feffer, J. (ed.), *Power Trip: US Unilateralism and Global Strategy After September 11* (New York 2003).

Gall, S., *Behind Russian Lines: an Afghan Journal* (London 1983).

Gerges, F.F., *The Far Enemy: Why Jihad Went Global* (New York 2005).

Gerth, J. & Natta, D.V., *Hillary Clinton Her Way: the Biography* (London 2007).

Gorbachev, M., *Perestroika* (London 1988).

Greenberg, K.J. (ed.), *Al-Qaeda Now: Understanding Today's Terrorists* (New York 2005).

Gurdon, C., *Sudan at the Crossroads* (Wisbech 1984).

Hamilton, N., *Bill Clinton: Mastering the Presidency* (London 2007).

Harclerode, P., *Fighting Dirty: the Inside Story of Covert Operations from Ho Chi Minh to Osama bin Laden* (London 2001).

Harclerode, P., *Secret Soldiers: Special Forces in the War Against Terrorism* (London 2001).

Harik, J.P., *Hezbollah: the Changing Face of Terrorism* (London 2005).

Heffelfinger, C. (ed.), *Unmasking Terror: a Global Review of Terrorist Activities* (Washington D.C. 2005).

Hoefer, M., Rytina, N. & Baker, B.C., 'Estimates of the Unauthorised Immigrant Population Residing in the United States: January 2008,' *Population Estimates*, US Department of Homeland Security/Office of Immigration Statistics Policy Directorate, February 2009.

Isby, D., *War in a Distant Country, Afghanistan: Invasion and Resistance* (London 1989).

Isby, D., *Russia's War in Afghanistan* (London 1986).

Jackson, General Sir M., *Soldier: the Autobiography* (London 2007).

Jennings, C., *Midnight in Some Burning Town: British Special Forces Operations from Belgrade to Baghdad* (London 2004).

Kampfner, J., *Blair's Wars* (London 2004).

Katz, S. & Russell, L., *Armies in Lebanon 1982–84* (London 1985).

Kean, T.H. (Chair) & Hamilton, L.H. (Vice Chair), *The 9/11 Commission Report* (London 2005).

Khan, A.U., *The Terrorist Threat and the Policy Response in Pakistan*, SIPRI Policy Paper No. 11 (September 2005).

King, G., *The Most Dangerous Man in the World: Dawood Ibrahim* (New York 2004).

Laffin, J., *The World in Conflict War Annual 7* (London 1996).

Laffin, J., *War Annual 1* (London 1986).

Laffin, J., *The War of Desperation: Lebanon 1982–85* (London 1985).

Laffin, J., *Holy War: Islam Fights* (London 1988).

Landau, E., *Osama bin Laden: a War Against the West* (Brookfield, Connecticut 2002).

Lee, R., *Terrorism, the Future, and US Foreign Policy* (Washington 2002).

Mackey, C. & Miller, G., *The Interrogator's War: Inside the Secret War Against al-Qaeda* (London 2005).

Macy, E., *Apache* (London 2008).

Martinez, L., *The Algerian Civil War 1990–1998* (London 2000).

Medvedev, Z., *Gorbachev* (Oxford 1986).

Melvin, N.J., *Conflict in Southern Thailand: Islamism, Violence and the State in the Patani Insurgency*, SIPRI Policy Paper No. 20 (September 2007).

Meyer, C., *DC Confidential: the Controversial Memoirs of Britain's Ambassador to the US at the Time of 9/11 and the Iraq War* (London 2005).

Micheletti, E. & Debay, Y., *War in the Balkans* (Poole).

Monger R. & Macreadie, B., 'Nonimmigrant Admissions to the United States: 2008', *Annual Flow Report*, US Department of Homeland Security/Office of Immigration Statistics Policy Directorate, April 2009.

Moore, R., *Task Force Dagger: the Hunt for bin Laden* (London 2003).

Moore, R., *Hunting Down Saddam* (New York 2004).

Munro, A., *Arab Storm: Politics and Diplomacy Behind the Gulf War* (London 2006).

Murray, C., *Murder in Samarkand* (Edinburgh 2006).

Musharraf, P., *In the Line of Fire* (London 2006).

Naughtie, J., *The Accidental American: Tony Blair and the Presidency* ((London 2004).

Nichol, M., *Ultimate Risk: SAS Contact al-Qaeda* (London 2003).

Omand, D., *The National Security Strategy: Implications for the UK Intelligence Community* (Institute for Public Policy Research, February 2009).

Orizio, R., *Talk of the Devil: Encounters with Seven Dictators* (London 2004).

Pettiford, L. & Harding, D., *Terrorism: the New World Order* (London 2003).

Phillips, K., *American Dynasty* (London 2004).

Pimlott, J. (ed.), *Guerrilla Warfare* (London 1985).

Polman, L., *We Did Nothing: Why the Truth Doesn't Always Come Out When the UN Goes In* (London 2004).

Al-Qahtaani, S., *The Levels of Jihad* (London 1997).

Randall, J., *Osama: the Making of a Terrorist* (London 2005).

Rashid, A., *Taliban: the Story of the Afghan Warlords* (London 2001).

Rashid, A., *Jihad: the Rise of Militant Islam in Central Asia* (London 2003).

Rees, S., *Dining with Terrorists: Meetings with the World's Most Wanted Militants* (London 2005).

Reeve, S., *The New Jackals: Ramzi Yousef, Osama bin Laden and the Future of Terrorism* (London 1999).

Rentoul, J., *Tony Blair* (London 1995).

Richardson, N., *No Escape Zone* (London 2000).

Ripley, T., *Conflict in the Balkans 1991–2000* (Oxford 2001).

Risen, J., *State of War: the Secret History of the CIA and the Bush Administration* (London 2006).

Robinson, A., *Bin Laden: Behind the Mask of the Terrorist* (Edinburgh 2001).

Rogers, P., *Iraq and the War on Terror: Twelve Months of Insurgency, 2004/2005* (London 2006).

Rose, M., *Fighting for Peace: Bosnia 1994* (London 1998).

Saikal, A. & Maley, M. (eds), *The Soviet Withdrawal from Afghanistan* (Cambridge 1989).

Schiff, Z. & Ya'ari, E., *Israel's Lebanon War* (London 1986).

Schwartz, S., *The Two Faces of Islam: The House of Sa'ud from Tradition to Terror* (New York 2002).

Shepherd, B., *The Circuit* (London 2009).

Sifaoui, M., *Inside al-Qaeda* (London 2003).

Smith, C.S., *Bad Men: Guantanamo Bay and the Secret Prisons* (London 2007).

Smith, S., *Allah's Mountains: the Battle for Chechnya* (London 2006).

Smucker, P., *Al-Qaeda's Great Escape* (Washington D.C. 2004).

The 9/11 Commission Report, Final Report of the National Commission on Terrorist Attacks upon the United States (New York).

Thompson, L., *The Rescuers: the World's Top Anti-Terrorist Units* (Newton Abbot 1986).

Unger, C., *House of Bush, House of Saud: the Secret Relationship Between the World's Two Most Powerful Dynasties* (London 2005).

Urban, M., *War in Afghanistan* (London 1988).

Waldman, M., *Falling Short: Aid Effectiveness in Afghanistan* (Oxfam International, March 2008).

Williams, P.L., *Al-Qaeda: Brotherhood of Terror* (USA 2002).

Windrow, M., *The Algerian War 1954–62* (London 1997).

Woodbridge, J., *Sizing the Unauthorised (illegal) Migrant Population in the United Kingdom in 2001*, Home Office Online Report 29/09.

Woodward, B., *Bush at War* (London 2003).

Wright, R., *Sacred Rage: The Wrath of Militant Islam* (London 1986).

Journals

Barber, 'Ending the Thirty-Year War', theworldtoday.org, April 2009.

Brookes, A., 'British Air Power in Iraq', *Air Forces Monthly*, 20 October 2003.

Brookes, A., 'Lessons from Afghanistan', *Air Forces Monthly*, 26 April 2002.

'Special Report Pakistan: the Man in the Middle' & 'Spain: Terror before an election', *Economist*, 13 March 2004.

'In the Name of God: a Survey of Islam and the West' & 'Morocco's Islamists: Fighting Not to Win', *Economist*, 13 September 2003.

'Kosovo and Macedonia: Fag-ends or Freedom Fighters?' *Economist*, 13 September 2003.

'Saudi Arabia Wakes Up to the Reality of al-Qaeda', *Economist*, 17 May 2003.

'Terrorist Finance: the Needle in the Haystack', *Economist*, 14 December 2002.

Kalic, S.N., 'Combating a Modern Hydra: al-Qaeda and the Global War on Terrorism', *Global War on Terrorism*, Occasional Paper 8, Combat Studies Institute Press, Fort Leavenworth, Kansas, 2005.

McGirk, T., 'Tracking the Ghost of bin Laden in the Land of the Pashtun', *National Geographic*, December 2004.

Milivojeviæ, M., 'Algeria's National Popular Army', *Armed Forces*, April 1989.

Quinn-Judge, P. & Zarakhovich, Y., 'Terror in the Dark', *Time*, 16 February 2004.

Raman, B., 'First Maritime Terrorism Attack of 2006', *International Terrorism*, Monitor Paper No. 13, 8 January 2006.

Smith, J., 'Biological Warfare Developments', *Jane's Intelligence Review*, November 1991.

Smith, J., 'Chemical Weapons Proliferation', *Jane's Intelligence Review*, May 1991.

Sperling, J. & Webber, M., 'NATO: from Kosovo to Kabul', *International Affairs*, 85:3 (2009).

Stuart, C., 'Why Kabul is Holding On', *Survival Weaponry and Techniques*, January 1991.

Stuart, C., 'USSR – the Ailing Bear', *Survival Weaponry and Techniques*, December 1990.

Tucker, A.R., 'Armed Forces of the Afghan Conflict', *Jane's Intelligence Review*, March 1990.

Tucker, A.R., 'Operation Magistral', *Jane's Intelligence Review*, October 1989.

Tucker, A.R., 'Counter-Insurgency in the Philippines', *Armed Forces*, August 1989.

Tucker, A.R., 'The Strategic Implications of the Iran-Iraq War', *Middle East Strategic Studies Quarterly*, Spring/Summer 1989.

Tucker, A.R., 'Problems Remain in the Philippines', *Jane's Defence Weekly*, 22 July 1989.

Tucker, A.R., 'The Soviet War Over Afghanistan', *Jane's Intelligence Review*, June 1989.

Tucker, A.R., 'The Mujahideen Guerrilla War', *Survival Weaponry and Techniques*, February 1989.

Tucker, A.R., 'Saudi Arabia's Military Build up', *Armed Forces*, February 1989.

Tucker, A.R., 'Conflict in the Horn of Africa,' *Jane's Defence Weekly*, 17 December 1988.

Tucker, A.R., 'Chemical Warfare ... a Reality', *Survival Weaponry and Techniques*, March 1988.

Tucker-Jones, A., 'The Great Escape', *intersec*, Journal of International Security, October 2009.

Tucker-Jones, A., 'Moscow's Last Stand in Afghanistan', *Military Illustrated*, February 2010.

Tucker-Jones, A., 'Allah and the Kalashnikov', *intersec*, Journal of International Security, January 2010.

Tucker-Jones, A., 'Al-Shabaab: Somalia's Taliban', *intersec*, Journal of International Security, November/December 2009.

Tucker-Jones, A., 'Hunting Terrorists at Tora Bora', *Military Illustrated*, October 2009.

Tucker-Jones, A., 'UK Commandos Return to Afghanistan' & 'Maritime Terrorism: the Gathering Storm?' *Warships International Fleet Review*, April 2006.

Tucker-Jones, A., 'Tour of Duty', *Classic Military Vehicle*, March 2006.

Tucker-Jones, A., 'Navies to Become Enforcers' & 'Full Dress Rehearsal', *Warships International Fleet Review*, March 2006.

Tucker-Jones, A., 'Fleets Tackle Flood Tide in Med', *Warships International Fleet Review*, February 2006.

Tucker-Jones, A., 'Navies Urged to Combat Pirates', *Warships International Fleet Review*, January 2006.

Tucker-Jones, A., 'Silent Killers', *Air Forces Monthly*, December 2005.

Tucker-Jones, A., 'Africa's War on Terror Off the Radar Screen?' & 'Bitter Afghan Harvest for US Navy SEALs', *Warships International Fleet Review*, October 2005.

Tucker-Jones, A., 'Syria on the Brink?' *Warships International Fleet Review*, May 2005.

Tucker-Jones, A., 'Strike from the Sky', *Air Forces Monthly*, March 2005.

Tucker-Jones, A., 'Future Eyes for the Navy', *Aviation News*, February 2005.

Tucker-Jones, A., 'Taliban Tanks', *Classic Military Vehicle*, February 2005.

Tucker-Jones, A., 'Algeria: Crucible of Terror?', *Warships International Fleet Review*, January 2005.

Tucker-Jones, A., 'Terror in the Malacca', *Warships International Fleet Review*, October 2004.

Tucker-Jones, A., 'Goodbye U-2?' *AIR International*, September 2004.

Tucker-Jones, A., 'Flags of Inconvenience Pose Terror Threat on High Seas' & 'A Bulwark Against Terrorism – Cyprus Squadron to Stay', *Warships International Fleet Review*, September 2004.

Tucker-Jones, A., 'Suez Attack Could be Catastrophic', *Warships International Fleet Review*, August 2004.

Tucker-Jones, A., 'Waiting for Watchkeeper', *Air Forces Monthly*, June 2004.

Tucker-Jones, A., 'US Navy SEALs & UK SBS Spearhead Coalition Hunt for bin Laden' & 'Albania's Gift to Italy', *Warships International Fleet Review*, June 2004.

Tucker-Jones, A., 'NATO's War on Terror', *Warships International Fleet Review*, May 2004.

Tucker-Jones, A., 'Can the Libyan Leopard Really Change His Spots?' & 'Coalition aims to put al-Qaeda through Cold Turkey', *Warships International Fleet Review*, March 2004.

Tucker-Jones, A., 'Yemen – A Cursed Corner' & 'Balkan Ambassadors', *Warships International Fleet Review*, February 2004.

Tucker-Jones, A., 'US Airborne Spying', *Air Forces Monthly*, January 2004.

Tucker-Jones, A., 'Gibraltar Between the Rock and a Hard Place', 'Drugs & Terror: The Nexus of Evil' & 'Good Friend … Bad Foe – Saudi Navy', *Warships International Fleet Review*, December 2003.

Tucker-Jones, A., 'UK Air Intelligence Capabilities', *Air Forces Monthly*, November 2003.

Tucker-Jones, A., 'West Would be Foolish to Turn its Back on Saudi Arabia' & 'Terror Ships of the Lebanon', *Warships International Fleet Review*, November 2003.

Tucker-Jones, A., 'Searching for a NATO Spy Plane', *Air Forces Monthly*, October 2003.

Tucker-Jones, A., 'US Navy SEALs in Hunt for Saddam', *Warships International Fleet Review*, October 2003.

Tucker-Jones, A., 'Global Choke Points' & 'The WMD Threat on the High Seas', *Warships International Fleet Review*, September 2003.

Tucker-Jones, A., 'Sixteen Days to Baghdad', *Classic Military Vehicle*, July 2003.

Websites

www.Aljazeera.Net
www.Allafrica.com
www.cpn.gov.uk
www.defenselink.mil/news
www.fbi.gov
www.the-hutton-inquiry.org.uk
www.icc-ccs.org
www.intelligence.gov.uk/agencies
www.irinnews.org
www.jamestown.org
www.janes.com
www.mi5.gov.uk
www.mi6.gov.uk
www.muslimuzbekistan.com
www.News.bbc.co.uk
www.pinr.com
www.rferl.org
www.un.org/news

Index

Aba Island massacre, 109
Abdirahman, Sheikh Mohamed
  Mukhtar, 52
Abdullah, Abdullah Ahmed, 165
Abdullah, Mohammed Ahmed Ibn al-
  Sayid (The Mahdi), 109
Abu Ghraid prison, 155, 187
Aden Abyan Islamic Army, 56
Afghan Mujahideen, 14–24, 35–9, 66–7,
  121, 186
Afghan National Army, 139–40
Afghanistan, viii, 14–24, 35, 141–7, 155,
  189
African Union Counter Terrorism
  Convention, 108
Ahmad, President Abdullah Yusuf, 50
Ahmad, Tariq Anwar al-Sayyid, 5, 11
Aideed, General Mohammed Farah, 48
Akram, Mohamed, 144
Albania, 57, 67–8, 92–9
Albanian Democratic Union for
  Integration (see also KLA), 98
Albanian National Army (AKSh), 97–8
Algeria, viii, 14, 20, 73–80, 108, 155,
  211
Algerian Hezbollah, 75
Alkhanov, Alu, 89
Allen, Charlie, 8
Amal militia, 105–06
Ansar al-Islam, 148, 150, 180
Arab Ansar in Chechnya, 86
Arafat, Yasser, 105, 116, 174, 186, 193,
  195
Armenia, 28–9, 81
Assad, President, 173
Atef, Mohammed, 5, 11, 48
Atta, Mohammed, 54, 204
Aweys, President Hassan Dahir, 50, 170
Azerbaijan, 26, 29, 81, 86
Azzam, Abdullah, 14, 113

Baku, 29
Bali bombings, 158–9
Baluchistan, 166–8
Bangladesh, 121
al-Banna, Hassan, 112
Barre, General Mohammed, 46
Basayev, Shamil, 83
al-Bashir, General Omar, 110
Beirut, 22, 101, 104, 175
Bekaa Valley, ix, 101–02, 104, 175, 177
Bensakhria, Mohammad, 73
Berger, Sandy, 6, 8, 55, 126–7
Bernsten, Gary, 126, 143
Beslan school massacre, 90
Bihac, 62, 65
Bin Abdullah, Mahommed (Mahdi or
  Mad Mullah), 46
Bin Laden, Osama, vii, ix, 31, 33, 44,
  47, 59, 71, 73, 85, 108, 112, 126–7,
  132, 151–2, 155, 162, 168, 182,
  186–7, 189–93, 204
  attempts to kill him, 2–13, 141, 165
  declaration of Jihad, vi, 3, 41, 47–8
  in Afghanistan, 19, 54, 110, 143, 146
  in Albania, 92
  in Bosnia, 66
  in Pakistan, 19, 163
  in Saudi Arabia, 119
  in Sudan, 41, 47, 110, 149
  in Yemen, 59
Binalshibh, Ramzi, 54
Black Hawk Down incident, 48–9, 53
Black Ops, 7, 65, 164, 174
Blair, Tony, 2, 148–9
Boko Haram, 157
Bosanski Samac massacre, 63
Bosnia, viii, 8, 14, 20, 49, 62–72, 87, 92,
  121, 140, 155
Bosnian Army, 64–5, 67, 69–70
Bosnian Croats, 63, 70–1

Bosnian Mujahideen, 67, 79
Bosnian Muslims (Bosniaks), 62, 65, 68, 70–1
Bosnian Serbs, 62–3, 69–70
Bouteflika, President Abdelaziz, 74, 77, 79
Bush, President George H., 47
Bush, President George W., 2, 12, 59, 127, 148, 182

Ceku, Agim, 96
Cengic, Deputy Defence Minister Hasan, 71
Central Intelligence Agency (CIA), vii, viii, 5, 6, 15, 26, 35, 48, 59, 64, 98, 164–5, 184, 203
   CIA Predator Ops, 8–12
   CIA training jihadists, 20, 23
   CIA weapon supplies to the Mujahideen, 15, 17, 22
Chébouti, Abdelkader (Lion of the Mountains), 75, 77
Chechnya, x, 14, 81–91, 140, 155
Chelbi, Driss, 174
China, 33–4, 42
Chinese weapons, 39, 95, 207
Christmas Bomber, 161
Clarke, Richard, 7, 9, 10, 66, 127, 132
Clinton, Bill, 5, 6, 9, 55, 63–4, 93, 126, 191

Dabas, Mohannad Almallah, 174
Dagestan, 81, 84
Darul Islam, 158
Dayton Accords, 67, 70, 98
Defence Intelligence Agency, 203
Defence Intelligence Staff, 65, 160, 182, 203–4
Dostum, General Abdul Rashid, 37, 39, 132
Drenica Valley, 93–4
Drug cartels, 101
Drug Enforcement Agency, 93, 117
Dudayev, President Dzhokhar, 81–2
Duhajman, Abdullah (aka Osama bin Laden), 121

East Africa Embassy bombings, 6, 50, 125
East Africa Counter-terrorism Initiative (EACTI), 129

East Turkestan Islamic Movement (ETIM), 33–4
East Turkestan Liberation Organisation (ETLO), 34
Egypt, 22, 112–14, 140, 182
Egyptian Islamic Jihad, 4, 80, 86, 108, 111, 149
Egyptian weapons, 39, 207
Ein el-Hilweh refugee camp, 102, 105
Eritrean Islamic Jihad Movement (EIJM), 111
Eritrean Islamic Party for Justice (EIPJ), 111
Eritrean Islamic Reform Movement (EIRM), 111
Eritrean Islamic Salvation Movement (EISM), 111
Erk Party, 31
Ethiopian attacks on AIAI, 49–50

Fallujah, battle of, 181
al-Fatah, 105–07, 174, 193
FBI, 52, 60, 165, 178, 203
Fedayeen Saddam, 152
Fergana Valley, x, 25, 26, 28–9, 31
Franchise Terrorism, viii, 4
Frey, Scott, 8
Front Islamique du Salut (FIS), 74, 76

Gaddafi, Colonel, 150, 178–9
Al-Gama'a al-Islamiyya, 112–13
Gaza, 107, 169–70, 195
Ghalyounnd, Ghasoub al Abrash, 174
Golden Chain, 71, 121
Gorazde, 62, 66, 69
Gorbachev, President Mikhail, 15, 24, 26
Government Communications Headquarters, 2
Grachev, General Pavel, 83
Grand Mosque occupation, 118
Gromov, General Boris, 14
Groupe Salafist Libre (GSL), 77
Groupe Salafiste pour la Prédication et le Combat (GSPC), 73, 77–8, 130
Groupement Islamique Armé (GIA), 73, 76–8
Grozny, x, 81–4, 87
Guantanamo Bay, 33, 56, 73, 145, 155, 187–8, 194

Hadley, Steve, 10
Hafe, Wadih el, 128
Hafs, Abu, 86–8, 90
Hamadan, Salim Ahmed, 54, 144, 216
Hamas, 11, 102, 106, 108, 120, 173, 176, 178, 180, 182, 186, 189, 191, 193
Hamza, Abu, 57, 67
Hamza, Mustafa, 113
Handzar division, 67
Harakat ul-Mujahidin, 4, 41, 168
Hariri, Rafik (assassination of), 175, 177
al-Harthi, Qaed Senyan, 59
Hassan, Abu, 57–8
Hassan, Sayyid Muhammed Abdullah (The Mad Mullah), 46
Hatshepsut massacre, 113
Hekmatyar, Gulbuddin, 12, 15, 16, 25, 36, 40, 119
Hellfire missile, 9–11, 59
Hezbollah, ix, x, 11, 17, 21, 35, 51, 101–02, 106, 108, 113, 126, 176, 178, 182, 186, 189, 191, 193
Hizb ut-Tahrir al-Islami, 31–2, 191
Al-Houthi, Abdel Malik, 61
al-Houthi, Hussein Badreddin, 60–1
al-Houthi rebellion, 56, 60, 194
Husain, Ed, 191
Hussein, President Saddam, 148–54, 162, 175, 180, 185
  links to bin Laden, 126, 149–50, 152
  links to Abu Nidal, 150–51
  links to al-Qaeda, x, 148–9
  links to al-Zarqawi, 151
Hussein, Uday:
  praises bin Laden, 126

Inter Services Intelligence Directorate (ISI), 15, 16, 20, 25, 35, 38–9, 165
International Islamic Brigade, 87
International Maritime Organisation, 112, 130
Iranian Revolutionary Guards, ix, 21, 64–6, 71, 104, 106, 182
Iraq, vii, viii, x, 8, 37, 61, 180–5
al-Iraqi, Abd al-Hadi, 183
al-Iraqi, Abdul Rahman, 183
Iraqi Mujahideen, 152
Islamic Army of Aden, 57
Islamic Balkan Centre, 95
Islamic Defenders Front (FPI), 158
Islamic Group, 112–13

Islamic militants:
  in Afghanistan, 20, 21, 32, 35, 40–1, 56, 117, 135, 140, 142, 157
  in Albania, 94–5
  in Algeria, 73, 77, 178
  in Bosnia, 66–7, 71–2
  in Central Asia, 21, 25–33, 73
  in Chechnya, 86–7, 89, 157
  in China, 33–4
  in Egypt, 112–13
  in Indonesia, 158
  in Iraq, 79, 152, 173, 180
  in Italy, 78–9, 92, 99
  in Kosovo, 95
  in Lebanon, 51, 103
  in Macedonia, 97
  in Mauritania, 77–8
  in Mexico, 184–5
  in Morocco, 156, 178
  in Nigeria, 157–8
  in Pakistan, 23, 40
  in Somalia, 47, 178
  in the Soviet Union, 25–33
  in Spain, 73
  in Sudan, 108, 110
  in Syria, 51
  in Tunisia, 157
  in the UK, 159
  in Yemen, 59, 178
Islamic Movement of Iraqi Kurdistan, 150
Islamic Movement of Uzbekistan, 4, 30–3, 41, 117, 133–4, 165–6
Islamic Renaissance Party, 30–1
Islamiyya al-Gamat, 189
Israel, vi, 3
Israeli Defence Force (IDF), 102, 105–06, 176
al-Ittihad al-Islamiya (AIAI), 47, 49
Izetbegovic, President Alija, 64–5

Jaish-e-Mohammed, 4, 41, 168, 172
Jalalabad, 4, 6, 44, 135, 141
Jamiat-i-Islami, 108
Jemaah Islamiah, 158–9
Jihad Air, 92
Joint Intelligence Committee, 4, 203, 218
Joint Terrorism Analysis Centre (JTAC), 160
July 7 (7/7), 159, 161

Jumblatt, Walid, 176–7
Jundullah, 166–7

Kadyrov, Akmad, 89
Kandahar, 4, 7, 11, 39–40, 87, 135, 141
Karimov, President, 31, 32
Karzai, President Hamid, 137
Kashmir, viii, 17, 158, 168
Kataeb el Qods (Jerusalem Brigades), 75
Kateebat al-Mujahideen, 67
Kazakhstan, 18, 25, 28–9
KGB, 21
Khalifa, Mohammed Jamal, 190, 193
Khan, Abdul Qadeer, 164
Khan, Akhtar Abdul Rehman, 15, 36
Khartoum, 47, 108, 111
Khattab, Emir, 85–7, 90
Khobar Towers, 44, 49
Khomeini, Ayatollah, ix, 36, 38, 104
Khost, 6, 19, 20, 24, 35, 44
Khurmal, 150
Kikambala Paradise Hotel bombing, 125
Kosovo, viii, 14, 67, 87, 92–100
Kosovo Army Corps, 96
Kosovo Liberation Army (KLA), 93–9
Kosovo Mujahideen (Abu Bekir Sidik), 95–7
Kosovo Protection Corps, 96
Kravchuk, President Leonid, 30
Kyrgyzstan, 10, 18, 25, 26, 32

Lake, Anthony, 48
Lashkar-e-Tayyiba, 4, 5, 41, 158, 168–9, 172
Lebanon, vii, ix, x, 101–07, 174, 213
al-Libi, Abu Laith, 169
al-Liby, Anas, 5
Libyan Islamic Fighting Group, 35, 179
Lockerbie bombing, 177–8

Madrid train bombings, 159
al-Mahdi, Sadiq, 109
Manningham-Butler, Eliza, 155, 163
Maqtoom, Qari Rashi, 165
Maskhadov, General Aslan, 82, 84, 89
al-Masri, Abu Ayyub, 183
al-Masri, Abu Hamza (*see* Abu Hamza)
al-Masri, Abu Obaidah, 169
Massoud, Ahmad Shah, 15, 16, 19, 20, 22, 25, 37, 39–41, 45

Mazar-e-Sharif, 138
Medvedev, Zhores, 24
MI5, 2, 155, 160, 187, 203, 218
MI6, 2, 160, 203
Middle East Peace Process (MEPP), 107, 147, 191
Mieh Mieh refugee camp, 105
Milosevic, President Slobodan, 96
Mogadishu, 47, 51
Mohamed, Khafan Khamis, 128
Mohammad, Nek, 164
Mohammed, Abu, 165
Mohammed, Fazul Abdullah, 125
Mohammed, Khalid Sheik, 2
Moro Islamic Liberation Front, 23, 206
Moro National Liberation Front, 23, 206
Moscow theatre siege, 89
Mouvement Islamique Armée (MIA), 75
Mouvement pour l'État Islamique (MEI), 76
MQ-1 (*see* Predator)
Mubarak, President Hosni, 110, 114, 116
al-Mugrin, Abdul Aziz, 123
Al-Muhajir, Abdul Rahman, 169
Muhtar, Amir, 87
el-Mujahed, 67, 121
Mumam, Abu, 184
Mumbai bombings, 169
al-Mumineen sect, Shabab (*see also* Houthi), 60
Munro, Ambassador Sir Alan, 119
Murray, Ambassador Craig, 31–3
Al-Musawi, Sheik Abbas, 193
Musharraf, President, 38, 166, 170
Muslim Brotherhood, 23, 109, 112
Muslim World League, 115

Nagorno-Karabakh, 28–9
Najibullah, President, 14, 15, 24, 35–6, 38, 41
Namangani, Juma, 11, 31–2
al-Nashiri, Abd al-Rahim, 55
National Islamic Front (NIF), 110, 120
National Security Agency, 5
National Security Council, 65, 221
Nawaz, Maajid, 190
New York 9/11, ix, 1–3

Nidal, Abu, 116, 150, 174
North Atlantic Treaty Organisation
    (NATO), vii, 2, 65, 68–71, 74, 79,
    96, 98, 112, 139, 188
  NATO International Security
    Assistance Force (ISAF), 139
  NATO Implementation Force
    (IFOR), 71
  NATO Mediterranean Dialogue
    Programme (MDP), 177, 179
  NATO Stabilisation Force (SFOR),
    92
Northern Alliance (United Front), 4, 5,
    10, 30, 39, 41, 45, 132, 135

Obama, President, 170, 184
Odeh, Mohamed Sadeek, 128
Omar, Mullah Mohammad, 2, 25, 39,
    41, 43, 73, 133, 141, 146, 163,
    168
Operations:
  Active Endeavour, 99, 112
  Anaconda, 146, 164
  Anvil, 147
  Cast Lead, 107
  Desert Shield, 119
  Desert Storm, 175
  Enduring Freedom, 4, 139, 147, 194
  Full Throttle, 146
  Iraqi Freedom, 106, 175
  Lightning, 154
  Mountain Blizzard, 163
  Mountain Storm, 163–4
  Peace for Galilee, 104
  Protective Shield, 107
  Provide Comfort, 66
  Quick Strike, 153
  Restore Hope, 47
  Sphinx, 100
  Thunder Run, 151
  Veritas, 4
Organisation of Islamic Countries, 64
al-Otaibi, Saud bin Hamoud, 123
al-Oufi, Saleh, 123
al-Owhali, Mohamed Rashid Daoud,
    128

Pakistan, vii, viii, 15, 17, 23, 24, 35,
    44, 59, 73, 121, 140, 142, 151,
    163–72
Pakistani Taliban, 169, 171, 219

Palestinian Intifada, 107
Palestinian Islamic Jihad (PIJ), 11, 102,
    106, 108, 126, 173, 176, 182
Palestinian Liberation Army, 103, 174
Palestinian Liberation Front, 174
Palestinian Liberation Organisation
    (PLO), 17, 22, 37, 102–04, 116,
    120, 150, 174, 177, 191
Panjshir Valley, 19–20
Pearl, Daniel, 188
Philippines, 20, 147, 206
Podujevo massacre, 94
Popular Liberation Army, 105
Powell, General Colin, 2, 48, 127, 149,
    175
Predator drone, 7, 9, 10, 12, 59, 164,
    204–05, 210

al-Qaeda, viii, 1, 14, 23, 33, 50–7,
    71–2, 66, 85, 98–9, 101–03, 126,
    135, 141–7, 149, 155–61, 186–9,
    191
al-Qaeda in Afghanistan, 141–7
al-Qaeda in Bosnia, 66
al-Qaeda in Iraq, 103, 151, 180–4, 186
al-Qaeda in Saudi Arabia, 115–24, 194
al-Qaeda in Spain, 73
al-Qaeda in the Land of Two Rivers,
    114
al-Qaeda in Tunisia, 157
al-Qaeda losses, 155, 159, 166–7, 171,
    184
Quilliam Foundation, 190–1

Rabbani, President Burhanuddin, 30,
    39–40
Racak massacre, 97
Rahman, Omar Abdel, 65, 112
Rawalpindi, 22, 37, 172
Rice, US Secretary of State
    Condoleezza, 127, 176
Riyadh, 68, 115, 121
Rugova, Ibrahim, 72, 94

Saada insurgency (*see* al-Houthi)
Sabra and Shatila massacre, 104
al-Sadah, Amal, 13
Sadat, President Anwar, 104, 113, 207
Sadda training camp, 23
al-Sadr, Moktada, 182
Salafia Jihadia, 156

Saleh, Mohammad, 5, 11
Saleh, President Ali Abdullah, 56, 60–1
Sarajevo, 62–3, 65, 68, 121
Saudi Arabia, vii, viii, ix, 3, 14, 17, 37,
    44, 56, 62, 73, 115–24, 140, 170,
    194
  seeks to radicalise the PLO, 116
  support to the Mujahideen, 17
Sayyaf, Abdul Bari, 165
Sayyaf, Abu, 23, 180, 206
Scheuer, Mike, 6, 12, 127
September 11 (9/11), vi–ix, 1–6, 10,
    12–3, 122, 155–6, 159–60, 162,
    186, 188, 190–1, 203–04
Serbian intelligence, 95–6
al-Shabaab, 51–3
  threat to Australia, 53
Shuskevich, President Stanislav, 30
Somali National Movement, 47
Somalia, 20, 46–53
Soviet Afghan War losses, 15
Soviet Afghan War veterans, 26, 29, 31
Soviet weapon supplies to Afghanistan,
    36
Soviet weapon supplies to client states,
    28
Soviet weapon supplies to Yemen, 28,
    54
Special Air Service (SAS):
  in Afghanistan, 162–3
  in Bosnia, 69
  in Kosovo, 94
  in Yemen, 59
Srebrenica massacre, 70, 210
Stinger missile, 21, 22, 35, 205
Strasbourg Christmas market plot, 78
Sudan, vii, 35, 65, 108–11, 149
Sudanese Hezbollah, 110
Sudanese People's Liberation Army
    (SPLA), 109–10
al-Suri, Abu Bakr, 169
Swat Valley, 171
Syria, vii, x, 51, 103–07, 173–7, 182

Taha, Rifai Ahmed, 113
Tajikistan, 18, 25–7, 32
Takfir Wal-Hajra, 56, 75
Taliban, viii, 2, 3, 8, 25, 30, 33, 38–45,
    87, 132–40, 142, 189, 219
Taliban air force, 134
Taliban armed forces, 45, 133, 216

Taliban drug trade, 42–4, 189
Taliban take power, 31, 35, 41
Tarnak Farms, 5, 8, 135, 204
Task Force, 121, 162–3, 218
Task Force Dagger, 162
Tehrik Taliban Pakistan (TTP), 171
Ten Dollar Taliban, 186
Tenet, George, vi, 5, 6, 8, 9, 10, 45, 55,
    127–8, 148
Thaqi, Hashim, 95–6
Third World Relief Agency, 65
Tito, Josip Broz, 62
Tora Bora, 11, 137, 140–7, 162, 170
Trans-Sahara Counter-terrorism
    Initiative (TSCTI), 130
al-Turabi, Dr Hassan, 110, 119–20
Turkmenistan, 25–7
Tuzla, 65–6

Uighurs, 33, 42
UN Counter-terrorism Branch, 155
UN Office on Drugs and Crime, 101,
    118
Union of Islamic Courts, 50
United Arab Emirates, 7, 44
United Tajik Opposition, 4, 30, 42
UNPROFOR, 68, 70
US National Counter-terrorism Center,
    52, 159
US Special Operations Command, 9,
    10
Ushtria Clirimtare e Kosove (UCK – *see*
    Kosovo Liberation Army)
USS *Cole*, 8, 44, 53–6, 59, 74
Uzbekistan, 25, 26, 29, 32, 147

Vietnam, 37

al-Walid, Abu, 88, 90
War of the Camps, 105
Warsi, Baroness Sayeeda, 195–6
Watson, Dale, 11
Wilson, Charlie, 15
Wolfowitz, Paul, 10
Woolsey, James, 64, 159

Yakawlang massacre, 140
Yandarbiyev, Zelimkhan, 87
Yarkas, Imad Eddin Barakat, 174
Yassin, Sheik Ahmed, 193
Yeltsin, President Boris, 30, 81

Yemen, viii, 14, 20, 28, 54–61, 73, 108, 112, 147, 194
Yemeni Mujahideen, 56
Yousaf, Brigadier Mohammad, 16, 22, 36
Yousef, Ramzi, 3, 8, 193, 204
Yugoslav Mujahideen, 66
Yugoslav People's Army, 62–3
Yuldashev, Abduhalilovich, 31, 164–6

Zaeef, Mullah Abdul Salam, 194
al-Zarqawi, Abu Musab, 103, 150–1, 173, 180–3
al-Zawahiri, Ayman, 2, 11, 66, 80, 86, 109, 112, 162, 165–6, 168, 170, 181, 184, 192–3
Zhawar Kili training camp, 6, 11, 20, 135, 145
al-Zulfikar, 37